Donald Clarke is the editor and principal au[...]
Penguin Encyclopedia of Popular Music. He lives with his
wife and son in Norfolk, England.

Billie Holiday

Wishing on the Moon

DONALD CLARKE

DA CAPO PRESS
A MEMBER OF THE PERSEUS BOOKS GROUP

Cataloging-in-Publication data for this book is available from the Library of Congress.

First Da Capo Press edition 2002
This book was originally published as *Wishing on the Moon: The Life and Times of Billie
Holiday.*
Reprinted by arrangement with the author.
ISBN-10: 0-306-81136-7   ISBN-13: 978-0-306-81136-4

Grateful acknowledgment is made for permission to reprint excerpts from the following copyrighted works: "I Wished on the Moon," words and music by Dorothy Parker
and Ralph Rainger. Copyright © Paramount Music Corp. and Famous Music Corp.,
USA, Warner Chappel Music Ltd, London. Reproduced by permission of International Music Publications Ltd. "Strange Fruit," by Lewis Allan. Copyright © Edward
B. Marks Music Company, 1940. Copyright renewed. Used by permission. All rights
reserved. For UK, Commonwealth (exc. Canada and Australia), and Eire, lyric re-
production is by permission of Carlin Music Corp., Iron Bridge House, 3 Bridge Approach, London NW1 8BD.*
*The author is grateful for the use of archive materials compiled by Linda Lipnack
Kuehl, courtesy of Toby Byron/Multiprises.

Published by Da Capo Press
A Member of the Perseus Books Group
http://www.dacapopress.com

Da Capo Press books are available at special discounts for bulk purchases in the U.S.
by corporations, institutions, and other organizations. For more information, please
contact the Special Markets Department at the Perseus Books Group, 11 Cambridge
Center, Cambridge, MA 02142, or call (800) 255-1514 or (617) 252-5298, or e-mail
j.mccrary@perseusbooks.com.

*For Ethne, who makes
everything possible, with
all my love*

Contents

We must respect the living, but nothing but
the truth is good enough for the dead.

— Voltaire

The author is grateful for the use of archive materials
compiled by Linda Lipnack Kuehl, courtesy of Toby
Byron/Multiprises

Preface to the First Edition (1994)

In 1955, an album called *I Like Jazz* was released in the USA, one of the first samplers ever issued, with twelve tracks by Columbia jazz artists, mostly from the vaults. Probably intended to test the market for jazz reissues, it sold for 98 cents when a 12-inch pop LP was $3.98, and sold so well it reached the top five in the *Billboard* album chart. One of the tracks was "I'll Never be the Same," made in 1937 by Teddy Wilson, with Billie Holiday and Lester Young; and that was my introduction, at the age of fourteen, to the music of Lady Day. (Lady was still working then, but we didn't hear her on the radio. We heard Patti Page instead.)

A couple of years later, another teenager called Linda Lipnack bought a Verve album of Lady's 1956 Carnegie Hall concert at Sam Goody's record shop, and was permanently smitten, as I had been.

In 1990, my editor at Viking/Penguin in London, Jon Riley, suggested that I write a biography of Billie Holiday. I liked the idea, but I was also awed by it. I knew that I would have to try to dispel the conventional image of her as a tragic black woman: her recordings, the primary source of evidence, reveal that she was nobody's stereotype, but a character as fascinating as any ever created by a novelist. Her ghost-written autobiography (*Lady Sings the Blues*, 1956), written to sell to the movies, was hopelessly inaccurate, and the 1972 film did even more to perpetuate the stereotype. Discographies and John Chilton's 1975 book *Billie's Blues* would be good guides to chronology, but neither could tell me anything about the first twenty years of her life. Where would I begin?

Before the contract was signed, Jon and I heard from separate sources about a Holiday archive. John Jeremy, in making his revelatory but now dated TV film *The Long Night of Lady Day*, had found in his research that everywhere he went he was following a path already trodden by Linda Kuehl.

Linda Lipnack Kuehl had interviewed nearly 150 people, some of them exhaustively, and many of whom had since died. She did most of this in 1970–72 and subsequently had a contract for a book, but she died before she had written it. I went to New York to look at Kuehl's material myself, and Viking/Penguin made a deal with the present owner for access, we thought, to the complete archive. This book could not exist in its present form without Kuehl's work.

Kuehl was good at interviewing people, allowing their voices and personalities to come through. But she was clearly emotionally involved with Lady Day. Having discovered Lady through the Carnegie Hall concert that included reading from the ghost-written autobiography, Kuehl gave the book too much credence. I was not able to hear the tapes of the interviews. Some of the interviews were not transcribed completely, and Kuehl didn't always know what was important. She sometimes didn't know who was being talked about; Jimmy Luntsford was obviously Jimmie Lunceford, but I worried about Wallace Stein until I realized it was Ted Wallerstein, a record industry executive. Carl Drinkard talked about the 1954 European trip; there is a single sheet headed "vocabulary from Europe tapes," with a note to the effect that "Paris was a drag," and "I never could be certain if she did run out of stuff. I think she was screaming and crying wolf—as usual." This would indicate that they were using drugs in Europe, but no one now living has heard the entire Drinkard interview. Finally, since the interviews are usually not transcribed with both questions and answers, we cannot be sure of some of the testimony. For example, did Wee Wee Hill volunteer "that summer of 1927" as the date that Eleanora Gough left Baltimore to become Billie Holiday, or was he prompted in some way? I hope the tapes survive for future historians.

The interviewees themselves are priceless, and each different. Big Stump was a terrible name-dropper, while Pops Foster enjoyed dwelling on the scurrilous. Bobby Tucker and John Levy (the bassist) are clearly two of nature's gentlemen, Jimmy Fletcher is completely trustworthy, and Jimmy Rowles is a gas. And above all, the women—Mae Barnes, Marie Bryant and many more—were valuable observers, and full of love.

Kuehl discovered that Sadie Fagan's name at birth had been Harris, but she did not look for Lady's birth certificate; I hired Susan F. Koelble in Philadelphia to do that. Not knowing what the rules were in the USA in those days, I told Susan that my mother-in-law was Irish, that I was doing research on the Fagan family, and that this particular Fagan might be a Harris, all of which was true. Susan immediately found it, and when I told her whose birth certificate it was, she was delighted and subsequently did research for me in the census records for Baltimore and Philadelphia.

John Jeremy allowed me access to his research materials, and I found that his clippings file was much better than Kuehl's, to say nothing of a complete set of admission documents from Alderson. As well as all of the people mentioned above, I have to thank Ernie Anderson, Jean Bach, Beryl Bryden, Thelma Carpenter, Leonard Feather, Delilah Jackson, Max Jones, Professor Robert O'Meally, Chris Parker, Mary Schoonover, Bobby Tucker and Laurie Wright, who have put up with me writing and telephoning them and in some cases darkening their doorways. It was my honor to meet and talk to Johnny Fagan in Baltimore, and to Tondaleyo Levy, Ron Levy, Helen Clark and Jimmy Monroe in New York.

And most of all, there is Lady herself. One of the perks of writing about music and musicians is the excuse to listen to all the records. I thought I knew her work, but I have discovered all over again that, as one of the greatest recording artists, her work is all of a piece, and repays the study of it from beginning to end. I can only hope and pray that I have done justice to her.

Norfolk, England

Introduction to the
Da Capo Edition (2002)

A long and mostly happy relationship with Penguin UK having come to an end, I am pleased that a new edition of this book will be published by Da Capo Press. Since its first publication, Ernie Anderson, Beryl Bryden, Thelma Carpenter, Leonard Feather, Max Jones, Jimmy Monroe, Jimmy Rowles, and Tondaleyo Levy (gracious lady!) have all left us. So time marches on; but this author at least will never forget them.

Also since 1994, there have been more books and TV programs about Lady Day. Not only is she more than ever an American icon, but it is even more obvious how difficult it is to keep the truth alive and in perspective. To illustrate—a slight digression:

Nearly forty years ago, in my home town, I had a lady friend who was unmarried and pregnant. Her erstwhile man friend had shipped out of Great Lakes Naval Training Center without leaving a forwarding address; she was the sister of a friend of mine, and as we were each lonely for different reasons, we held hands for a few weeks. Later, when she went to the hospital to have the baby (which she was giving up for adoption), she was pleased and surprised when I kept a promise, coming to the hospital to cheer her up and bringing some flowers. It crossed my mind as I sat there on her ward, nurses and other visitors coming and going, that somebody might get the wrong idea; and I remembered the gag line from Fats Waller's "The Joint Is Jumpin'": "Don't give your right name, no, no, no!" But nobody asked my name.

Many years later, obtaining a certified copy of Billie Holiday's birth certificate, I was charmed to see someone called Frank DeViese listed as the father. Of course it's possible that some nurse just wrote down a name so that the space would not be blank, but I preferred to think that Sadie had someone there with her, a boyfriend, a friend of the family, whatever; and I thought it was a shame that Eleanora, who grew up to become an American icon, probably never knew that her mother was not entirely alone at the time of her birth.

Then another book was published. Stuart Nicholson had found his own copy of the birth certificate, and to be fair about it, in his book (*Billie Holiday*, 1995) he did not claim to have discovered the true identity of Billie's father. But for whatever reasons of his own, he did write that "Whether or not DeVeasy was Eleanora's true father will never be known....There could be any number of reasons why Sadie refused to acknowledge [Clarence Holiday's] paternity at the time she registered her daughter's birth. In the Southern States they have a saying: "Mother's baby, Father's, maybe!"

Now for 80 years, nobody had doubted that guitarist Clarence was the baby's father· not Sadie, not Eleanora, and certainly not Clarence, who bragged about it to his friends, and who was proud of his daughter some years later, when she became a singing sensation in Harlem. Clarence's wife, Fannie, who he married in 1927, and all their circle of friends and acquaintances took for granted Clarence's paternity. Not, however, the reviewers of Nicholson's book. John Jeremy wrote in *Jazz* magazine that "it now seems all but conclusive that Clarence Holiday was not her biological father." Someone called Sandra Parsons wrote in *The Daily Mail* that "who her father was is a mystery" and that "on the birth certificate Sadie herself wrote that the father was Frank DeViese...." The only copies of the birth certificate in circulation are merely certified evidence from the authorities in Philadelphia of the fact of the baby's birth; it is a safe bet that Sadie wrote nothing at all on the birth certificate, did not "register" the birth and probably never even saw any birth certificate. Nicholson had done some good research, and I have acknowledged some of it in this, my latest edition (pp. 34 and 36); but research and the interpretation of it are two different things. I think I will stay with the paternity of Clarence Holiday.

At the end of his book Nicholson goes off on his own bat again. Earle Zaidins was a naïve young lawyer fresh out of the University of Wisconsin who knew little or nothing about the music business; he met Lady as they walked their dogs in the park, and she gave him very limited authority to try to collect her record royalties. He also negotiated the contract for the book *Lady Sings The Blues* on behalf of Lady and her ghost-writer, Bill Dufty. So unaware was Zaidins that he thought Lady had been off drugs since she had allegedly gone "cold turkey" in the Flanders Hotel in 1956, so that when he was interviewed on the radio after she was arrested on her deathbed in 1959, he was able to swear up and down that she must have been framed. It was only a dozen years later, at a party in New York City following the completion of John Jeremy's film, that Lady's housekeeper Alice Vrbsky tipped him off: Lady was never off drugs very long, but she didn't want Zaidins to know, first so that he wouldn't be disappointed in her (she had a long history of mothering naïve young people), and secondly in case she got busted again and needed him to act as her lawyer.

Meanwhile, Louis McKay, Billie Holiday's last husband, was a violent man who beat her up and stole her money, just like every other man with whom she'd spent any length of time. Two of Lady's female pianists in the mid-1950s, Memry Midgett and Corky Hale, despised McKay and feared him; Maely Dufty called him "Decay." After Lady died, McKay had plenty of good reasons to portray himself as a diamond in the rough, so he lied about Zaidins and everybody else, including Lady. Lady and McKay had been arrested together for possession of drugs in 1956, before they were married; the notion that McKay left Lady a couple of years later because Zaidins had helped her get back on drugs is just ludicrous. (They split up after Lady discovered that McKay was running a string of whores, whereupon he became so violent that she ran to Zaidins' nearby flat to hide.) McKay accused Zaidins of making sexual advances to Lady; he complained that Zaidins had not looked after her financial interests properly, whereas in fact he had very little authority to do so, and was no more a match for Joe Glaser, Lady's manager, than was McKay himself.

Lady owed Zaidins money for legal services rendered, which he wouldn't have bothered to try to collect since she didn't have any money anyway. After she died it was a different story. Glaser thought he controlled the film rights to Lady's so-called autobiography; Zaidins disagreed. Ellis & Ellis were a reputable law firm who had employed Zaidins and whose services Glaser had also used; but now

Glaser suckered McKay in order to blind-side Zaidins: he offered to pay for another lawyer if McKay would agree to dump Zaidins. The wanna-be gangster agreed, and suddenly Ellis & Ellis were out and another lawyer, Florence Kennedy, who basically didn't like anybody, was in. And for some reason, Nicholson decided many years later to accept McKay's version of it all, and Kennedy's: she thought McKay's string of whores was "not unusual...in the black community," according to Nicholson. McKay later became an advisor on the 1972 film *Lady Sings The Blues*, one of the worst movies ever made; while among Kennedy's contributions to Lady's welfare had been to draw up a contract for her participation in an exploitative film, *No Honor Among Thieves*, when she was on her deathbed, as Nicholson also points out. Why was he was so impressed with these people? I think we should be told.

As this new edition of my book goes to press, there has been a BBC TV film about Billie Holiday· a decently-made picture 57 minutes long which was scrunched, cut, voiced-over and generally butchered by A&E for American viewers in February 2002, but still contained plenty of Stanley Crouch drooling over the thought of two women together on a bed, or maybe even three. And there is talk of a new TV biopic for Showtime or HBO if they can get a star, today's TV moguls being more adept at buying stars than at making them, and oblivious to the fact that the reason there are not many bankable black female movie stars is because of decades of neglect on the part of, er, American TV moguls. I hope Lady's spirit is looking down from somewhere and laughing at all of us.

Austin, Texas

1

An African-American Nation

In August 1619 a Dutch man-of-war stopped in Virginia and sold the residents twenty Negroes. They were not slaves, and were free after seven years of indentured labour; at least one of them later became a landowner. But slavery was legitimized in Virginia statutes in the 1650s, as British sea power and the slave trade increased: over 6,000 Africans were sold into slavery in Virginia alone between 1699 and 1708.

The slaves were from the Yoruban, Ashanti, Mandingo, Angolan, Wolof, Ibo and other tribes, but in America they were spread out and separated: they could not maintain their tribal identities, so that their many languages and customs were poured into a common pot. The circle dance is a case in point: it had come from all over central and western Africa, almost always shuffled in a counter-clockwise direction, except for women from Togo, for example, who on some occasions danced in a clockwise direction. But in America the circle dance became the slaves' ring shout, and the clockwise direction disappeared completely, because of the overwhelming desire of the Africans for the other direction. In this way they were detribalized by the experience of slavery, and at the same time a new nation was being created: the African-American.

Its creation was easily kept a secret. Slave-owners did not of course believe that the slaves had any culture at all. Some of the early researchers on the lives of the slaves tell of waiting for years before witnessing a ring shout, and former slaves interviewed as late as the 1920s testified that it had not been considered a good idea to tell any person half of what you knew: if the white man thought that slaves were incapable of cultural or spiritual values, so be it; no doubt the slaves felt safer that way, as well as better able to retain a sense of their own identity.

An African-American culture has been developing on American soil for over 350 years, shaped first by slavery and then by naked racism; and it is from that culture that the subject of our story comes. Therefore neither her life nor her works can be judged by the standards of European Puritanism, which yields far too much evidence of ignorance and hypocrisy.

In 1630 a Virginia court decided that one Hugh Smith was 'to be soundly whipped before an assembly of negroes and others for abusing himself to the dishonour of God and shame of Christianity by defiling his body in lying with a negro.' Despite social disapproval of miscegenation, the existence of the priapic white man was soon acknowledged by the law, for in 1662 the question of the status of children begotten by Englishmen on Negro women had to be settled: '. . . all children born in this colony shall be bond or free only according to the condition of the mother.' The principle of slavery as an inherited condition was thus reinforced, as well as an inherent element of racism: if a child had black blood it would be a slave no matter who its father was. In 1705 the legislature had to define 'mulatto'; and it was not long before the slave society's own practice of miscegenation led to the placing of the white Southern woman on a pedestal, for she was the only one who could guarantee the perpetuation of the superior race. A Reverend Thomas Hawley was quoted in a book in 1839: '. . . I can say that I have been in respectable families (so called) where I could distinguish the family resemblance in the slaves who waited upon the table. I once hired a slave who belonged to his own uncle.' And not too long after that, Rebecca Fagan was born; a son's death certificate a century later gave her maiden name as Hammond, but one way or another the name Fagan had been bestowed by the Irish on an African-American family of Baltimore, Maryland.

2

Baltimore

Despite economic and social differences between the north and south of the state, Maryland had experienced a transition to free labour for decades. Cereals had become the state's main crop, requiring gangs of labour at harvest time but not providing steady work for the rest of the year, so that there was no economic reason for landowners to support large numbers of slaves. By 1810 Maryland had the largest population of free blacks in the USA, and by the time of the Civil War the free black population was nearly as large as the slave.

While blacks outnumbered whites in some Latin-American slave societies, so that free blacks formed an important economic element of craftsmen, shopkeepers and small landowners, in the USA the white majority was always substantial, never falling lower than 62 per cent in Maryland (in 1810). But if blacks were easily kept in the margin, Baltimore was never imprisoned by the slave economy that retarded the development of other cities further south. The increase in the state's population between 1830 and 1840 occurred almost entirely in Baltimore, and 40 per cent of that increase was comprised of free blacks; by 1850 Baltimore had almost half the population of the northern counties and over a quarter of the population of the entire state.

Of course the civil rights of free blacks in Maryland, as elsewhere, were grossly violated. Those who refused to work for white employers could be bound and sold at annually renewable terms by the courts; free blacks were not allowed to own dogs, liquor, firearms or ammunition, and were not allowed to sell most merchandise of value, especially foodstuffs, without written proof that they had acquired it honestly; and so forth. Yet these rules seem to have been intended to encourage good behaviour rather than being strictly enforced. Baltimore had thousands of slaves along with free blacks, but its commerce in labour had many gradations: a slave-owner might not feed a slave at a time when he had no work for the slave to do, forcing the slave to find his or her own employment. Southern cities all differed from rural areas in these respects, but Baltimore to a greater degree, and all this relative social fluidity had a cumulative effect, in that Baltimore offered blacks greater anonymity, more freedom and more responsibility for their own fate than most places.

Baltimore's strategic location had put it on the map during the Revolutionary and Napoleonic Wars. In the 1830s the Baltimore & Ohio Railroad became the first to use an American-built locomotive; and by 1845 it was possible to travel from New York to Baltimore in a day: it was a strenuous sixteen-hour day to be sure, but the town was further knitted to the prosperous Northeast rather than to the relatively backward South. Maryland did not secede from the Union during the Civil War of 1861–5 and so did not suffer the destruction that the deeper South did; but its large black population suffered the same reversals as the rest. A new state constitution adopted in November 1864 followed Abraham Lincoln's lead in abolishing slavery, but as one historian put it, 'A border state to the end, Maryland yielded with bad grace ... had it not been for ballots cast by soldiers in the field – in a procedure that many considered irregular – the inevitable would have failed to muster a majority in Maryland.'

The new constitution echoed the federal document of 1789 ('all men are created equally free'), but it was soon replaced by that of 1867, which did not; and in any case practice was more important than theory. Former slaves found that they could be denied permission by an employer to attend the distant funeral of a loved one, just as if they were still chattels. And even the constitution of 1864, by remaining silent on the question, preserved the incompetence of black witnesses in legal proceedings and explicitly reserved suffrage to whites. With the new constitution of 1867, the southern counties of the state cheated: they counted their black citizens in order to gain more representation in the state legislature, so that voteless blacks contributed to the power of their worst enemies. As elsewhere in the USA, there was now no difference between free black men and former slaves: all were second-class to the same degree.

Baltimore was always a lively place in every way, with a well-deserved reputation for rowdyism and outbreaks of mob violence; around 1850 there were gun battles between rival fire stations. There were a lot of foreign immigrants, and nativist sentiments contributed to a lively political stew: the Baltimore Plug-Uglies was a prominent local club, while the national (and nationalist) Know-Nothing or American Party had an effective machine in Maryland and in Baltimore in the 1850s, and had its greatest political successes there during a decade of political instability. Sanitation in Baltimore was a matter of individual initiative, which meant that for much of the nineteenth century the streets were full of garbage, and pigs to eat it; and at the time of Billie Holiday's birth in 1915, it was still the largest town in the USA without a municipal sewage system.

The family home of Henry Louis Mencken, the Sage of Baltimore, who deserves to be the patron saint of American writers, was connected to a private sewer in the 1880s, but outdoor conveniences were common, with private sinks under them:

The one in our yard was pumped out and fumigated every Spring by a gang of coloured men who arrived on a wagon that was called an O.E.A. – i.e., odourless excavating apparatus. They discharged this social-minded duty with great fervour and dispatch, and achieved non-odiferousness, in the innocent Aframerican way, by burning buckets of resin and tar. The whole neighbourhood choked on the black, greasy smoke for hours afterward. It was thought to be an effective preventive of cholera, smallpox and tuberculosis.

Mencken played with black kids as a lad, and 'We boys subscribed to all the traditional Southern lore about them ... that their passion for watermelon was at least as powerful as a cat's for catnip, and that no conceivable blow on the head could crack their skulls, whereas even a light tap on the shin would disable them.' Baltimore was sometimes still called Mob Town in Mencken's youth, though by then the violence had lessened considerably. He bragged in the 1930s that there had never been a race riot there,

6

though I am by no means easy about the future, for a great many anthropoid blacks from the South have come to town since the city dole began to rise above what they could hope to earn at home, and soon or late some effort may be made to drive them back. But if that time ever comes the uprising will probably be led, not by native Baltimorans, but by the Anglo-Saxon baboons from the West Virginia mountains who have flocked in for the same reason, and are now competing with the blacks for the poorer sort of jobs.

The irascible and controversial Mencken was never easy on anybody, and may not have been aware of the extent to which blacks had always headed for Baltimore. He was accused in later life of racism; he rarely used 'coloured', the polite term in those days, but 'Aframerican' or 'blackamoore', precisely because these words were then ridiculous. Mencken was among the first to point out that nobody in American culture could be without racism, which is the beginning of wisdom on the subject; and the great black novelist Richard Wright began his reading with Mencken, who as editor of a Baltimore newspaper was well known for making impertinent remarks about the South.

John White, in his useful book *Billie Holiday* (1987), quotes another, anonymous journalist on a Baltimore paper in 1896, writing about a slum called Pigtown:

Open drains . ashes and garbage   cellars filled with filthy black water . . villainous-looking negroes who loiter and sleep around street corners and never work; vile and vicious women, with but a smock to cover their black nakedness, lounging in doorways or squatting upon the steps, hurling foul epithets at every passer-by; foul streets, foul people, in foul tenements filled with foul air

You could wring a quart of racism out of these few words. There are always journalists who pander to what they think is received opinion; the reminder here is that a century ago the USA already had its urban underclass. But Mencken loved Baltimore, and some of its black natives also had fond memories of it in later years; its segregationist laws were no different from those of many another town.

*

In the census of 1880, Rebecca Fagan was living at 42 Little McEldery Street in Baltimore. She gave her age as twenty-eight, which would make her born in about 1852; she did washing for a living. There were four children, of whom the oldest was Charles, aged eleven, which would make him born around 1869. Rebecca reported to the census that she had been married in 1880, but there was no male in the household, and we do not know anything about Mr Fagan. A few doors away, at 36 Little McEldery Street, Henry and Ginnie Harris lived with three little girls, Fannie, Lottie and Josephine; Ginnie also did washing, and Henry worked on a tugboat.

The census of 1890 was destroyed in a fire; in the census of 1900, Rebecca was living at 710 North Spring Street, and all the older children had left home; four children at home in that year included Rose (born 1881) and John (born 1895) In 1900 Rebecca gave her age as forty-two (born c. 1858) and said that she was a widow; she also said that she had had a total of eight children, of whom five were still alive.

Charlie Fagan, Rebecca's first-born, does not seem to have been living in Maryland in 1900; Fagan family lore has it that he had a lengthy relationship with a woman in another state. We do not know whether he was married then or not, but he certainly had a liaison with a woman named Harris to whom he was not married, which resulted in the birth of Sara, on 18 August 1896.

At some point Charlie moved home to Baltimore. His death certificate says he was born in 1871, but in the 1920 census he is said to be aged forty-five, which would make him born in about 1875. In 1920 he was working as a waiter and living in rented accommodation with his wife Mattie, who had been born in Virginia about 1880 and was working as a laundress.

Charlie and Mattie were Catholics; the rest of the Fagans were Methodists, placing them a social notch above the store-front ghetto Baptists. They were an African-American family who struggled successfully for respectability: even in the worst times, the men found employment; they worked packing seafood on Baltimore's waterfront, or they canned vegetables at Lord Mott's, or they worked as porters. Today's generation of Rebecca's descendants include teachers, policemen, a social worker and so forth.

Charlie's siblings lived in a poorer ghetto neighbourhood on Baltimore's East Side, but Charlie was the first to move upwards.

He worked in various Baltimore hotels, and towards the end of his life as an elevator operator in the B&O Building. He earned and saved enough money to purchase his own home in West Baltimore, at 1117 Brevort Road. Mattie may have converted Charlie to her higher church, although the impulse to Catholicism may just as well have come from a Fagan Irish ancestry; we do know that Mattie ruled the roost, no doubt in large measure responsible for Charlie's relative prosperity. She also looked down at her Methodist in-laws, never accompanying Charlie on his visits to the East Side or opening her door to visits from the others. And in particular she would have nothing to do with Sara Harris.

The whole history of the African-American nation has been a struggle to keep families together, beginning with the terrible absurdity of slavery: Louisiana even had to have a law prohibiting the sale of a child under ten away from its mother. An unrelated Anne Harris, interviewed in Virginia at the age of ninety-two, three-quarters of a century after slavery, told her interviewer that no white person had ever set foot in her house.

> Dey sole my sister Kate. I saw it wid dese here eyes. Sole her in 1860, and I ain't seed nor heard of her since. Folks say white folks is all right dese days. Maybe dey is, maybe dey isn't. But I can't stand to see 'em. Not on my place.

The unbearable heartache of uncounted sundered kinships was not healed by generations of institutionalized racism. There was always pressure on black families to behave in socially acceptable ways, so that they would have wished to do so, but the social and economic disadvantages of second-class citizenship often made it simply impossible; thus the second-rate nature of black citizenship was confirmed, completing the circle.

To study only the history of black music is to see evidence of it everywhere. Charlie Parker and Dizzy Gillespie were both musical geniuses; Parker, born in 1920, died a physical ruin at the age of thirty-four, while Gillespie, almost three years older, was with us until 1993, a much-loved grandfather of American music. The big difference was that Parker's father was absent, while Gillespie had a stern, loving father in his formative years, and so himself made a stable marriage. The black female blues singers, Ma Rainey, Bessie Smith and the rest, were accompanied at the piano; perhaps they worked indoors as children. But the legendary black male blues singers, nearly all of them, accompanied themselves on the guitar, a portable instrument, and many of them were itinerant. This is because the black female was less of a threat to the white man than the black male, who was therefore even more marginalized, to the point where he was effectively emasculated, often unable even to play the traditional male role as head of his family.

This is a problem for which America is still paying today in its inner cities and which has only been exacerbated by a paternalistic welfare state. The orthodoxy of the 1960s and 1970s was that it is lack of a paycheck rather than lack of the wage-earner that damages families; yet every sociological study of any value on the subject of homes without fathers adds to a catalogue of heartache. This has nothing to do with race, but everything to do with the whole history of the human species. Many black families have struggled successfully to attain an American ideal of respectability, and then struggled to maintain it; the courage and strength of character the struggle has required, and still requires, is bad enough, but some people just don't have any luck.

We do not know anything about Sara Harris's early life, but she was one of the luckless. Somewhere along the way her name became Sadie, a common American variant ('Sarey' was known in England in the seventeenth century, corrupted to 'Sairey' by the nineteenth.) Perhaps in her desire to identify herself as a Fagan, Sadie adopted her father's Catholic religion; but she was already kept well outside the family's inner circle when, in the summer of 1914, while working as a live-in maid with a white family, she went to a carnival or a dance, and was seduced there by a younger teenager, Clarence Holiday.

When she found herself pregnant at the age of eighteen, Sadie went to Philadelphia to have the baby; to get there, she took what was called a transportation job, a contract between a white employer and a black servant from further south, perhaps because she wanted to have the baby away from the Fagans and maybe because a ghetto midwife was not good enough.

Sadie was admitted to obstetrics at Philadelphia General Hospital on 14 February 1915; we do not know why she was admitted so early. Elinore Harris was born at 2.30 a.m. on 7 April 1915; the doctor's name was Samuel R. Stillman. The baby's name is spelled 'Elinore' on the birth certificate, 'Elenoir' in the doctor's report, and 'Eleanor' in the hospital's records; it was spelled various ways throughout her life, but 'Eleanora' is the most common variant, so that is the spelling I shall use in this book.

Sadie was living at 331 South Broad Street in Philadelphia at the time; she had passed her nineteenth birthday by the time of the birth, and her occupation is listed as housework. The hospital was an almshouse type of establishment, where the indigent were cared for; its registration record states that Sadie had 'no friends', and instructed '*Notify Social Services – letter in folder*', but the records of the social services have not survived. Mother and daughter were discharged on 19 April, and the birth was registered on 24 April.

The only real surprise on the birth certificate of the child who became Billie Holiday is that a putative father is listed. Frank DeViese was living at 1131 South Broad Street: he was twenty years old, and worked as a waiter. There is no doubt at all that Clarence was the father, but Sadie had evidently made a friend, so that she was not entirely alone, and at least there is a name on the birth certificate rather than a blank space. Whether or not Sadie hoped for something more from her relationship with Frank DeViese we do not know, but the 1920 census listed a Frank H. DeVeasy, twenty-four years old, renting at 817 North Burns Street in Philadelphia; his occupation is listed as driver, and he was married to Jennie, who was the same age and whose parents were both born in Maryland. Perhaps Frank was a friend of the family to begin with, and just lending his sympathy The sad thing is that Eleanora probably never knew that somebody had been there when she was born, standing up for Sadie.

In 1900 Nelson and Mary Holiday were forty-three and thirty-five years old respectively and had a son, Clarence, whose age is given as two, but his birth date is listed as April 1892: this is probably a mistake on the census-taker's part or in the transcription of the records. Clarence was born in Baltimore on 23 July 1898 and is thought to have been living with his parents in 1915, delivering groceries after school to pay for banjo lessons.

Baltimore was full of music: its citizens have ranged from drummer and bandleader Chick Webb (1900–39) to rock's *enfant terrible* Frank Zappa (b. 1940). But two of its most famous emigrants were pianist/composer Eubie Blake (1883–1983) and multi-instrumentalist/bandleader Elmer Snowden (1900–73). Blake formed a partnership with bandleader Noble Sissle, writing and producing hit Broadway shows; Elmer Snowden moved to

Washington, then to New York, where in 1923 his band, the Washingtonians, included Duke Ellington on piano, and was the beginning of Duke's career.

Snowden ran so many bands in New York that he got in trouble with the musicians' union and moved to Philadelphia for several years. But long before that, Clarence and Elmer were both playing banjo in Baltimore as teenagers, and Elmer remembered getting a gig with Blake because Clarence could not yet read music. Elmer and Clarence attended a boys' school together, in a converted tin factory, and 'we used to lay for the girls who went to school a block around the corner, to the Cafly Street school.' After eighth grade they went to separate high schools.

I was in Northwest Baltimore, and he was in East, so the only time we saw each other was when we'd play a dance. We played Mary's Casino on Preston Street, St Mary's Hall, and a lot of time we would have battles of music. That's when we was kids in short pants . we went to school in short pants, and then when we went on the job we changed to long pants.

In 1917 Clarence told Elmer, 'You know, I'm a daddy now.'

I said, You're a *what?* . The first time I saw [Eleanora] was in 1918 or 1919. A fellow named Joe Rochester, a piano player, took the band over to Jefferson Street in East Baltimore; Clarence was living there . When I saw her when she was about three years old, Clarence asked me to be her godfather. I was too young to even know what it was, so I asked the piano player, who was a man, and he told me it meant that I had to take care of her. So I thought, uh, uh. I couldn't take care of myself with the money we was makin' then ... I thought she was an ugly little thing, a homely looking baby, but she turned out to be a beautiful girl .
And all through her life she always thought of me as her godfather, even though I never said yes or no, and anywhere I was playing, she would come to me and look to me as her second daddy.

Clarence infrequently visited, and he helped Sadie with her rent even less often. There is no evidence that they ever lived together, but Sadie tried to keep track of him; she took transportation jobs not only because they paid better, but also to chase Clarence. In the 1920 census a Clarence Halliday, aged twenty-one, was living as a lodger in Baltimore and working as a porter in a factory. Sadie probably never knew that Clarence (his surname again spelled 'Holliday') married an eighteen-year-old Baltimore girl, Helen Bouldin, on 16 October 1922. The same year, Clarence left Helen and Baltimore for Philadelphia, where he ran an elevator in a ballroom to pay for his music lessons, and was soon gigging with South Philadelphia's jazzmen; in that city he had already met Fanny, his second wife.

Sadie continued to search for security· she worked hard and kept herself tidy; she never wore fancy clothes, but tried to provide what she could for her daughter. In the census records for 1920, a Sadie Harris is listed as living in West Chester, a suburb of Philadelphia, with a black family and several other young boarders; Eleanora is not there, and Sadie's age is listed as nineteen. This may be the wrong Sadie, or she may have been fibbing about her age to make herself more employable; and as researchers in this field are aware, census information from those days is only as good as the person giving it: the census-takers spoke to whoever opened the door. The same year's census for Baltimore lists Sadie and Eleanora living there, with Robert and Eva Miller, forty-three and thirty-three years old, and their two children, Charles and Dorothy All the censuses were supposed to have been taken in January; the Millers may have listed her as living with them even if she was in West Chester, reasoning that Baltimore was her permanent home. The Baltimore census has Sadie's age right, and has her name as Sadie Fagan. She is described as being a sister-in-law and working in a shirt factory

Billie Holiday did not write her autobiography, and bragged that she did not even read it; *Lady Sings the Blues*, written by journalist William Dufty, was published in 1956. The book says that Sadie had worked in a clothing factory during the First World War and then took a job out of town, leaving her with a Cousin Ida and her two children; perhaps it was Eva who became Ida in Billie's book. Billie complained that Ida was a tyrant, but Eva must have had her hands full with a wilful little house guest who was already aware that she did not have much of a family

Billie's book also says that her grandparents and her great-grandmother lived in the same house, but the census does not mention anyone else living there, and there is no evidence that

Eleanora ever lived with any Fagans. Sadie had decided to start calling herself a Fagan by this time, and that was one of her typical mistakes: it was the custom that a natural child took the name of its mother, and nothing would have irritated Aunt Rosie more than someone appropriating the Fagan name who wasn't entitled to it.

Sadie's closest brush with family approval came when she was twenty-four: she married a twenty-five-year-old longshoreman, Philip Gough, on 20 October 1920, and Charlie provided them with a house, at 1421 North Fremont Avenue in West Baltimore. But Sadie's temporary state of grace ended when Gough abandoned her three years later. In 1923 the Emory Street Permanent Building & Loan Company sued for an outstanding mortgage loan of $2,500; Charlie took over the annual rent of $48, a weekly mortgage payment of $9.25 and $2.19 a week for taxes, ground rent and water; and Sadie moved out.

Sadie's household was poor, but she made clothes for Eleanora and sent back second-hand clothes from the rich people's houses she worked in: Eleanora was not exaggerating when she claimed years later to have been 'the sharpest kid in the block when I was dressed up' But there was never enough money, nor a complete family At one point Sadie is said to have worked with her cousin John's wife in a factory (or perhaps with his sister, another Rebecca) and paid that family rare Sunday afternoon visits; this may have been when Eleanora got to know her great-grandmother. But Sadie and Eleanora got no closer than that.

The boss of the Fagans and the guardian of their respectability was Aunt Rosie, the fire-eating and unflappable matron who was also custodian of the family Bible, in which, everyone was led to understand, the family's roots were to be discovered in 'very good people' from West Virginia. But the roots went back to slavery, and nobody wanted to discuss that; no Fagan dared ask Rosie for more information. And Rosie would have nothing to do with Sadie and Eleanora.

There is evidence that Charlie Fagan loved his daughter and granddaughter, and that Clarence was also fond of them, in his careless way Clarence became a well-known big-time musician, and Sadie held them up as figures of fantasy· the prosperous home-owner and the romantic travelling artist. Both men were weak, if we want to see them that way, or they were ordinary men like us, if we do not. Rather than struggle one way or the other, perhaps hopelessly, against what others decreed the norms of family life and blood relationships, they allowed themselves to be looked after by strong women.

In Baltimore in the 1920s, economic stability was hard won and hard to maintain: Charlie and his brothers took whatever work they could get, the work was often seasonal, and there were no labour unions to protect them. John Fagan died in 1951; as Johnny Fagan, Eleanora's uncle, put it many years later, 'We were substantial people. Pop was nothing but a porter all his life, but he fed us and put us through junior high school. He did a pretty good job.'

After Eleanora became famous as Billie Holiday, on one of her visits to the Point, Johnny saw her in a bar on Pratt and Bethel.

I buy her a drink. She asks me how's the family, and I go my way and she go hers. One time she tells me, 'Send for your Pops.' But Pops won't come. He has to be working in the day; he can't be going to no nightclub at 2.30 in the morning when she gets off work. Anyways, he expects her to come and see him in his house. It was her duty to visit him.

And on another occasion, Johnny says, when several Fagans turned out to see her, she told them, 'As far as I'm concerned, all the Fagans are dead.' They were offended, and got up to leave, one of the women calling back over her shoulder, '*You're* the one who's dead, girl.' Billie did not put on airs when she visited Baltimore, but she resented the family's rejection of her and her mother, and the breach was not to be healed. Eleanora, become Billie Holiday, a big name in show business, now belonged for ever to a different world from the senior Fagans. Her Uncle Johnny had a lot of her records and enjoyed her singing, but he was also proud of his own church-going wife and the children they were raising; to have a strong woman to come home to, far from being something to apologize for, was a great improvement on the old slavery lament:

This world is not my home.
This world is not my home.
This world's a howling wilderness,
This world is not my home.

Johnny Fagan remembered the old days:

Sailors came through to see things. This was a seaport town
... When Billie Holiday got famous singing 'I Cover the
Waterfront', that song had a certain meaning for us, and for
her too. She knew where she came up.

Today it's like a jungle. I can walk into a bar and I don't
know a soul in there, believe me! I'm a stranger to people
three houses down. But then we had togetherness. The Point
had finesse. Ethel Moore had a famous good-time house;
Ethel was very congenial. She was pretty good with the
officials. You didn't have to worry about running out the
back door; she paid for her protection. All the years she run
her house, she never went to jail. You could say she run it like
some people run Wall Street.

Billie Holiday used to look up to Ethel like an older sister.
She used to come back here to play the clubs and she always
used to visit Ethel. 'Cause Eleanora sung in Ethel's house. She
worked in it, too, sure, naturally What else was she going to
do in them times? It was a way of life. I knew how to take a
sting when I was ten years old. You had to make ends meet.

I know several guys still living here who was her boyfriends.
Burley used to go with her. Burley used to be an amateur
fighter years ago, but he wasn't all that glamorous . . Penny
used to go with her. Piano-playing Penny – what's his right
name? That's another thing you got to put up with,
nicknames. I know people all their lives only by their
nickname. It's togetherness, has roots in the neighbourhood.

Billie Holiday was very pretty in the bloom of her youth.
Got her colouring from my Uncle Charlie – that's her grandfather, my father's brother . He looked mulatto. My father
was a pretty light fella too, but my Uncle Charlie was lighter
than him, so you know he had to be almost white. Our name
is Irish, the guys in school used to kid us about it. Pop
mention some people in the Civil War days that was good
that came from some parts of Virginia, but families don't like
digging up things. Whites can go back, but blacks can't.
Some people are clannish. It's pride, that's what it is, pride.
Some things I ask the family that they don't even tell me. If
you could get into the family Bible that would be a treasure;
you'd know more about it than I do. But I don't think they'll
get up off none of it .

See, Sadie and Eleanora wasn't too close to the Fagans. The breach came from how they treat Sadie kind of cool like 'cause of the kid. They give her a hard time. It wasn't so much Pops as it was a woman's thing. It was a friction between the women.

Ethel Moore (1906–68) had indeed been a prominent resident of the neighbourhood. Johnny also said that most of the children had been delivered at home by midwives, which is why Sadie had gone to Philadelphia to have Eleanora.

Another story told in Billie's autobiography was about her unnamed great-grandmother, who had had sixteen children, all of whom were dead except Charlie, and who was ninety-seven or ninety-eight years old (in a radio interview Billie said she was 109 when she died). The great-grandmother had dropsy and had to sleep sitting up. She was so tired on one occasion that she lay down just for a few minutes while telling Eleanora a story; and a few hours later the child woke up locked in the arms of a dead woman. This story turns out to be based on fact.

Rebecca and a lot of other Fagans all lived together in one house for a number of years, in Fayette Street, until John Fagan Sr decided that things were getting too crowded, and moved his family round the corner to Dallas Street, taking his mother with him. But Sadie and Eleanora never lived in either of these houses. John had about seven children; Johnny was born in 1916. Johnny Fagan was interviewed again in 1992, and he remembered his grandmother's death.

Rebecca lived to be over seventy, and she did suffer from dropsy (oedema, or water retention, a symptom of liver or kidney trouble). So she did indeed have to sleep sitting up; she had had a lot of children, starting at a very early age, and it was no wonder that her health was failing. But quite a few of her children were still alive when she died, and Billie certainly wasn't there. Johnny remembered it well, because it was about Thanksgiving time and he was excited.

There wasn't any sound from her room, and I was about to go in there and wake her up, but my father stopped me and said, 'That's all right, son.' She was a light sleeper and there hadn't been a sound, and my father knew what had happened.

By 1992 Johnny regretted even more not knowing anything about his family. Rose had died in the 1970s; she had had three children called Fagan and several more with a different surname; the whereabouts of the family Bible are uncertain. Johnny had an aunt called Sophonia Smith, he remembered.

She used to tell my father, 'You ought to be ashamed of yourself, calling those children Fagans. I'm gonna tell 'em who they *really* are.' And she used to say that she was going to tell me the truth about my family But I was just a kid, and I wasn't interested; I wouldn't listen. I regret that now; I regret the *hell* outta that.

Johnny had outlived two wives and never had any children of his own, but they had raised an adopted daughter and one of Johnny's brothers' boys. 'This is no way to raise kids,' he grumbled, meaning that he wished he could tell the younger generation more about their own family. He was more emphatic than he had been in 1972 about Eleanora's grandfather: 'Charlie was a *mulatto*,' he stated flatly Charlie had almost certainly had a different father from the younger Fagans, perhaps a white man; and the African-American community had its own prejudices. Even the attitude of the census reflected it: in 1880 Rebecca and her children are described as 'mulato', in 1890 they are simply black. In fact, the 1910 census was the last one to allow the mulatto designation; the bureaucracy henceforth demanded more rigid racial bifurcation, and while swarthy Europeans and even some Asians and Hispanics came to be regarded as white, a few drops of African blood remained powerful stuff.

Light skin is commonly assumed to have meant more social status, but it could be confusing: Lena Horne, born in Brooklyn, moved to Georgia as a child, and found that her light skin (as well as her speech) were made fun of. 'To some Negroes light colour is far from being a status symbol   it is evidence that your lineage has been corrupted by white people.' She also wrote, 'On the one hand much money was spent on hair-straighteners and skin-lighteners, on the other you were put down for being naturally closer to the prevailing ideal of beauty I did not know whether I was supposed to be proud of my colour or ashamed of it.'

The irony for people who are 'brown all year round' is further compounded by white people who spend money on chemicals to darken their skin and who talk about men who are 'tall, dark and handsome'. Perhaps Charlie's lighter skin, along with Mattie's standoffishness, had one way or another contributed to cool feelings in the family. At any rate, in the twenty years between Johnny Fagan's interviews, the whole attitude of the African-American community had changed: black studies had become an established academic discipline, and Alex Haley's *Roots* had had enormous impact: Johnny had read it several times. But the older generation of Fagans was gone and had taken its secrets to the grave.

There had been Mattie to rule the roost in Charlie's house, and Rosie to help keep Sadie at bay; and soon Clarence had a wife in New York. The child Eleanora yearned for her handsome grandfather and her dashing father, men who achieved things and got respect; but what she saw was that all Sadie's hard work went for very little, and her good intentions for even less: Sadie remained poor and rejected, while Bible-thumpers like Mattie and Rosie looked to Eleanora like hypocrites, living on pedestals. In her autobiography many years later, Eleanora/Billie remembered Philip Gough affectionately and told her ghost-writer that he had died; we can only imagine why he abandoned Sadie and what effect this had on the child. When he was gone, Eleanora began to find her own way, to make her own decisions. She began seeking her philosophy of life in the street.

She was registered in the fourth grade at Public School 104 in West Baltimore, but when she had been nabbed once too often playing hooky, a probation officer named M. Dawson brought her to juvenile court. For the court record, Sadie gave their names as Sadie and Eleanora Gough, and Eleanora's guardian's name as Philip Gough, whereabouts unknown; a magistrate named Williams judged Eleanora a 'minor without proper care and guardianship' and committed her to the House of Good Shepherd for Colored Girls.

On 5 January 1925 she entered a forbidding red-brick building on Calverton and Franklin, operated on a shoestring by the self-sustaining Little Sisters of the Poor. She received the protective pseudonym of Madge (which she changed many years later to Theresa). For some reason Good Shepherd thought she was born in Baltimore in 1914, but testified years later that Sadie had given them the correct information: Eleanora was only nine, much younger than the usual age, which ranged from about thirteen to eighteen. Many of the girls were already streetwise and familiar with petty crime; as the youngest and prettiest, Eleanora may have discovered lesbianism. As her girlhood chum, Pony, casually explained, it was simply the way things were.

Mary 'Pony' Kane was the only woman in Baltimore who would talk to Linda Kuehl in 1971 about Eleanora. 'Others were cautioned not to – one by a husband, another by a school psychologist daughter, others who claimed not to know anything, and sent me packing with cryptic smiles.' Perhaps, Linda speculated, Eleanora's life resembled theirs too closely, when many a poor girl worked in the street; but Pony, a feisty survivor of sixty years, did not bother to defer to morals imposed by others. She had also played hooky· 'All my mother could say was that she sent me to school, but the Principal put in a report.' A little younger than Eleanora, she went to Good Shepherd a little later.

> The state put me in there too   Then they throwed me out 'cause I cussed Mother Margaret. Mother Margaret was mean, hit me on the fingers with a ruler. So I say, 'If you hit me again, goddam if I don't hit you back.' Well, she gets my little skirts and blouses together and called my mother right up and she say that I am on my way. She say, 'If you be bad again, you sure ain't comin' back here. You going to that *other* place' [a tougher reformatory]. It sure didn't make me unhappy, nope.
>
> Some of the older girls was tough, though. The older girls fuck the younger ones. Sneak 'em candy, talk nice to 'em, and when they catch 'em in bed, they fuck 'em. Some would cry, and a lot would tell their parents, but a whole lot wouldn't tell nobody ... I mean the average girl goes to bed with another girl just for kicks. I knowed a few women who started doing it just to be doing something .

In this not entirely salubrious place, where the no doubt hard-worked regime could not keep everything under control, both devils and angels lived, as in the real world: Eleanora was baptized there, in the Sacred Heart Chapel. As Sadie could not present formal proof of Billie's baptism at birth, Father Edward Casserly gave her conditional baptism and absolution on 14 August 1925; and in the eyes of the Church at least, Eleanora became legitimate. A godfather was listed as Oliver Welsh; her godmother was Christine Scott.

Good Shepherd received $3,000 a year from the state; to make ends meet the Sisters took in laundry and raised chickens, and the inmates had chores assigned to them. Christine Scott worked in the kitchen and spent the rest of her life in institutions, a compromise which gave her security, but did not encourage a lot of expertise in the godmother line. Interviewed at the age of eighty-four, she was living in St Martin's, an old-age home run by the Little Sisters of the Poor, and her memory was sharp, everything agreeing with the records:

> I'm not an affectionate person . . . You get into a lot of trouble when you have a lot of friends flocking around. The only place I went with the girls was to Mass every day. I took my meals in the kitchen . They used to call me stuck up, but I don't know, there was always something in me . . .
>
> Madge and me wasn't the same. I was a growed-up person and Madge was nothing but a child, but she was right plump and tall as any fourteen-year-old girl. Very nice-looking brown skin. Her features was even and light. She wasn't as light as me, but she was light, and she had a very nice suit of hair. Neat and clean was she . . . Took no interest in anything but sewing. Always down in the dumps, very seldom had anything to do with nobody else . . . Then one Monday morning was the first communion and I went down to the chapel .. the chaplain came in and beckoned me with his finger. 'Come inside with me for a few minutes.' He asked if I was baptized and confirmed; I said, 'Yes, Father.' He asked me would I stand up for a girl and pointed to Madge . . . I don't think I [had] said two words to her before, but I said, 'Yes, Father, I will.' She was to be baptized and I was to be her godmother.
>
> Everybody in the place knowed how much she wanted to be baptized. She expressed herself. She told the Father she'd been baptized down at St Francis Xavier [a church on the Point where Sadie and Eleanora had attended Mass], but her name wasn't there and her parents' names wasn't there.
>
> She was so happy, poor child. She was in there with the rest of the girls, all of them in white dresses and veils; she was grinning from ear to ear, you could almost see her back teeth. She was just as light as a feather. And after she went down to

see the Sisters, and the Sisters gave her Mary rosary beads. She was so tickled. Oh, and yes, I gave her a prayer book. I almost forgot that. She must of appreciated it 'cause she always kept it in her hand.

After that she used to come from dinner and sit right on the floor beside me. I'd be sewing or looking in a book, and I would say, 'Hello, how you getting on?' or something like that . . . I didn't ask her a thing about herself or her parents. If she was going to tell me, I was going to listen. She never told me anything and I never asked. I don't know nothing about her private life at all.

When she left I don't know who took her. I don't know where she went. We never correspond. That was the end of Madge. She was a right good girl. Next thing I hear she come back for a visit [in 1953] . . . I was down in the yard with the chickens or someplace, but nobody came for me. The next thing I read, she died . . . When I seen her picture, I said to myself, 'That's my godchild. That's my Madge.'

3

The Point

On 3 October 1925 Eleanora was released to her mother's custody, and they moved to the only part of Baltimore they could afford. In 1778, so an immigrant to Baltimore testified to the Maryland Historical Society in 1844, Fell's Point had been a sparsely settled outpost of the town, separated from it by forest and farmers' fields; in 1925 the Point was still separated: it was the wrong side of the tracks and included a red-light district.

'You know Freddie?' Pony asked. 'His girl just got into trouble.' Freddie was elusive, because he was protecting a barmaid who had shot a girl whose brothers were looking to even the score. Linda Kuehl met him in a private club.

Freddie remained a sporty dresser and a fan of Eleanora's. According to him, Sadie and Eleanora started out in the 600 block of Bond. 'It was a beautiful neighbourhood, one block this side of Johns Hopkins hospital.' That end of Bond was on the opposite side of town to the Point.

> You're getting it from the horse's mouth, 'cause when I found out who Eleanora was, that she was Billie Holiday . . . I was buying her records and having a ball with 'em and I didn't know it was the same girl I came up with, you dig? 'Cause Billie was the same age as me.
>
> She and Miss Sadie sublet from my mother. They used to use my mother's kitchen. On Sunday mornings it was tripe fried in batter and eggs and hot biscuits and bacon and a dish of molasses on the side. Miss Sadie was such a great cook. She was a short neat pretty little lady, everything always in place.

She used to go to Catholic church on the 600 block of Eager, and I remember she used to have a little tiny statue of the Saviour on the wall. I can't recollect but I think she used to do day work 'cause my mother did the same out at Roland Park. Money was so measly . . . Miss Sadie was making weekend trips to New York, but she never left Eleanora too long. I think that's when she met that musician Holiday. My mother said, 'I know Miss Sadie is going there weekends so she must have a friend' . . . but he came after Baltimore.

By this time Clarence was indeed living in New York, but he was from another part of town, and the only Eastsiders who knew that he was from Baltimore, and that he was Eleanora's father, were the Fagans. Pony had never heard of him, either. Freddie went on:

Then I helped 'em move down to the Point. Miss Sadie told my mother she found a little home, and she say, 'Well, Freddie can help you move.' I paid two dollars and a half for a harness team, and one load did it. I use to go there for dinner on Sundays, only you had to fight your way to their end of town. That was the bottom of the Point. That's what they called the *bottom*.

Sadie took a room for them in Spring Street, until she met Wee Wee Hill, a good-natured reprobate, whereupon they moved to the second floor of 217 Durham Street, a row house owned by Wee Wee's mother, Miss Lucy Hill, known to one and all as Miss Lu. Pony and her mother lived on the third floor, 'in the attic, like. It was an ordinary old row house,' said Pony. 'Bath out back. Wasn't too good. Shit. Nope. Take the water up from the summer kitchen.'

Sadie continued taking transportation jobs, which meant leaving Eleanora with others. She tried to be enterprising; somewhere along the way she is said to have opened a restaurant in Baltimore on Pratt Street, though all this meant was hanging out a sign that said 'East Side Restaurant'. She cooked pigs' feet, red beans and rice in her kitchen, and served it with bootleg whisky in her living room, while still working during the day as a domestic. In their restaurant *manqué* Sadie and Eleanora had gas and electricity, and Eleanora never forgot it. Many years later, she told *PM* magazine,

We were the first family in the neighbourhood to have gas and electricity. Mom had worked as a maid in New York and Philly. She'd seen all the rich people with gas and electric lights and decided we had to have them, too. So she saved her wages for the day.

But Sadie's time on the Point was a disappointment, and Wee Wee was another rejection. He was eight years younger than Sadie and remembered the time well; for a while Eleanora regarded him as a stepfather, and nearly fifty years later he voiced pangs of remorse over his misspent youth, while also forgiving himself, according to the eternal double standard:

> My mother tried to get me to do the right thing by Sadie, and that's the truth. She said, 'If a woman's good enough for you to live with, she's good enough for you to marry.' I guess I was a bad fella. I was gambling, running around, running different women. Sadie tried to fight me a couple of times, but I wouldn't hurt her . . . She came rapping on a house in Bond Street. I looked out the window and seen her with a gun. It surprised me; I didn't think she cared that much to hurt me. I didn't go home till her cousin, John Fagan Sr, Johnny's father – he's dead and gone now – come and got the gun and brang it to me. When I came home she grabbed a wooden cigarette stand with trees on it, you know, like prongs like, and swang it and cut my wrist. She was short but she was strong. Eleanora tried to stop her, tried to talk sense to her, but I run.
> Sadie said she wanted to marry me . . . I guess I never did have my mind set to getting married. So she said that she would never stay with me no more in Baltimore, and went up to New York. We correspond back and forth and finally I did go up there. She was working as a maid-cook for a family name Levy in Cedarhurst, Long Island, and we live like husband and wife. They got me a job as a porter in a cotton goods store in Times Square. I didn't stay long; my mother was sick. She fell and broke her leg on ice and it never did set proper. When I came back to Baltimore, I met Viola, and she came between me and Sadie. I promised my mother I'd marry Viola.

Sadie used to buy goods and stitch her and Eleanora clothes and stitch me silk shirts   . She didn't do no drinking or messing up.

On the one hand, banging on somebody's door and waving a pistol in the air while looking for her boyfriend couldn't have done Sadie's social standing with the Fagans much good; but on the other, Wee Wee seemed to understand that if he married Sadie his own good times would be over. Men like Charlie Fagan and his brothers had strong women to look after them and kept their end of the bargain; and men like Wee Wee had women to look after them, period. After Wee Wee's mother died he married Viola, and in 1971 Viola was dead, but Wee Wee had another woman to look after him (who said grumpily, 'I don't know nothin' 'bout no Billie Holiday').

Sadie knew that Wee Wee would never marry her, and Clarence was in New York; so she stayed on Long Island and left Eleanora with Miss Lu for a while. It was during this period that Eleanora found her role models. Miss Lu was an invalid and could not go upstairs in her own home, much less look after an increasingly mischievous child. 'Miss Lu was cripple,' said Pony. 'She fell coming through the alley, and they don't know nothing about cancer then. And this hole just ate and ate.'

Eleanora loved her mother in her way, although she could have no respect for her in the most important sense. Indeed, she became and remained a mirror image of her mother, tied to her by her very rebellion. If Sadie tried to maintain some semblance of respectability despite being rejected, Eleanora rejected the hypocrites, leaping over the fence in psychological terms and remaining outside conventional respectability in one way or another for the rest of her life. If her mother went as a servant to white men for their money, the men, white and black, came to Eleanora; they gave her money willingly, and she rolled them for the rest. Even the pimps gave her money, because they liked her, because they knew they could not control her and because she could sing. And if the most important men in her life rejected Sadie, Eleanora chose her own men according to how tough they thought they were and then rejected them before they could reject her. But as Eleanora began to become Billie Holiday, it is clear that she also became a hero, not a victim. Like many of the greatest artists, she roared through life like an express train, staying sane by remaining faithful to the sub-culture in which she found herself, never asking for anything, and certainly not for permission.

Sadie was short, knock-kneed and inclined to be matronly, though Wee Wee and others praised her skin and her straight hair. Eleanora was only ten or eleven years old when she was turned loose on the Point, but she was big for her age, taller and better-looking than her mother. 'She hung in there with Ethel Moore,' Wee Wee recalled, referring to the good-time house. 'Ethel was a hustling woman and Eleanora looked to her like she was a mother. She hung in there with Alice Dean and them girls, so she had to be doing what they was doing. I guess she had to get money somehow.' Yet expressing his own double standard, Wee Wee went on to exaggerate the help that Sadie and Eleanora got from him and from Charlie, saying, 'She didn't have to hustle, no.' The only one to be the judge of that was Eleanora.

> But she became a fast woman. She wanted fast money, fast life, that's right. I knowed one boy she used to went with: Dee Dee. He live with his mother and work in the wholesale fish market in the oyster house and pack orders. He liked Eleanora, but she was too fast for him. After Dee Dee she went with a hustler. People knowed it; that's what give her a bad name. My mother loved Sadie so naturally she loved Eleanora too; she tried to talk to her, you know, about being a good girl. But Eleanora didn't like it either. [Did Wee Wee mean by 'either' that he didn't listen to his mother any more than Eleanora did?] She come to the house to spend a night and get a meal and listen, but she never did give a damn.

Years later, in her autobiography, Eleanora/Billie described scrubbing the marble steps of Baltimore's famous row houses, and claimed to have made more money than the other girls because she brought her own bucket and rags. This much may have been true: Pony says that they both scrubbed steps. But Eleanora soon found that there were easier ways to make better money. 'Sadie work, but I didn't see Eleanora work,' said Wee Wee. 'Never knowed Eleanora to scrub steps.'

In 1971 Pony was living in a peeling row house, but by then there were holes in the row: on one side of her was a rubble-strewn lot where Ethel Moore's good-time house had been, and on the other side the house where Johnny Fagan had grown up was gone:

Shit, no work in them days. No work down here except in packing season ... I used to go up and down Pratt Street where them Jewish people live. Scrub them steps and a whole house for a few pennies. I didn't knowed Eleanora to go in too much for that. I never knowed about her working, nope. She wanted fast money, yep. She was getting a meal, missing a meal, catching a trick or two. She came back to Durham Street, take off a pair of stockings, wash 'em out, put 'em back on half dry and go out to where the happenings is.

Pony described the scene at Durham Street: Wee Wee stayed with Sadie when he felt like it, but mainly just kept his clothes there, and took most of his meals with his mother. 'He was a handsome guy, had other girlfriends. A lot of women, yep. So he and Miss Sadie couldn't make it too much.' Sadie left Eleanora there, and 'When Miss Sadie be gone, she be gone too.'

Eleanora was getting around fast. You know the kind of people that say, 'I'm gonna get cussed out anyways, so what's the difference? What the hell?' Well, Eleanora just went out and done what she felt like doing 'cause she was just don't care-ish.

I used to follow her. I was younger and teeny and fat; she was a big noble-looking girl. I followed her to the five-and-ten-cent store on Broadway ... We stole a skirt. She put it under my coat. My mother beat me about it, but Eleanora tell her she bought it with money she got cleaning .. she was young and rough in her way. She just come out of this home where they put coloured girls ...

After describing her own stay at Good Shepherd and the goings-on there, Pony said, 'I never knowed Eleanora to be with girls.' Not in those days, but Pony also said that later she went up to Harlem to visit, and thought that Eleanora went with women. 'I know a few women who started using dope and then they started likin' women.' But in the early days in Baltimore,

Nope, Eleanora dug them guys. She liked a whole lot of boys

and a whole lot dug her. Like Dee Dee ... Dee Dee had bread 'cause he was the only boy in his family. His family used to be crazy about him. But Eleanora called them 'country boys'. Eleanora would just get the money, and she have no time for 'em. She was running down to Alice Dean's with the girls, down there to the 200 block of Dallas where they have a house. She can get herself a dollar a trick, a quarter a trick, and if she get herself a good wallet, then, oh then, she can make herself plenty of money.

Let me tell you something. You see a man coming around the neighbourhood looking for sport, there's no telling how rich he be. White guys, straights, squares mostly. Coloured have no money, they have nothing. But them white guys come up from the waterfront to Pratt and Dallas, and down from Broadway to Dallas, and the women be waiting. They walk 'em into Alice Dean's and clip 'em.

They go in with the girl expecting to give her what few pennies they was going to give her, but she has a chair sitting like this by the door in front of the bed. Okay, so when he pulls off his pants, she goes in and takes the wallet out, takes out the money and puts the wallet back. If the guy don't take off his pants, her hand is working on the wallet like this. They never do nothing but fuck, 'cause if a man go down on her she can't beat him. Then he is on his own. She might have to jive him, like tell him, 'Go ahead and do such-and-such a thing till I get it hard, or till I get my own self straighten out,' till she can get around and beat him. Or Alice Dean or one of the girls has to sneak behind and help her beat him.

No telling how much money they make. You never see people getting so rich so quick. Eleanora was doing it. *I* wasn't – not then. Then I was learning the trade, by working in the house and watching. Alice Dean never learned me nothing, I just watch what she did. I did anything to be in there, *just to be in there*. Takes me a whole day to scrub outside one room so's I can peeps in to see how it goes.

They don't have too much oil cloth then, so I scrub the floor until it be yella. You can eat off the floor. I used to starch and iron them drapes. Alice have white drapes in one bedroom, everything was white, the furniture, everything. The other was all blue. Alice Dean have beautiful clothes in

the closets. Fur coats, Chinese furs, Hudson seals .. There
wasn't no minks then, honey. She used to wear house dresses.
No pants cause they was too much trouble to take off. She wear
them big brim hats with flat tops and birds-of-paradise feathers,
and Casablanca hats during the war. She have nice long hair,
straight, parted in the middle, made her look like an Indian.
    Oh, Alice Dean have everything. A graphophone in the
living room that they used to wind up and put a record on.
Play 'Black Bottom' and 'Stormy Weather' and a whole lot of
blues Susie stuff – whatchyou call it? – Butterbeans and Susie?
They have all them Florence Mills records and Bessie Smith
and Mamie Smith. They wasn't too much with Louis
Armstrong, nope. They was mostly with blues singers, them
women blues singers, right. They would have pianos in people's
houses and sing and booze and dance. Mary-Mary on
Lombard Street – her sister Esther, and Billie Holiday used to
go to carnival over there on Carver Street. They used to have
block carnivals and do the Lindy Hop and all that stuff.

Pony's chronology slips a little: 'Black Bottom' was a hit in 1926,
but 'Stormy Weather' not until 1933; the Lindy Hop and
Casablanca belong to later years. But her details are interesting.
Pony includes Florence Mills, who made it to Broadway before she
died in 1927; Mills never recorded, but fifty years later Pony
would have remembered the name of the great black star for
whom Duke Ellington wrote 'Black Beauty'. Butterbeans and Susie
were Joe (or Jody) and Susie Edwards, a vaudeville team who
began recording their off-colour blues in 1924. 'Love Me and the
World Is Mine (Hit Me and the Jail Is Yours)' was made in 1926,
'I Wanna Hot Dog for My Roll' in 1927, and they made an
album in 1963, the year Susie died.
    The girls would have liked the women blues singers, but Louis
Armstrong, though he would be a profound influence on Eleanora,
had begun his rise to national fame only in 1926. People in
Baltimore would have used the word graphophone to describe a
gramophone (just as most Americans used the word phonograph),
because the graphophone was a variant of Edison's original
phonograph, and the successful Columbia Graphophone Company
was the Maryland, Delaware and District of Columbia franchise
that became Columbia Records.

Pony remembers the clothes, and how good everyone looked:

Miss Sadie and her was always keeping theirself looking good. Eleanora always wear nice things more than the average girl out there. Miss Sadie used to bring her nice clothes from New York and Philadelphia, pleated dresses – navy, black, red. Stockings in the wintertime – dark brown, ginger brown, brown toast. Silk [stockings] was only a quarter [25 cents]. Eleanora used to wear satin slips and panties. Most of the sporting women do. All colours – red, orange, black, lavender, green, yellow – so when they pull up their dress . . .

In her autobiography in 1956, Eleanora/Billie told the famous story of how she was desperate for a job, and was discovered as a singer in Harlem, at Pod's and Jerry's, trying out first as a dancer. But Pony and everybody else on the Point remembered her singing from the time she hit the street. Freddie recalled,

We had a wind-up victrola [another generic term, from Victor's trademark for their gramophone], and when Eleanora was living with us I put on records and Eleanora sung along. They was records by Bessie Smith and her sister Mamie Smith. [The Smiths were not sisters, but everyone thought they were.] Eleanora always like the sad ones. She could pick up tunes just like that. Then I lost track of her, and the next thing I hear she comes back to Baltimore to play the Royale Theater with Count Basie.

Pony goes into more detail about the partying:

Specially on Monday night. Yeah, Monday was Blue Monday . . business is slow after the weekend, so they used to go to the different clubs and party and ball and go around to the different houses. Drink theirself to death. The best-dressed hustlers used to come around the neighbourhood to get Eleanora for the sing. They be wearing the pinstripe suits and caps from Matteburgs and leather nob shoes with the wing toes, and red garters of velvet on their shirt-sleeves. A lot of hustling men liked Eleanora; they pick her up and take her to the good-time houses.
    A couple of the boys used to sing too . . but Eleanora take the cake. She was the big attraction. Everybody pile in when

she sing. She do the popular tunes of the day, fast and slow numbers. They have a place on Caroline Street where a man play piano in the back room; Eleanora could pick up a couple of bucks there.

Skinny 'Rim' Davenport was one of the pimps. In 1971 Skinny was a school janitor, 'a toothless, caved-in, stringbean of a man', according to Linda Kuehl:

> His voice is mellow as vintage brandy and his line of jive as smooth as the blackberry wine he sipped with Billie at Ethel Moore's. He was one of Billie's earliest patrons – the pimp as patron of her art. That art gave her leverage and equality, for Skinny gave *her* money rather than the other way around. I know he spared Billie obligatory moralizing because retrospectively he happily spared me.

These people were not ashamed of the lives they'd led, because life was simply a fact, not a fairy tale. Skinny left 'the life' when he returned from the Army to find his girls and possessions whisked away to Cleveland by another hustler, but he'd had his good times. 'My mother,' he said, 'she work for her living cleaning other people's houses.'

> But I give her money. That's why I live so long, 'cause I was good to my mother.
> I was pimping then, yeah. All the fellas was pimping. Didn't have no cars, didn't want to throw away no money on no cars. Wanted that money to pile up so's we could spend it balling. Eleanora liked us. Eleanora lived the fast life; she loved the fast life. That's what I loved too.
> No telling how much I blowed in one night. However much my girls gave me, that's how much I blowed. I saw 'em each every day, they give me whatever they make. They was glad to give it to me. They love me, that's what they say. I was a young man; I satisfy 'em in bed. They don't want nothing else. I give 'em whatever they need to keep 'em presentable for trade.
> They didn't go too many places. I'm the one has to sport; they didn't do no sporting. Now and then I take one of 'em to a nightclub, but I never let 'em see no other cats. If they'd of

done that I'd of beat 'em up. Oh, they love that; they be so proud of their black eye. 'Look, look what my man done to me!' That's what they like, baby. You have to treat 'em rough. I don't know why. Some people like it that way. You can't be calm or else you lose 'em. Lose 'em? I can't afford to lose 'em. You kidding? Not unless somebody come to town and steals 'em. I have to fight to keep 'em in line; I don't just sit there looking cute. And another thing: a woman likes for her man to keep her out of jail regardless of the fine, just to keep her out of jail. Otherwise, hell, when she comes out some other cat's going to get her for sure.

But I have no stable; my girls live in different parts of town Two I have thieving on the Point. My white girl, Babe, I keep in a room. Some nights they clip cats for three, four hundred bucks. Sometimes I take a girl up to Langston, Chester or Philadelphia and leave her there for a week. Pretty good hustling in them big-time houses. Big sporting action in Baltimore is the Middle Section Club on Lexington, between Forrest and Eastern; that's the big-time club where all the hustlers come from out of town to skin all night. Club lets out at six, we go sleep, sleep till afternoon, take a bath, go to some bar, mess around.

Sunday morning we go out on the street. People in the neighbourhood be cooking; they say, 'Come on over for some salad, hot chicken and some bread.' They was the good people, people what worked, like my mother knowed his mother and his mother knowed somebody else's mother and like that.

My father, he work at Sparrow's Point in the steel mill, but I make more in one night than he make in six months, maybe. I never knowed no Depression. I have more money in the Depression than I ever have in my whole life.

On Monday we go sport. Everybody balls on Blue Monday, even working people. I dress up real sharp. I like them double-breasted suits with monkey backs, purple suits, suits with pinstripes in it. You got to have that pinstripe. Mike Turk on Green Street custom-make mine. I like Hamburger hats, white, big ten gallon. And Florsheim shoes. All the pimps have the best clothes.

We hire cabs and pick up cute chicks along the way.

Eleanora used to go with us. I like Eleanora as a friend. I give
her money; there was nothing she could give me. I just like
her company. We smoke reefers, good stuff then. I was no big
drinker; maybe a glass of blackberry wine with ice and
lemonade. Now and then I snort some coke. Use to like to
smoke with Eleanora. Let her go ahead, you know, get high
and have a ball.

She was a good girl. She wasn't messing with hard stuff, I
mean. She used to sing; she have singing on her mind. She tell
us where she be and we follow her from club to club. First she
sing at the place on Bethel and Pratt that's tore down now
and she come up Central and Pratt, and then she go up here
on Baltimore and Dallas where the barbershop is now. The
clubs close up and we take her to the good-time houses.

Take her to Ethel Moore. That's where she start in smoking
reefers. Ethel have a bar upstairs with a graphophone; take a
trick, smoke, drink, play records. Eleanora sings if we ask. Put
a record on that has no words and she sings 'em. Or she sings
without music.

Six o'clock come again and people start in getting tired.
They go home, go sleep; I go back to the York Hotel. I don't
know where Eleanora go. Maybe with Tootie or Nitey, or one
of the latest guys . . . they dead now. I'm the only one still
living.

'Diesel' Haskins was the manager of Baltimore's Apollo Club in
1971. He remembered, 'You take two or three piano players with
us to somebody's house where they have a piano. And the parents
sit around and listen, and then go to bed, and we just play into the
early morning, singing, dancing. And then we go home and wash
up and change and go to school.' It is not clear exactly when this
was, but Diesel thought that the stevedore Gough was Eleanora's
father; the other children may have gone to school, but soon
enough Eleanora was a drop-out. Charlie Ray, present at the
Apollo Club interview, said that her first singing job was at Buddy
Love's, at Orleans Street and Wayside, 'after hours'. He
remembered eating bowls of beans with her in a lunchroom at
Caroline and Monumental at three in the morning; you got all
you could eat for 15 cents. One of her boyfriends was Calvin
Atkins, who Charlie thought was about ten years older and

smacked her on the side of her head for wearing his shoes. 'Mostly all of her men was hustling type of men. That's the only kind of men that she liked, because they understood her life. Whatever she did or wherever she'd go, there were no questions asked. These guys understood life because they was out in it.'

Pony's memories just won't stop. 'She used to go down to Broadway to this Custer Movie for Amateur, sing shows at the Star Theater too. Sing in Reverend Scott's Baptist Church and all them little old store-front churches what they used to have on Dallas Street.' It's impossible to know how much of this is literally true, but Baltimore was full of music, and the cumulative detail is impressive. Eleanora was already a singer.

And if we needed proof of sexual abuse, we now have that too. Lady's autobiography said that she had been sent to the Good Shepherd Home because she had been raped; we know that she was initially sent there because she wasn't attending school, but British journalist Stuart Nicholson has discovered that the story about the rape is true. Early on 26 December 1926 Sadie and Wee Wee came home from a night out to find a Wilbert Rich having sexual intercourse with Eleanora. Later that day she was examined by doctors, Rich was arrested and Eleanora was sent back to the Good Shepherd Home as a 'State Witness', and no doubt also (as Nicholson points out in his book *Billie Holiday*) because the quality of her 'care and guardianship' was once more in question. She was held there until 27 February 1927, and apparently baptised again; meanwhile, on 18 January, Rich was found guilty of 'Rape — Carnal Knowledge of 14–16 year old' (although Eleanora was only eleven) and received a custodial sentence of three months.

Pony remembered a child who was big for her age and lived in a place where children grew up young.

She was young then; all the girls was young, but she was the youngest. She was tall, shape pretty nice, and by her being so young and singing so good, different fellas liked her. She was light-complected like her mother. Miss Sadie was a light brown-skin lady, but short and chunky with knock-knees and like that. She have a good quality hair but not so good as her daughter. Eleanora used to wear it back with a ribbon 'round a bun. One time she have it in a pageboy like, and another time she have it cut in a real boyish bob with a clip in back. Both of 'em didn't straighten it – didn't have to.

Oh, I can tell you all the women was jealous of her. Used to beat her up sometimes. Somebody go tell somebody else that such-and-such a girl is out with your man last night, women talk, you know. And they be out looking for her until she get in with 'em and she get rough too; then she be swinging out this a-way with Hilda and Tooty and Nitey and all of 'em . . . Eleanora stay with Nitey next door [Eva 'Nitey' Beasley, at 219 Durham]. Nitey used to sing too. All of 'em sung, at Miss Ella's after hours and Pop Major's. Sung and boozed and smoked them real skinny reefers that seamen used to roll for the foreigners, Isaac and Miss Laura out on Caroline. Sell 'em three for a quarter. Eleanora used to smoke 'em. Eleanora used to love that bootleg whisky too, that corn liquor, that white lightning. I imagine she be feeling good, pretty high, and she come out on the street cursing and hollering, 'You motherfucker, cocksucker, kiss my ass, kiss my ass.'

A child, eleven or twelve years old, shouting the worst words she knew in the street, anxious to be grown up. She already knew all about hypocrites, and she knew what kind of world she lived in. She told in her book about some 'nosy bitch' accusing her of doing 'that thing', and about her own salty answer causing still more trouble: 'She thought it was terrible for me to say what she had been thinking.' If the world seemed to be a howling wilderness, Eleanora was going to tame it the best she could. Pony went on:

A lot of people don't like you calling 'em motherfuckers; they beat you for it. A lot of men, a lot of women. Not everybody cuss their men. Hilda don't; she knowed she was going to get her ass beat. But Eleanora say it anyways: 'Suck my ass, suck my ass . . .' She be half a block aways, and some would let it slide, and some would say, 'I *am* going to suck your ass, bitch,' and beat her ass too . . .
      Eleanora didn't say much. She must have liked the men beating on her. The fellas that was crazy for her, she didn't have no time for, and the ones that have somebody else was the ones she wanted. She wanted who she wanted. They was lovers, they was young, they have women hustling for 'em, giving 'em money. Tidy was one. That's one she went with;

he didn't have no job, women took care of him. Then there was Beans. Beans has a wife, but I guess you could call him a pimp too. In his later years after he came out of the service, then he work. But when he was young, he was nice looking and dark and small and solid and looked good in clothes. And Freddie. You know Freddie? . . .
They slap her around a lot, her men did, yep. Beat her up when they can ketch her. *I* seen it. *I* seen her come back to Durham Street looking like she be put through the mill. Her eyes was made up so you won't notice too much. The house was dark 'cause Miss Lu didn't have no electricity, she only have cobalt lamps. But *I* can see. That's when Miss Lu write Miss Sadie to come down to Baltimore and carry Eleanora away, 'cause Eleanora is getting too much for her to handle. Different peoples come back to tell her things. Eleanora's face broke out in big red splotches and peoples say she has disease . . .
And I'll never forget when Eleanora leave Baltimore. She have on a white voile dress with a red shiny belt.

We cannot be sure when Eleanora left for New York; some say it was in 1929, at the age of fourteen. Diesel Haskins said she sang 'Sentimental Baby' in Baltimore, a song not published or recorded until 1928; but he was interviewed over forty years later, and he also thought she was fifteen or sixteen years old. Elmer Snowden said that he met her in Harlem in 1927 and he didn't recognize her at first. Wee Wee remembers, 'Finally she left Baltimore and that was that summer of 1927. Her last night she stayed in our house; I took her to Pennsylvania Station. She was glad to go . . .'
Eleanora/Billie herself remembered comparing her solo 'flight' to New York to the famous solo flight of Charles Lindbergh across the Atlantic, which had taken place in May 1927 and was the biggest news story of the year. From this point on, her ghost-written autobiography, though careless about details, is considerably more believable.
She says that she stayed on the train past her stop, intending to go straight to Harlem (perhaps to look for her father?); that when she disembarked in New York she got lost, and was picked up by kindly welfare authorities, to whom she refused to give her name; and that she was finally reunited with Sadie, who was still working

for the Levy family, who (we know from Wee Wee's testimony) were not imagined. Sadie then found a job for Eleanora as a maid. Many years later Billie admitted that the chores were not onerous, but she soon got herself fired, having decided against domestic service as a career. All of this rings true, for Eleanora was a wilful, intelligent child who was used to doing as she pleased.

Then, we are told, Sadie agreed to board her in Harlem, no doubt giving in to the child's importuning, and settled her in an apartment house off 141st Street. This, Billie said, was a fancy building where high rents were paid, and where her landlady was Florence Williams, the biggest madam in Harlem. It is hard to believe Billie's claim that her mother was simply naïve, but whatever the circumstances, for the first and probably the last time Eleanora was actually an inmate of a house of prostitution, something she hardly would have allowed in her book if it wasn't true. And her description of it (or Dufty's) is priceless. Still very young, and perhaps not too crazy about sex, she found her white customers easier to tolerate.

> With my regular white customers, it was a cinch   When they came to see me it was wham, bang, they gave me the money and were gone. I made all the loot I needed. But Negroes would keep you up all the damn night, handing you that stuff about 'Is it good, baby?' and 'Don't you want to be my old lady?'

The hard facts, as researcher Stuart Nicholson discovered, are that Sadie and Eleanora were both arrested working in Florence's brothel in the spring of 1929. Eleanora was barely 14 years old but claimed to be 21 and got away with it. For some reason Sadie was released, but Eleanora was sent to Welfare Island until October.

The next verified testimony about Eleanora's activities comes from tenor saxophonist Kenneth Hollon, who years later played with Billie on recording sessions. In 1930 or 1931, when he was first gigging professionally on clarinet, apparently with Hat Hunter's band, he took her to the Gray Dawn, a cabaret at Jamaica Avenue and South Street in Queens. He said that the audience in this place threw money on the floor, and 'Billie made her first dollar in New York that night.' Or, he said, it might have been 1932, at the Paradise on Prospect and South. But she sang Fats Waller's 'My Fate Is in Your Hands' and 'Honeysuckle Rose',

38

and 'How Am I to Know' (by Jack King and Dorothy Parker, from 1929). Billie had a boyfriend then named Ham who was insanely jealous, said Hollon; he was a pimp, but Billie wasn't on the game. She and Sadie were living in Brooklyn, at 7 Glenada Place in the heart of Bedford Stuyvesant; but the subway ride under the river was only a nickel, and Billie was familiar with Harlem by then.

And from about that time, there is some final testimony from Wee Wee Hill:

Sadie came back [to Baltimore] when she heard about her father being sick. She came to me at the B&O Building where I was working as a porter to ask me would I go across the street to ask him to come out so she could see him. See, Sadie had an awful bad stepmother and I knowed she never did go to their house. I knowed she never went there 'cause the woman was pretty mean. I say this 'cause when I went in there she wouldn't allow me to go upstairs to his bedroom; she made Mr Fagan come downstairs with his robe on. I told him I want to borrow some money and he slip me ten. But I didn't want the money, I want to talk to him. But *she* was sitting there. Finally she left, and I told him that Sadie was waiting outside. He said, 'I can't go, I'm too weak. Tell her I said to take care of herself, but I'm too weak. I can't go out.'

I went to tell Sadie and she sit and cry, and talk and cry. She tell me to keep in contact. 'Let me know how my father is getting along.' She went back to New York, but I didn't do it. I didn't keep in contact with her. See, instead of me writing to tell her her father pass, she write and tell me. It tore me to the heart; I guess I could of did that little bit for her . . . I should of went back to the house to see how he was getting on.

But see, for one thing, when he die, his wife never did notify any of his people. Even his own brothers didn't know he was dead. When Sadie find out, he was dead and buried in the ground.

Wee Wee reiterated that Charlie had loved Sadie and Eleanora, that Sadie could get help with her rent from him, Wee Wee, and that Charlie used to come to Durham Street and give Sadie a little money.

Charlie paid off the mortgage at North Fremont, the Gough family home, on 31 March 1931, four years after Sadie had left Baltimore, and just a few months before Charlie himself died, on 8 July. By 1931, Clarence Holiday had played banjo, then guitar for several years with Fletcher Henderson, one of the best bands in the business; and Clarence's daughter was poised to become one of the greatest American artists of the century.

4

Harlem

The world's most glamorous atmosphere. Why, it is just like the Arabian Nights!

– Duke Ellington,
on first seeing Harlem in 1923

Harlem in the nineteenth century had been a prosperous and well-kept community of white bourgeoisie, but as urban rail transport brought the north end of Manhattan Island within reach of the downtown business districts, speculators built too many tenement buildings, and where profits were at risk, racism did not prevent empty flats being rented to blacks. By the 1920s Harlem had become the largest black city on earth.

When Sadie and Eleanora got there, the so-called Harlem Renaissance had been going for some years. It seemed as though black literature and music were bursting out of their confines: black plays and musical shows had made it to Broadway, while black writers and artists were patronized by white socialites like Carl Van Vechten.

It was at a Vechten soirée that the hostess told Bessie Smith, 'You're not leaving without kissing me goodbye!' Whereupon Bessie, drunk as a skunk, knocked her to the floor, saying 'Get the fuck away from me! I ain't never *heard* of such shit!' Bessie knew when she was being patronized, and she also probably knew that being clasped to the bosom of the white establishment, even if that had been possible, would have destroyed her art. Vechten published a novel in 1926; it was a critical success and fairly realistic about Harlem, but only a white patron could have been foolish enough to call it *Nigger Heaven*, using a word he claimed he never used. The few blacks who read it no doubt wrapped a plain brown cover round it first.

Meanwhile, African-Americans had fought well and bravely in the Great War of 1914–18, told that they were helping to make the world safe for democracy; they no doubt expected things to change back home. Small hope: the black troops were treated as inferiors during the war itself, and in the summer of 1919 they were welcomed home with the first national wave of race riots. They were urged by their own newspapers to mind their own business, but also to take up arms if necessary and defend themselves. A prominent black Mason in California asked, 'If the Negro could afford to die to liberate the serfs of Europe, can he afford to do less to protect his own home and loved ones?' After a riot in Washington in July, the *Pittsburgh Courier* wrote: 'A bullet in Washington has no more terrors than in the Argonne.'

Times were changing, all right. The Harlem Renaissance had been built on sand, soon to be washed away by the Great Depression. As David Levering Lewis's book *When Harlem Was in Vogue* (1979) makes clear, many of the literary figures were ambivalent about their own place in society, some of them travelling to Europe and back and never feeling at home anywhere. The African-American community was simply not big enough to support a literary movement based on the essentially European forms of poetry and the novel; by the 1950s the early scholars in what came to be called black studies questioned whether there had ever been a Harlem Renaissance at all.

British critic Dave Gelly, writing about the saxophone in 1992, pointed out that most forms of art are created when important and authoritative people want nothing to do with them.

The saxophone developed into the marvellously flexible and expressive instrument it is today precisely because proper musicians [in the 1920s] would not touch it with a bargepole. It was not taught in music colleges, there was virtually no 'serious' music written for it . . . As a result, there was no correct way to play it and no correct sound to aim at . . .

In fact, the saxophone doesn't really have much of a 'core' sound; it merely responds to the way you blow it . . once you learn to control the instrument reasonably well, this apparent

42

limitation turns out to be a most precious quality. It means
that you can imagine the sound you want to make and, with
time and practice, it will emerge.

Similarly, forms in art are fusions to begin with, which happen
naturally. Jazz itself was a fusion, and so was rock'n'roll in the
mid-1950s. But naturalism is easily eroded: today too many young
saxophonists sound the same, because they have been taught to
play 'correctly' and have not looked for their own voices. Similarly,
recent self-conscious fusions, such as third-stream and jazz-rock,
have not amounted to much, because they are forced.
In the 1920s the Harlem Rush was far more important than the
Renaissance. This is the term used to describe what took place in
the streets and in the clubs, not at meetings of glitterati or at the
swanky parties of slumming aesthetes. While African-Americans
had been kept in the dark about their own culture and pressured
to make their 'culture' conform to the white, they carried on
creating it where nobody was looking. Not that there weren't a lot
of hip white people. Harlem was integrated in those days, at least
as far as entertainment was concerned, and there were plenty of
movie stars and other swells who knew where the best entertainment was to be found. As with African-American culture since the
beginning, the nation as a whole paid little attention, but it was
the Harlem Rush that swept the world in years to come.
Black music is always happening everywhere; the traditional up-
the-river-from-New-Orleans approach to the history of jazz has its
deficiencies, but as a rough outline it will do, and the centre of
black music in the late twenties was moving from Chicago to New
York. Freddie Green, Eleanora's old friend from Baltimore, who
had lived in Harlem for a while, said in 1971 that Harlem
compared to the Point was, as we Americans used to say, the same
thing only different:

Coming off the Point and going to 125th Street was the same,
only a different town . . It was a larger town, and more
night life, more clubs in Harlem. Harlem is a harder place –
dog eat dog – you'd have to struggle. You had to squeeze
more. People had their own thing, didn't help one another
. . . It's rough.

In the booklet accompanying *The Sound of Harlem*, a 1964 compilation of recordings on Columbia, Frank Driggs and George Hoefer described over a hundred Harlem clubs, cafés and dance halls without exhausting the supply Indeed, a great many joints could not have been described, because they were essentially private; if you had the room, you made use of it the best way you could. It was this milieu in which Sadie and Eleanora found themselves.

According to the marriage bureau, Clarence had married Fannie Lee Taylor, from Fredericksburg, Virginia, on 5 July 1927. Her name was usually spelled Fanny; Eleanora/Billie later said in her book that she was West Indian, but Fanny said:

> I'm from Virginia. We're the meanest women in the world. I first met [Clarence] at the Waltz Dream Ballroom in Philadelphia. I went to a dance that night and he was up there runnin' the elevator. He wasn't playin' with no band then. He was about twenty-one, in 1920 or '21. I came to New York in 1924 – Clarence and I came together. He had a room here then, and I was working that summer in the Pocono mountains, and I came here to visit him in his room. We lived together, and we got married.

Later Fanny decided it was 1922 when she met Clarence in Philadelphia. Clarence had gigged there, when he wasn't working to make ends meet; among others, he'd worked with reedman Russell Procope: they later worked in Fletcher Henderson's band together, and Procope became better known in Duke Ellington's band from 1946 until Duke's death. Clarence was never a soloist, but he became a first-class player of rhythm guitar, an art that is now almost lost. Jimmy Crawford, drummer with Jimmie Lunceford's very popular band, praised Clarence's playing: 'He was just a rhythm man, he had that left foot going, stomping, yes he did, he had all that going, and he was swinging!'

The greatest of all rhythm guitarists was no doubt the other Freddie Green, who worked with Count Basie for over forty-five years. He was a married man, but also one of Billie Holiday's many lovers; more to the point, as the young trombonist Dennis Wilson said many years later, 'It's as if in the Bible they said, "Let there be time," and Freddie started playing.' Much of today's music business can't tell a human rhythm section from a computer-generated beat, but the rhythm guitar of the Swing Era has been described as 'the clock that laughs'. Its importance to the music of the period can hardly be overestimated; the acoustic guitar, playing four beats to the bar, was felt rather than heard, and the recordings of the time weren't very good at capturing the sound, but on Basie's records you can hear Green stroking away, not only an integral part of the beat but playing chords, adding harmony to the rhythm.

It is in this illustrious company that Clarence Holiday belongs, for when he joined Henderson in 1928 it was probably the best-loved band in the black community, and as Benny Carter put it many years later, it was the best band with the best music: if you could make it in that band, you could make it anywhere. It was also prolifically recorded. The records are full of joy, and it was good work; as Driggs said, racial equality was not on offer anyway, and a musician in a top band could live very well in those days.

Clarence (whose nickname was Lib-Lab, meaning ad-lib, after his gift of the gab) played with Henderson until 1933, except for a short period of illness in 1932. He later played with Carter and with Don Redman; it was Redman who had written most of Henderson's arrangements until 1927, helping Henderson towards the big time. It is often said that Clarence also played with McKinney's Cotton Pickers, a Detroit-based band of which Redman was music director 1927–31, but this is not true: his absence on the road with the Cotton Pickers was an excuse made up by Eleanora in her book many years later for the failure of her parents' marriage, which itself never happened.

From 1929 Clarence and Fanny had a three-bedroom flat at 79 St Nicholas Place, and the rooms were available. Bassist/ bandleader John Kirby used to bring white girls to Fanny's place; Jimmy Crawford was a roomer there. Fanny made it clear that she and Clarence had a flexible relationship. 'What was Clarence gonna listen to me for? He was the boss. He was my boss. I listened to *him*.' But when Clarence became a successful musician and was on the road a lot, Fanny wasn't sitting around doing nothing. And Clarence was always a tomcat: Atlanta Shepherd, a white woman who worked in a dance hall, gave birth to Clarence's daughter Mary on his birthday in about 1932, according to Fanny. Fanny liked Atlanta and called her 'wife-in-law'. Fanny liked Eleanora too: earlier it had been proposed that Eleanora come to live with

Fanny and Clarence, but she was already too wild for Fanny. Yet when Eleanora had become Billie Holiday, she always sent drinks to Fanny's table when she was in the house.

Fanny first met Sadie and Eleanora when they came for a visit to 144th Street between 7th and 8th Avenues. Fanny said that Eleanora may have been twelve or thirteen, a 'fat thing with big titties'. Everybody liked her, but they stayed all day and Clarence got bored. There is no reason to doubt that if Sadie had played her cards right she could have made a friend of Fanny, but soon enough she began making a pain in the neck of herself. Trombonist J.C. Higginbotham said, 'Clarence was one of the swellest guys you could ever know – friendly, joking, have a drink and have fun.' (Drummer Walter Johnson had never seen anybody drink as much as Clarence; he put away tumblers of straight whisky, but 'I never saw him drunk.') As the years went by, it seemed that every time the easy-going Clarence sat down in a club for a drink, Sadie materialized. Asked about the famous fight, when she was supposed to have laid into Sadie with a handbag, Fanny freely admitted that she had got fed up:

A club – 101 Lenox Avenue. Clarence was there mindin' his own business; he was in with a party of us, and Sadie came in and you know she was always around me, and she looked as if she was trying to agitate me. My temper went up. I didn't need no handbag; I took up my fists and beat her. That's when the guy picked me up and took me outta the club and wouldn't let me back in.

Back when Fanny lived on 144th Street, Clara Winston had two apartments at 135 West 142nd Street, one to live in and one for business. Clara had known Clarence for a long time and was a good friend of Fanny's. Clara's other flat was a good-time house, like Ethel Moore's in Baltimore: not a brothel, but food and drink were available there, and a room to use if a guest had brought a woman with him. Sadie and Eleanora stayed in Clara's first flat, the one she lived in; Sadie was Clara's housekeeper, and Eleanora did as she pleased.

I used to have a business and people used to come into my house from the best to the worst – even Tallulah used to come to my house. You didn't have to worry about anything being stolen, about being stuck up, you know what I mean? Things have really changed.

Clara loved to reminisce. She was one of many elderly people interviewed many years later to croon about the Harlem that used to be. She slipped back and forth in chronology: she was married to a 'no-good skunk' who got beaten to a pulp in the street; and 'You heard about this woman who put five bullets in this man that lived in this building.' But all this was much later: her no-good husband was beaten up after the war, and the man who got shot 'ain't been dead a year'. The Harlem that Clara knew in her heyday was different. If there was a shoot-out in a joint on Lenox Avenue in the old days, they were gangsters, 'big-time Italian fellas' In the good old days, ordinary people were mostly safe in Harlem, both black and white. 'I used to have a lot of beautiful company comes to my place.'

When it came to the arrangement with Sadie and Eleanora, Clara was coy about the details: Sadie 'was a very nice person in trying to give a helping hand . . . lots of times I'd try to give her a little money . .' The idea of Eleanora doing any work was ludicrous, 'But listen, darlin', as far as I know about [Eleanora] doin' any prostitution, I don't know nothing about that. But better to sell it than give it away, that's what I say.'

But whatever else Eleanora was doing, she was singing. 'We worked in the latter part of the twenties in a club in Harlem called the Nest Club,' said Mae Barnes, 'which is where I first met Billie, way before it changed to Monroe Uptown House.' The Nest was at 169 West 133rd Street; it was a popular joint, and there were a couple of gangster shootings there in 1927. Elmer Snowden had bands there, then Luis Russell; the great Ellingtonian Barney Bigard played clarinet for Russell, and Ellington first heard him at the Nest.

There is not room enough in this book to list all the personalities and musical treasures that came and went in these clubs, and it is no wonder that Mae Barnes, over forty years later, got some of them confused. By 1932 the Nest had become Dickie Wells's Shim Sham Club; Clark Monroe's Uptown House was a few blocks away Barron's Exclusive Club was where Ellington worked with Snowden in 1923; Barron Wilkins was a prominent Harlemite who was murdered because he refused to bribe gangsters for his booze;

his older brother Leroy was one of Willie 'The Lion' Smith's first employers, and the Lion told in his wonderful book *Music on My Mind* (1964) how a tubercular cocaine addict, Yellow Charleston, was commissioned by the Mob to kill Barron and died before he could be put on trial.

Mae Barnes had a lot of memories. She started in show business at the age of twelve, going to Europe with a 'big fat blonde' white singer, Ethel Whiteside, and her Ten Pickaninnies. She worked in black vaudeville in the TOBA circuit (Theater Owners' Booking Association, or 'Tough On Black Artists', or 'Tough On Black Asses'). Her stock role in the chorus line was at the end, for comical antics as the girl who was always out of step and racing to catch up with the others. She appeared on Broadway in *Shuffle Along* (1921), *Runnin' Wild* (1923), this or that edition of *George White's Scandals* and *Ziegfeld Follies* (with Tallulah Bankhead). She was a life-long friend of Billie's:

> I don't know when Billie came from Baltimore to New York, but it was 1928 when I met her. Then she wasn't doing her own style. She was doing everything that Louis Armstrong was doing. She knew his records backwards, every one of them ... 'West End Blues', 'Heebie Jeebies', 'Sweethearts on Parade' ... She wasn't imitatin' his style, she was using all his numbers. That's what she got her kicks out of, singing his songs. That was her beginnin' of changing Louis's style to her own, only she used his numbers to do it. Like, 'Two by two, we go marchin' through', and she'd do that Louis br-r-r-rmmm kind of thing, and she'd do her own thing right behind it. Louis would be her kick-off kind of thing.
>
> She always had this deep voice, this double tone. She could do it just like him, almost exactly like him, because she had this heavy voice, this gravelly tone, even when she had her own style ... 'I Surrender Dear'. She'd slide, and do the Louis run as if he'd do it on the trumpet, only with his voice. You couldn't tell the difference .. She did 'Them There Eyes' at the Nest.

'Them There Eyes' was published in 1930 and recorded by Louis Armstrong in April the next year; by then the Nest had changed its name. But it became one of Billie's best-known tunes, and now we know, if we needed any evidence, who was Billie Holiday's greatest influence: Louis is probably still the single most influential stylist in the history of American popular music.

Jazz musicians were already swinging when Louis came along – they called it 'getting off' or 'taking a Boston' – but Louis couldn't even talk without swinging, and he made it part of the air everyone breathed. Playing second cornet in King Oliver's band in 1923 in Chicago, he knocked out white kids still in short pants who went on to invent the Chicago style; the young people who heard him there included Benny Goodman. In 1924 he went to New York to spend a year with Fletcher Henderson's band, then no more than a good commercial dance outfit, and showed them the direction to take. With his own incandescent series of Hot Fives and Hot Sevens from late 1925, Armstrong had set the world of music on its ear, becoming the first great solo star, swinging entire recording sessions by himself, bending notes and phrasing as he pleased; he did not invent stop-time choruses, scat singing and all the rest, but did it all so naturally that music itself seemed to belong to him. And in 1929, fronting big bands that were no more than showcases for his playing and singing, he embarked on a series of hit records that totalled over forty in the 1930s alone. He could make anything his own, from a great pop song like 'Body and Soul' to the Mexican hit 'The Peanut Vendor' to the schmaltzy 'Sweethearts on Parade' (already a number-one hit for Guy Lombardo), all recorded in 1930.

From childhood Eleanora had loved the blues singers; in a 1956 interview she told Willis Conover:

> I think I copied my style from Louis Armstrong. Because I used to like the big volume and the big sound that Bessie Smith got when she sang. But when I was quite young, I heard a record Louis Armstrong made called the 'West End Blues'. And he doesn't say any words, and I thought, this is wonderful! and I liked the feeling he got from it. So I liked the feeling that Louis got and I wanted the big volume that Bessie Smith got. But I found that it didn't work with me, because I didn't have a big voice. So anyway between the two of them I sorta got Billie Holiday.

Bessie's innate musicianship and ability to put a song to her own service had its effect, and in Armstrong Billie's art had found its true inspiration, the final piece of the puzzle.

They would start at the Nest, Mae said, at about two in the morning. Mae had turned to singing after being injured in a car crash; she opened the show

> You'd go around to the tables – me, Billie, an Italian girl who wanted to pass as coloured, her name was Audrey. She twisted her can and took dollars off the tables. That's the kind of club it was. Billie didn't take money off the tables. She'd go and sing, but she wasn't a dancer; she took tips with her hand. Audrey sang risqué songs, like that; we all did it. But Billie wasn't that type . . .
> Billie Haywood, a jet-black girl like you never saw, teeth white as pearls and the deepest dimples . . . Billie Haywood and Cliff Allen were a team, they played all the places downtown . . . She could sing 'This Is My Last Affair', and they'd do comedy like. He'd play a ballad, and she didn't want a ballad, and she'd hit the ground, and he'd start carryin' on fast, and she'd sing it – hell of a rhythm singer. They were singing at a place called Don's Basement, 137th Street I think, and I'd go down to their club during intermissions, with Billie, and they'd come to see us. We'd finish 7 or 8 o'clock in the morning, any kind of time, and then we'd go to the gin mills till about 12 o'clock in the afternoon. We'd go to Pops – 132nd Street and 7th Avenue. We'd go to all we could find that was opened. A place on 141st Street and 7th – Mike's – and other little gin mills – I forget the names. And from there we'd go to apartments, buffet flats, and buy whisky and drink, and that's what we did at 12 o'clock. We'd buy reefers. We'd get to bed 4, 5 o'clock, and we'd sleep, and go to work at 2 o'clock in the morning. Worked seven nights a week, no nights off. Didn't want no nights off. We could make sometimes $100-odd dollars a night.
> Billie Haywood and I were more together, because Billie Holiday had the slower kind of singing. Billie Haywood and I were fast rhythm. As friends, the three of us were unbeatable. We agreed on everything, I don't think we ever had an argument. We'd fight at the drop of a hat, so nobody else bothered us . . . I was the funniest of the three. All three of us was pretty peppy. If we just wanted to do anything

individually, we'd just walk off and say, 'I'll dig you.' The evilest was Billie Holiday.

Billie called her Maisie. 'Yeah, and she called me a whole lot of other things. Bitch, motherfucker, uh, huh. All of us were into that. "Ah, bitch, do so-and-so." '
Film stars like Franchot Tone and Burgess Meredith used to come to the Nest, Mae said, and hung out with the girls. Meredith and Mrs Tone were especially crazy about Billie Haywood, and Mrs Tone would sometimes tip the girls $50 apiece. (Tone married Joan Crawford in 1935; the Mrs Tone Mae remembered was probably the actor's mother.) Forty years later, Mae said that Billie Haywood had worked as a maid for Mae West, had been in a car crash and now her mind was going; but they had good times when they were young. Mae told a story about the two Billies getting arrested:

> We were playing the Nest, around '29 or '30. What attracted the cops was loud talking. Lady used to carry on in the streets, yes. Break of dawn. They were talking loud, and hollering, and laughing, and cursing each other. And a cop came over and tried to quiet them down, but they wouldn't keep quiet and got louder. And they wanted to lock them up, so they were screaming, 'I don't believe it, take me!' and they refused to go and sat down in the middle of the street and refused to get into the patrol wagon. 'I ain't going to take a step till you take me in the car.' So they had to bring around a police car . . . So they took them down and booked them on disorderly conduct and the judge gave them a little talking to and let them go right away, 135th Street, and there's a police station right there. I was standing there watching them raising Cain; I couldn't move . . . we used to try to drink twenty-four hours a day.

Eleanora/Billie was at the Nest for about a year, Mae said, and then went across the street to Pod's and Jerry's. It was during this time that she changed her name. She said years later that she had named herself after Billie Dove, a movie star of the period, but now we know that she had a chum called Billie; and also that some of her friends already called her 'Bill' or 'William'. (In her book she said that her father had called her Bill when she was young,

but he was not around much.) The name Fagan had never done
anything for her, but she was reluctant to trade on her father's
fame, so for a time she spelled it Halliday. By now she was coming
more into her own style as well, said Mae; did she ever sing the
blues?

No. That's what I'm trying to tell you. She don't. She's not a
blues singer, oh no. She never spoke about her singing. She's
a stylist; everybody that's tried to do her can't do it . . . Even
the finest have tried to do it, but I'm sorry, she had a style *all
her own*. The faggots, like Sam Lords, later than her time: he
was a singing waiter at Lucky Roberts' and there everyone
could sing, and beautiful operatic voices, in the thirties and
forties. You'd be served a drink and suddenly you'd hear a
voice break out operatic. One waitress sang Madame Butterfly
out of this world. Sam Lords still imitates Billie; he's out on
the coast [in 1972]. But he's the only one that can sound like
Billie Holiday . . it makes me mad when I heard Patti Page
and Peggy Lee and them try to get her style.

Charles Luckyeth Roberts was a pianist and composer who wrote
shows, ran society orchestras and had an upmarket club for many
years; Sam Lords was only imitating. I suppose Patti Page had
certain *longueurs*, but Peggy Lee is a stylist in her own right. None of
them would be able to ignore Billie's influence when the time
came. Mae was an entertainer who was present at the advent of
Billie's greatness and witnessed its decline: her memories of it were
priceless to her, but her complaining about Billie's influence is
pointless, like complaining that Henry 'Red' Allen and Jabbo
Smith sounded like Louis Armstrong. They couldn't help being
influenced, but even so they had their own musical personalities.
Asked who played for Billie at the Nest, Mae replied, 'A man
she loved.'

The only man I think she ever loved in her life – a boy named
Bobby Henderson. A beautiful pianist. God that man could
play piano .   he played Duke Ellington's 'Sophisticated
Lady' like no one else ever played it .. the chords he'd get
out of it. Where Duke would play runs, Bobby would chord
it, and make the pretty chords in between
    I wouldn't say he was so quiet, because Bobby could juice a

lot, you know. He was very lively; he'd go out with someone he wouldn't know, maybe then he'd be quiet. But when Billie and him and I would go out together to clubs, like that, like we used to do a lot . . . he was aloof, though, from people.

Bobby Henderson was an observer who knew how to look after himself. He was also a man with a lot of feeling – for his native New York, for music and for people. 'One point I want to make,' Bobby said,

I always had a habit of walkin', and in Harlem I used to go by the Hudson River by myself or with somebody who liked to walk, and I used to stop off and get a bottle of wine. People used to wonder why I'd get over there – it's calm, you get away from that night life, get away from all of it, and that's what I used to do. Central Park – I know every path in every park in New York City. I'm one of the few people that walked from the Battery to the Bronx, from the Hudson River to the East River. Through Chinatown. I don't think there's a street in New York I haven't walked on. It's a big city, but since I was a kid I knew it. And thank God I could always hear some music where I was walkin', whether a juke box was playin' or not, whether I was in Central Park, I was hearin' sounds. And when I came to the piano at night, the girls would say, 'Where you been today? Whatchu been doin'? You sound mighty fresh on those keys!'

He quit studying bookkeeping, just walked out of high school one day, because he knew he could make a living at music.

I said, who's goin' to keep whose books in *this* administration? And it was the night after I was listenin' to Duke Ellington, and I'm sittin' in the back row, and I was hearin' nobody but Duke playing 'Sophisticated Lady', and my teacher's name was Mr Marquet, and he kept callin' my name: 'Mr Henderson, Mr Henderson.' I looked up, he said, 'Where are you?' And right then I knew I said, 'I can't tell you, but –' and all the class turned around and they're laughin'. . '. I picked up my books and I said, 'Mr Marquet, give these to the Principal with my best regards, 'cause I'm leavin' school right now.' He said, 'You can't do that,' and I said, 'I'm

doin' it, right now . . .' I hopped on the back of one of those
open streetcars and I rode right up to Harlem.

Bobby described his mother as a janitress. She was disappointed,
because she wanted Bobby to go to college, but who was going to
pay for that? Bobby hugged her and kissed her and told her that
he was already making money playing the piano at parties.

I was workin' with Stanley Payne, and Stanley was playin'
violin then . . . So we're playin' these parties and the guys are
hearin' me and sayin', Well, this cat can play a little bit. I
went downtown and got me a job cleanin' refrigerators, and I
went to work in the garment district. And this cat Jack Sneed,
who was playin' the four-string guitar and was one of the
most mischievous cats in the whole world – but the hippest
too – he told Jerry, 'The Lion's gonna leave.' 'Cause at this
time Jerry's was jumpin', man, and the Lion was the place.

Stanley Payne must have learned his stuff, for he played tenor sax
in Benny Carter's band at a recording session in 1940, sitting next
to Coleman Hawkins. Jerry was Jeremiah 'West Indian' Preston,
whose career as a nightclub impresario had begun more than a
decade earlier at the Orient. With his partner Charles 'Pod'
Hollingsworth, he ran one of the most popular speakeasies in
Harlem from around 1925; its name was the Patagonia Club, but
as Frank Driggs put it, during Prohibition they didn't go in much
for neon lights outside, and nobody ever called it anything but
Pod's and Jerry's. Willie 'The Lion' Smith was the legendary
keyboard tickler and composer who had already encouraged Duke
Ellington and Fats Waller; he played on Mamie Smith's 'Crazy
Blues' in 1920.

So Jack Sneed woke me up at eight o'clock in the mornin'
and said, 'I got a job for you,' and my mother said, 'what
kind of a job at eight o'clock in the mornin'?' But I understood, so I got dressed and that's the first time I worked
Jerry's.
    The Lion was sittin' there, and I froze right by the door
and I'm lookin' around and I'm sayin' Wow, and my eyes are
poppin' . . I didn't know who the Lion was . . and Jack got
the boss and brought him over, and he said, 'Hello, son, can

you play the piano?' And I said, 'A little bit.' I was nervous, you know, so I said to myself, play what you can play, and that's all you can do . So the boss said to me, 'See that guy sittin' over there at the piano?' I said, 'Yeah.' You know who that is?' I said, 'No.' 'That's Willie "The Lion" Smith, and he's made plenty of money but he's goin' to move downtown to another spot. Play a tune, kid.'

He found out later that Tommy and Jimmy Dorsey were also there, before their national fame but already well-known musicians. 'My ignorance saved me, man, 'cause I didn't know who these cats were.' He played about twenty choruses of 'I Got Rhythm', and people started saying, 'Who's this kid?' and 'You're all right, kid.' The boss said, 'Don't stop now. Play a little blues. I like you; whatchu drinkin'?' He asked for ginger ale and whisky. He got the job, starting that night.

Everybody encouraged him, including the Lion. He was advised to drink water instead of ginger ale with his whisky, because he'd feel better in the morning. Told that the pay was $14 a week, he said, 'You're out of your mind, 'cause I make seven bucks a night when I play a party.' The Lion growled, 'You don't understand, kid. Take the job.' The girls went from table to table singing, and there was a mirror over the piano, and Bobby thought that was nice; he could watch the crowd. But the Lion had put the mirror there so he could watch the girls, to make sure they didn't forget to share their tips with him. A waiter looked after Bobby.

One of the girls said, 'I ain't got no more.'

So he started to go underneath her pants, so she said, '*I'll* get it.' She had sixty dollars. He said, 'Now give him his.' And he handed me thirty dollars. Nobody handed me thirty dollars in my life to play I said, 'Man, what's goin' on?' 'Put it in your pocket, kid.' I'm playin' like mad, you know. Then the next girl got up, and that was the first time I seen 'em take the money off the table, and my eyes popped to death, and this went on all night. And I started to feelin' the club, and people would come and give me requests.

So I work from eleven o'clock that night to ten the next mornin', and that's the first time I ever saw my fingers swell up, but they was gettin' endocrinated, you know And I had money in all my pockets – shirt pockets, back pockets, pants pockets, nothin' but money. I had so much money it scared me. And I turned around to see if the waiter was lookin' out for me. And he laughed. I said, 'Look, I made a whole lot of money tonight; and you were lookin' out for me, so why don't you take some of this money?' He looked at me and said, 'Kid, don't worry about it.' He reached in his pocket and pulled out a roll big enough to choke a horse and said, 'I got mine.'

When he got home, Bobby threw most of the money on the dresser and was asleep as soon as he hit the pillow He awoke to a yell from his mother, wanting to know where he'd got all that money. He burst out laughing, assured her he hadn't stolen it, and that he'd explain later, but he had to go back to sleep, and she should go out and buy herself a new dress. 'And I didn't even empty my pants pockets out. So look in there and you'll find some more.' And later, after he'd had something to eat, 'We were four blocks from Central Park, and I took me a ten-dollar bill, and I'll never forget, I bought me a bottle of white wine, and I got a row boat, and I pay the cat, and I get out there, I row far out, and I sat there thinkin', Wow, what a job. You know? I was *talkin'* to myself.' He went back to work that night.

But he had to satisfy his mother, and he couldn't describe the musical side. So one night he told her to get dressed up, and sent a cab driver friend for her.

So I'm playin' and I turn around and who's laughin' and who's havin' a great big ball but my mother. The girls are all around her, and the boss brought out fried chicken for her, and she had a drink. So later, one of the girls came over and said, 'Your mother's tired, I can tell.' So I come over and I say, 'Are you enjoyin' yourself?' And she said, 'Oh, wonderful, the girls are so nice. Now I know where you work.' So my cab man which is my buddy is standin' by the side, and I say, 'Now I gotta go back to play, but when you're ready to leave, you tell the girls, and make sure you get home' . . . and when I got home the next day, she was like a little girl: 'I never had such a good time, those girls are so nice, and you played – pretty good.'

Bobby brought everybody home to meet his mother. One night

there was a white guy who'd been sitting by the piano. He was Charlie Barnet, a saxophone player from a wealthy family and highly regarded by the musicians; he played the chimes on Ellington's 'Ring Dem Bells' in 1930. Bobby said, 'He sat there all night, and we left Jerry's at about ten in the mornin', and I said, Big John's is right around the corner, that's where everybody goes, let's go to Big John's.'

Big John Reda was a heavy-set Italian and a friend to all the musicians His café was at 2245 7th Avenue, and there was always a pot of pig's feet and beans cooking and a place to sleep after the job, or more importantly, if a man temporarily didn't have a job.

All the musicians had accounts with him, and I think Fletcher Henderson and Duke's men, whenever they was in town, that was their headquarters, at Big John's And everybody would have a jug on the table and the juke box was full of good sounds that everybody just made, and everybody's wavin', come over and have a drink with me.

Horace Henderson, Fletcher's equally talented brother, wrote a tune called 'Big John's Special' in 1934 that became an anthem of the Swing Era.

Around noon Bobby and Charlie had had enough, and Charlie didn't think he could get home to Long Island, so they got in his cream and blue roadster convertible and drove to Bobby's place, where Charlie went to sleep. Bobby had to put him to bed, and a few hours later Bobby's mother gave him breakfast In a few years Barnet was leading one of the best bands of the era, 'And I read about him and I wondered if he remembered. But that was the way my mother was.' And that was the way Harlem was.

The girls at Pod's and Jerry's didn't try to cheat Bobby, because they liked the way he played for them. The Lion was one of the all-time great piano players, but the girls said Bobby was a better accompanist. 'I got to like to play for 'em, like Mattie Hite, and Mary Straine, and Detroit Red.' Red was Laura Livingstone, also known as Big Red; she first met Billie Holiday in 1928, and like Mae, became a life-long friend. Like Mae too, Red worked 'stock' in Harlem theatres, one of which later became the Apollo, and worked in all the clubs as a dancer and a singer.

We could have met at the Black Cat – all the performers

would gather there after we got out of work, and they had jam sessions, and everyone would get up and do a number, like Mae Barnes, who at that time was considered one of the greatest dancers.

There was three of us rated, I was rated third, Alice Whitman was rated first, and Mae Barnes second. We was coloured tap dancers . .

The Hot-Cha was an after-hours place. During them days after-hours places was legal and Harlem was a town within a town. Peoples was comin' from all over the world to see Harlem. And we was makin' an awful lot of money   Tips. Your salary was nothin' I had two apartments in town – one for my mother and my children, and one for my husband and myself. And I'd go and give my mother a couple of hundred dollars for expenses for the children .

In the *Daily News* I was written up as the Hot Harlem Girl. I wasn't no shake dancer, but even in my menstruals I could roll my stomach, and let my behind go up and down like this; I'd tell 'em I was from Detroit and I had to shift them Detroit cars, and I'd shift from right to left, and shift in reverse, and throw it in high!

The after-hours places weren't legal, but the cops were paid off. Pod's and Jerry's often had sidemen sitting in, Bobby said; there was plenty of entertainment.

Five, six girl entertainers, and the musicians were comin' in after they got off their jobs, guys like Roy Eldridge, and Roy used to bring his horn and take it out . . Then there was a place across the street called the Coal Bin where they had Billie Haywood and Cliff Allen, and Cliff used to play in F sharp, and this chick got so she couldn't sing in no other key, 'cause she used to come over and I used to love the way she sang, and I used to ask her, 'Come on, Billie, sing a tune.' And she used to say, 'Bobby, I'd love to sing one but I'm F-sharp crazy.' It was wonderful.

But the other Billie was special.

The chronology of Billie's activities in the early 1930s is not certain, and some of the witnesses, forty years later, had some of the clubs mixed up. It doesn't matter; all the clubs were so close together, and Billie probably sang in most of them. Her face and her voice were becoming part of the scene.

The Harlem vocalist Monette Moore was a prolific recording artist and a friend of Bobby's. Clifton Webb and Patsy Kelly were stars of Broadway musicals, and Webb, who was later swaddled in Hollywood's sentimental film comedies, was a familiar face in Harlem. Bobby describes his first meeting with Billie:

I went down with Monette Moore to see Clifton Webb and Patsy Kelly, 'cause Monette was a very good friend (there wasn't no eyes or nothin' like that), and she took me to Dickie Wells' Clam House. Well, there was a place Billie was singin' in – if it was the Clam House or Brownies, 'cause the clubs were so close together, see, then, and you could open a club with a quarter, so long as you had some corn liquor . . . so wherever it was, I saw this well-built girl over there, she was a woman, 'cause Billie, boy, she was well-groomed, she was a woman.

Billie was – which I didn't know until I read her book – she was about sixteen at that time, and Dot Hill was the piano player, a tall girl, played like a man, and Monette introduced me to Dot, and told her that I played, and Dot said, 'Come on, why don't you play a tune?' I said, 'No, I'd rather listen to you.' But eventually I did sit down and played somethin'. And the tune – I never forgot – was 'Sweet Sue', and I did somethin' in there, and Billie was standin' and watchin', and she said, 'Do that again.' And I said, 'What?' And she said, 'What you just did.' So I went over it again, and she said, 'That's what it is.' And I remember that thing – I could do it now – it was so – So I looked at her, like, man, you know, she sings. And I played something for Billie to sing, and we all went up the street.

I was aware of her. She was a beautiful woman. She was the kind of woman that you would admire. You would say she was statuesque . . . She wasn't dressed in the most beautifullest gowns, you understand – in later years, that came out. But we went up the street and stopped in a couple of places and we played . . . Then we went up to Jerry's, and they made her sing a song there, and Jerry liked her, and

Jerry said, 'Why don't you come up here and work?' So he hired Billie.

So much for the story in Billie's autobiography that she wandered into Pod's and Jerry's one winter day, half frozen, and she and Sadie had nothing to eat, and she auditioned as a dancer and couldn't do that, so Jerry asked her to sing, and she was discovered on the spot. She had been singing for years, yet she was still only sixteen or so. She and Bobby often left the club together; always cavalier with the facts, she let people think they were married, or engaged, or living together; in fact, Bobby stayed with his mother, and Billie was living with Sadie.

'We had a liking for each other,' said Bobby. 'I never met anybody like Billie. Wasn't too many girls I met, goin' to school.' In fact, Bobby was already married, and his first marriage had already failed; but I don't think Bobby is being disingenuous here. I think he was a gentle, sensitive man who could have been manipulated by a woman; I think he soon saw that Billie was too much for him, and to her credit she did not manipulate him. 'She was much more of a hip woman than I was a hip young man. And it surprised me when I knew she was sixteen years old. She didn't tell me much about her early life, but I sensed it. She had a tough time when she came up.'

He soon learned that she could be hard to get along with:

The thing, how can I say it? The thing that I found out about Billie was not to arouse her temper. Now, she had a lot of patience, the people that she worked with, and the people that she knew. But if some guy insulted her, you had it . .
The musicians liked her and the entertainers liked her
When you liked Billie you got to know that she had a way of her own and a mind of her own, and I think she respected me because I respected her mind of her own. I might have asked her questions in my mind but I never questioned her actions or decisions. I just said, 'Well she's got to have a reason for it,' and I tried to be understanding.
I brought Billie to the house to meet my mother because I wanted my mother to know that Billie was one of the greatest people I ever met in my life .   Billie never told me nothin'
.. She didn't try to do anything extra with me. It's just the

way she naturally carried herself. You could see Billie at times when she let her guard down – she was like a little girl. As if nothin' bad had ever happened in her life – to hear her laugh – she laughed from the soles of her feet to the top of her head, plus some   .
I used to love to watch Billie eat. She was very dainty, and Billie was what could you say, a full-bodied woman, and she was very graceful in everything she did. She was very clean, very neat. (In later years I don't know.) And if she had had the money in younger years, she always knew what she wanted to wear. The point I'm getting at is, she could say, 'I like that.' The way she handled a fork, the way she did eat. I used to sit down and eat – we'd be in a restaurant, and we'd be eatin'. And somebody would say to me, 'What's the matter with you?' I'd say, 'Nothin'.' But deep in my mind I'm sayin', 'You do things in a beautiful way.'

And of course there was the musical side. Bobby had discovered at their first meeting that Billie, a born musician, was one of them, listening to them rather than simply using them as a background.

If we were both born in a different set of circumstances it would have been a lot different, 'cause – well, I'd already been married . . . So maybe people will blame you principle-wise, but I don't care any more. But on the conscious level I was trying to do the right thing. 'Cause it might have been different for us if we'd gotten together. We had a beautiful thing there, 'cause, when I went in there to play, she didn't say, 'Play for me to sing,' like if you're sittin' there playin' the piano, another entertainer would say it. No, she's listenin' to what I was doin', she's listenin' to the musicians, see. That was the most remarkable thing.
She kept perfect time – you could go anywhere and she'd be there. Perfect time and perfect diction. And I knew that even at the raw stages of the vocalist you could see it was there, and that's why I used to try to encourage her. I used to play full chords for her, I did everything, I had a knack, I guess, I *felt* a singer, and I could stay just behind her – you don't pay no attention to the piano, 'cause you just listen to the singer. That's why the girls didn't steal anything from me.

If Bobby took Billie home to meet his mother, he was simply doing

the expected thing, but his home life was very different from
Billie's Bobby's mother was supportive; like a lot of musicians'
mothers, Bobby pointed out, she always welcomed the others who
came by. 'My mother never judged me. She never tried to tell me
how to live. But she used to give me warning signals.' She once put
him in the YMCA, because he was an only child and she wanted
him to be thrown in with his peers for a while. And Bobby had a
father figure, Uncle Fred, though he didn't know the whole story
until he was seventeen years old.

'He used to come to the house all the time and every time he
came to the house he acted like a little chippie girl' – Bobby means
flirtatious, perhaps a bit foolish, like someone in love – 'and my
mother was well in years then.' Uncle Fred had a musicians' club
above Barron Wilkins' old place, and Bobby and his best friend
Stanley Payne would hang out there, and 'he's on the telephone
there, gettin' gigs for different people, and he says, "This is my
boy." And he puts his hand around my shoulder, and he had a
piano there, and he says, "Why don't you sit down to play?"' When
Bobby was seventeen he found out that Uncle Fred was his father.

Billie also did the correct thing and took Bobby home to meet
Sadie. And many years later, Bobby made the polite gesture: 'She
was a wonderful woman, a very simple woman, kindhearted.' But
Billie had grown up without a father; and then Bobby describes at
length how Billie and Sadie used to scream at each other. Clearly
he did not like it or understand it; and this relationship may well
be one of the reasons why there would never be any happily-ever-
after for Billie Holiday. Without being too hard on poor Sadie,
there is no relationship more likely to be fraught than that of a
mother and an only daughter

Sadie seems to have been effectively abandoned, working as a
domestic servant when she was little more than a child. Many
mothers have suffered from sexism: the father of a large family may
be making babies carelessly, as though he were raising chickens; in
Sadie's case she was rejected by her own father, then by the
careless father of her child; one can only speculate about why
Philip Gough left her, and even Wee Wee Hill rejected her. The
result of all this rejection, beginning at an impressionable age, will
be that such a woman is emotionally retarded, like a child who can
never grow up; and having a daughter, she may cling to her like a
child to its doll.

Sadie's judgement had always been poor, and it never improved. She had decided to call herself Fagan instead of Harris, appropriating a family name to which she was not entitled by law or custom, making it even less likely that she would be admitted to full membership in that family; then, chasing her shiftless boyfriend Wee Wee, on at least one occasion she made a public fool out of herself waving a pistol in the air, not a way to gain entrance to the ranks of the respectable. Later she made an enemy of Fanny, Clarence's wife. She seems never to have done anything right.

Some witnesses said that Billie was good to her mother, some that she was not; she apparently helped her to open a restaurant in Harlem at one point and then perhaps regretted it: Sadie couldn't operate a business to save her soul. Asked about the relationship, John Hammond said:

Billie wasn't terrible to her mother but she wasn't good to anybody. Billie was horribly abused by life, and if she had a little extra dough – I mean, she felt sorry for her mother, and she couldn't bear the idea that her mother was working for Mildred Bailey, and Mildred was just a bitch about it of course, complaining about what a lousy and sloppy housekeeper and cook Billie's mother was, and she was, but this was Mildred's way of getting back at Billie because Billie was so good – she couldn't stand it. Mildred told this to me among other people.

Hammond has not stuck to the question, and in the end is unclear: Mildred complained about Sadie, but it is unlikely that she said that she did so because she resented Billie's talent. Hammond was critical of many people, often without much understanding; most people say, for example, that both Sadie and Billie were good cooks. But Billie's hackles would have been raised by criticism from outsiders about her mother, especially from someone as hard to get along with as Mildred.

Clara Winston said, 'At one point she wasn't so good to her mother,' repeating several times that Sadie 'used to run along behind her – "Billie, Billie, Billie" – just like a little baby.' (Linda Kuehl wrote that Clara's imitation of Sadie sounded like a chirping bird.) Clara concluded philosophically, 'Well, that's a mother,' but added, 'Mam should have put her foot up her behind.' But such a mother, cling though she might, has no moral authority:

the child has learned early to pay little attention. Billie 'was a grown woman, she did what she wanted'.

Sadie and Billie were stuck with each other, as if with the original sin of having been born; Billie escaped from Sadie (and other demons) through music and by becoming addicted to alcohol, drugs and danger: she was beaten by many men, shot at by cops, and acquired scars from needles all over her body; and on top of all that Sadie managed to bestow upon her a burden of guilt which she carried all her days.

In the early thirties, Sadie made Billie so angry, said Bobby,

You'd think she was gonna go through the roof. I didn't know enough about their business to have any feelings about what they were arguing about. I just didn't like to see them hollering at each other as mother and daughter. Small things, maybe where Billie had been out and didn't come home .

Bobby was pained by some of his memories; this is the only place he is a bit unclear: 'We'd get off from work and I had to fight – luckily I had the kind of mother that I had who instilled in me all of the right things that a guy should be   ' Here he may have referred to trouble that could begin in a club – Billie was never reluctant to mix it up with anybody who crossed her – or to their relationship, or to Billie and Sadie.

This was something I never understood and I never interfered with. A couple of times I'd say, 'Billie, don't holler at your mother like that,' or 'Don't argue so loud.' And I tried to say, 'Sadie,' I'd try to make an excuse, but I couldn't say anything .   I made up my mind: keep your mouth shut, 'cause you don't know what they're *really* arguin' about.

What Billie liked about me was that I never tried to say 'Your mother's wrong and you're wrong.' I just said I didn't like to hear you hollerin' or arguin', and I'd rather leave. I always had that respect for people, 'cause it's private and it don't have nothin' to do with me.

In her autobiography Billie mentioned Bobby as her accompanist, then a few pages later referred to the pianist she'd loved when she was young, who already had a wife and kids, without mentioning his name: 'It was the only time I was ever wooed, courted, chased after. He made me feel like a woman. He was patient, and loving;

64

he knew what I was scared about and he knew how to smooth my fears away.' Nobody doubted that she was referring to Bobby, though plenty of pianists loved her. But her fears were already too great, and Bobby could not look after her; she needed a combination of strength and tenderness that might have been beyond any man, and she had already shown signs of preferring the kind of men who wanted to show her how tough they were, so that she could fight with them and then reject them, the way she herself had been rejected. They drifted apart, and when it was over, the *New York Age* reported, on 1 December 1934, 'Bobbie Henderson, pianist, no longer engaged to Billie Halliday'.

5

The First Records, and Triumph at the Apollo

Billie resembled her father physically, Clara Winston said; 'Only thing is she was taller, he was a little shorter. And you know, she had them freakish lookin' eyes, sort of slanty eyes, like Clarence did He was a handsome man ' Billie also resembled Clarence in her liking for a drink and a good time; her father had become a successful musician, and now it was time for his daughter to find more success: Sadie's status as an outsider would become even more pronounced.

Professionally speaking, Billie was already mixing with experienced company: some of the others who sang at Pod's and Jerry's were recording artists. Mary Straine and Mattie Hite had begun as keyboardists; coincidentally, they had each played on one take of 'Elder Eatmore's Sermon on Generosity', a hit in 1919 by the comedian and Broadway star Bert Williams. After the astonishing success of Mamie Smith's 'Crazy Blues' in 1920, the record companies cut a lot of blues: as a vocalist Mary Straine made five sides in 1922–3, accompanied by Fletcher Henderson at the piano; Mattie Hite cut seven sides during the acoustic era, often working for Henderson, and got a last chance in 1930, making two more blues for Columbia, accompanied by Cliff Jackson. The nonsense words of her 'Texas Twist' were intended to be slightly risqué:

> Saw two frogs prancing on a stump.
> And I heard something go bumpity-bump
> It was the Texas twist,
> Froggy's bliss,

Hoppin' and jumpin', to the Texas twist.

Nice and easy, but do it long,
Just spread your butter and you can't go wrong,
'Cause it's the Texas twist,
Tight like this,
Keep on, don't you stop it, do the Texas twist.

But the blues was going out of style; even the immortal Bessie Smith's sales were falling off: Bessie made only six sides in 1931, and she hadn't had a hit since 1929. Anyway, the blues wasn't Billie's type of material.

Monette Moore was a successful entertainer, but her recording career was slowing down, too; she had made over fifty sides between 1923 and 1928, and was supposed to sing 'Someone Stole Gabriel's Horn' in April 1933, when English bandleader Spike Hughes came to New York to record his own arrangements with an all-star black band, but she didn't show up, so Benny Carter sang it. On one more date in 1936, she made her last recordings with a small group called Her Swing Shop Boys, on Decca; these probably did well on Harlem juke boxes.

In the early 1930s the Depression had almost destroyed the record business, and anyway in those days making records was not such a big deal. It was good for publicity, but the records themselves were only pocket money, because even if you got a hit you didn't get any royalties at this end of the business; these entertainers made their living performing live. But the music itself was changing. John Hammond was a fan of Monette's and described her as a 'very good blues singer'; but it was Hammond who assembled the band for those Spike Hughes recording sessions, and no doubt put her up for that job, so he knew that she was more than a blues singer Her last two recording sessions of the 1920s, in early 1927 and again in early 1928, were interesting: nearly all the recordings in this market were with small groups or just solo piano, but these of Monette's were with Charlie Johnson's Paradise Ten, the house band at Smalls' Paradise.

This club, at 2294 7th Avenue, had started in 1925 and was still going decades later. (Ed Smalls had sold out to run a liquor store; the Paradise in the 1960s was operated by basketball star Wilt 'The Stilt' Chamberlain.) In its heyday Smalls' was a high-class spot, like the Cotton Club; he encouraged the band to park their cars in front on slow nights to make the place look busy. The Paradise had waiters who could do the Charleston while balancing a tray of drinks; unlike the Cotton Club, the Paradise admitted blacks, if they could afford it; and unlike the Cotton Club, the Paradise had no radio wire for broadcasts: Johnson later regretted that he never had a chance to become as famous as Duke Ellington.

In 1955, at a rehearsal session with pianist Jimmy Rowles when a tape recorder was running, Billie told a story about herself auditioning to sing at Smalls'. She said she was about thirteen years old: she may have exaggerated her youth for effect when telling the story, but it is easy to believe that she already knew at that age not only that she could sing, but that her singing might be her strongest suit. At any rate, her technical knowledge was not yet adequate for an audition at one of Harlem's top clubs. She was asked what key she wanted to sing in; 'I said, "I don't know man, you just play." They shooed me out of there so fast, it wasn't even funny!' That, she added, was when she made up her mind to learn something about keys. This further contradicts her own story of her later discovery at Pod's and Jerry's; Billie already knew a good band when she heard one, and certainly knew that not everything was the blues. (It is interesting to speculate that in making up the famous story about her audition at Pod's and Jerry's she was reliving that earlier experience at Smalls' and giving it a happy ending.)

Johnson's was a very good band, and Billie probably knew Monette's records with it. 'You Ain't the One', for example, made in 1928, was a rhythm novelty in the demotic style that had grown out of the 'coon song', a combination of ragtime and black vaudeville that had a big influence on the songs of our century Billie's first records would use similar tunes.

Monette had worked at Covan's Club Morocco, at 148 West 133rd Street, in 1932, accompanied there by pianist Garland Wilson. This was the club where Mae Barnes first met Franchot Tone; John Hammond knew the club and remembered in his book, *John Hammond on Record* (1977), that he always stopped off somewhere to use the men's room before he got there, because all Covan offered was an outhouse in the back yard.

Hammond was a young socialite, a Yale drop-out, a campaigner for racial equality, a jazz and blues enthusiast and a fan of Garland Wilson's piano playing. The first records he produced, at the age of twenty in 1931, were 12-inch Columbia sides by Wilson, and part of the deal was that Hammond had to buy 150 copies. According to the discographies, they didn't even get catalogue numbers, but were called 'Specials'; maybe they weren't issued commercially. 12-inch 78s didn't sell very well anyway, and Hammond subsequently became more practical, but the experience was the beginning of his illustrious career. Garland Wilson went to Europe in late 1932 with vocalist Nina Mae McKinney, was back in the USA from 1939 until early 1951, and worked in Paris until he died in 1954. Wilson was also gay, a fact of which the greenhorn Hammond had been unaware. The union scale for recording being very low, Hammond had made Garland a present of an expensive watch; and Hammond remembered, 'For weeks after our record date Garland went around showing off his new watch saying, "Look what John gave me!" It took me a while to live that down.'

In 1933 Monette opened Monette's Supper Club on 133rd Street. Some have speculated that Clifton Webb might have been a backer, but the club could have been a temporary arrangement: Prohibition was not repealed until the end of the year, and all the clubs were still illegal. Joe Helbock, who opened the original Onyx Club in 1927, was quoted in Arnold Shaw's invaluable book, *52nd Street: The Street of Jazz* (1971, originally called *The Street That Never Slept*):

> Even when you paid off the cops, you'd sometimes be raided by the feds. Then you had to take care of the agents so they'd change their testimony before the commissioner To make sure he'd allow it, you had to take care of him too. Crazy days, they were!

If you did get in trouble with the law, you could change the name of the club and carry on as usual. In any case, Monette was busy: lyricist Howard Dietz (who co-wrote 'Dancing in the Dark', 'I Guess I'll Have to Change My Plan' and many more standards) had heard Monette the previous year and got her a spot in a show with Webb; this was *Flying Colors*, which opened on Broadway in September 1932 and ran for 188 performances. It starred Webb and Patsy Kelly, with songs by Dietz and Arthur Schwarz including 'Smokin' Reefers'; 'A Shine on Your Shoes' was a piece of

Depression-era hopefulness, and was sung by Monette. Most of Monette's business at her club was conducted after midnight, but she was also busy as the hostess, so instead of doing the singing herself, she hired Billie Holiday. Whatever the circumstances, the club only lasted three weeks, but John Hammond was there every night.

He later wrote that Monette might have been put out with him because he was so knocked out by Billie. Her accompanist was Dot Hill, who, Hammond says, was an alcoholic but a wonderful pianist; he didn't hear her accompanied by Bobby until later, at the Hot-Cha, and soon decided that the better her accompanist the better she sang. One of the songs she sang was 'Wouldja for a Big Red Apple', which Hammond liked; he later learned that it was the second song Johnny Mercer had ever written. Hammond wrote in his autobiography:

> She was not a blues singer, but sang popular songs in a manner that made them completely her own. She had an uncanny ear, an excellent memory for lyrics, and she sang with an exquisite sense of phrasing ... Further, she was absolutely beautiful, with a look and a bearing that was indeed Lady-like, and never deserted her ... I decided that night that she was the best jazz singer I had ever heard.
>
> My discovery of Billie Holiday was the kind of accident I dreamed of, the sort of reward I received now and then by travelling to every place where anyone performed ..
>
> Night after night I went to the Yeah Man, the Hot-Cha, Pod's and Jerry's Log Cabin, the Alhambra Grill, Dickie Wells', and other Harlem speakeasies to hear Billie   I brought everybody I knew to hear her   I had found a star and I wrote about her in *Melody Maker* .   there was little I could do for her immediately. No one would record her   She was unknown outside Harlem, and, indeed, a vocalist who did not play an instrument – like Armstrong – was not even considered a jazz singer. I could not forget her, but all I could do was talk and write about her

There is a story about a demo record, supposed to have been made with Billie and Bobby; and that Bobby was arrested on the way to the date for spitting on the subway, and Dot Hill was drafted in a hurry But no trace of such a record has been found, and Hammond doesn't mention it in his book.

Among those Hammond brought to Harlem to hear Billie was his close friend Artie Bernstein, later to play bass with Benny Goodman, and Goodman himself, as well as British actor Charles Laughton, then making his first appearance on the stage in America, and Laughton's wife, Elsa Lanchester, soon to become a legendary image as *The Bride of Frankenstein*. And there was Spike Hughes, Burgess Meredith, producer Joe Losey and others. All became Holiday fans.

In 1972 Hammond elaborated on his discovery of nearly forty years earlier.

I heard something that was completely – the phrasing, the sound of an instrumentalist. I was of course a Bessie Smith fanatic at the time I was listening to Billie, but I really didn't like girl singers very much because most of them were very corny. Except for blues singers, who I loved. I was a vaudeville freak, so all the people like Sophie Tucker and Dolly Kaye and Bea Palmer – who brought Eddie Condon's band to the Palace from Chicago, she was the shimmy queen – and Annette Hanshaw, who was from my home town. I heard a lot of Negro singers in shows, but those I heard in nightclubs were . . . you know, people who picked up dollar bills from tables, which Billie had to do later on at Dickie Wells' but not at the Hot-Cha. She didn't have to. The Hot-Cha was a marvellous place; people went there who really dug music . . in '35 at Dickie Wells' she did that because that was the kind of place it was – strictly a Gladys Bentley type of clientele there.

What Hammond is getting at is the way music was changing. The vaudeville stylists were corny, but they were entertainers with outsized personalities, and the object was to have a good time: Sophie Tucker was of course long since a vaudeville headliner in 1933, 'the Last of the Red Hot Mamas', not a very good singer and not even particularly pretty, but a great entertainer. Dolly Kaye had hit records during the acoustic era; her big one in 1923 was also a Tucker hit the same year: 'You've Got to See Mama Ev'ry Night (or You Can't See Mama at All)'.

Annette Hanshaw was a star of radio and records, rather than vaudeville; she had hits in the late 1920s. Here Hammond's interview is unclear: he said that Hanshaw was 'that bad', meaning as corny as the others, but Hanshaw was regarded in her day as a unique stylist, having her own way with a song: elsewhere Hammond, who knew her well, said 'I don't think she realizes how good she is.' At any rate, his point was that these were not jazz singers: Al Jolson was famous as 'The Jazz Singer', from the title of an early talking film, but he wasn't a jazz singer, either.

Interviewed again in the early 1980s by Ted Fox (see Fox's book *In the Groove: The People Behind the Music*), Hammond thought that Billie had just arrived from Baltimore and said, 'I heard Billie before anybody else heard her,' putting her Harlem fans in their place. More interestingly,

> I couldn't believe it. In the first place, you couldn't have a microphone in a speakeasy because the noise might filter out to the street. So Billie was just singing   to customers at tables .. she sang the same song at each table completely differently I had never heard a really improvising singer until that time. So I knew that she was unique. I can't say it was any big deal. I just happened to be around at the right time.

Hammond, who had connections at record companies and wrote for a British music paper, undoubtedly did more than anyone for Billie as her career began, but he certainly was not the first to hear her and may not even deserve all the credit for discovering her. Two young pals, Ernie Anderson, who worked in advertising, and Bernie Hanighen, a songwriter from Nebraska, knew all about her from Pod's and Jerry's. Ernie wrote about their pub-crawling:

> Bernie was an undergraduate at Harvard, he played the hot fiddle and had a collegiate jazz band. I think Eddie Condon introduced us   Bernie used to take a train down from Cambridge every Friday and we'd hit the after-hours joints in Harlem all weekend. Pod's and Jerry's must have been about 130th Street just east of 7th Avenue . . It was a speakeasy; you were supposed to be a member, but nobody was fussy about that formality. It was on the ground floor of a brownstone, and after being checked through a grill in the door under the stone stoop, you entered into a large room with about forty small tables.

There are still a lot of brownstones in New York. They are imposing houses, originally private residences, with a stone staircase rising from the footpath in front in effect to the second floor (the first floor in Britain). Underneath the front steps is the entrance to the ground floor, where the kitchen was and where the servants would have accepted deliveries. A lot of 'speaks' started in brownstones.

An upright piano was played continuously by Willie The Lion Smith or Teddy Wilson, as a singer prowled the tables, which were almost always packed. There'd be two singers who alternated, Billie Holiday and Jazzbo Jimmy. The singer would sing a chorus of the song at each table, and somebody would hand out a tip of a dollar bill or a five or even a ten-spot. The singer would fold the bill through the fingers, so that as the singer worked the room there'd be a cluster of folded bills sticking out of each hand. Thus they'd do about forty choruses of each song. The music just kept going . . . As one piano player slid off the bench, another slid on.

That's where I first heard Billie Holiday, and she was marvellous. I never heard her in better voice in all the years I knew her. Singing the same song for chorus after chorus she seemed to build the excitement . . I have no idea what happened to Jazzbo Jimmy. He was a solid performer . . .

Be the details as they may, it seems likely that Hanighen, already a songwriter, probably knew Hammond, another Harlem habitué, and it seems unlikely that Hammond had never heard of Billie before setting foot in Monette's. In any case, they had discovered one of the great artists of the century.

Billie was the first singer who was herself a great jazz musician, as opposed to a musician who also sang. She was singing some of the newer American popular songs the way they deserved to be interpreted, and she was discovered just as the Swing Era was coming together: dance bands, arrangers, vocalists and everybody else would be jazz-influenced during the 1930s, as jazz became the centre of popular music during a new golden age.

The British were the first to read about Billie, thanks to Hammond, writing in *Melody Maker*, and this no doubt contributed to the myth, to which Hammond himself subscribed, that Europeans appreciated jazz more than Americans did. In fact a great deal had already been written about jazz in the USA, but it is true that Europeans, soon discovering that most of the best jazz was played by blacks, were less racist in their attitudes, and that the British record industry had been less badly hit by the Depression than the American.

In 1921 the American industry had sold $106.5 million worth of records, sales not exceeded until 1947 During the 1920s records suffered from periodic economic slumps, as well as from competition with radio, where the music was free and the sound quality probably better than that from home record players.

Hammond's autobiography is valuable partly because he was, as far as his ego would allow him, an honest man; instead of taking all the credit himself, he wrote that it was bandleader and executive Ben Selvin, recording director at Columbia, who told him at a party one night in 1932 that the company had been getting requests from England for jazz records and asked him if he had any ideas. If nobody could afford to make jazz records for the USA, Hammond was not slow to leap at this opportunity; at the end of that year he recorded for the English market with Fletcher Henderson's band, a hair-raising experience because of that band's nonchalant attitude: they straggled in late to the studio, so that only three sides were made instead of four.

Hammond then sailed to England for a personal visit; on his return he went straight to Benny Goodman to tell him that he had a deal with Columbia. Goodman called him a liar – Goodman liked to call people liars – and said that he'd just been to Columbia, where Selvin had told him that the company was bankrupt; Hammond hastened to explain that the deal was with English Columbia, now a separate company and still in business. Goodman had not recorded as a leader for anybody since 1931, but the result of Hammond's efforts was delightful Goodman records with vocals by Jack Teagarden. The expenses having been covered by the English deal, the records were issued in the USA as well, and 'Ain'tcha Glad?'/'I Gotta Right to Sing the Blues', made on 18 October 1933, was a two-sided top ten by the end of the year.

Hammond wrote in his book that Columbia were so pleased with Goodman's hit that they immediately agreed to make some more records, and luckily Goodman wanted to record with Billie. But Hammond's memory telescoped events; things actually happened more quickly than that. Goodman's second 1933 Columbia session was later the same month, on 27 October; and Billie's first record was a month later, not long enough even then to have seen Columbia's accountants leaping with joy

The session of 27 November 1933 was an Ethel Waters session, accompanied by the Goodman band; Billie was literally squeezed in. Waters was a difficult person, and she and Billie took an instant dislike to each other; but she had recorded since 1921 and was the biggest black star on Broadway and radio: she was not a jazz singer, but a more elegant stylist than the vaudeville belters, one of the first modern pop singers, and some feel that she must have been an influence on Billie. The Holiday record 'Your Mother's Son-in-Law' was issued under Goodman's name, backed by an instrumental, 'Tappin' the Barrel', recorded on 4 December. At that session, Billie recorded 'Riffin' the Scotch' and Jack Teagarden sang 'Keep On Doin' What You're Doin''; both takes were rejected, but remade on 18 December and issued back to back.

All these were thought to have remained obscure, but we have to remember the terrible condition of the record business of the period. In 1986 Joel Whitburn's Record Research Inc. published *Pop Memories 1890–1954*, compiling lists from many different sources, including the record companies themselves, to make pop charts going all the way back to the beginning of the commercial record industry (the modern *Billboard* charts did not begin until 1940). The book is not very clear about exactly how the material was manipulated to produce chart listings, but at any rate it rates 'Riffin' the Scotch' as another top ten, the fourth Goodman hit title in a career that by 1953 totalled over 160 of them. But Goodman's name was already well known among jazz fans, and a sale of 5,000 copies in those days, wrote Hammond, was a hit.

Shirley Clay, an excellent trumpet player in Don Redman's band, certainly admired by Goodman, was the only black musician on the Holiday sides; Goodman was still nervous about using black sidemen, his sensational commercial success with Teddy Wilson and Lionel Hampton still a few months away Goodman's pianists on the dates in October had included Chicagoan Joe Sullivan, Frankie Froeba and possibly Arthur Schutt, but Billie was positive in later years that Buck Washington had been the pianist on her first records, crediting him with chasing away her nerves: he said, 'You're not going to let these people think you're a square are you? Come on, sing it!' Buck was a good pianist, half of the popular black duo Buck and Bubbles, but the discographies have always credited Sullivan. He seems to play a lot of notes behind Billie's vocals, but that was typical of the period.

As its title implies, 'Son-in-Law', written by Alberta Nichols and her husband, Mann Holiner, who specialized in vaudeville material, was a rather silly novelty; it came from Lew Leslie's *Blackbirds of 1933*, which was a flop. (Leslie was trying to recover the success of the first edition, in 1928. Curiously, although most sources refer to 'Blackbirds of 1933' and the show opened and closed in December of that year, the record label on English Columbia described it as *Blackbirds of 1934*.) Many years later, Billie told Willis Conover that she had got a bang out of the record. 'It sounds like I'm doing comedy, my voice sounded so high and funny ' These arrangements were credited to Arthur Schutt, who had played acceptable piano on jazz records in the past, but Hammond wrote that the arrangements were terrible, and time had to be wasted at the recording sessions twisting 'Ain'tcha Glad?' and 'I Gotta Right to Sing the Blues' into shape.

Both Billie's first two sides benefited from the authoritative and unmistakable Teagarden trombone. By the time of the 'Riffin' the Scotch' dates, the arrangements were by Deane Kincaide, who had been writing since 1929 and was becoming one of the top arrangers of the Swing Era; thus 'Riffin' the Scotch' deserved the greater success of Billie's two sides, skilfully combining the period novelty effects (in this case a phoney Scottish effect at the beginning and a popping cork at the very end) with a lot of good jazz, and at exactly the right tempo.

'Scotch' had been written by guitarist Dick McDonough. Goodman grabbed a credit, since it was his date, and someone called Buck also got a credit. One source amplifies this to 'Ford Lee Buck', who must be Ford Lee 'Buck' Washington; and the pianist on 'Scotch' seems more relaxed than on 'Son-in-Law'. But that may be because it's a less frenetic arrangement; Buck seems to have been involved, but it's probably Sullivan playing.

The words were written by Johnny Mercer, who was twenty-four years old and working for Paul Whiteman at the time. He remembered, in Shaw's book about 52nd Street, that McDonough came to him with a tune he called 'Riffin' the Scotch' that needed words; so Mercer wrote something he called 'I jumped out of the frying pan and into the fire' And those are the words Billie sings, although they kept McDonough's title, which had nothing to do with the words. Billie didn't have to sing as high as on 'Son-in-Law' and sounds more like herself. And Mercer, like Billie, was a

Southerner, a fact to which Gene Lees (no mean lyricist himself) credits much of Mercer's genius: maybe the way he put words together appealed to Billie. 'She was quite a pretty girl,' Mercer remembered. 'But there was something about her – not just the torchy quality of her voice – that made you want to try to help her.'

Billie was paid $35 for her first record, she said later, but she talked about the sides in her book as though they had both been recorded on the same day. Maybe she was paid $35 for each. Anyway, then it was back to the clubs, where she did not add either tune to her repertoire.

Mae Barnes said that it was at the Nest in the late twenties that Bobby accompanied all of them, leading a band of five or six pieces, and after that that Billie moved to Pod's and Jerry's. Mae goes on to say that Billie was at the Nest about 1928–9 and that her accompanist at Pod's and Jerry's was 'a house piano, a light fella'. John Hammond wrote in his 1977 book that her accompanist there was Garnett Clark, 'who was good though not in the Bobby Henderson class', but he had said in 1972 that Clark was 'one of the best accompanists that ever was. He went to Paris in '35, made some records with Bill Coleman [a fine trumpeter who had gone to France the same year] and died of drugs.' He also said that Clark had been one of 'the very few jazz pianists I've ever known who wasn't straight – he was a homosexual.'

Clark led a quartet at a recording session in November 1935 in Paris with Coleman and Django Reinhardt, and recorded again in the hospital in 1937: he had suffered some sort of breakdown late that year, spending a year in the hospital before he died. Unless he was confusing Clark with Garland Wilson, that makes two gay jazz pianists Hammond knew. By his own admission, Hammond was a bit of a prig; he told Linda that Billie had sung songs like 'Round the Clock Blues' and probably 'Hot Nuts' at Monette's, and that this would have turned him off somewhat. He asked her to turn off the tape recorder and told her that Benny Goodman had slept with Billie and complained that she 'couldn't come'.

Hammond met Sadie, too:

Billie set her mother up in this beat-up flat on 99th Street between Central Park West and Columbus, and I went over there once or twice, after hours. Awful place. She was an ignorant Catholic. And Billie had sold her soul to the devil. And [Sadie] thought of me – though I was an atheist – as being spiritual, because I didn't smoke or drink or carry on with chicks and the rest, and I was somebody she could trust. Sure, I was a square.

That sounds like Sadie, approving of someone who was about as hopelessly unsuited to Billie as possible. Hammond loved to gossip, but he had a sense of humour about it all, and in 1972 he knew how much he had accomplished. In November 1933, just before he was supervising Billie's first two sides, he had also produced Bessie Smith's last four, released on Okeh. He thought the labels probably regarded him as a nut, but a nut with money, and they couldn't afford to disregard him; his track record in the end was unrivalled.

Nevertheless, although now a recording artist, Billie still had to make a living, and it seems to have been in 1933 or 1934 that she joined Pops Foster's unit. Foster was not the New Orleans bassist of the same name, but a singer, dancer and would-be comedian who got together a group of entertainers that went round the clubs performing wherever they were allowed, for tips.

I got her and Honey Coles and Baby Lawrence together. We worked at a place called the Log Cabin – Pod's and Jerry's Log Cabin. We played there every night. We got no money Just every night waffles and chicken. We only got the money people would throw. We'd pick up $10, $15, $20, because the elite used to come in there. All the stars: Tommy Dorsey, Jimmy Dorsey, Tallulah Bankhead – all the big white stars used to come up to 133rd Street from downtown. There were eight or ten little joints in a row – like the Strip.

Foster was quite a gossip, too. When he first met Billie, he said, she was 'doing a little prostituting, along 136th Street, that was kind of the main drag . . .' and that 'She was a hustler. Out of the clubs. But the night she learned she could sing, she stopped hustling.' Baby Lawrence was Lawrence Jackson then; he was a singer, about eleven years old, and Billie 'loved him to death', according to Foster; he was later better known as Baby Lawrence, the dancer. Honey Coles was Baby's inspiration, a very good dancer indeed, and there was also a comedian called High Jivin' Smiley·

He was a big black boy with great big white teeth and a great big broad smile He tried to jive his way through everything. Billie used to pass out when he started, used to die, because he used to make her laugh He used to make everyone laugh because he was so *un*funny . . .

I was a kid singer I started out singin' I dug her for her singin' ability Her vocabulary and vibrata – a funny vibrata – some people didn't dig her But her vibrata had something so warm about it that she was just lovable. And a person that is in love, naturally sings about love . .

Foster said that Bobby was playing piano at Pod's and Jerry's when his unit worked there. 'I would go on, and introduce Honey, and then Baby Lawrence, and always have Billie close the show.' He thought he had first met Billie at Big John's, and they were both marijuana smokers, and it was some time later that he got up his group and included her. He loved to talk about the night life, including the buffet flats, or railroad flats.

We had a place we all used to go to, and Billie went there too, what they called the Daisy Chain. It was a house of prostitution and drinks and everything. Billie used to frequent it just to see what was happening And *eeev'rything* was happening. It was *faaaantastic*! Women goin' with women, men goin' with men, nobody paid it any mind, everybody was gay and havin' a ball. Stayed open twenty-four hours a day On 141st Street between Lenox and 7th They had a girl there called Sewing Machine Bertha and she'd go down on all the girls. The girl that owned the house – Hazel Valentine – very, very pretty girl; she was the landlady; she was an ex-chorus girl. The Daisy Chain was a big railroad flat house, with these rooms over here and rooms over there and a long hall, and you'd see people on the floor gettin' their thing   . you had to pay $5 apiece, and everybody got buck naked and everybody was ballin'. Go from room to room Entertainers went up there Half coloured, half white. Hell yeah, real integrated. All the lesbians went there I couldn't quote names because some of them was real big-time stars, so it was husha-husha. The public didn't know anything about it. It was only show people.

The Daisy Chain was a popular hangout for quite a few years;

when Fats Waller recorded several wonderful piano solos in 1929, he called one of them 'Valentine Stomp', after Hazel, and Count Basie recorded 'Swingin' at the Daisy Chain' in 1937 The joint was not included in Frank Driggs's list of Harlem spots, because it seems to have been 'livelier' than most, and on the private side.

Foster also describes the tea pads: '. . And they had Reefer Mae, a girl called Reefer Mae   she moved down to 114th Street. Kaiser's was in a basement, in a railroad flat, and they had big chairs, and you didn't see nothin' but marijuana being passed around there. Mostly show people.' Foster is another one who emphasizes that Harlem was different then.

That's when Harlem was Harlem and you needn't be afraid to come up there. They used to sing a song called 'Harlem Must Be Heaven 'Cause My Mother Came from There'. The breakfast would start about 2.30 in the morning – that's when it was really swinging – up until twelve, one o'clock in the day. And everyone would be ballin'. And it was very much integrated then. At that time Billie started drawin' white people.

Again and again in all these reminiscences there is the feeling that Billie wasn't doing anything that a lot of other people, black and white, weren't doing; it was just that, as Pony said back in Baltimore, she was just 'don't care-ish'. Foster describes Billie as a happy girl, but 'when she was evil she was really evil'.

Fight at the snap of your finger. She was always trying to have some fun, but if anybody crossed her she was really bad . . .

We used to smoke pot a lot together   She was quiet, you know, in a way of speaking. Unless somebody flusterated her, then she was a bitch. She'd raise hell. But she wasn't a loud girl. She was kind of a shy girl, until she got loaded . .

Honey Coles was on the staff at the Apollo many years later. Foster loved to reminisce and scandalize, and skips from one story to another and back and forth in time, but Coles is more down to earth and his memory probably more accurate.

We worked around all those clubs – a foursome thing – around Harlem for what you could pick up off the floor, maybe some nights you'd pick up $40, $50 ... We were hustlin' in those days, trying to get the rent money together. In those days they called us buskin'. Every night we'd go to another little club, like the Log Cabin. This had to be around 1933, '34, because I had just come to New York. I would be able to pay my rent, get my suit pressed. Baby Lawrence was a boy tenor and he sang things like 'Gypsy Fiddles Are Playing'. Had a beautiful little voice. It was Pops Foster's unit, he got it together. And we'd go to a little club and ask a guy, could we go on, and if he said yes, we'd go on ... I would do tap jazz — kind of modern. Pops was old then [he was about thirty-one]. Real funny guy. Billie would do things she later recorded — 'Miss Brown to You', 'Them There Eyes'. ['Miss Brown to You' wasn't published until 1935.]

At that time there was a place up on 7th Avenue called the Hoofer's Club, where all the dancers got together and traded steps and danced. It was really a poolroom and a lunch room, but the guy gave us a back room because he liked dancers ... And I met Pops there. It was between 131st and 132nd Street on 7th Avenue. Pop knew Billie because they smoked, so that's the connection. And the other comic named Smiley, Pop knew him also. He needed a dancer.

Late at night, at that time Harlem was booming all night. You never ran out of places to go. A thousand little places in between the blocks ... We used to work all of them. Primarily the Log Cabin was sort of our home base. I think it was Pod's and Jerry's then ... There was a piano player in each club. Everybody knew everybody's thing. All I required was somebody to play an introduction in stop time. And everybody knew Billie's tunes — they were standard things. And if they didn't know them, you'd run through them once and they got it. I don't see how this could have been before 1934 because the first time I saw Billie Holiday was at the Yeah Man or the Hot-Cha on 137th . At this time Harlem was as white as it was black. At night everybody from downtown came up, after everything closed downtown. And they walked the streets like anybody Diamonds and minks and furs. Nobody thought of mugging anybody .. They were after-hours places and a guy would have maybe a piano and a singer . . Dickie Wells always had regular shows, so we never worked there.

When I first heard Billie sing, it didn't move me at all. I was used to the Ethel Waters type singing where you had clear singing and enunciation, and Billie kind of left me cold at first, until I listened for a while and began to dig what bag she was in. I wound up liking her very much.

Along with many others, Coles thought Billie was older than she was.

She must have been extremely young . . Very attractive. Very cool, very gentle. But she was mature acting for a young girl, which is why I thought she was about twenty To my recollection, she was an extremely quiet person who liked to laugh. But quiet. Sort of even shy. She never impressed me – even in later years when she became famous – as an extrovert, like people in show business who are always on . .

She was definitely unsophisticated. She was a nice person – like you would think of a younger sister – but she had some maturity about it. She knew what she wanted to do as far as a song was concerned; she had *that* confidence   . I'm talking about her shyness off stage, sort of a shy approach to audiences, that hesitation, like 'Who wants to hear me?' That type of attitude   like some singers will go into a club and want to sing regardless of who's working there. I'm sure she was the type of person that had to be asked. I think basically she was a shy person, and this may be one reason   aside from associations – that got her on drugs, to give her that false courage. [She wasn't] like a Lena Horne, who attacks a song and an audience. Ella's shy, but so secure in the knowledge of what she's doing   absolutely, positively secure in what she does. But I think Lady Day was always a little shaky in what she had to offer. When we were doing our little thing, I think she was a little reluctant then; she'd go on, but it was a sort of timid approach to going on.

Ella Fitzgerald said after decades in the business that she still suffered stage fright. But there is plenty of evidence that Billie liked to be asked. Two of Billie's close friends a little later were Irene Wilson, Teddy Wilson's wife, and Callye Arter, an old friend of Irene's from Chicago, who described a party which must have taken place in 1935 or possibly 1936.

Irene had this surprise birthday party for Ted   When the band gets off – Benny Goodman's – they come to the house. Half of Benny's band was there; and Lionel Hampton's wife Gladys, and of course Lionel was playing with the band then. And Miss Kathryn Perry, who was Earl Hines's first wife – she's a personal friend of Irene's, and at that time she was known for her singing. Kathryn Perry's song was 'More Than You Know' You know how a party is. So Kathryn gets up and sings that. And different ones were doing their thing, and Billie's sitting there, and nobody is saying one word to her. Billie wasn't famous there, she was nothing but a kid. But Billie couldn't stand it any longer, and she gets up and says, 'Teddy, will you play "These Foolish Things"?' I can always remember her saying that to him. And Ted played it and do you know that she broke the party up . . . Then she sang more.

But she had wanted to be asked. There would always be an ambiguity about Billie's attitude towards her fame. A lot of people, including Pops Foster and Honey Coles, thought that Billie had played amateur night at the Apollo in the late 1920s, when she was twelve or thirteen years old; but the Apollo as we know it, with its Wednesday amateur night, didn't open until 1934. It was in a former burlesque house, moving to its present location the next year. In any case, as 1935 came on, Billie's fame began to grow, with all the problems and ultimate glory it would bring, and her success at the Apollo, when it came, would be a bigger thrill than the first records could have been.

She is thought to have had a short engagement at the Alhambra, at 2110 7th Avenue, but she soon settled in for a longer stay at the Hot-Cha Bar and Grill, up the street at 2280. The Hot-Cha in those days was a gin mill with the entertainment in a back room; John Hammond said it was a better place to hear her than Pod's and Jerry's. Don Frye was playing piano; according to Frank Driggs, she was already appearing at the Hot-Cha in 1934, on a bill with Billy Daniels. Ralph Cooper, who had been a bandleader and later became a famous disc jockey, was an MC at the Apollo in the mid-thirties; he heard her at the Hot-Cha and reported to the Apollo's owner, Frank Schiffman, in one of the most famous bursts of enthusiasm in all music: 'You never heard singing so slow, so lazy, with such a drawl – it ain't the blues – I don't know what it is, but you got to hear her' Schiffman was sold, and booked her for the week of 23 November 1934, with Bobby Henderson on piano. This was the beginning of a sequence of milestones: Billie had appeared as an extra in a Paul Robeson film, *The Emperor Jones*, in 1933, and she had played some bit parts on a radio soap opera produced by Sheldon Brooks (who wrote 'Some of These Days' for Sophie Tucker); now on 12 March 1935 at Paramount Film Studios in New York she made a short film with the Duke Ellington band. This was her first exposure as a singer outside the clubs of Harlem (not that many people saw the film). *Symphony in Black* has her knocked to the pavement by her fancy man (played by dancer Earl 'Snakehips' Tucker), whom she accosts as he goes out on the town with another woman. She sings only a few bars of Duke's 'Saddest Tale', but it is enough to convince anyone that the wrenching drama of which she was capable was already fully formed. She was not quite twenty years old.

Schiffman then booked her return for the week of 19 April 1935; this time she sang with a band. Cooper says he had bought her a gown and slippers for her April appearance, as well as rehearsing the house band for her. Comedian Pigmeat Markham, soon famous for his 'Here come de judge' routine, had been in the business for over fifty years when he talked about Billie in 1972. Her weight was evidently going up and down; when Pops Foster first knew her, he said, she was 'a big fat slob', and a year or two later she was said to be around 200 pounds, but in the Ellington film she is quite slim, and Pigmeat says she was skinny at the Apollo. He also says that 'she was a simple lookin' girl. Nothin' glamorous about her looks   you could see that she was a girl that hadn't been around, weren't hip, she didn't know how to make up real good, you know, the things that girls do to pretty up, she didn't know nothin' about it. So she looked like a plain ordinary girl, but she was attractive.' He had already seen her in the Hot-Cha:

She had somethin' different, a different style from any other singer I've ever heard. She had a weird voice. One thing attracted me to Billie so much was that she never sang on the beat with the music, she always slurred behind the music, the music was ahead of her at all times, but she sang behind the music. Even in her slow records. It was fascinatin'.
Billie came on right before the big band closed the show,

'cause that was the big attraction in those days – the big bands. There was no secret about no smokin' reefers in those days; she loved those reefers. Oh, she was so high that mornin' for her first show; I guess she was tryin' to get her energy to go on stage. She was standin' in the wings before she went on; the music comes up; she froze – she just stood there. And I give her a shove – a hard shove and I didn't intend to shove her as hard as I did, and I guess she would of fell, but she grabbed on to the mike and finally she got herself together and she started singin' . .

In those days the Apollo would be packed on Friday morning for that first show. It was cheap – no more than 25 cents . . . the Apollo was just a haze of smoke. I'll never forget, when Billie came out to sing, they put a green spotlight on her and you could see that smoke all over the house . . . you could get a contact high if you wasn't smokin'. When she got herself together she tore that house down.

She sang 'If the Moon Turns Green', a Bernie Hanighen song, 'something about "the shadows come up and down, would you be surprised"',' said Pigmeat – and 'Them There Eyes', and some say she did 'The Man I Love' for an encore, because the audience wouldn't let her off the stage. The Apollo held perhaps 2,000 people, and she had probably never sung for more than 200 before, but she won over what was then already one of the most discerning audiences in the world.

Pigmeat says he put her under contract: 'She wanted me to handle her.' But he was too busy working at the Apollo, and he knew he didn't have time to hustle work for her; she went back to the Hot-Cha for the time being, and he went over there one night and tore up the contract.

Billie had seen Clarence from time to time. She said in her book that she would go to wherever he was playing and get some money from him whenever she and Sadie were hard up, and that he would pay up because he didn't want her hanging around, lest the groupies of the period learn that he was old enough to be their father. The night after he first heard Billie, Hammond said, he went to the Congress Ballroom on Broadway between 51st and 52nd Street where Fletcher Henderson was playing:

I came bouncing up to the stand, and I said, 'Clarence, you didn't tell me you had a daughter. She's the greatest singer I ever heard.' I was bubbling. Afterwards, when the band got off the stage, Clarence came up to me and said, 'For Christ sake, John, don't talk about Billie in front of all the guys. They'll think I'm old. She was something I stole when I was fourteen.' You know, I was so naïve, I didn't know what 'stole' meant. I never heard a parent referring to a child with so much contempt and horror. So I knew there was no relationship between the two, so I never talked to him about her again.

This is Hammond's puritanism talking. Clarence was busy having a good time, and he helped Sadie and Billie out a little now and then even though he thought Sadie was a pain in the neck. Elmer Snowden says that Clarence and Billie always had a warm relationship. But there had certainly not been any natural children in Hammond's (Vanderbilt) family; what did he know? For someone who had had his name removed from the social register because he regarded it as anti-semitic, Hammond remained remarkably naïve. Drummer Kaiser Marshall later said that Clarence was irked that his daughter's recording sessions used every guitar player in town except him; and Hammond said that he was the one who called the musicians. Thus it seems that the reason there are no records with Billie and Clarence together may be Hammond's lack of a certain kind of understanding.

In the spring of 1935, Billie's father came to the Hot-Cha to congratulate her. Experienced in show business, he was impressed by her success at the Apollo, but even more by the fact that she had already been booked for a return engagement. He hadn't known what to make of her singing at first; he himself had occasionally sung, but in a shouting gin-mill style that he would have learned in Baltimore. He heard she had been listening to all Louis Armstrong's records and was concerned at first that she was copying somebody else instead of finding her own style. But now he must have realized that she wasn't copying anybody, and he had to be pleased that so many people were excited about her. For Billie's part, seeing that her father was pleased with her, she now changed the spelling of her stage name to Holiday.

And after that second Apollo engagement, something even more important happened. Now a fully mature artist, she began making one of the century's most incandescent series of recordings.

6

The Teddy Wilson Era

At the end of 1933, Utah had put across the crucial vote for the amendment to the Constitution repealing Prohibition; it was after that, some say, that Pod and Jerry decorated the outside of their place with a phoney log effect and changed its name to the Log Cabin. The electric coin-operated multi-selection record player had become practical, and when taverns legally opened up across the country, they all needed juke boxes.

Homer Capehart, later a two-term Senator from the state of Indiana, had been experimenting with automatic record changers for years; the company named after him marketed the most elaborate and expensive home record player on the market, which turned the records over, playing both sides of each one (and sometimes breaking it). But business was poor at the beginning, and Capehart was squeezed out of his own company, so he bought the rights to another automatic changer and in 1933 went to work for Wurlitzer, whose organs and player pianos weren't selling too well during the Depression. Wurlitzer began making juke boxes, and sales of 5,000 machines in 1934 became 30,000 by 1939, while Seeburg, Rock-Ola and several others also did good business. This new outlet for records revived the American record business, just as the worst of the Depression was over.

The Columbia group had gone bankrupt (not for the first time) and been swallowed by the American Record Company, whose flagship label was Brunswick; the Columbia label was retired for a while. Victor had begun recording Fats Waller and his Rhythm in 1934, and half a dozen sides from Waller's first sessions were big hits on the new juke boxes; this probably made it easier for John

Hammond to talk Brunswick into making jazz records for that market. Already a famous entertainer, Waller sang on his own records; his sidemen were on his payroll and he probably had a royalty deal, but Hammond's idea was even cheaper: Teddy Wilson was hired as a contractor to make small-group sides using any jazzmen who happened to be in town. A bit later, in early 1937, Victor also started a long series of small-group sides led by Lionel Hampton, with constantly changing personnel; the rationale behind all these hundreds of wonderful records was that experienced jazzmen could cut four sides quickly and cheaply, without any expensive arrangements or rehearsal time.

Pianist Teddy Wilson was born in Texas in 1912, but his background was very different from Billie's: his parents were schoolteachers. His style of single-note lines in the right hand had been influenced by Earl Hines and Art Tatum, but was spare and elegant, made to order for the Swing Era: not that there was anything wrong with his left hand either, and his time was effortlessly swinging. John Hammond first heard Wilson on the radio, subbing for Hines at the Grand Terrace in Chicago; Benny Carter went to Chicago to fetch him.

Hammond recorded Wilson with Red Norvo, who was then married to Mildred Bailey (they were called 'Mr and Mrs Swing'), and it was at Bailey's home that Hammond first brought together Benny Goodman and Teddy Wilson. In mid-1934, Goodman formed his own band, as opposed to the *ad hoc* groups he had recorded with; Wilson had already played on Goodman's first hit recording of 'Moonglow', made in May for Columbia, and would soon be a star in Goodman's trio and quartet on Victor, but not in the big band. In August 1935 the Goodman band suddenly hit the big time on a coast-to-coast tour, touching off the Swing Era with the sort of music black audiences had been dancing to for years; but Wilson and Hampton were presented separately during the intermission, like a vaudeville act, helping to avoid the racial problem.

Wilson also made some piano solos for Columbia in May 1934, his first recordings under his own name, but the label didn't release them at the time. In mid-1935, just twelve days before making his first trio records with Goodman and Gene Krupa, Wilson began making making a series of over 140 sides, most of them on Brunswick, but on Columbia after the Columbia Broadcasting System bought ARC in 1938 and revived that label. This total does not count alternate takes, piano solos, trio sides and a few big-band numbers in 1939, but includes those on which Wilson played that were released as 'Billie Holiday and her Orchestra'. Wilson's short period as leader of a big band was not successful, but his classic series of small-group records was ended only by the musicians' union strike against the record companies that began in 1942, although by then the USA had entered the Second World War. Shellac was rationed and the recording of black music probably would have suffered anyway.

Some of these Wilson sides were instrumentals, but all were chamber jazz at its best, most of them including vocalists: Ella Fitzgerald, Lena Horne, Mildred Bailey, Helen Ward, Thelma Carpenter and several more. Altogether, thirty-eight of the Wilson sides are calculated to have been hits. The sides with vocals gave the vocalist equal billing, but leaving plenty of room for solos; and by far the greatest number of vocals were those of Billie Holiday It is important to remember that she was one among equals: Wilson said, 'Billie would do one chorus, like a horn. The horns were featured equally with the voice.' He first met her at Pod's and Jerry's, with Bobby Henderson, when John Hammond took him there.

> She took turns singing with a girl called Beverly White and the three took turns and were the whole show Beverly and Billie were as different as night and day, and the two on the same show were terrific. Beverly was a great ballad singer, I think one of my favourites that I ever heard. And Billie had this beautiful rhythm singing, you know, faster tunes.

Wilson praised Bobby Henderson as 'a solid rhythm player', and also Henderson's successor Garnett Clark for 'a very facile technique, a lot of embroidery playing and a lot of runs'

Hammond wrote in his book that Brunswick did not object to Wilson recording with Goodman, who was becoming more famous: the association could be nothing but good publicity for the Brunswick records. But Hammond wanted the favour returned. Goodman had begun recording for Victor in April 1935, and Victor would not be so cooperative; neither was Goodman himself. When he sat in with Wilson at Brunswick he often used the name John Jackson; he didn't really want to do it at all, but he owed

Hammond too much, and he was too good a musician not to play beautifully when he showed up. Before the first session, Hammond said, 'Benny kicked like a steer.' He wrote in the *Melody Maker* that Goodman was five minutes late when he called to say that he wasn't coming. 'Just at that moment,' wrote Hammond, 'I put on a greater burst of temperament than the New York Telephone Company has ever before had to suffer. Result: in ten minutes Benny was sitting and playing in the studio better than ever.'

Billie's first four tunes with Teddy, made at his first session as a contractor, were 'I Wished on the Moon', 'What a Little Moonlight Can Do', 'Miss Brown to You' and 'Sunbonnet Blue', in that order. The group was all black except for Goodman: Roy Eldridge on trumpet, Ben Webster on tenor sax, John Trueheart (playing with Chick Webb's band at the time) on guitar, John Kirby on bass and Cozy Cole on drums. Kirby was one of the best bassists in jazz, again and again contributing a melodic line as well as keeping the time with authority; Cole was a popular session drummer who was still recording with Billie in the fifties. Goodman had arrived late and left early, pleading a dinner date, so played only on the first three sides.

'I Wished on the Moon' was written by Ralph Rainger, who had been arranger and accompanist for torch singer Libby Holman and for Clifton Webb; Billie would record more of Rainger's songs. The words to 'Moon' as Billie sang them are worth quoting; they were written by the acerbic playwright Dorothy Parker, a good versifier who was also a troubled woman, to whom Robert Benchley once said, 'Dottie, if you keep committing suicide, you're going to damage your health.'

> I wished on the moon, for something I never knew;
> Wished on the moon, for more than I ever knew;
> A sweeter rose, softer skies,
> > Warm April days, that would not dance away
>
> I begged on a star, to throw me a beam or two;
> Wished on a star, and asked for a dream or two;
> I looked for every loveliness,
> > It all came true: I wished on the moon, for you.

This is a good example of a modern pop song, a complete marriage of words and music: poetry has little to do with it. On this record there are only the two verses, but together with the melody they serve all the necessary functions; the second line would appear to be repetitious, but it is relieved by a beautiful chord change.

It is said that black recording sessions had to take their pick of songs that were left over after the white recording stars had their choice; Wilson seemed to confirm this, saying on one occasion, 'That's why many of those songs we recorded you never heard anybody singing besides Billie.' This was no doubt sometimes true, but far too much has been made of it. Many of her songs were well-known ones, and in any case she and Wilson picked them from a selection: she recorded the ones she liked the best. Not all of the songs from that golden age could be masterpieces, yet for decades cabaret artists have been discovering and rediscovering the more obscure ones; it is no doubt true that some of the songs Billie recorded have survived because she made them her own, but every song needs an interpreter. The very first, 'I Wished on the Moon', was introduced by Bing Crosby in the film *Big Broadcast of 1936*, and there were two other hit recordings of it in 1935, including Crosby's; it was hardly a throw-away In fact, if many of the tunes have been forgotten today, some of them were chosen at the time because they were already hits, and the punters shoving nickels in juke boxes would recognize the titles.

In another interview, Wilson pointed out that 'all of us were working from lead sheets because the tunes were brand new; no point in memorizing them if they weren't hit tunes.' Most of the songs didn't turn out to be hits, 'but they were pretty good songs' They would rehearse in Teddy's apartment, because he always had a piano; one afternoon would be time to go through thirty or forty songs, and Billie would choose the ones she liked the best, for both words and melody. They would choose three or four for the next recording session and spend an hour on them.

And we rehearsed them until she had a very good idea of them in her mind, in her ear, but there'd be no rehearsal with the musicians; there was no need for rehearsals. They were all expert improvisers. Her ear wasn't phenomenal, but she had to get a song into her ear so that she could do her own style on it. She would invent different little phrases – all great jazz singers do that, do variations on the melody, and they have to know the melody inside out in order to do that.

Billie clearly liked the words and the sentiment of 'I Wished on the Moon'. On her very first syllable, the first-person pronoun, she comes in ahead of the beat, then lapses into her swinging version of Southern languor: she has announced that the song is worth listening to, so that we tune in. In the second line of each verse, she omits the pronoun entirely; as for the last line of each verse, 'Warm April days' and 'It all came true' have the same number of syllables, but entirely different accents: she makes short work of that little inconvenience, and we don't even notice it. Her singing is not so much lazy as conversational, yet never at the expense of the song; her vocal colour is unique: it is not slick but has a rough edge on it, like the voice the girl next door might have. And her time and her phrasing are that of a musical genius. This is both pop singing and jazz singing at their best; but then it is largely thanks to Billie that the two became almost synonymous, at least for a while.

At this first recording session, after a few notes of introduction from the piano, Goodman introduced the first three tunes, casually caressing them with easy swing; Webster did the same for the last. After Billie sang, the horns take the tune out, everybody playing at once in what was essentially the Chicago style, which had become standard operating procedure for jazz combos at the dawn of the Swing Era and which some years later, in lesser hands, became Dixieland. But in this company nobody got in the way; these people knew how to listen to each other, and not one note too many was played. No arrangements and no amount of rehearsal could have resulted in better music, for these musicians were not only among the best of their kind, but they made a living performing every day for live audiences. They were recording their own work, not manufacturing product.

The records were well made; even Trueheart's rhythm guitar is well recorded. 'I Wished on the Moon' received the slowest tempo of the session, but not too slow: a gently walking pace, perfect for its wistfulness. 'What a Little Moonlight Can Do' was by Harry Woods, from a British film called *Roundhouse Nights*; Woods was born in Massachusetts in 1896, and wrote a lot of the sort of songs that were transitional types, halfway between the earlier Tin Pan Alley tradition and the more modern style, and which were big in vaudeville, such as 'When the Red Red Robin Comes Bob-Bob-Bobbin' Along', and 'Paddlin' Madelin Home' This one was taken at a cracking pace, as quick a beat as Billie ever sang over, but of course Goodman and Billie made it sound easy, while the rhythm section did the work. The last two sides were taken at a slightly quicker walk than the first, just about perfect for a crew of jazzmen like this. 'Miss Brown to You' was by Rainger, Richard Whiting and Leo Robin, and remained in Billie's repertoire for the rest of her life. (The studio was at 1776 Broadway, and during Goodman's introductory solo on 'Miss Brown to You' we can hear the horns of cars going round Columbus Circle just outside.) 'A Sunbonnet Blue (and a Yellow Straw Hat)', far from being hack work, was a song by Sammy Fain and Irving Kahal, a team who also wrote 'I Can Dream, Can't I?', 'When I Take My Sugar to Tea' and others; Webster's introduction alone makes you want to hear the rest of the song.

At the second recording date, on the last day of July, Goodman was replaced by Cecil Scott, who had been a bandleader, employing both Bill Coleman and Don Frye, the pianist at the Hot-Cha. Lawrence Lucie replaced Trueheart on guitar and played a more retiring role, sticking like glue to the rhythm section. Hilton Jefferson, subsequently less well known than other jazzmen but very highly regarded by his peers, was added on alto sax. Three vocals were recorded, and Wilson had written out some unison passages for the horns; he later professed to be disappointed with the results, and it's true that it's a slightly different kind of date, but no less delightful. Given Kirby's splendid bass and the absence of the Chicago-style ride-outs, the sound seems more modern; and partly because of the quicker tempos there is room for solos from everyone.

The three songs Billie sings, all by Tin Pan Alley stalwarts, are of the sort supposed to be second-rate. But their innocent high spirits offered the crew on hand just what was needed: unlike earlier Tin Pan Alley products (all those waltzes from around 1910) and unlike today's rock hackwork, they were tunes worth improvising on. 'What a Night, What a Moon, What a Girl' (changed by Billie to 'boy') is a happy, uptempo romp, perfect for jitterbugging sweethearts. 'I'm Painting the Town Red' is slower, but still a jaunty, carefree lope; 'It's Too Hot for Words' picks up the tempo again, with an appealing lyric: it's never too hot to make love if you're young enough.

On 25 October the horns were Eldridge, Benny Morton on trombone and Chu Berry on tenor sax; Dave Barbour (later

married to Peggy Lee) was more evident on guitar, like Trueheart
on the first session. The rhythm section was unchanged. The first
three pieces were no doubt silly novelties, but with good tunes, and
again, if these people had this much fun with them, how can we
complain? '24 Hours a Day' is a nursery-rhymish love song about
a music-box; the soloists skitter up and down the melody line like
kids skipping rocks on a pond: Berry in particular is a delight, as
he always was. Billie's vocal is one of her most typical of the
period: on the words 'old-fashioned' in the first line, and again and
again at the ends of phrases – 'song about you', '24 hours a day' –
she does as she pleases with the beat; it is as though the words
aren't going to fit, yet they do, and the swing is inexplicably
carefree. What Whitney Balliett wrote about Lester Young is as
true of Billie: they had 'absolute mastery of broken-field rhythm
and phrasing – the ability to emphasize the beat simply by eluding
it'. 'Yankee Doodle Never Went to Town' (co-written by Bernie
Hanighen, and also recorded by the Goodman band) and 'Eeny
Meeny Miny Mo' get the same treatment; 'If You Were Mine',
written like 'Eeny' by Johnny Mercer and Matt Malneck, is a fine
ballad. Wilson indulges in arpeggios behind the vocal on the latter
that are reminiscent of society bandleader Eddy Duchin.

On 3 December there was another instrumental along with
three vocals; changes in personnel include Johnny Hodges on alto,
who convinces us that 'These 'n That 'n Those' is not a bad tune,
and bassist Grachan Moncur, a Hammond discovery. 'You Let
Me Down' is a torchy love song by Al Dubin and Harry Warren,
and was already a Jimmy Dorsey hit; 'Spreadin' Rhythm Around'
is by Ted Koehler and Jimmy McHugh and was recorded by Fats
Waller: the way Billie lets the words slide across the beat, the
rhythm is spread like butter, while drummer Cole plays a 2/4
backbeat that would survive in rhythm & blues and beyond. On
'24 Hours a Day', Kirby plays 4/4 on the bass while Barbour on
guitar preserves a 2/4 feeling, resulting in a happy, loping beat;
this was New York jazz just before the rhythm sections began to
smooth it out, as 'modern jazz' began to be born

But Billie is the star What she brought to American popular
music complemented the quality of its songs. She sang and recorded
songs by all the greatest writers; soon one of her favourites would
be 'Yesterdays', by Jerome Kern, perhaps the greatest of all, who
began by trying to write operettas in an American style, but soon

combined his shapely melodies with the work of the best lyricists to invent something new. These composers couldn't help it: they were Americans, not Viennese (though it must be pointed out that Kern obtained valuable experience in England in his early years, where a lot of experimentation was going on, and that P.G. Wodehouse, creator of Jeeves and Wooster, was one of the influential lyricists).

Richard Rodgers spent his pocket money as a schoolboy attending matinées of Kern shows. New songwriters were influenced equally by Kern and by black songwriters such as Sheldon Brooks ('Some of These Days', 1910), and Henry Creamer and Turner Layton ('After You've Gone', 1918), who continued to develop demotic songwriting after the ragtime or 'coon' hits of the 1890s. About Harold Arlen, Johnny Mercer said, 'It sounds terribly inventive to us, terribly difficult, what he does, but not to him. It's like turning on a tap. It just flows out of him.' Alec Wilder described the quintessentially American Arlen style as a 'don't-worry-about-the-mud-on-your-shoes' attitude. Mercer wrote with Kern, Arlen and almost everybody else.

Kern and Arlen were Jewish; George and Ira Gershwin were the sons of Jewish immigrants; Irving Berlin was born in Russia. Many of the greatest American songwriters who were not Jewish were also from immigrant families: the tunesmith Harry Warren, a successor to the Tin Pan Alley tradition rather than a Broadway composer, was Italian, his real name Salvatore Guaragna. He wrote 'Jeepers Creepers' and 'You Must Have Been a Beautiful Baby' with Mercer, both big hits in 1938; with Mack Gordon, in 1941 alone, he hit with 'There Will Never Be Another You', 'I've Got a Gal in Kalamazoo', 'Chatanooga Choo Choo', 'Serenade in Blue' and 'At Last', the last four for the Glenn Miller band.

Cole Porter was one of the few who wasn't born poor. Sammy Fain and Ralph Rainger had been born in New York around 1900, Richard Whiting in Peoria, Illinois, in 1891; Whiting had become a successful businessman when he wrote 'Till We Meet Again' in 1918, and there were five hit recordings of it the next year.

All these songwriters had more than talent going for them: they were working in a historical window. They celebrated a love affair with the English language, learning to sing and shout and play stickball in American English, drawing on the optimism of what was then, for all its warts, the most easily, carelessly optimistic nation in the world. They began long before television, and even before radio, so that they were uninfluenced by advertising jingles or media fads, but were able to write songs in the language of their streets and neighbourhoods. But there is no point in complaining that songs are not written like that any more, for that golden age of popular music was of that time and cannot come again, any more than the classical music of Haydn and Mozart can be re-invented.

In Billie Holiday this great American style of songwriting found its most influential interpreter. She sometimes recomposed a song to suit herself, but even when she did not do that, she subtly altered it harmonically, making it a personal vehicle, all the elements of the art of singing at the service of swing. She was not well educated, and even her speaking voice, to judge from surviving radio interviews and studio banter, was different when she was not singing. She could show a unique wit, but she was also shy, and it was the words to the songs, with their freedom, their sweetness with substance, that set free her heart and soul, and her genius. Again and again those who knew her say that she was entirely herself only when she was singing. Not for nothing did Frank Sinatra say to *Ebony* magazine in 1958, talking about hearing her on 52nd Street when he was young:

> With few exceptions, every major pop singer in the US during her generation has been touched in some way by her genius. It is Billie Holiday who was, and still remains, the greatest single musical influence on me. Lady Day is unquestionably the most important influence on American popular singing in the last twenty years.

Trumpeter Bill Coleman, who heard Billie at the Hot-Cha before leaving for France, said that he knew instantly that she was different from any other singer he had ever heard. Hazel Scott, a singer and pianist who later had a successful career of her own, was present at the first Apollo engagement; just fourteen years old, she was playing hooky from school, and later remembered, 'I couldn't believe the way she sounded . . . I stayed through three shows just to hear her again.' Mildred Bailey, hearing Billie for the first time, said 'That girl's got it,' and thereafter resented her. Sarah Vaughan, Dinah Washington, Peggy Lee, Dick Haymes, Perry Como and all the rest came up in Billie's wake, to say nothing of all the fine singers who never became household names: Billie was idolized by Sylvia Syms, who in turn was described by Sinatra as 'the world's greatest saloon singer' Perhaps only the great Ella Fitzgerald, with her unique and different talent, may not have been directly influenced, and even she must have been listening.

Apart from Louis Armstrong himself, the only major American pop singer whose career began before Billie's and outlasted hers was Bing Crosby, the number one recording artist of the century by a very wide margin, with well over 300 hit records in less than twenty-five years, and he had to have been affected by her. Like Armstrong, he was one of the first who understood how to use a microphone, so that he sang intimately in his appealing baritone; and he had already been influenced by jazz musicians, such as Bix Beiderbecke and the great guitarist Eddie Lang. But his recordings from the early thirties sound self-conscious compared to his later ones: in the late thirties and in the forties, after many of the classic Holiday records had been made, and when no one in the music business could have been unaware of her, he had become the Crosby we know, singing in that wonderfully casual American way, as though he were inventing the words as he went along.

In mid-1935, Teddy Wilson was only twenty-two, and Billie just twenty. They made fourteen sides together that year, and they had already made history.

7

The Street That Never Slept

It is all very well for people who were there to talk about how wonderful Harlem was in the old days, but its residents did not have much of a stake in it. Many visitors to Harlem, especially the black ones, noticed that most of the shopkeepers were white. Irene Wilson, Teddy's wife, had written to her cousin Callye Arter that compared to Chicago, 'all the business is run by the white man and the places, I mean everything except the restaurants here all have white help. Groceries and all.' With the repeal of Prohibition the booze business was regularized, after-hours clubs began to disappear and there was less reason for white people to go up to Harlem to have a good time, while the resident African-Americans were simply stuck there, with as little economic stake as they had anywhere else. The music scene began to move downtown.

The new scene, on 52nd Street between Fifth and Sixth Avenues, was another musical miracle. When Long Island and other outlying areas were developed, people began moving out of New York City, becoming commuters, and eventually the well-to-do people who still lived in the brownstone mansions on 52nd Street in the 1920s noticed that the neighbourhood was going downhill, with gangsters and their kept molls living next door and the occasional shooting. By 1925 the street had its first speakeasy, and according to Arnold Shaw, some time in the early thirties Robert Benchley and a friend decided to do a survey, drinking their way up one side of the block and back down the other: 'Several days later, when he had recovered from the night's research, his notebook revealed the not quite legible names of no fewer than thirty-eight Judas-hole establishments.'

After 1927, in the wake of the first Onyx Club, there were soon more and more joints featuring music. For many years any taxi driver in New York needed only to be directed: 'Take me to the Street.' Old-timers still grieve that property speculators wrecked the Street in the fifties – there are modern bank buildings there now, with their ugly glass and aluminium entrance lobbies – but by then the clubs were closing or turning into strip joints, because after the war a lot of things had changed, and anyway it was changing property usage that had created the Street in the first place.

By the end of 1935 Teddy Wilson and Billie Holiday had appeared on the Street, though Billie's first gig there was short. The Famous Door, owned by a syndicate of musicians including Gordon Jenkins, Glenn Miller, Lennie Hayton and others, had opened in February; trumpeter, singer and inspired clown Louis Prima inaugurated the place with a long engagement and had several hit records in July and August. In September the white New Orleans trombonist George Brunies took over; Teddy and Billie were booked during this run, hoping to perform for booking agents and talent scouts. 'We were partners for a while,' said Wilson.

Billie's stay there lasted only a couple of weeks. It was a feature of the Street that many of the joints were opened as hangouts for musicians only to be overrun with tourists; Billie still lacked confidence, and on her first attempt she did not capture the attention of the Famous Door's no doubt noisy crowd. Wilson and Holiday were a sensation with musicians, reported *down beat*, but 'the Park Avenue crowd which supported Prima didn't like her.' And she was not allowed to mix with the customers and took it as an insult. Trumpeter Max Kaminsky found Billie sitting disconsolate upstairs in the foyer, just outside the club's toilets, and said, 'What are you doing here all alone?' He remembered seeing her singing and waiting on tables at the Alhambra, and she was pleased to see someone who knew Harlem. Arnold Shaw and John Chilton have pointed out that this anti-mixing policy was a surprising one for a club that was nominally run by musicians, and a lot of clubs on the Street were integrated.

In fact, the Onyx, the Famous Door and a lot of other places moved around and changed owners; and nearly all the places Billie ever worked on the Street were owned, or managed for the owners, by various combinations of a group which included lawyers, a former liquor salesman and so forth. Some of these people were interviewed by Arnold Shaw for his book on 52nd Street, which is priceless for this kind of information: as Billy Daniels, later so famous for his interpretation of 'That Old Black Magic' that he was mimicked by stand-up comics, told Shaw,

> Alexander was married to Ralph Watkins' sister, Beatrice, who was related to Artie Jarwood's first wife. Beatrice got Artie's wife to persuade him to lend money to Alexander. That's how Artie was involved in the Stable, which was actually run by Irving and Ralph. Oscar Rubin, who was a Mob guy, also had a piece – the checkroom . . .

One of these insiders, Beatrice Watkins Alexander Colt, talked about Billie many years later:

> My husband she called Jack until after the Famous Door and after that she made believe she didn't know him. Even in her autobiography I think she slighted him because he fired her, because they were fighting all the time . every night it would be the same thing: 'You don't let me sit outside because I'm coloured.' But the Famous Door was a very small place, and the policy was that no entertainers could mingle. Even Maxie Kaminsky and Louis Prima and Bunny Berigan. But she didn't care and that's the way she acted. I always felt that she felt, 'I'm better than anybody else, but just because I'm coloured I'm not better.' She was bitter. She felt like the world let her down, because she really did have a tremendous talent.

Despite this inauspicious beginning, Billie would conquer the Street and become its biggest star.

It was at this point that Billie began her long business relationship with Joe Glaser, who ran a booking agency with Tommy Rockwell, who had begun as a record producer, responsible for many of Louis Armstrong's classics from the 1920s; the Associated Booking Corporation is still going today. Unlike some of his kind, Glaser looked after his clients and kept his word; his stable already included Louis Armstrong: perhaps Louis recommended Glaser to Billie. The first thing Glaser did was to insist that she lose weight; she had gone back up to around 200 pounds.

Barney Josephson, later an important figure in Billie's life, remembered Joe Glaser's visits to his club, Café Society.

Joe was a roughneck, uneducated crude man. He came from Chicago. Owned some clubs out there with the Mob, or his wife, whore-house days .. But he comes down to the Café one night, and I was sitting with him, and this was one of those nights when half the house was black, and he looked around and said, 'Why do you allow so many jigs to come in here?' I said, Watch your language. He would use the word and not mean the same thing So I said, this is the kind of joint I'm running, but he said it's not good for business to have so many of them. 'Now look,' he says, 'don't get me wrong. Nobody likes a little nigger pussy better than Joe Glaser. But in business it's another matter; it's not good for business.'

I heard stories that he owned Louis. That he paid him a salary and owned him, which is not unusual   .

There were the Moe Gale guys – brothers – they had a talent agency like Joe Glaser, and they had the Ink Spots for many years on a deal   . they paid the four of them $500 a week, guaranteed fourteen weeks, and they'd send them out to Hollywood to hype up a picture with some coloured talent, and they got their $500 a week and the agency got $18,000 for the week. I had Hazel [Scott] out there in those days for $4,000, $5,000 for five, six days So for four weeks, $20,000. I was told that Joe had this kind of contract with Louis and that Louis never saw a cent.

The Ink Spots were one of the biggest of all black acts in the 1940s, with over forty hit records starting in 1939 But that's what the business was like then In any case, Glaser was a more complicated and more interesting man than Josephson thought, and the old story about Glaser taking advantage of Louis is also not that simple

Glaser had not begun as a roughneck, but came from a well-to-do family on the north side of Chicago. His father was a doctor, and Glaser rebelled early by refusing to go to college; his family indulged him, and when he discovered that his mother owned the land on which stood places like the Grand Terrace, the Lincoln Gardens and the Dreamland Café, he began to inhabit that part of town, fascinated by boxers, gangsters and girls. At the Lincoln Gardens he got to know King Oliver, and Ernie Anderson says that Louis told him that it was Glaser who gave Oliver the money to bring Louis to Chicago from New Orleans, leading to the classic recordings of Oliver's Creole Jazz Band in 1923, with Louis on second cornet, and also that it was Glaser's idea as much as anybody's that Armstrong should leave that band and go solo. So Armstrong and Glaser had known each other for some time. But Glaser was not primarily interested in music or artist management. He managed some boxers in Chicago, he chased women and he took on the speech and the manners of the gangsters he admired, until he had to leave Chicago suddenly. Anderson heard that Glaser had a used car lot. One faction of gangsters would buy a touring car from him, drive off and shoot up some other faction, and then sell the car back to Glaser. Another story concerns the Dreamland, where Glaser hung out with his girlfriends and, according to Anderson, had an opium pad upstairs. One group of musclemen hijacked a truckload of liquor and stashed it on the Dreamland's dance floor for a few hours, taking rather large advantage of Glaser's friendship; the rival group from whom the booze had been stolen got wind of this, and Glaser felt it an · opportune time to go to Paris for a year or so. At about that time his mother died, and when he returned to the States he was broke and had no prospects.

Meanwhile, Armstrong made his first trip to Europe in 1933, managed by a small-time gangster named Johnny Collins, who stole his money and didn't pay the bills. The story is that Collins left Louis flat in London without even a passport; Louis told Anderson that he expected a white man to steal his money, but when the bill collectors were waiting in the wings while he performed, the situation had begun to interfere with his music, and that's where he drew the line. Back in the USA, Anderson wrote,

Louis went out and found Glaser. 'His pants were raggedy and his ass was showing,' Louis told me. He told Joe he wanted him to be his manager. Joe said he couldn't possibly do it as he didn't have any money. Louis said, 'Don't worry, the money will come in. You just book me, I'll play the job, then you collect the money and pay me. All I want is a thousand dollars a week. You see to it that the musicians are

paid, and the taxes and expenses, and you keep the rest.'
That's the deal they made, and that's why they never needed
a contract. And Louis never had to worry about a thing, and
if he'd had any money he would have given it away anyway.
He gave away envelopes full of money to anybody who had a
sob story He even gave away trumpets, until Glaser put a
stop to it.

So according to Anderson, that's how Glaser got into management.
He handled Louis so well that the money rolled in, and Glaser
soon had lots more clients. Milt Gabler, who produced records at
Decca in the forties and recorded Billie, Louis and the Ink Spots
there, said about Glaser:

> He would call me and say, 'I have so-and-so. Could you use
> him . . .?' And I would say, 'How much? Great. You've got a
> deal.' He was a terrific businessman. I could work with him
> like I could work with Billie or the musicians. I took him at
> his word; his word was his bond. We let the two lawyers,
> Associated Booking and Decca worry about it. No matter
> what act it was, including Armstrong.

Men like Joe Glaser and Irving Mills were tough businessmen, but
they also appreciated the talent they were handling: all through
the 1930s Mills handled Duke Ellington and published his music,
and provided the band with its own Pullman car; almost alone
among black bands, Ellington's band (and Cab Calloway's,
another Mills act) never had to worry about where they were
going to sleep on the road. Joe Glaser was a great improvement on
the managers Louis Armstrong had been used to, and he saw to it
that Louis began to appear in better films. Glaser made a lot of
money on Louis, but he also travelled with him in the thirties and
left Louis a huge sum in his will. Billie's relationship with Glaser
lasted the rest of her life partly because his self-image was consistent: he didn't pretend to be anything he wasn't. He also usually
gave her money when she asked for it.
    The first booking he got for Billie was a revue at Connie's Inn.
Connie Immerman's club, like the Cotton Club, had been famous
in Harlem for its floor shows – Fats Waller's *Hot Chocolates*, packed
with hits like 'Ain't Misbehavin'', had started at Connie's and
moved to Broadway in 1929, and was the beginning of Louis

Armstrong's greatest fame. Like the Cotton Club, Connie's had moved downtown, to 48th Street between Broadway and 8th Avenue. In 1936 the revue included Louis, with Luis Russell's band; Billie's feature was 'You Let Me Down', which she had recently recorded, and was a success; but she came down with what was said to be ptomaine poisoning and had to leave the show, replaced by Bessie Smith. Of Billie's two idols, Louis admired her singing, but Bessie was not noted for paying compliments to other entertainers, and her opinion, if she had one, is unrecorded.

Next she went to upstate New York for theatre dates with the Jimmie Lunceford band, whose 'Rhythm Is Our Business' had been a national smash hit in 1935. There was some talk about work in Europe, and on 4 April *Melody Maker* ran a picture of her with her eyebrows pencilled in, because she'd been trimming them and accidentally cut half of one off.

In June 1936 she went to Chicago to appear at the Grand Terrace with Fletcher Henderson's band: Clarence had left, but she had many friends in the band. The gig turned out to be short. Ed Fox, who rented the venue from Glaser or managed it for him, hated Billie's singing and told her so after every performance. Billie tried to keep her temper for a while, and Fox, experienced in Chicago show business, was a tough fellow, but he must have thought he'd met his match when she finally began throwing the furniture at him in his own office. He fired her on the spot; she didn't even have travelling expenses back to New York, and Henderson, true to form, kept his head down. Some years later, she said in her book, Fox tried to hire her again for the Terrace; needless to say he had no luck. (But in fact she did work for him again later, at a different venue.)

Her first Chicago experience discouraged her, but she got no sympathy from Glaser, who, she later recalled, wanted her to 'speed up the tempo, you gotta sing hot stuff'. Finally, she said, she told him, 'Look, you son of a bitch, you sing it. I'm going to sing my way, you sing your way.'

Early in September she opened at the Onyx Club on West 52nd Street, sharing the bill with Stuff Smith's sextet. There was a personality clash, and on top of that Billie was finding her fans, and Smith began complaining about her encores. Joe Helbock let Billie go, because Smith had doubled the club's attendance during the slow summer season and was good for business, so now she had lost a job thanks to a member of her own race. But Helbock liked her and brought her back in December, while Smith was away on tour, to sing with the Spirits of Rhythm, who included the sensational and innovative Leo Watson.

About Billie on the Street, Bea Colt said:

> When she walked in, she walked in with her head high and straight ahead. I could tell you about Lena Horne, too, because she had the same attitude. She was married to Lennie Hayton, who was my husband's best friend. When she married Lennie, and she came to Kelly's Stable, a fella who was a very well-known theatrical agent who handled Loretta Young and people of that calibre, called and he wanted to take them to dinner. She said no, that just because I'm coloured, he asks me where I want to have dinner, but he wouldn't ask me if I was white. She had the same attitude as Billie Holiday
>
> Years ago we didn't figure it was a militant attitude, but in retrospect I would say that Billie was militant. Maybe that's what made her such an individualist – her style and her arrogance – because she *was* a marvellous entertainer. When she walked out you knew she was somebody, and she was going to be somebody . . If you asked her for a request, she might sing it if and when she got good and ready That was her way She sang what she wanted to sing.

Horne came from a middle-class background; she had a long and happy marriage to Hayton, who was white (he won an Oscar in 1949 for his Hollywood work). Horne's expression of her attitude was on the whole different from Billie's, but of course they were militant. Bea Colt's generation didn't think Billie was militant at the time; they just thought she was a pain in the neck. But Billie and Lena were practising black pride thirty years before it became fashionable. In Billie's case, despite her lack of confidence, she knew what she did with a song, and she knew that if she took too much nonsense she might not find her fans, and on top of everything else she had to put up with people telling her how to sing! Of course she had an attitude; she was making progress and finding her downtown audience, and in order to do so she had to stick up for herself. And the recordings continued.

On 30 January 1936 Wilson recorded 'Life Begins When You're in Love', a ballad with a vocal by Billie, and an instrumental; for

some reason there were only the two sides cut. Rudy Powell, a
Waller sideman at the time, played fine clarinet. On 17 March
Billie was upstate, and a Wilson session included two vocals with
Ella Fitzgerald. She is accurate, charming and little-girlish on 'My
Melancholy Baby' and 'All My Life', not quite eighteen years old
and already much more than a pop vocalist. This was another
session full of good tunes; admittedly 'Melancholy' was already
twenty-four years old at the time, but 'All My Life' was a big hit
in 1936, one of its authors being Sammy Stept, who also co-wrote
'I'm Painting the Town Red'· there were three hit versions of 'All
My Life', including Wilson's and a number one by Fats Waller.
(Waller must have liked the song, for it was one of the few he ever
sang absolutely straight, without kidding it.) Ella's records did
well in England, but English fans briefly worried that the Wilson–
Holiday partnership had come to an end.

On 14 May Wilson was in Chicago, and almost the entire
personnel was from the recently revamped Henderson band, then
playing at the Grand Terrace; the date might have included Billie
if it hadn't been for Ed Fox's tin ears. On 30 June, back in New
York, four Holiday vocals plus an instrumental were squeezed into
the date, and again Billie's are all good songs.

Driggs is one of those who complain that the music publishers
were in control, passing out their 'plug tunes', but he also points
out that when dominance passed to the radio stations a few years
hence the result would be a disaster. How can anyone complain
about 'It's Like Reaching for the Moon', 'These Foolish Things',
'I Cried for You', and even 'Guess Who?'? Kirby and Trueheart
are back, and it must be said that Kirby was a much better bassist
than Moncur; Cole is again on drums; trumpeter Jonah Jones was
then making a name for himself on the Street with Stuff Smith,
and introduces the loping, happy 'Guess Who?' with a muted solo
statement. The Ellington band must have been in town, because
Hodges on alto and Harry Carney on baritone and clarinet are
definitely assets. Billie's dying fall in pitch on the ends of many of
her phrases is especially pronounced on 'These Foolish Things'
and 'I Cried for You', adding an extra passion of resignation, a
habit for which she remained famous even after she stopped doing
it.

Wilson's session in Los Angeles on 24 August was just five days
before the second, epochal recording of 'Moonglow' by the Good-

man Quartet, and the date used entirely Goodman players, including the boss. Two Rainger tunes were recorded by Helen Ward, credited as Vera Lane for contractual reasons; they are nice records, but not a patch on Billie's, and there were also two idiosyncratic vocals by somebody called Red Harper, evidently a local club favourite, on which Goodman did not play.

Back in New York, on three dates in October and November with two different lineups, seven Holiday vocals were recorded. Cole Porter's 'Easy to Love', Kern's 'The Way You Look Tonight' (words by Dorothy Fields), 'Pennies from Heaven' (by Johnny Burke and Arthur Johnson; the song had seven hit recordings in 1936–7), and 'I Can't Give You Anything But Love', by Fields and Jimmy McHugh (the tune perhaps originally by Fats Waller) all continue to refute the orthodoxy about second-rate material, while 'With Thee I Swing', 'That's Life I Guess' and 'Who Loves You?' continue to use contemporary pop material to make records that were first-class because they were Billie's, and Teddy's. 'The Way You Look Tonight' is the first for which an alternate take has survived; the issued take was the second recorded, a better one, with lovely introductory clarinet from Goodman sideman Vido Musso. It is one of Billie's prettiest records. The ensemble introduction and ride-out on 'Pennies' are a little corny, but Webster plays a lovely solo, and Goodman a nice obbligato behind Billie's vocals on that and on 'That's Life I Guess', a title which might have appealed to Billie, given that she had just lost the job at the Onyx.

Wilson had another date in December, which included two vocals by Midge Williams. So 1936 saw twenty-seven Wilson sides, with twelve Holiday vocals; but meanwhile there was a sure sign of gathering stardom: Billie also began recording under her own name.

When Benny Goodman signed with Victor in early 1935, Hammond said, he got a 5 per cent royalty deal, one of the first for a jazz musician; Wilson and Holiday got no royalties on any of their work of the period. Yet for all the mythology about these records being obscure at the time, and for all the incredibly tight profit margins in the record business, ARC was so pleased that the company put Wilson under contract at $3,000 a year, which meant about $60 a week whether he recorded or not. Billie got $100 for four sides, and each of six or seven sidemen $20 each, and there were no arrangements to pay for, so the records were cheap to make. Hammond remembers what the business was like:

After four or five of these Teddy Wilson sessions, the American Record Company finally realized that they had something, so they signed Billie under the Vocalion label under her own name. And although they didn't give her royalties, what they did do was put her under a yearly contract for about $5,000, $100 a week, which was something . .

The Teddy records on Brunswick sold about eight or nine thousand, and they sold for 75 cents each. Vocalions sold for 35 cents. Arbitrary difference; they were both pressed out of the same terrible material. The company was making so little money it was tragic; there was no profit on the 35-cent record.

The full-price record, Hammond said, went to the distributors for 17 cents, the pressing costs were about 9 cents and a penny and a quarter a side went for the song royalties, and the recording sessions had to be paid for. The profit was 8 cents, so if they sold 20,000 copies (which was a lot) they made $1,600 profit on a hit. The big money in today's record industry simply wasn't there, and the whole thing more risky, because the cheap records were sold on a sale or return basis, like books. If they pressed too many they might get most of them back, and of course nobody dreamed that some of them would still be selling long after everybody involved was dead and gone: with those tight margins they had to look for short-term turnover.

Yet in 1936 records began appearing by Billie Holiday and her Orchestra. Basie's drummer Jo Jones remembered years later that the musicians were happier to work for Wilson, who was a star with Goodman and had money in his pocket; with Wilson they'd get paid on the spot, whereas they had to wait two weeks for their $20 from a Billie date.

Bernie Hanighen was the producer on the Vocalion sessions, though Hammond attended them as well. She had been singing 'If the Moon Turns Green', and soon recorded 'When a Woman Loves a Man', co-written by Hanighen with Paul Coates and Billy Rose respectively; in 1946 Hanighen and Raymond Scott co-wrote a Broadway show, *Lute Song*, which ran 146 nights and was revived in 1959. Johnny Mercer also co-wrote with Hanighen, and many years later said he wished Bernie hadn't stopped writing.

Billie said in her book that Hanighen almost got himself fired, fighting for money for her: they were lovers; maybe Hanighen helped to get her under contract. On the other hand, there was more than one way to get into trouble at Brunswick. Hanighen, like Billie, smoked marijuana, according to Hammond; at any rate,' the musicians, many of them, certainly indulged. Hammond said that the executives usually didn't show up at these sessions, because it was 'only jazz', but that John Scott Trotter was an ARC executive who disapproved strongly of pot (at that time in New York smoking pot had become a misdemeanour). Trotter went to Decca in 1937 and was Bing Crosby's music director for many years, but meanwhile Hammond also says that one session almost got cancelled because unnamed executives walked in and smelled something suspicious in the studio.

The first time Hammond went on salary at Columbia, he got himself fired. He was sales director for the classical Masterworks line (which, he said, nobody had bothered to try to sell to the big New York record shops), the company fired his secretary for trying to organize the office, so he told them to fire him, too. It wasn't only black people who had to kiss the boss's behind, although of course black people were less likely to get the job in the first place. But Billie was doing well, and many years later she was still grateful to Bernie Hanighen.

Billie also continued recording with Wilson, both under her name and his; but her own first session was on 10 July 1936, only a year after her first records with him. This long-established fact ought to lay to rest any legends about the records not selling well; ARC simply didn't have any money to invest in artists who were unlikely to break even. The first session had Cole on drums, but all the other personnel were white: Bunny Berigan on trumpet, Artie Shaw on clarinet, Joe Bushkin on piano, Dick McDonough on guitar and Arthur 'Pete' Peterson on bass. Berigan was already well known for his solos on Goodman records, and Shaw was an experienced and sought-after freelance musician who would become one of the most famous bandleaders of the Swing Era; indeed, fans would soon squabble over who was the better clarinet player, Shaw or Goodman. Shaw loved Billie's work and told her that he wanted her to sing with his band some day, but she had already heard that from Goodman and probably wasn't impressed. Bushkin, who sold albums well into the LP era, is still a highly rated musician; later on, Ernie said, 'Benny Goodman made him his musical director, not a title Benny awarded easily, but Joey always has insisted that he can't stay where he's not having a good time, so he vamped Benny.'

The tunes were 'Did I Remember?', 'No Regrets', 'Summertime' and 'Billie's Blues'. Again, these are hardly leftovers. 'Did I Remember?', by Harold Adamson and Walter Donaldson, was a film song nominated for an Oscar that year; 'No Regrets' was likewise a contemporary pop tune that was being played by Tommy Dorsey and the Casa Loma Band. The ensemble sound on these is indubitably white and harks back to a Chicago sound. The tour-de-force was 'Summertime', a new song at the time, from *Porgy & Bess*, the Gershwin opera which had just flopped on Broadway because audiences didn't know what to make of it: this recording was one of the first to give a sultry treatment to a song that began as a coloratura lament. From its introduction by Berigan's muted growling trumpet, with a passionate Shaw obbligato and Cole's drums rolling out a jungle beat, and followed by Billie's vocal, it would never be the same again.

When it came to it, nobody liked the tune that had been picked for the fourth side, so Hanighen suggested that Billie sing a blues, and 'Billie's Blues', her first copyright, was improvised on the spot.

On 29 September, a similar crew was assembled, with Irving Fazola replacing Shaw, Clyde Hart on piano and Artie Bernstein on bass. This is a session that must be described as somewhat ragged. All the tunes were pop tunes of the day, and all were treated in the same off-hand way by the band, though Billie does her usual wonderful job. 'A Fine Romance' was from a Fred Astaire/Ginger Rogers film of that year and has become a standard, as almost any song by Kern and Fields deserved to do; Billie's laconic treatment serves it well. In the film, we know that Fred and Ginger are going to end up together, so a fairy-tale quality is acceptable; but most people's love-lives aren't like that, and Billie's certainly was not: even the pauses between Billie's stanzas are eloquent. 'I Can't Pretend' has disappeared so completely that no reference to it can be found in the usual sources, but it has interesting chord changes. 'One, Two, Button Your Shoe', and 'Let's Call a Heart a Heart' were both by Johnny Burke and Arthur Johnson, from a Bing Crosby picture of 1936; neither is a world-beater. There are nice moments on these sides from Fazola, McDonough and Berigan; but on the first two Cole becomes a nuisance, especially on 'I Can't Pretend', with ricky-tick effects on his rims and his cowbell during Hart's piano solo. Yet his soft press-rolls behind Faz's and Berigan's shared chorus are very nice; again, something that's not heard any more. Trombonist Benny Morton, quoted by John Chilton, told a story about a recording session at which the composer of one of the songs showed up:

> He heard a playback on his composition and then said, 'That's a nice job, but it isn't my tune.' Billie said, 'That's the way I've done it. If you don't like it we'll just cancel it, we have several tunes here we could do instead.' The man said, 'Oh, no, oh no.' I can't remember what the tune was, but it turned out to be one of Billie's hit songs.

With hindsight it is difficult to understand the problem some composers had with her interpretation, but it did sometimes amount to recomposition, and 'One, Two, Button Your Shoe' is a good example. There is a radio aircheck of Ivy Anderson singing the song with Duke Ellington, and a comparison is instructive: in the melody as written there is a considerable, identical drop in pitch between 'one' and 'two', and between 'your' and 'shoe'; the effect is see-saw, nursery-rhymish, similar to that of the childlike melody of '24 Hours a Day', which Billie had done more or less straight the year before and to charming effect. On 'One, Two, Button Your Shoe', however, she ironed out the first phrase, ignoring the first interval entirely. Maybe she didn't think much of the song, and for once the critics are right: something else should have been chosen. Unusually, the record begins with some vocal jive between Cole and Billie; then the soloists ignore the tune entirely, and whereas the aforementioned Ellington arrangement treats it fairly as a piece of swing-era jive, Billie's record is too 'don't care-ish'.

Hammond says that he picked all the musicians for the dates, adding that Hanighen didn't even know them, which is ridiculous. Hanighen and Anderson were fans of white musicians as well as black, and Hanighen had been hanging around the jazz joints for years at this point; others have said that Hanighen picked them, and on the Wilson dates Teddy, who was always very much his own man, may have done the choosing. By the 1970s Hammond had been taking bows for many years for discovering Billie, and there are those who think it could just as well have been Goodman who heard her first; for that matter, Hanighen and Anderson must have been spreading the word. Hammond's success went to his head to some extent.

On Billie's first two dates, however, it is unclear who the real leader was, which is probably why the results are a notch below what she had been achieving with Wilson. In any case, several of them sold well, and things soon improved. Wilson played on Billie's next session, and as we have seen she continued to sing on his; things were back up to standard for some time.

It may have been at about this time, with things improving a bit and money coming in from recording sessions, that Billie and Sadie moved to 99th Street and Central Park West, and Billie set Sadie up with a restaurant. Some say the restaurant was directly downstairs; in 1941 it was a few doors away, but still close by. Sadie specialized in soul food, especially ribs; keeping her busy was no doubt a good idea, but the business was probably not too profitable. Anybody who was hungry got a hand-out, and visitors came and went upstairs, generating a party atmosphere that Billie must have liked; Babs Gonzales said that Billie and Sadie fed everybody in New York for years. Both Sadie and Billie were open-handed by nature, and nothing in their experience had taught them to plan for the future; in later years witnesses would suggest that Billie simply gave away a large part of her income over the years to anybody who was temporarily down on his or her luck. Billie wrote in her book that Sadie would take in any hooker off the street who had a sob story; and many a musician had cause to be grateful for a free meal and maybe a bed when he was out of work.

After her return engagement at the Onyx Club, Billie went back to Harlem at the end of 1936 to the Uptown House. This is the downstairs room that began around 1915 as Barron's Exclusive Club. It then became the Theatrical Grill, managed by Dickie Wells with Jimmy Mordecai as host; they had been members of a well-known dance team, and this was the beginning of Wells's career as a club operator, while Mordecai had played 'St Louis Jimmy' in the famous short film made by Bessie Smith in 1929. The club's name changed again to the Pirate's Den, then the Red Pirate, and finally became Clark Monroe's Uptown House in 1936. Somewhere along the way the front entrance moved round the corner so that the address changed from 2259 7th Avenue to 198 West 134th Street. Monroe encouraged after-hours jam sessions, and his club was one of the places where the music evolved into be-bop, or bop, or 'modern jazz', the participants including Dizzy Gillespie and Charlie Parker. In 1943 the Uptown House moved to 52nd Street, and in the sixties the old address was the site of baseball player Roy Campanella's liquor store.

Clark Monroe, known to his friends as 'the dark Gable', was a handsome man; trumpeter Harry Edison says they used to call him 'Money' Monroe. In the sixties he was back uptown, managing Count Basie's Lounge, and in 1971 was said to be running an elevator in a hotel; but in his encouragement of the musicians during a critical period in American music he became one of its unsung heroes. Clark's brother, Jimmy Monroe, was also very good-looking. He had been married to Nina Mae McKinney, a well-known vocalist, and had been to Europe with her. (She had appeared in *Hallelujah!*, an early MGM talkie in 1929, a film ahead of its time, about a black cotton-field worker who accidentally kills a man and becomes a preacher. Nothing so realistic about black people would come from Hollywood for thirty years.) The house band at the Uptown included Joe Guy on trumpet.

Both Jimmy Monroe and Joe Guy would play important parts in Billie Holiday's choice of paramours, but it seems that all of these people had known each other for a long time. Claire Leybra was a long-time friend of Billie's; she married Aaron Liebenson, whose pharmacy was at 142nd Street and 8th Avenue, when Billie and Sadie lived in the block. Claire, Carmen McRae and a girl called Lorraine, who was a baker and a caterer (the pharmacy had a luncheonette), were pals. Aaron recalled:

> The block was the most densely populated in Harlem. That's why they knocked it down, and they built a project there now, that's how I got out, in '59 . . . When I came there there were some Jewish people still living there and had businesses there like laundry, candy stores, a dentist lived on 141st. Very few black doctors there in those days. Many refugees had come to Harlem and practised, but it was a typical ghetto block. I was there for twenty-six years.
>
> I think her address was 232 or 242 West 142nd Street, on the second or third floor.

The people were marvellous to me. Outwardly it wasn't crime-ridden at all. People, some of them turned to crime, a knifing now and then ... You know, black people were being mugged and raped a long time before the white people were. It makes the papers when white people get it; never made news then because it was black people. Cops would ride around and stop off at the candy store to get paid off by the numbers runners. But hundreds of people from that block went to work every day, because we opened at 7 o'clock. In menial jobs, but they worked, not hustling. People played numbers, but everybody in Harlem plays numbers.

But Billie hustled. Willie worked in a grocery store right next to my store, and he delivered groceries to Billie one time, and she propositioned him when he was delivering groceries, and he had an affair with her, in her mother's house. I know for a fact that there was a bandleader who was Blue Barron who was up there, and Lorraine knows it. And there were others I don't know by name. There was goings on all the time, but I never heard neighbours talk about it. She didn't stand out, though. You had to be rough to get along. Everybody was.

Claire talked about the Monroe brothers; she said she didn't think they were very much alike.

Jimmy was a suave kind of cat and [Clark] Monroe was kind of soft and quiet . He [Jimmy] was very nice and we used to go down the beach all the time and then he got on the stuff too. And that's when he started going with Billie. The beach was Rockaway. Everybody used to go to Rockaway at that time. We'd meet at a certain spot. Take the train or go in a car sometimes. A bunch of us. John Levy. She went with him, too. He used to smoke hop, so did Monroe, so did Dickie. Billie always used to go up to Dickie's place to see Dickie .. Nina was very knowing, very beautiful, very sharp.

Aaron said, 'She only became popular because she made that picture, *Hallelujah!* That was all she ever really did.' Claire added:

Nina was so ignorant, just common, but beautiful brown. Just hit her on the head and her legs would fly open. Jimmy was out and out a hustler. But Dickie was top drawer, he could have anybody he wanted.

Blue Barron was a white bandleader named Harry Friedland, originally from Cleveland, who had a Mickey Mouse sweet band and a few hits from 1938; George T. Simon wrote that Barron had a sense of humour about the schlock music. Pops Foster talked about his time in Europe, when Monroe had left Nina Mae McKinney there: she was a 'dope fiend', had turned lesbian and took Foster's girlfriend away; but the more scurrilous his stories were, the better Foster liked them.

Claire also talked about Tondaleyo, a show girl turned nightclub hostess, who was a dear friend of hers. Her real name was Wilhelmina Gray; for a while there was a club called Tondaleyo's.

Dickie was a good-looking man, and John was fair and nice looking, but Dickie was a sexy cat and looked as if he might give you a very good time. John was very independent and would beat his women – he beat Tonda, all of them. Tonda had more class to her than Billie, fair vocabulary.

Aaron and Claire loved Billie. They talked about her kindness and her generosity, and the closeness of the friendships among the girls: 'She gave me a ring I admired. It was in her dressing room on 52nd Street. Carmen was mad because she didn't get one.' Carmen McRae's birthday was the day after Billie's, and they used to celebrate together; Carmen said years later, 'I'd start out with her on hers and never could make mine because I got so loaded I had to go home. I spent most of mine in bed.' But having found each other and made a lasting marriage, the Liebensons were frank about the bad habits of some of their old friends.

Billie tried, and mostly failed, to find love through sex. She had no conventional hangups, but she also had had no childhood to speak of, either; she gave love freely, but could not accept it. Her vulnerability was there, everyone knew, but so deep that no one could reach it, for she was afraid to reveal it. As the years went by, she began to make terrible, destructive relationships, each man apparently worse than the last: Jimmy Monroe, Joe Guy, John Levy and Louis McKay, in that order, and the evidence is that she had known all of them a long time. Having made a circle of friends in Harlem, she could not trust anybody outside that circle or look outside it for what she had not found inside it.

Neither her romantic problems nor her drug problems started just yet. 'She enjoyed singing so much,' Wilson said. 'She was bubbling at those recording dates. Very nice and cheerful person. In those days there was none of the blues and despairing, none of the stuff that came out in that book.' Billie's first engagement at Monroe's Uptown House lasted three months and could have lasted longer, but other events intervened.

Her first three recording sessions of 1937 all had Wilson at the piano. The first, on 12 January, had Cole, Kirby, Ben Webster, Jonah Jones, Goodman sideman Allan Reuss on guitar, and Edgar Sampson on clarinet and alto sax. Sampson was the author of 'Stompin' at the Savoy', 'Blue Lou', 'Don't Be That Way' and several other enduring classics of the Swing Era, including 'If Dreams Come True', which Billie would later record; but on this session he was almost wasted. 'One Never Knows, Does One', 'If My Heart Could Only Talk' and 'Please Keep Me in Your Dreams' were new so-so pop songs. There's nice trumpet, both open and muted, from Jones. But 'I've Got My Love to Keep Me Warm' was a brand new standard from Irving Berlin, and easily the best of the date: the tempo is just right, there's a nice solo from Webster, and Berlin should always have been so lucky with his singers: Billie's phrasing is exactly right for staying indoors on a cold winter night, and her dying pitch on the ends of phrases, on the words 'storm' and 'form', is even more apposite than usual.

The next session, a Wilson date on 25 January, is an epochal event and a new high in the Holiday canon. Goodman returns, and whatever else may be said about him, his greatness is proved by the fact that he holds his own in this company, for the rest are all from the Basie band, which had reached New York at the end of 1936. The world's greatest rhythm section, Walter Page on bass, Freddie Green on guitar and Jo Jones on drums, brings a new finesse to Billie's discography; Page's accents in particular are wonderful. Buck Clayton on trumpet and Lester Young on tenor sax complete a list of some of the best friends and best accompanists she ever had; she even sounds younger than she did two weeks earlier.

The first side is a cute novelty by Berlin: 'He Ain't Got Rhythm' ('so no one's with 'im, the loneliest man in town'). But then the beauty begins. 'This Year's Kisses' is a wistful ballad, also by Berlin, and it is no wonder that other songwriters said, 'Irving

Berlin *is* American music.' How an immigrant singing waiter, who started out writing songs about Yiddle and his fiddle and Marie from sunny Italy, could have gone on to write words as simply memorable and apposite as these (to say nothing of his tunes) is an American miracle. It begins here with a solo from Lester, which only Billie could follow: he seems to sum up all the best in twentieth-century art, so spare, so evocative, so beautiful is he.

'Why Was I Born?' is by Kern and Hammerstein, from 1929; it begins with Buck's muted horn. It is a ballad of unhappy romantic love. Or is it? Listen to the words: it could be any kind of love. The song in her hands transcends category; its passion is understated, and lies in her art, not in her obvious expressions of emotion. The matching of song and singer is as good here as it ever gets.

'I Must Have That Man!' is by Fields and McHugh, from 1928, and another of Billie's classics: we do not need to hear anyone else sing 'I need that person/Much worse'n just bad/I'm half alive and it's drivin' me mad . . .' And there is another solo from Lester, and Goodman at his best. The music in Heaven is like this.

The next session, on 18 February, could not have measured up, but in fact it's pretty good. Four good contemporary ballads were played by Cecil Scott and Prince Robinson on reeds and Henry 'Red' Allen on trumpet; there are those who say that Allen did not fit on a Holiday date, but his strength of character does not seem so very intrusive (though Billie may have felt differently). The rhythm section has Jimmy McLin on guitar, with Kirby and Cole. The tunes were 'The Mood That I'm In', by Abner Silver and Al Sherman; 'Sentimental and Melancholy', by Johnny Mercer and Richard Whiting; 'You Showed Me the Way', credited to Bud Green, Teddy McRae, Chick Webb and Ella Fitzgerald (Fats Waller had a hit on it); and 'My Last Affair', by Haven Johnson, introduced by Billie's old pal, Billie Haywood, in *New Faces of 1936*.

Billie had a steady gig at the Uptown and was making great records. The year was off to a good start. Then on 1 March she received a telephone call at the Uptown. It was long distance, from Dallas, Texas; the caller asked if he was speaking to Eleanora Billie Holiday, daughter of Clarence Holiday; and then she was told that her father was dead. Clarence had died on 23 February; they learned the details from drummer Sid Catlett. Touring with Don Redman, Clarence had caught a cold which turned into what the death certificate described as influenzal pneumonia.

Billie said in her autobiography that Clarence's lungs had been damaged by a gas attack during the First World War, causing him to give up the trumpet. In fact we know that he was already playing the banjo when he was a teenager. He was, however, in the US Army; his service number was indeed 4105715, as printed in John Chilton's book, *Billie's Blues*; he served from 22 August 1918 to 7 July 1919. There are no more details of his military service because of a fire in a government office in 1973, but the Armistice came on 11 November 1918, and it is unlikely that Clarence was trained, shipped to Europe and injured in a gas attack in less than three months.

Clarence was a heavy drinker and not a man to look after his health: his friends fondly remembered crazy pranks like wading into the surf to dig up a bottle of gin that somebody had buried in the sand while the tide was coming in, emerging with his clothes soaking wet. And as his illness worsened in Texas, he had to find a veterans' ward that would take him in; by the time he got to Dallas it was too late: pneumonia can still be a killer today, and it was far more dangerous in 1937. Billie said bitterly in her book, 'It wasn't the pneumonia that killed him, it was Dallas, Texas.'

Now she would never get to know him any better; the father whom fate had cheated her of from the beginning was gone for ever. Clark Monroe took care of the funeral arrangements, with some help from Jimmy, and the funeral itself turned almost to farce: Fanny was joined by Atlanta, the unofficial wife, who now had two of Clarence's children, a boy and a girl. Sadie managed to play the fool, according to Billie; refusing to ride in a car with Fanny, she rented her own car and got lost, so that she didn't arrive until it was all over. For the rest of her life Sadie tearfully told friends that she had never loved any other man: her martyrdom was now complete.

Billie said in her book that Atlanta's children were so light they were passing for white, but we do not know the truth of this. She also described Atlanta as wealthy, but she had worked in a dance hall. Billie cannot be denied, however, when she reflects on the racism practised in public places like the Roseland Ballroom; if the management saw a black musician looking at a white woman, he'd have been out of a job so fast his feet wouldn't touch the floor, while here was proof that they couldn't really do anything about it at all if two people wanted to get together.

Not long after the funeral Billie left town. She was on the road with the Basie band.

8

On the Road with the Big Bands

John Hammond was a music fan with money in his pocket; he could afford the biggest and best of car radios. On a January night in 1936 in a parking lot in Chicago, he was listening to a Motorola with nine tubes and an extra-large speaker, no doubt a custom installation, when he heard a nine-piece Count Basie band broadcast from the Club Reno in Kansas City. Nowadays most of us can afford a good car radio, but Hammond had a privilege that is gone for ever: in 1936 there was live music broadcast every night.

Hammond being Hammond, he had already heard both Basie and his tenor saxophonist, Lester Young. Basie, born in Red Bank, New Jersey, had taken organ lessons from Fats Waller in a cinema when they were both still in short pants; he played with Elmer Snowden at Ed Smalls' first club, somewhere on Fifth Avenue in New York. He worked his way to Kansas City in vaudeville, played in Walter Page's Blue Devils and in the prolifically recorded Benny Moten band; Moten had appeared at the Lafayette Theater in New York, and Hammond met Basie there in 1932, and at Covan's, which was behind the theatre. Moten died in 1935, and Basie ended up at the Reno as a leader.

Kansas City was a wide-open town, where twenty or thirty clubs operated right through Prohibition and the Depression; the musicians played all night, swinging the blues and forging their chops, while Tom Pendergast, the corrupt political boss in charge of it all, went to bed every night at nine. Having heard the band on the radio, Hammond convinced Basie to enlarge it and head East; big bands were already the flavour of the era, and Hammond gave credit in his book to Willard Alexander of the MCA booking agency for being willing to take on an unknown bunch of Midwesterners.

Lester Young was from Mississippi; the family moved to New Orleans, then to Minneapolis in 1920. The father was a music teacher, and Lester began on drums in a family band; he played tenor sax in the late twenties, doubling on alto and baritone. Hammond had heard him once, briefly, with King Oliver; then Lester came to New York in 1934 to work for Fletcher Henderson, lasting less than four months. It was then that he met Billie. Coleman Hawkins had finally given up on Henderson's lackadaisical ways and gone to Europe; Lester must have been miserable in New York, for Henderson's men (and Henderson's bossy wife, Leona) wanted somebody with a big fat tone like Hawk's. Hammond wrote that he had given the money to Henderson to bring Lester to New York, but Henderson and Hammond were the only ones that liked him. Like Billie, Lester had his own way of doing things, and there was more that was different about his music than just his light, airy tone, which he once described as 'alto/tenor'.

He gratefully moved in with Billie and Sadie, who lived in what Billie described as a railroad flat, with rooms off a hallway: one room she called her playroom, where she kept her records and an old piano, and Lester had a room of his own. Having a man around who had a great musician's sensibility, a unique sense of humour and genuine affection for other people, and who was in no way a threat, must have been delightful beyond words; it no doubt mellowed Sadie and brought out the sweetness in Billie.

She had occasionally been called Lady since the early days in Harlem clubs, when she was reluctant to take the tips off the tables: not that the other girls necessarily resented it; that's just the way she was. Lester had nicknames for everybody: he called Basie 'Holy'; he called his younger brother, drummer Lee Young, 'Little Pea'. It was Lester who called trumpeter Harry Edison 'Sweets'. Will Friedwald says that he dubbed Ella Fitzgerald 'Lady Time'. Jazz already had an Earl, a Duke and a so-called 'King of Swing'; a Kansas City radio announcer was said to have ennobled Bill Basie to a Count (but there is evidence that Basie had called himself that much earlier). Anyway, this was America, and as Franklin D. Roosevelt was the biggest man around, and as Lester was the president of the saxophone, Billie called him Prez for short. He thought that she must be the First Lady, named her Lady Day, and reasoned that Sadie, a Lady's mother, must be called Duchess. All the names stuck for the rest of their lives.

From then on her oldest friends continued to call her Billie, but increasingly she liked to be called Lady, the title Lester had given her; strangers in clubs who addressed her as Billie would be scolded for assuming familiarity. She was indeed a Lady, and henceforth that is what she will be called in this book.

Everyone is unanimous that Lady and Lester were not lovers; they were instant soul-mates, and he must have been like the brother she never had. Perhaps they had the kind of love that a man and a woman should be able to offer each other, but which neither could offer; they understood each other's fears so well that they may have thought that romance would get in the way. In any case, Lady had learned to go for tough guys, or guys who thought they were tough, and Lester was anything but tough. He affected 'nancy' ways, and some thought he was gay; but his mincing walk may have been caused by syphilis. Researcher Frank Büchman-Møller says that in 1937 Lester and three other members of the Basie band were diagnosed with it, and that in 1944 a US Army medical examination confirmed it, adding that he occasionally had epileptic fits, a side-effect of the disease. In any case, unlike many men, Lester was not afraid of the feminine side of himself: he could play anything he wanted on his horn, and didn't have to compete in any other way.

If Lester had a demon, it was racism. He'd once quit the family band rather than tour the South. He was a gentle man, and no doubt racism, being beyond understanding, simply represented to him the forces of darkness. His musical intelligence, like Lady's, was related to his sensitivity, which began very early; as with Lady, music set him free.

Lester's brother Lee said that he was an introvert.

It really stems from his childhood. My mother was a teacher; my father had been a school principal. He knew one way: 'Do it because I say do it.' It was perfect for me; if he'd been any other way I'd have been the world's worst cat. But Lester was such a lovable person, he couldn't stand it. You don't deal with kids in the same manner, because of their individual personalities. Lester used to run away from home every time he'd raise his hand to strike him; he ran away six or seven times. He felt that to be struck was to be unloved. It never occurred to my dad that that was the wrong method.

Lee mostly worked on the West Coast and didn't meet Lady until 1939, at the Uptown House. He had taken his drums from Los Angeles to New York on a Trailways bus, and went to a lot of jam sessions.

It seemed that every place I'd go to where they'd have a session, Lady would be there . . She was like a musician. I think if you listen to the things that she and Prez did together, you'll realize that she was like a musician; she thought like a horn. She and Prez complemented each other   They were like brother and sister. They inspired one another. On most of the record sessions, he would play the bridge; that's because of the thing they had between them. If you'll listen closely, he played the way she sang, and she sang the way he played.

It is often said that Lady sang 'like a horn', but Lee is more precise: she *thought* like a horn. Her recomposition of a song was never just for the sake of it; as with Louis and Lester, as Martin Williams wrote, '   for her, dramatic effect and musical effect are one and the same thing.' Her phrasing and her time were those of a jazz musician; her instrument was her voice.

Claire Liebenson talked about Lady and Lester, remembering how she met Lady at the Hot-Cha.

Carmen used to go around with all the musicians. And Prez and Art Tatum. We'd find out from Les where she'd be. Even if she was married, he could always put his hands on her. They were that tight. Carmen would be singing where he'd be and so and so; 'Lady's around here,' she'd say   .

But regardless of what man she would be with, if Prez called her or needed anything, they'd see each other. They would talk about it; she would talk about Prez: 'Greatest motherfucker I ever met.' That's the way she used to talk about him, loved him. And I don't think it was any more than friendship. They adored each other. And they wouldn't always kiss like people do today – hug and kiss. But when they'd see each other, I guess they knew they were happy to see each other. Their faces would light up or something, and they didn't even always shake hands. They'd look at each other and say 'Goddam son-of-a-bitch,' it was one of those things [in a low husky tone]: 'How you doin', Daddy.' 'Baby ' She called him 'Prez' or 'Daddy' She didn't call most men Daddy, not that I remember. But him, yes. The way she said it. Quite a rapport between those two. He had a wife and everything too, you know . . .

I saw Prez and Billie jam at Kelly's, oh yes. Play behind her, and other clubs late at night until 7 o'clock in the morning

Jimmy Rowles, bright, funny, opinionated and one of the best accompanists who ever lived, is fascinating on Lady and Lester. separately and together:

I was at the Trouville [in Hollywood] about a week. and I had just met her, we had just come from rehearsal, and I didn't know what to make of her, whether she came out here to fuck Lester Young, or what she did. One night I was sitting at the end of the bar and called her – 'Lady, can I buy you a taste?' So she sits down beside me, I bought her a gin and Coke. Can you imagine drinking that shit? I didn't know what to talk to her about. So I think back to when I was listening to Andy Kirk's band . So I remembered a tenor player with Kirk, and for some funny reason I ask her about Dick Wilson. She put her drink down. 'Did I ever know Dick Wilson?' Now this is the first time I talked to her alone. 'I'm gonna tell you something. I was going with Freddie Green, and I was faithful to that motherfucker, but every time I saw Dick Wilson I just had to take him out and fuck him.' The first time I'd heard anything come out from a chick like that. Crazy chick. She had me then. What can you do after that? You have to love her. Too much chick.

The way Lester played behind her, these fill-ins, she would feel like she was just in her mother's arms. If he had not showed up for work that night, she would have been strayed. She would have sung, but she wouldn't have been Lady Day 'Cause she was always happy when she knew Prez was standin' right there, playing for her. Because what he did was for her.

Perfectly matched. Regardless of how great any tenor player is – and how I love Ben Webster, beautiful – now I'm thinking like Lady Day, because I'm just thinking of her mind, how she thought – her boy was Lester Young, Uncle Bubba. That's what we all called him in those days, because all his nieces and nephews called him Uncle Bubba. He was married to a girl named Teddy, but I haven't seen her since '42. Small, dark girl, very very pretty, called his Teddy Bear.

But the way he and Lady got along was really strange. If there ever was a unique individual, this man was it. And his language. You couldn't understand him unless you worked with him for three months. He invented all the gimmick talk, like 'I have eyes for that.' When he didn't like something he'd go like this [Jimmy does a puffed-up-cheeks-and-sullen look] 'No eyes, no eyes.' His name for the fuzz was Bob Crosby If the fuzz came in, Lester would come by and touch you on the shoulder and say, 'Bob Crosby's in the house.' People would be looking around for Bob Crosby

At other times the police were 'Alice Blue Gown' White people were 'greys' in the black argot; Lester decided that black people were 'Oxford greys' Racism or any discomfort was 'I feel a draught'. Another expression of dislike, Lee Young said, was 'No momma, no poppa.' Meeting another man's new chick, he might say, 'Does madam burn?' (Can she cook?) A difficult situation would bring out 'Give me a taste. This is making me lose my groove.' Sylvia Syms said, 'He was the first person I ever heard say to his piano player, "Just play vanilla, man. Just play vanilla," which meant cut out the embroidery and play the proper chords behind solos.'

'He wasn't really vulgar, considering all the m.f.s and s.o.b.s musicians use,' said Lee. 'He had an expression for a fine chick. "What a fine hat," or "How'd you like to wear that hat?"' Rowles remembered that too.

You could be on the stand, and he'd turn around and look at me and say, 'Startled doe at three o'clock.' And I'd look around at three o'clock and there'd be a chick with big eyes. I had to decode it as I went along, like learning Japanese. And chicks were hats.

Like a cat comes in one night with a new chick, and Prez

looked at him. 'Bubba, I'll buy you a taste.' He was drinking at that time Old Schenley Bond, straight, a water-glass full, 100 proof. And a water chaser. So Prez sits down. The waitress has to go to the office for this drink, comes out with a water glass. Prez would start, take that much of a first swallow. 'I see you're wearing a new hat.' And the cat who knew – he wouldn't do this unless the cat knew – he would say 'Yeaaah.' And Prez would say, 'Skull cap?' 'Well, uh . . .' 'Homburg?' 'Uh . .' 'Mexican hat dance?' And the chick in the meantime is sitting there smiling, wondering what they were talking about. They were discussing her pussy, you see.

And Lady Day had her little shit she'd throw in. They'd go together almost like that praying mantis, that devours the old man when they're through making it. That's my own image for them. Lady Day was happy, she was on her own. She was there because Prez was there, but she was never all over him, like where are we going to go now, or always sitting together. She went her way, and he went his. 'Well, Prez, I can smell him. I know he's here, so it's good.' Out of this dressing room comes this beautiful brown-skin bitch over to the bar. And she's rough. I mean rough. And he'd come around from behind a pillar, and he'd be nancy, you know. They'd meet and stop, and he'd say, 'How are you, Miss Lady Day, Lady Day?' And he'd give her this silly look. She'd be saying, 'Hey, you motherfucker.' And she'd back off, and they'd come together, and she'd be hugging him, and she'd move back, and like they would mate just so much. Like she was going to eat him up. And they mate but just that much. Like goldfish or something. And they went through their little trip. You put the two of them together, it's pretty wild. But they'd just touch, and they'd get their guns off, and it was cool, until the next time they bumped into each other around the club, when they'd come again, and like 'Christ, I'm going to come again.' And they'd grab each other, and they'd split. Like accidental joy And she was happy all the time.

It was like brother and sister, but another thing. He was so strange. He was like a visitor. And she was too.

Lester Young was twenty-seven years old when his first recordings were made, in Chicago in October 1936, while the band was playing at the Grand Terrace on its way East.

In a tiny studio that had only one mike, Hammond recorded a quintet of Basie, Page, Jones, Lester and Carl 'Tatti' Smith on trumpet (the show at the Grand Terrace was so tough that Buck Clayton had split his lip). Smith was a perfectly good trumpeter, who remains obscure because he went to South America and never came back.

When the records were released on Vocalion as 'Jones Smith Inc.' it was clear that this was a new kind of music. 'Economy, "less is more": these are the ideals pursued,' wrote Gunther Schuller many years later. With regard to some of Billie's records with Teddy in 1935, I wrote a few pages ago about the beats in a bar, the transition from 2/4 to 4/4: New York jazz in the 1930s was still deeply influenced indirectly by ragtime, through the New York 'stride' piano style of Willie 'The Lion' Smith, his friend The Brute (James P Johnson) and The Brute's acolyte, Filthy (Fats Waller). It was the Basie rhythm section of Jo Jones on drums and Walter Page on bass (who was already being called 'Big 4') who would smooth it out. Jones was not the only drummer to carry the 4/4 beat on the cymbals in the mid-thirties, but he did it with such insistent finesse that he began to change music; these men would have an influence on jazz similar to that which Billie had on vocalists. It is no wonder that Billie's sessions with Basie sidemen were among her best.

The Smith–Jones ensemble recorded two vocals by Jimmy Rushing, and two instrumentals featuring Lester; of 'Lady Be Good' Jo Jones stated flatly, 'This was the best solo Lester ever recorded.'

Schuller transcribed the solo for his masterful book *The Swing Era* (1989), and wrote about it at length, describing 'the lineariza-tion of melodic content' It was as though all the thrilling vertical arpeggios that a Hawkins might play had been laid on their side, and the melodic intervals compressed into a narrow range: just as jazz musicians were improvising endlessly and brilliantly on chord structures, and would continue to do so for many years, Lester was already pointing the way forward, free from the harmonies, and with a simplicity and an effortless swing that came from the hothouse of Kansas City and the wide-open spaces of the Southwest. Lester's music, like Lady's, celebrated a love of beauty and a freedom of the spirit that was beyond racism, politics or even bravery· they performed where nothing could touch them.

In the Basie band, there was rivalry with the excellent Herschel

Evans, who played with a big tone like Hawkins. Evans told Young he should be playing alto: 'You got an alto *tone*.' Lester tapped his head and said, 'There's things going on up there, man. Some of you guys are all belly.'

The band did not take New York by storm at the end of 1936. It was in effect a new band: trumpeter Oran 'Hot Lips' Page (no relation to Walter) had gone off with Joe Glaser, who hoped to make a star out of him, like Louis Armstrong; alto saxophonist Buster Smith had refused to leave Kansas City; Basie had had to add a lot of new men and the band was still shaking down. Hammond stuck his oar in: guitarist Claude Williams was replaced by Freddie Green, because Williams also liked to play violin, and Hammond couldn't stand his violin: we got the incomparable Green, but it seems hard on Williams. Caughey Roberts on alto sax was soon replaced by Earle Warren; Schuller thinks that maybe Roberts's tone was more suitable in the ensemble, but Hammond had his way No wonder the band had to shake down; it was not the band Hammond had heard on the radio earlier in the year. They had been so poor for so long that they were playing beat-up instruments, held together with rubber bands; some of them were not good readers, and they sometimes played out of tune. There was a devastating review in *Metronome*; Clayton blamed it on their 'cheap and overused instruments', and also said that Joe Keyes' trumpet was so bad that nobody could have played it in tune.

Their first few records, as Schuller points out, were also somewhat raggedy; Clayton misremembered that his first recording session had been with Billie in late January 1937, it gave him such pleasure. In fact the full band's first record date had been four days earlier. And soon, on 7 July, the band recorded its first hit, 'One O'Clock Jump', which had begun in Kansas City as a head arrangement called 'Blue Balls'. Like Glenn Miller's 'In the Mood', it was just a riff that had been around for ever, but in Basie's hands it became an anthem; all the bands played riffs, but Basie's showed them how: it was swinging the blues, Southwestern style, and soon there were many recordings of 'One O'Clock Jump', several of them hits.

On 13 March 1937, Lady made her debut with the band, in Scranton, Pennsylvania, making more money than she had made at the Uptown: she was now on $70 a week, out of which all her expenses on the road had to come, and at that, Basie said, she was making more than anyone else in the band.

Hammond had taken Basie to hear her: 'I heard her and that was it.'

Musically, there was a great change, *great* change made in the band. Something added, a wonderful attraction that we had. Everybody loved her, everybody got along with her; she got along with all the guys, and that was something else that was wonderful . . . Playing for her was just too much . . . Billie was a musician. That's the way the guys felt about Billie – the guys really felt they could get in the bus and not say, you know, 'Watch out, fellas.' But anybody else who got in the bus would have to watch it.

A week after Lady joined they played the Apollo, 'and that's really where Billie starred,' said Basie. 'She just couldn't get off the stage.' A newspaper critic writing about the Apollo gig rated her higher than Ella Fitzgerald, whose hit records with Chick Webb were accumulating; at the Apollo, Billy sang 'I Cried for You', 'My Last Affair' and 'One Never Knows, Does One', the song's wistful melody overcoming its silly title lyric. On Sunday 11 April she appeared with Basie at the Savoy Ballroom, and by then the Holiday fans and the Basie fans were making common cause.

Basie must have been interviewed a great many times, but he was always a gentleman; life on the road was never easy, but Basie was laconic about that, too.

There were no outstanding incidents that happened. The average travel. We were just starting out. Really starting. What were the rough spots? Comin' to think of it, there weren't any. We were workin' and that's all we wanted to be doin'. And we had a fairly nice band . . . We were happy together. Then when Lady Day joined us, then we were a really happy crew . . The rough times – now I guess we can say, when you're doin' your one-nighters, possibly, in some parts of the United States where it was sort of rough. Now it seems that it was rough, but then we were younger and we were havin' fun. From year to year you'd be going here to there and you'd be lookin' forward to it. And you were used to the conditions. We were workin' and gettin' *paid* for workin'

.. Played then sometimes on good pianos, sometimes bad ones, sometimes very bad ones. Like now.

Basie, Benny Carter and many others have had to point out over the years that, as far as the saxophones being held together by rubber bands is concerned, 'They still use rubber bands now, when a spring breaks, till they can replace it.'

Lady called him Daddy Basie, and he called her William. Linda Kuehl referred to a TV programme made many years later, saying, 'You were tight. I saw it in *The Sound of Jazz*, the way she was talking to you.' And Basie's reply to this was anything but laconic; Linda made a note in her transcription about how deeply felt it was: 'We were tight. Much tighter than that. Much tighter. I loved Billie an awful lot. I loved Billie as far as love could go.'

On the road, the band tried to room together, sometimes renting a whole house to stay in, so they could all be together and cook for themselves. Lady was one of the best cooks. Asked if they all stayed in the same hotels, Basie replied, 'Sometimes. Most of the times. That's why we had so much fun ... we would have a little taste. Maybe like if we got into a town early we'd all go – the guys who were close to Billie – we'd go to Billie's room; she had a nice record player.' When they could not find a place to take them all, especially in the South, the cry of 'every tub' went out, meaning 'every tub on its own bottom', or 'every man for himself' (The band recorded the Basie–Eddie Durham tune 'Every Tub' early in 1937.)

In Detroit she had to 'black up' in a theatre, because she was too 'yellow' 'I have that picture in my scrapbook,' said Jo Jones. 'That's in the *Detroit Free Press*. I have the picture of what they did to us in the Fox Theater.' Harry Edison said that 'When I came out on stage, I laughed. It was funny to me, and then she turned around and called me a motherfucker.'

There is much testimony about Lady shooting craps on the band bus, and general agreement that she won her share of the loot. 'She didn't know how to shoot dice,' said Jo Jones. 'And they told her wrong. And however wrong they told her, she took all their money ' When people were broke they borrowed from each other, but they knew better than to ask Rushing for a loan. He would scold them for not looking after their own money, and he was right; in his memoirs, Basie said that it was Rushing's spirit that helped keep the band going in its earliest years, so in a way they all owed their jobs to Mr Five-by-Five.

Rushing remembered the incident when he'd refused to give Lady any money; he said he kept telling her that he didn't have any, while the truth was that he'd already lost it in the crap game. Harry Edison remembered it differently:

I think everybody put Rushing down one time or another, 'cause he wouldn't give anybody no money, no. He believed to each his own. But he was the type of guy who didn't drink, didn't smoke, so he always had money, you dig? 'Cheap fat motherfucker' she called him. That was funny. He was just as down as they were and didn't care what they said; she got really salty, but she didn't get no dough. He sat tight on that money. That ain't nothin'; Basie had the band, and he wouldn't lend Basie no money.

He never shot craps with us on the bus, maybe play some cards, but if he lost a few dollars, he quit, while we'd sit there till it was all gone. He had plenty of women, but he didn't splurge on them, while I'd blow my dough like that

Sweets remembered the places the band played:

They were the lowest. I can remember places in the Carolinas, in the tobacco regions Winston, Salem. And we'd play the tobacco warehouses. And that's all you could smell would be tobacco, because it would be hanging in the top of those huge barns, and they would rope off areas for dancing, and just the smell of tobacco would be in your clothes, and when they started dancing, the dust from the floor and the tobacco smell, well – I don't know how she made it, as a woman. She never got tired.

Knowing Billie was like having a friend for ever. 'Cause if she liked you, there was nothing in the world she wouldn't give you, and nothing anybody could say against you. She was like a man, only feminine, because she came out knowing how to protect herself.

There was fun on the road, but as trombonist Benny Morton put it, 'These people made their own fun because they needed it, a lot of the time these people were hurting inwardly . . . Billie laughed her life away, but I believe that this girl cried a lot too.'

Lady's free and easy ways were already well known, and there was speculation about her balling everybody in the band. On musical and other grounds, she admired Buck Clayton; he was a very handsome man, and Billie liked good-looking men. Some years later, on 52nd Street, according to Sylvia Syms, who loved to tell stories, Billy Eckstine said to Lady, 'Ain't I pretty?'

'You're pretty, but you ain't the prettiest,' said Lady

'Who's the prettiest?' Eckstine demanded.

'Buck Clayton is the prettiest man who ever lived.'

But Buck was surprised years later to read about that in her autobiography; she'd never come on to him with anything like that, he said. One witness said, 'She was an angel compared to what some girls got up to on the road.' Lady said that she would have been scared to fool around with them too much, because of all *their* promiscuity Her lover in the band was Freddie Green, who was married and had children: they would check into hotels together, but their romance was short-lived.

The biggest problem was that Lady was under contract to Brunswick, and this was important. Basie had a superb male vocalist in Rushing, but the 'girl singer' was an increasing attraction in those days, and although Basie had the best, the record industry of the time would not allow her to make records with the band.

The orthodoxy is that Lady belonged more naturally in a small-group context, or even in the smallest of clubs with just a piano player, and it is true that considering her body of recordings as a whole, the ones with the largest ensembles are the least important. But the Big Band Era rejected Lady, not the other way around; and in any case, the orthodox view ignores the unusual way she belonged in the Basie band. Basie said, 'She fitted in so easily, it was like having another soloist. All she needed was the routine, then she could come in with her eyes closed – no cues or signals.' Asked how it was planned that Sweets or Buck 'came in' to accompany her, Basie said, 'It wasn't in the arrangement. When they felt like it.' Clayton wrote in his autobiography, 'I would watch her mouth, and when I saw that she was going to take a breath or something I knew it was time for me to play between her expressions. It's what we call "filling up the windows" ' These people breathed together.

It is heartbreaking that we have only three airchecks, two from the Savoy Ballroom ('They Can't Take That Away from Me' and 'Swing, Brother, Swing!') and one from the Meadowbrook in New Jersey ('I Can't Get Started'. 'Even Basie had me to tea,' she sang). (There is also said to be a 'Dinah' from Meadowbrook.) But it is evident from these alone that the Basie band of the period was a wonderful setting for her: when she changes the words to 'Come on, swing me, Count!' she knew what she could depend on; during another aircheck from the Savoy, the instrumental 'Shout and Feel It', Lady can be heard in the background during Basie's solo, shouting encouragement. One of the great experiences of the Swing Era is lost to us because the record companies were too foolish to cooperate.

On 16 January 1938, Benny Goodman's Carnegie Hall concert was recorded (released in 1950, the two-LP set was a hit in the *Billboard* album chart) After the concert, Basie's men hurried uptown to the Savoy, where a 'battle of the bands' between Basie and Chick Webb took place.

Basie had had only one hit record at that point – 'One O'Clock Jump' – but Webb's band already had several, including Sampson's anthems 'Stompin' at the Savoy' and 'Don't Be That Way', and two vocals by Ella: 'Sing Me a Swing Song' and '(If You Can't Sing It) You'll Have to Swing It', also anthems in their way. John Hammond was there.

I always thought that Basie won. The newspapers – every Negro newspaperman – was on the payroll of either the Moe Gale agency, which handled black bands, or the Savoy Ballroom itself, which owned Chick's band. Moe Gale handled Chick and Ella, and they owned the Savoy, and every Negro newspaperman was on their payroll, and this is how they got their money, because Negro newspapers didn't have enough money to pay their salary, so they made money off performers. Now Basie was with MCA and was the only black artist that MCA had, so they didn't pay off the Negro newspaper press. Basie may have occasionally slipped somebody $10 or so, but it would be automatic in the *Amsterdam News* and *Pittsburgh Courier* to say that Chick and Ella won.

Basie said in his memoirs that although Webb as the house band used the main bandstand and had better equipment, there was something wrong with their microphone that night, so that Ella was at a disadvantage. But after these 'battles of the bands' the ballroom's patrons voted on their way out, and the press reports said that the vote was a comfortable win for Chick Webb, the local hero who had more hits.

Then Lady was fired – 'asked to leave' – in early 1938. Her last gig with Basie was ironically at the Apollo, already the scene of some of her greatest triumphs. The jazz press blamed Hammond, and there was immediately a press release from MCA in which Willard Alexander claimed responsibility for firing her, and was quoted in *down beat* saying that it was Hammond who'd got her the job, and if it hadn't been for Hammond she'd have left six months earlier: 'The reason for her dismissal was strictly one of deportment, which was unsatisfactory, and a distinctly wrong attitude towards her work. Billie sang fine when she felt like it. We just couldn't count on her for consistent performance.'

But the mystery deepens. Alexander was less forthcoming many years later: 'You better ask John about this . . I'm not aware of any problems   John may have been on the outs with Billie at some point but I'm not aware of it . . . frankly I didn't have that much direct experience . . your best source would be John.'

Hammond emphasized the terrible working conditions and the racism on the road, but Lady had put up with the racism, the hotel rooms and the long hot bus rides for nearly a year. She held her tongue at the time, quoted by *down beat* as saying only that 'Basie had too many managers – too many guys behind the scenes who told everybody what to do. The Count and I got on fine. And the boys in the band were wonderful. But it was this and that all the time, and I got fed up with it.' But she regretted leaving Basie and blamed Hammond, and she wasn't the only one. Jo Jones was in no doubt:

She was fired. John Hammond. But nobody's got guts enough to tell the people that because he's the great white father. Bullshit. I tell it to him every time I see him. No, he says, he didn't fire her. You're a garbage-mouth liar, I tell him. Put it in print and quote me . . He fired her because he wanted her to sing the blues. He wanted her to be a coloured mammy. ,

'Cause I'm pained about this shit . Bessie Smith coulda been the greatest opera singer – singin' the blues. Miss Mahalia Jackson, who has replaced her – Will you sing in a

nightclub? – No. We'll give you $100,000 – No. They love to
do that. All they think is, that as a black person you're
supposed to sing the blues. Stay in your place, little boy.
Northerners do it, not Southerners. The liberal ones. I go
through this. I sleep with it every night.

Jones was an angry man, but his thesis is also developed by others.
That black artists were bossed around by the industry even more
than white ones is beyond dispute. Billy Eckstine said that he
wanted to see a book bringing out the theme that they were black
singers:

> Oh, Eckstine, he's a black singer Not Peggy Lee, she's a Slav
> singer, or Barbra Streisand, she's a Jewish singer. You don't
> get that. When we first started on records, you didn't even get
> a ballad, you sang blues   The white critics are blues freaks,
> they'll go into days of research on Huddie Ledbetter, and we
> black people – I don't remember going across the street to
> hear Huddie Ledbetter .. Look at these people. Just this
> week I was listening to the Sonny & Cher show, and here's
> this girl sang something, and why Jesus Christ, baby, there's
> no black person in the world with an accent that broad.
> When she talks she's talking very proper, yet when she sings
> she's straight out of McComb, Mississippi .   Tom Jones
> openly declared that he got his style from Otis Redding, from
> Jackie Wilson, from Chuck Berry, and that he started in
> learning to sing ballads by listening to my records. Now all
> four of us – where's our compensation? Where are we? Where's
> ours?

Lester Young was a lyrical player who said he liked to have the
words of a song in mind while he was playing; Lee thought that
Lester was badly recorded in the 1950s, because the white record
business wanted blues.

> He wasn't aware of Jimmy B. being such a great bass player.
> When we were working, I would tell him that Jimmy B. is
> 'Prez'. So we had a session and Jimmy picked up the bow and
> played 'Stardust' and 'Body and Soul', and it flipped him out.
> He says, 'Give me another taste; Little Prez has bruised my
> man.'

All Norman Granz could hear was blues. 'D.B. Blues', 'N.Y. Blues', blues blues blues. You're just playing twelve-bar phrases all the time, you're not really playing a love-story theme, and he was great at playing melody.

There is little doubt that John Hammond had a power complex. A lot of people thought that he pulled Basie's strings, but Basie was already thirty-two years old when he reached New York with the band that would make him famous; he knew a lot about being poor and he had already signed a bad contract with Decca because he didn't know any better. He may very well have decided to let Hammond call the shots as far as the business side was concerned. He was not very forthcoming in his memoirs, published not long before he died in 1984. In an interview he said that Billie 'was always doing her job, always singing, never juiced or out of her mind', which would seem to contradict Alexander's 1938 comments on her deportment. But then Basie was nice about everybody: 'less is more' in Basie's music may very well correspond to that old African-American tradition of not telling everything you know.

Hammond's work on behalf of racial and left-wing causes in those years was fearless and his triumphs in the music business undoubted, but like many liberals he could be bossy. Not for nothing did Lester call him 'the Holy Main'. Lee Young said,

> When Lester and I went to New York to play Café Society, Benny Goodman had taken Jimmy Rowles from us, so I got Clyde Hart for piano. John never cared for Clyde. He just didn't like him. He had this man in such a state that he could tell even with his back to us the minute John Hammond came into the house. He'd say, 'He's here.'

Hammond said that Billie left Basie because 'She wasn't making enough money. It's as simple as that.' Linda Kuehl replied, 'Jo Jones said you fired her because she wouldn't sing the blues. He said you fired Billie at Lafayette Hall.' Caught off guard, Hammond blurts out, '133rd Street and 7th Avenue,' as though the address of the hall was important.

> Absolute lie. How could Jo say a thing like that? Did you talk to Jo? Jo's out of his mind . I never could have said

anything about her not singing the blues, because they had a blues singer, so called, Jimmy Rushing. And you could sing only so many blues, and there was a real problem between Billie and Basie, and this is the principal reason she left the band.

I love that 'so called'. Jimmy Rushing was a superb blues singer, he was almost as much the backbone of the classic Basie band as the rhythm section, but he was a Kansas City blues singer, a swinging shouter (though in Rushing's case the shouting was a powerful yet intimate, friendly gravel). What Lady said was that if they had Jimmy Rushing to sing the blues, they didn't need her to sing them. And although Jimmy Rushing was also a superb pop singer, of course he was black. In 1991 PolyGram issued a two-CD compilation called in France 'Le Blues de Billie Holiday'; of thirty-five tracks, two are blues. There's no escape.

Willard Alexander told Linda Kuehl to talk to Hammond about why Billie was fired, and Hammond told her to talk to Alexander. Rushing referred to Alexander and Hammond as 'the Gestapo' and stayed well away: 'My contract wasn't with them, it was strictly with Basie. I'd go to him with my problems and we'd straighten them out.' Although not a witness, Benny Carter knew Hammond, and indicated that he was willing to believe Jo Jones's story.

Yet the business about Hammond wanting Lady to sing the blues can't be the whole story either; from the first time he heard her, Hammond knew perfectly well that she was a jazz singer rather than a blues singer. A final clue is offered in a compilation of Billie's recordings, *Legacy*, published by Sony Music in 1991 The notes are by Michael Brooks, who says that Jo Jones's version was confirmed by Dickie Wells and Dan Minor. Hammond is referred to as 'a figure with connections to the New York publishing world'; why it is necessary to be so coy about it five years after Hammond's death is a mystery Lady, 'as a sop to commercialism, sang the pop standards of the day.' The mysterious figure 'suggested that she revive numbers from the 1920s which were associated with Ethel Waters, Clara Smith and other female blues singers.' Lady did say something like, 'Ah, hell, I ain't gonna sing that old shit! This is 1938!'

If Brooks got the story from Jo Jones, then he has to be referring to John Hammond; Dicky Wells spelled his name with a 'y' on his own memoirs (*Night People*, 1970, with Stanley Dance), but it was spelled 'Dickie' as often as not; he and Dan Minor both played trombone in the Basie band, though Wells joined only after Billie had left. And some of Brooks's assumptions must be challenged: anyone who thinks that Basie was not the leader of the band (as opposed to the business side) is simply wrong; there was nothing 'sinister' about Hammond, Ethel Waters was not a blues singer, and Lady did not sing contemporary pop songs as a sop to anything. There was no such thing as 'the pop standards of the day', a song did not become a standard until it had been around a while, and in fact in 1938 the concept of the 'standard' as a classic song of that golden era probably did not yet exist. But here perhaps is the nub of it.

Waters had many hit records between 1921 and 1923; they included songs like 'There'll Be Some Changes Made', 'Sweet Georgia Brown', 'I've Found a New Baby', 'Birmingham Bertha', 'Shine On Harvest Moon' and 'River, Stay 'Way from My Door'. Clara Smith, for that matter, although certainly a blues singer, recorded songs like 'Oh! Mr Mitchell', 'When My Sugar Walks Down the Street', and 'Ain't Got Nobody to Grind My Coffee', which were not always blues, technically speaking, and which in any case had a strong flavour of vaudeville about them; and we have Hammond's own word for it that he was a vaudeville freak. These earlier songs were the kind that Hammond grew up with; furthermore, there is not really much evidence that Hammond was a connoisseur of songs, as opposed to how they were delivered: his discovery of Bob Dylan in the early 1960s was probably prompted by Dylan's authenticity as an urban folkie in the Woody Guthrie mould as much as by the songs themselves; still later, one suspects, Hammond's championing of Bruce Springsteen was based on Springsteen's identity as an authentic working-class New Jersey rocker, and on the search for a new Dylan.

As for Hammond's connections with the 'publishing world', for a few months in 1934 Hammond had worked for Irving Mills, a publisher and plugger of his own songs who often subsidized recording sessions, with strings attached of course. And publishers like Mills had large catalogues of songs that Hammond must have liked perfectly well: money from a new performance of an old hit was easier than money from a new song, and any publisher as canny as Mills would have been anxious to keep his back catalogue before the public. Hammond's connection with Mills evidently lasted longer than a few months, for Midge Williams, who sang on two Teddy Wilson sides at the end of 1936, was a Mills protégé, and had recorded for Mills's Variety label.

Hammond no doubt did favours for people in exchange for support for this or that project of his own; it was during this period that Hammond was putting on his famous 'Spirituals to Swing' concerts. Hammond would not have sold his own musical judgement for any number of favours (he didn't share Mills's enthusiasm for Midge Williams, which is no doubt why there were only the two tracks with Wilson), but he may have been trying to pull too many strings at once: no one's judgement can touch all the bases all the time.

Knowing Hammond, we have to admit that he would have been quite capable of leaning on Basie to play certain tunes and complaining to his friend Alexander about this or that. As far as we can ever reach a conclusion, it certainly looks as though Hammond meddled between Basie and Billie and helped to wreck what must have been one of the era's greatest partnerships. He always thought that his artists did their best work as long as they took his advice, but he should have known by then that nobody was going to tell Lady what to sing

And finally, Hammond knew that Basie's lousy deal with Decca would run out, and when that happened he lost no time in getting him under contract to Columbia: Lady had been with Basie nearly a year, and only a year later, in February 1939, Basie made his last recordings with Decca and his first with the Columbia group. For three years after that, Billie Holiday and Count Basie were under contract to the same group and could have recorded together. For much of that time (after Helen Humes left) Basie had no girl singer at all, at the very time when the female vocalists were becoming increasingly important in the business; yet while Basie sidemen played on Lady's records, and Basie himself guested on Benny Goodman small-group sessions, and Basie and Lady sometimes appeared together in public, they still did not make any studio recordings together. American black music had come up with one of the greatest combinations in its long history, but the music business and one of its great white gods screwed up, and the loss is ours.

*

In late March 1938, almost exactly a year after joining Basie, Lady once again went on the road with a big band, joining Artie Shaw. This experience was even worse, and lasted only until December.

Born Arthur Arshawsky in New York, Shaw had suffered from anti-semitic bullying as a child and had very strong anti-racist views. He could be as irascible, self-centred and tight with a buck as Benny Goodman, but he was less bad tempered, so at least you knew where you stood with Shaw A successful freelance musician, he was asked in mid-1935 to assemble an opening act for a concert, and he put together a small group with a string quartet and original music, a mild sensation in musical circles. Encouraged by Tommy Rockwell, he then formed his own conventional swing band and began having hits on Brunswick in 1936, of which 'Goodnight, Angel' (a film song with a vocal by Nita Bradley) was big in early 1938. He had told Lady that he was going to form his own band and that he would ask her to sing for him, and he kept his word. His last recording session for Brunswick was in February and was apparently aborted for some reason; only one track was recorded, which was never issued. But just as Lady joined him, Shaw switched from Brunswick to RCA Victor; he complained later that he thought she was leaving Brunswick too. But why should she leave Brunswick? She was making records under her own name there, and becoming better known all the time. At any rate, they then had the same contractual difficulty that Lady had had with Basie.

She joined the band in Boston; bassist Sid Weiss remembered the time Shaw decided to play the blues for half an hour at the Roseland State Ballroom. 'Billie sang coming in and out of the different parts of the programme. That was one of the high points. I'm sorry no one ever recorded it.' She often rode in the car with Sid and Mae Weiss. In the early days, on the way to Boston, Lady was smoking pot, and Mae said, 'I was so naïve I thought the brakes were burning.' Mae added:

I was just thinking about how far ahead of her time she was. She was living 'black is beautiful' before it was fashionable. Her whole stature and the way she carried herself is what you see today, the pride in being black. She did it before she even knew what it was; that's the way she lived. She was a trail-blazer, without being conscious of what people make a thing out of today

In spite of its Brunswick hits the band was still struggling. At its first Victor recording session, in July 1938, the records included 'Indian Love Call', with a novelty vocal by saxophonist Tony Pastor, which was a hit in August; then disc jockeys turned it over and discovered one of the biggest hits of the whole era: Jerry Gray's arrangement of Cole Porter's 'Begin the Beguine'. In 1956 (in the nick of time) *Billboard* polled the nation's disc jockeys on their favourite records; Shaw's 'Stardust' (1941) was number one, 'Begin the Beguine' was number three, 'Summit Ridge Drive' (1941, with the Gramercy Five quintet) was number eight, and 'Frenesi' (1940) was number fifteen. One of the most successful careers of the era was launched at that first RCA session; and at that same session Lady made her first commercial recording with a big band. 'Any Old Time' is a nice ballad, written by Shaw and arranged by Gray; her vocal is lovely, and the record is still a good example of a swing band and its canary Clearly, far from being somehow unsuited to singing with such a band, she was one of the very best. But it was her only record with Shaw

Lady's stay with Shaw was ultimately more disappointing than her time with Basie. The entire Basie band had to put up with racism on the road, with all its insulting inconvenience with regard to food and lodging, so that at least Lady was not alone; but a black singer with a white band faced special problems.

Shaw's sidemen were all young then, enchanted with their sudden success and thrilled to be working with Lady, but somewhat in awe of her. Drummer Cliff Leeman says that she missed Freddie Green terribly He adds that Shaw was never easy to get along with, made few announcements from the bandstand and in general didn't seem to like people; he had bad breath, perhaps because of a nervous stomach, and Billie used to call him 'Breath' He also told a version of the famous 'Jesus Christ' story. Lady preferred riding with some of the other men, because Shaw talked constantly about how smart he was, the best-selling books he'd read and so forth; 'Artie was a pretty strong personality. He still is today,' said Leeman.

There was a time when he thought he might like to write a

book. He said, 'Geez, I went up to the Catskills, I went up to the mountains for two months, and it snowed. I stayed there and I wrote. I didn't shave, for about two months. Before I came back to New York I looked just like Jesus Christ.' That struck Billie. Whenever she had the chance she used to say, 'Jesus Christ, His Clarinet and His Orchestra.'

There are many road stories. Shaw had a ten-year-old Rolls-Royce; Lady called it the roller coaster: the back seat didn't decline backwards very much and Lady complained, 'Every time you go downhill, Shaw, I'm standing.' She couldn't stand bugs, flies or insects of any kind: she walked off the stage at the Eastwood Gardens in Detroit because the bugs were bothering her, and another time she almost got out of the car at seventy miles an hour because of a fly: they had to stop the car and let the fly out. Sometimes the band rode in a bus, and Lady was always yelling 'Rest stop!', so trumpeter Chuck Peterson got her a big bottle for her birthday.

'She used to play a shaker,' said Leeman. 'Either two shakers or one shaker. Keeping time, no rhumba.'

Count Basie had a thing going at the Reno Club, originally. One of the saxophone players, Buster Smith, when Prez was playing or Herschel Evans or somebody was playing, he used to take some of the beads out of the shaker, used to dampen it by putting some tape on it. Maracas are what I'm talking about. And they used to get a sound that used to blend with Jo Jones and they'd add it to the rhythm. That steady thing. Billie used to do that with us all the time; it was a gasser. Well, she thought that was great. She didn't have to sit on the bandstand, except that she loved music.

According to Avola:

She was not disturbed by the things which disturbed other singers and still do – too much brass or too much background. She cared for a great deal of rhythmic background and a lot of band. So did Shaw; so did all the people involved with jazz. She was not inhibited by this other thing going on, or disturbed by music going on behind her. Most singers don't like to be disturbed by too much background, especially on record dates, when you get some of these incompetents in the control booth. All they know is what the dials tell them. But she wanted a lot of that.

The Shribman brothers, Cy and Joe, booked the band, as they did so many others in the East, and also owned or controlled ballrooms, such as Boston's Roseland State. They took whatever bookings they could get for a new band, including schools; there is a story that Lady was not allowed to sing at a girl's school, but the truth seems to be that the school didn't want any vocalists at all. Leeman thought it was a funny place for a band to play anyway; saxophonist Hank Freeman agreed:

> All the bands started in Boston. That was the centre, not New York. All the bands broke in Boston, because there were so many ballrooms in that area in New England. So the band booker would book the bands indiscriminately. I remember one incident where we had Wingy Manone at a coming-out party in Boston; these old dowagers would come up to Wingy, and they'd ask, 'Mr Manone, would you play a waltz?' And he'd say, 'Shit, lady, we don't play no waltzes! This is a jazz band!' They didn't even know what the word meant.
>
> I recall a girls' school, it was in Newton, Massachusetts, where we played a thing, 'Jungle Drums' or some nonsense like that, and they called it indecent music because the girls screamed. They had orgasms. There were no boys, all girls. They danced with each other. They weren't allowed to have boys at the dance.

Wingy Manone was a white one-armed trumpet player and bandleader of the Chicago school. It was the white bands that broke in the Boston area; black bands like Fletcher Henderson's had played plenty of waltzes in the early years. In 1938, though, at a black ballroom in Chicago, according to Joe Shribman, the billing was 'Billie Holiday with Artie Shaw and his Orchestra', and Shaw hit the roof. 'It was very funny,' said Shribman,

> because they opened up and Artie really laid it on, 'cause he'd found out they didn't really know who he was. The band was tight; it was a great band. The reception was wild. When Billie came out, she tore the joint down. We had great

arrangements for Billie; she was an inspiration for an arranger.

Alto saxist Les Robinson remembered a battle:

> We were always bumping into other bands. Once we had a so-called 'Battle of Singers' with Billie and Mildred Bailey. Mildred was with Red Norvo. The two bands would alternate on the same night. Mildred and Billie were in some respects pretty similar in style . . . I think Billie won that night as far as applause, and she wasn't big. Mildred Bailey had a big name. It was just outside of Boston. We'd go on for thirty minutes, then they'd do the same thing. It was like applause-meter style. Oh, Billie broke it up – not that Mildred didn't get her share. Billie was the underdog, and she loved every minute of it; it gave her a chance to turn it on. She sang her heart out.

Leeman had a revealing attitude towards pop songs:

> All big bands had to do pop songs. I don't think Billie did any because it wasn't in her idiom, you know; they may have thrown a couple at her, and had a couple arranged for her, but that was part of the deal with big bands. The songwriters used to pick up a lot of cash, try to plug their songs, like you plug a record today. Not in the jazz idiom. That's a different idiom. Billie was a jazz singer. At some time in life, 'You Go to My Head' was a pop song, at one time. 'Back in Your Own Back Yard' was a pop song in its own time. 'I Cried for You' was a pop song. But they were so old that finally someone just grabbed onto them and made them jazz songs. They weighed good for musicians. To play jazz to, the chord progressions.

Leeman was a fine musician who eventually played with a lot of good groups, including the great Charlie Barnet band of 1939–41 (my favourite white band of the era by a wide margin), as well as combos on 52nd Street; he knew Charlie Parker well. Yet over thirty years later Leeman still thought that a song could only become a 'jazz' song if it was old and tired enough. In fact, the song-pluggers plugged songs, and some were better than others; it's as simple as that. Some critics seem to be unaware that they are influenced by often second-rate or downright bad performances by run-of-the-mill singers, which is not fair to the songs. Lady knew better than that.

The booking agents and ballroom managers were not slow to inform Shaw that he should hire a white singer, and anyway Shaw wanted a singer he could record with. Nita Bradley briefly came back; then Shaw heard a demo record that he liked and hired nineteen-year-old Helen Forrest, who turned out to be one of the better white girl singers, according to the critics; he also kept Lady on, and the men in the band chipped in from their own paychecks to pay her. Lady's attitude seems to have been characteristically generous, urging Shaw to get some arrangements written for young Forrest. In 1938–9, the band recorded 'Between a Kiss and a Sigh', 'A Room with a View', 'It Took a Million Years', 'I Want My Share of Love', 'You Grow Sweeter As the Years Go By', 'I Can't Afford to Dream', 'I Poured My Heart into a Song' and other now-forgotten ditties, all with vocals by Forrest. This was when Forrest learned her trade well, and if Shaw wanted to make records, he and his record company had to deal with song-pluggers; geniuses like Billie Holiday and Lester Young knocked their heads against racism and the music business, and they were changing the nature of American music, while the mainstream – the business – as usual had no idea what was really going on. So their records were restricted to 'minority' markets.

Meanwhile, there were the racial problems on the road. The band had a black bandboy, and either Shaw or the local ballroom manager would know where he and Lady could stay At one point Shaw had an extra drummer, Zutty Singleton, the black New Orleans veteran; the band pulled into one town and dropped Zutty off at a hotel that would have him, but Lady thought she'd try to stay where the others stayed. It didn't work, and they had to take her back to the first place; meanwhile, Zutty had got the only room with a private bath. Seventeen years older than Lady, he didn't want to be a trail-blazer

Sometimes Lady was allowed to sit on the bandstand, sometimes not. 'Especially in the South,' recalled Robinson,

> they didn't like the idea of a black girl sitting on the bandstand. They didn't care if she sang, as long as after she finished she returned to her place, as they would say.

She just sort of took it in her stride. The South didn't bother

her; it was the North where she flipped, and of course the guys in the band always stood behind her, to make sure of how she was treated. There was another hassle where they called the sheriff and the guys wouldn't go on till she was allowed to sit on the bandstand. It was the same old thing everywhere we went – hotels, restaurants. And the guys stood behind her. Artie did too.

Mae Weiss remembered playing in Canada:

We played the Royal York in Toronto, which would be comparable to the Waldorf in New York or the Plaza in Boston. It was wonderful to walk up to the front door and Billie walked in with us like anyone else, and she got a room. No problem, no question. We all felt marvellous about it . . . She took it as she should have taken it, that it was her right.

On a tour on the way to St Louis, part of the route was through the South, and it was there that the most famous incident occurred. Shaw described it in John Jeremy's television film, *The Long Night of Lady Day*. The band had a routine: if there was any trouble, Lady was supposed to keep her eye on Shaw and take her cue from him; the bus was parked next to the stage door, and they would hustle her out in a hurry. On this occasion, probably in Kentucky, she sang 'Travelin'', and there was enormous applause, and Shaw was relieved. But then as Shaw was giving the downbeat for an instrumental, somebody shouted, 'Let the nigger wench sing again!' And the irony was, as Shaw pointed out, that he was just a typical redneck and he liked her singing. But Lady was outraged. She called him a motherfucker; Shaw read her lips, and most people didn't hear it, but the redneck did and was astonished. The result was pandemonium. This was probably the fracas Robinson also recalled:

It was some town in the South . . . I do remember a cop or something started to bug Artie. Artie was bugged a lot anyway. He didn't like squares. We came there to play. He wasn't exactly a personality kid. I remember there was a helluva fight. I don't remember if Artie hit somebody over the head with his clarinet; he had three or four clarinets. It was over Billie. I think someone was calling her a nigger . . . it was a dumb incident. The majority of people were for the guys in the band. It was a heckler. Even today, you find that stuff.

Forrest joined the band in St Louis; they were playing at the Chase Hotel and stayed round the corner, but Lady had to stay on the other side of town. She told a story in her book that may or may not be apocryphal: the owner of the hotel was a little old racist in a wheelchair who usually was not on the scene, but turned up while the Shaw band was there and couldn't believe that he had a black singer on his hands. So Lady challenged him to let the band see what they could do: he could not refuse the challenge, and of course the band tore up the place, at a time when they were becoming nationally famous because of 'Begin the Beguine'.

With their sudden fame they soon went to the Blue Room of the Lincoln Hotel in New York. They opened there on 26 October 1938, and that was the beginning of the end for Lady. The hotel's manager, Maria Kramer, asked Shaw to ask Lady to use the freight elevator, so that the hotel's patrons would not assume that black people were staying in the hotel: this in the nation's first city, not the deep South, and at a hotel named after the President who'd freed the slaves. Even the reactionary columnist Walter Winchell remarked on that. This is what Robinson meant when he said that it was in the North she flipped.

Not only did she encounter racism on her own turf, but there were radio broadcasts from the hotel two nights a week, sponsored by Old Gold cigarettes, and she was not allowed to sing on the air. The cigarette people presumably allowed blacks to buy their product, but they didn't want a 'coloured' singer, and song-pluggers, anxious to have their songs broadcast, wanted them interpreted absolutely straight, and didn't want Lady Suddenly the band had huge hit records, a top engagement that lasted for months, and was making $25,000 a week; and having stuck with it while it was struggling, Lady was effectively shut out of its success.

There was no way the band could turn down any of these opportunities, but Shaw didn't fire Lady; she was obviously unhappy and finally told him she wanted to go off on her own. She worked out two weeks' notice and left the band in December. A press report quoted her as saying that she would never tour with a dance band again; the Swing Era and the Big Band Era were synonymous as far as the public was concerned, but the big bands had lost their last chance to feature the greatest of the era's vocalists.

Lady was angry with Shaw; she had probably expected him to tell Kramer what she could do with her freight elevator. (In truth, she would have been better off with Charlie Barnet, who would have done exactly that.) They contradicted each other about her exact reasons for leaving the band: she said she was tired of his 'snooty, know-it-all mannerisms', that he wanted her to sign a five-year contract, and that he never paid her for the single record she had made with the band. Shaw denied some of this, and finally they forgave each other She admitted that he was 'a good cat deep down'. As early as 1940, she wrote to a fan in England, 'Artie deserved it because of his treatment of me, still don't say he's not a good musician because he is good, one of the best, and I bet he will come back bigger than ever.' This was after Shaw had walked away from it all: he hated the music business and abandoned the band not long after Lady did, only to come back from Mexico in 1940 with 'Frenesi', one of his biggest hits (arranged for a large orchestra by black composer William Grant Still). Lady knew that it was having to listen to advice from hotel managers, sponsors and song-pluggers that had finally disgusted him beyond endurance. Shaw always spoke highly of her, and was one of the first to volunteer for her 'comeback' TV show in 1953.

Shaw also speculated, in an interview in 1973, that it was when she left his band that she began to realize that she would never reach a mass popular audience and that racism wasn't the only reason. She was an interpretative artist, and most of the public wanted its music cut to a formula (which is why Shaw put down his horn for ever in 1954). On 17 January 1939 she sang with Benny Goodman on his Camel Caravan show and, as John Chilton suggests, may have taken pleasure in being heard on the radio with Shaw's chief rival. But the surviving airchecks reveal that Goodman's arrangement of 'I Cried for You' was too busy and all wrong for her. She sounds bored and as though she's not allowed to phrase the song properly; and a lot of Goodman's music in those years stuck to a successful formula, the constant 'jeek-jeek-a-jeek' of the muted trumpets becoming tiresome. Martha Tilton, Johnny Mercer, Lady and Leo Watson had a little more fun taking turns

Around the table, probably at the Savoy Ballroom in 1940, *left to right:* Lady Day, Bob Bach, Dave Tough, Eddie Stein, Stein's companion, Mrs Tough and Lady's 'sister' Bach's radio show, *Jive at Five*, had a Basie arrangement named after it; Tough was one of the finest drummers of the era; Stein was a wealthy jazz fan (and, said Tondaleyo, 'the first white guy I ever went out with!'). When Dizzy Gillespie saw this picture, he said of the woman on the right, 'That's Billie's sister!' This is probably Ruby Helena, who was living with Lady and Sadie at the time, and who Lady liked to introduce as her sister (*Jean Bach*)

Lady and Sadie in a nightclub on 52nd Street in June 1941. If their relationship was never easy, maybe that's one of the things that made Billie a great interpreter (*Bobby Tucker*)

Lady with Art Tatum (piano), Oscar Pettiford (bass) and Big Sid Catlett (drums) at the first Esquire jazz concert, at the Metropolitan Opera House in 1944 (*Pictorial Press*)

The Apollo marquee in the mid-1940s, when Roy Eldridge was leading a big band. The theatre's spelling leaves something to be desired, but Tondaleyo's name has often been misspelled. Some say that it was a member of the Cats and the Fiddle quartet who, around 1940, first gave Lady heroin (*Delilah Jackson / Black Patti*)

Left: Sometime around the end of World War I, Billie Holiday was still little Elinore Harris of Baltimore (*Avalon Archives*)

Below: Clarence Holiday on the road with the Fletcher Henderson band in the early 1930s (*Avalon Archives*)

Teddy Wilson in 1935, when great records were made almost casually, and America still had a five-cent cigar (*Avalon Archives*)

A publicity shot of Billie Holiday in 1935, at the beginning of her fame and already glamorous (*Max Jones*)

The Danish-born jazz entrepreneur 'Baron' Timme Rosenkrantz took this picture behind the Apollo Theater in August 1935. *Left to right*: Ben Webster, Billie, 'Shoebrush' (with guitar) and Johnny Russell, with Roger 'Ram' Ramirez (kneeling). Willie Bryant's band must have been playing at the Apollo; Webster and Russell (and Stanley Payne) were all in the reed section and Ram was on piano. Bryant's guitarist was Arnold Adams; Shoebrush was probably a stage-hand or a bandboy (*Frank Driggs*)

Above: On stage at the Town Hall in New York in early 1946. Lady was the Queen of 52nd Street, had a major-label recording contract and a national hit with 'Lover Man'; this sold-out concert was the first of several artistic and critical triumphs during the very period when her habits began to catch up with her (*Avalon Archives*)

Below: Lady grabbed young Bobby Tucker off 52nd Street to play for her in late 1946, and inscribed this photo to him (*Bobby Tucker*)

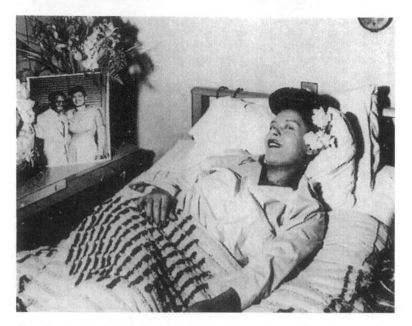

Above: In a high-priced clinic in early 1947, undergoing a worthless drug cure. It was a nice rest and it made Joe Glaser happy. Lady had just finished making a film with Louis Armstrong, hence the photo at her bedside (*Bobby Tucker*)

Below: Teddy Wilson and Lady being presented with their Esquire gold awards in 1947 by broadcaster Arthur Godfrey. That year's *Esquire Jazz Book* played down the black winners at the expense of the editor's white favorites; Esquire's jazz awards soon dried up and blew away (*Bobby Tucker*)

Left to right: Dorothy Donegan, Lady, Irene Kitchings, Kenny Clarke. Donegan, like Kitchings, began her musical career in Chicago; she was a very good pianist who also sang and became a popular lounge entertainer. 'Klook', the pioneering bebop drummer, looks pleased to be surrounded by such talented women (*Avalon Archives*)

Soulmates Lady Day and Lester Young, the president of the saxophone, in the prime of their lives (*Avalon Archives*)

Robin Carson was a highly rated photographer in the 1940s;
Greer Johnson liked to take credit for arranging the famous
series of photos of Lady, including the one on the cover of this
book, but Carson remembered it as just another assignment
(*Nancy Miller Elliott*)

Some of the best friends Lady ever had.
Left to right: Dickie Wells, Buddy Tate,
Count Basie, Buck Clayton, Jo Jones,
Freddie Green and Earle Warren.
They were all in the Basie band togeth-
er from 1939, when Tate joined, until
late 1943, when Clayton and Jones
were drafted; this picture may have
been taken later, at a reunion (*Nancy
Miller Elliott*)

Above: On stage at the Strand Theater in 1948, one of Lady's longest and most successful engagements, with Bobby at the piano (*Magnum Photos*); *Below*: Lady and Louis Armstrong at Decca Records, probably in September 1949, the only time they recorded together. Louis looks as though he's worried she might get a sound out of that horn (*Brown Brothers*)

The Club Ebony in New York City in 1949, when Lady wasn't supposed to be there: she didn't have a cabaret card. It was here she got involved with John Levy (*Avalon Archives*)

Lady and John Levy appearing in court in San Francisco in early 1949, charged with possessing opium. Their lawyer Jake Erlich is on the right (*Temple University Archives*)

Above: Jimmy Ascendio, Bobby and Lady in a US Commissioner's office in May 1947 for a hearing on the narcotics arrest. Bobby looks fed up, but he was not charged (*Temple University Archives*); *Below*: Lady and Bobby arriving at a Gene Norman Presents concert in Long Beach, California (*Bobby Tucker*)

Above: Lady on stage at one of the Carnegie Hall concerts in May 1948, with Bobby on piano. First she broke the hall's box-office record, then three weeks later she broke her own record (*Bobby Tucker*)

Below: In Greenwich village *c.*1948, *left to right*: Jane Tucker, Bobby's sister; Tyrone Power's ex-valet (name unknown); ex-boxer Izzy Grove; Jimmy Monroe; Lady; Freddy Taylor and Preston Ware, pals of Monroe; Bobby Tucker; and Tony Callucci, who operated both the Downbeat Club and the restaurant where this picture was taken (*Bobby Tucker*)

Above: An undated photograph of a pensive moment at the bar (*Brown Brothers*); *Below*: A photo of unknown provenance. Lady's addictive personality is catching up with her (*Donald Clarke*)

Above: One of Lady's last recording sessions, probably early 1958 (*AP/ Wide World Photos*); *Below left*: Lester Young in Paris in early 1959, a few weeks before he died. He had changed music forever, but his gentle spirit could not bear to grow old (*Herman Leonard*); *Below right*: Jimmy Monroe in 1987 He was supposed to be a bad guy, but for years he came running whenever Lady needed a friend, and he survived them all (*Nancy Miller Elliott*)

Left to right: pianist Jimmy Jones, Lady, Sarah Vaughan and dancer Bobby Johnson.
Jones was Sarah's pianist 1947–52 and again later in the 1950s (*Delilah Jackson/
Black Patti*)

On the Jazz Club U.S.A. tour, arriving at Stockholm Station in January 1954 after
an all-night train ride in a blizzard. *Left to right:* Beryl Booker, Inez Cavanaugh,
Lady and Leonard Feather. Inez was married to Timme Rosenkrantz; according to
Carl Drinkard, Lady and Inez did not get along (*Max Jones*)

Above: Arriving at Heathrow in London in February 1954: Carl Drinkard, Billie Holiday and dancer Taps Miller, who happened to be on the same plane and was searched by customs for drugs (*Max Jones*)

Below: A snapshot taken backstage in Nottingham in February 1954 by Louis McKay (*Max Jones*)

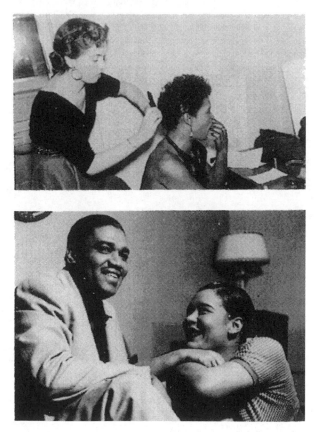

Louis McKay and Lady posing at home (*Bob Willoughby/Redferns*)

singing 'Jeepers Creepers': Lady sings 'Where'd you get that size', and Watson repeats her 'mistake'.

In Jeremy's film Shaw says he offered to help her if she needed money, for arrangements or whatever, but she had continued making her own records all along, and (according to *Pop Memories*) fourteen of them had been hits while she was on the road with Basie and Shaw. She knew she could make a living on 52nd Street. Big-time showbiz had rejected her, but a new phase in her career was about to begin: Café Society was beckoning.

9

1937–9: Strange Fruit

Between joining Basie and leaving Shaw, Lady had not been entirely absent from 52nd Street. While with Basie on one of the dates at the Apollo she participated in a jam session at the Hickory House, where the band was led by reedman Joe Marsala; at the 1955 rehearsal session recording, Art Shapiro reminded her of that occasion. She recalled that she hadn't had any money that night, so Marsala had bought her a steak, and she remembered the kindness.

During this period she also had fifteen recording sessions in New York, about half her own and half Wilson's, recording a total of fifty-six titles. The songs continued to be mainly contemporary tunes, most of them by no means second-rate by the standards of the time, and some of these records were among her finest; but after leaving Shaw there were several more sessions before 'Strange Fruit' marked a change in her career, and the quality of these records marked a temporary falling-off (admittedly from a high plateau), as though her failure to achieve the success of the Big Band Era had discouraged her.

From her first Wilson record date after her father died, on the last day of March 1937, all three vocals were hits: 'Carelessly', a nice ballad by Norman Ellis (music) and Charles and Nick Kenny (lyrics), was one of Wilson's biggest hits. The other side of that record was 'How Could You?', by Al Dubin and Harry Warren, and 'Moanin' Low', by Howard Dietz and Ralph Rainger, also did well. Of the two contemporary tunes, the sweet dance band of Anson Weeks also had a hit with 'How Could You?', but the big hit on 'Carelessly' was the only one on that title. The session benefited from the presence of Ellington sidemen.

'Moanin' Low' is a torch song from a 1929 revue in which it was introduced by Libby Holman, and a comparison with Holman's hit that year is interesting: the torch singers displayed their hearts on their sleeves; Billie could out-torch any of them, but used artistry rather than artifice. Drummer Specs Powell said in 1971:

She was one of the first singers that did not emote, no bouncing around, sang very quietly, snapped right hand, holding it close to her side. Snapped her fingers and tapped her feet very quietly, head tilted slightly to one side. The opposite to most jazz singers, who seemed to be choreographed. Her whole attitude was very cool.

This natural elegance continued to develop – in fact she soon gave up snapping her fingers. As far as men were concerned it was the same thing: 'The same cool attitude prevailed, nothing shocked her ... she could curse a person out and still make it sound like music. She could say the most vulgar thing but never sounded vulgar.' Powell goes on to describe the scene, talking about the early forties:

There was an attitude of jazz musicians then – cool, reserved attitude. Anybody who carried this attitude was very worldly, and to an eighteen-year-old boy this was something – very slow-moving matter-of-fact way of looking at life. We now know it was a lot of bull. What started as a happy business gave way to this cool, droopy I've-been-there-before attitude.
But Billie never affected anything. She was authentic.

Powell goes on to say that the male counterpart of cool was Lester Young, who was cool because he was high. Both Lady and Lester used a lot of liquor and marijuana, but Lester never used hard drugs, and Lady wasn't using them in the thirties. Later, in the forties, the music was changing from swing to bop, and narcotics contributed to the cool scene; some people were so cool they were nodding off. But Lady's and Lester's coolness was not simply an attitude: they were sure of themselves as artists, so that they became innovators in more than the musical sense, two of the handful of artists in twentieth-century popular music who inspired generations of followers.
Lady's next session, under her own name the following day, also had Wilson and Kirby, and was a little disappointing only by

comparison. Lady's vocals and the clarinet obbligatos by Buster Bailey are fine, but the tempos are a bit slowish and the songs either undistinguished or not right for her, and neither the arrangements nor the competent sidemen were at their best. Fats Waller had a hit on 'Where Is the Sun?', but 'Don't Know If I'm Comin' or Goin' ' disappeared without trace. The other two tunes were both Gershwin songs from the Fred Astaire/Ginger Rogers film *Shall We Dance?*: 'Let's Call the Whole Thing Off' had several hit versions, including Astaire's, but was a ludicrous choice for Lady: her audience didn't include a lot of people who said 'tomahto'. Lady's version of 'They Can't Take That Away from Me' is listed as a top-fifteen hit, but the lugubrious arrangement isn't a patch on the wonderful aircheck version with Basie, only reminding us of the tragedy of that partnership, unfulfilled by commercial recordings.

In May and June there were two Wilson sessions, in June a Holiday session with James Sherman on piano, and in September another with Claude Thornhill: all four of these included Buck Clayton and Lester Young, and the Basie rhythm section played on the last three. Songs such as 'I'll Get By', 'Mean to Me', 'Foolin' Myself', 'Easy Living', 'Me, Myself and I', 'A Sailboat in the Moonlight and You' and several others are still among Billie's best-known recordings. 'Sailboat' is one of those regarded as the sort of song which would not be remembered if Lady hadn't done it, but there were four hit recordings of it at the time, including Guy Lombardo's (it was written by Lombardo's brother, Carmen). Its imagery is not untypical of love songs in the days before they became lust songs: in the fourth decade of the century, all our innocence was not yet gone.

A comparison of Lady's version with one of the other hits is instructive. Helen Oakley was producing recordings by Ellington small groups for Irving Mills's Variety label; at a nominal Johnny Hodges date, they struck it lucky with 'Sailboat', sung by Buddy Clark. He became a very good pop singer before he was killed in a plane crash in 1949, but in 1937 he sang 'Sailboat' absolutely straight. After many years of familiarity with Lady's record, the song as written turns out to be a craftsmanlike but uninspired piece of work: one thinks, 'Oh, of *course* that's the way it goes.' But in this instance as in others, Lady's essentially harmonic changes made a different though still recognizable song of it, at the same time endowing it with an unforced yet guarded wistfulness of which the song's composer was incapable. The lyric of 'Me, Myself and I', by some people called Gordon, Roberts and Kaufman, smacks of novelty; but Lady turns it into an incantatory chant, and Lester is playing behind her: they could have recorded the phone book together and made it work. 'Getting Some Fun out of Life' has just the right summertime languor in it. Hodges played on the first of these sessions, the clarinettists included Bailey and Edmund Hall, and all concerned were scaling the peaks of pop.

Richard Whiting's 'He's Funny That Way' was less than ten years old when Lady first recorded it; although it had had two hit recordings in 1929, it was perhaps less familiar in 1937 than it is now. It still sounds remarkably fresh for a song published over sixty years ago; while Lady's version of a song always had its own integrity, it is probably an example of a great song that she could not improve: Frank Sinatra's treatment of the original 'She's Funny That Way' is more faithful to it and, interestingly, so is Lady's later version, made in 1952.

But in the case of 'I'll Never Be the Same', by Gus Kahn, Matty Malneck and Frank Signorelli, she made a classic statement. The singer has been dumped by her lover; the lyric as written says 'life has lost its meaning for me' and so forth, and concludes, 'I'll never be the same again.' In the way the last two syllables fall on different notes, the song really needs two different words, rather than 'a-gain'; Lady not only recomposes the lyric but makes it her own: 'I'll never be the same, all day' is not only a musical improvement, but sarcasm for the faithless lover, and a delicious affirmation: she is susceptible to heartache, but no mere man is going to keep her down for long.

On the first day of November, at a Wilson session, Clayton and bassist Walter Page are the only Basie men present; Reuss and Cole fill out the rhythm, Prince Robinson and Vido Musso are on reeds. Kern and Hammerstein's 'Can't Help Lovin' Dat Man' is memorably introduced by Clayton's muted horn; 'Nice Work if You Can Get It' and Billie's first version of 'My Man' are outstanding. 'Nice Work' is a Gershwin song, as is 'Things Are Looking Up', which (she told Greer Johnson some years later) remained one of her favourites among her own records.

'My Man', by Maurice Yvain, introduced in Paris in 1920 by

Mistinguette, is an unforgettable French tune: the English words by Channing Pollock have been sung by Fanny Brice (another torch singer), Alice Faye and Barbra Streisand, and Lady sang various verses in the years to come. Feminists love Lady, but they have an understandable problem with a song about a man she cannot give up even though he beats her: there was too much violence in Lady's love life, but on her first version of the song the direct reference to physical violence is absent. Either the violence in her life had not yet come to the fore, or perhaps the tougher lyrics would have been less acceptable in 1937.

Two sessions in January 1938, one for Teddy and one for Lady, have identical personnel, entirely Basie men except for Teddy; there are alternate takes of seven of the eight tunes, so there is twice as much of everybody. Songs like 'My First Impression of You' and 'Now They Call It Swing' were contemporary pop stuff; the first masterpiece was 'When You're Smiling': this was a corny hit from the 1920s, but in this mid-tempo version, introduced by Benny Morton's smooth-as-silk trombone stating the melody, Lady banishes Pollyanna from the room, and Lester's solo closes the door. Jimmy McHugh's 'I Can't Believe That You're in Love with Me' is just right. Edgar Sampson's 'If Dreams Come True' has the riff-laden flavour of his more famous instrumentals; if the words don't have a lot going for them, this lineup tosses the tune off with the required lilt. 'On the Sentimental Side', 'Back in Your Own Back Yard' and 'When a Woman Loves a Man' are masterpieces: the first, by Johnny Burke, was from a Crosby film, and in this version has some rare solo strings from guitarist Freddie Green; 'Back Yard' was introduced by Al Jolson in the late 1920s, and from him was no doubt more kitschy, but Lady makes you believe it, as though remembering an idyllic childhood that she should have had, but didn't. 'When a Woman Loves a Man' is a great song from 1934, by Johnny Mercer, Gordon Jenkins and Bernie Hanighen: on a session for Lady, Hanighen was entirely justified in slipping in his own fine tune.

Her next two sessions, in May and June 1938, had Thornhill on piano; Eddie Anderson on trumpet, Buster Bailey on clarinet and Babe Russin on tenor sax play a lot of ensemble, the pastel colours in the writing sounding like Thornhill's work: he had already formed his own first band, and in the next decade his experimental sounds, in the context of what seemed to be an ordinary white dance band, would be profoundly influential, with such people as Gerry Mulligan, Gil Evans and Lee Konitz involved. The sessions resulted in workmanlike versions of eight contemporary pop tunes; perhaps the best was 'You Go to My Head'. During this period she joined Shaw, and the members of that band remembered her doing this tune in particular; Joe Shribman loved it, and years later she would sing 'You Go to My Head' in a club if he was there.

In July she made her single recording with Shaw, and in September there was another date with the Basie alumni, with Margaret 'Queenie' or 'Countess' Johnson on piano: some collectors thought this was Basie moonlighting, but she plays far more notes than Basie would have used. (She played as a teenager with Lester, and died in 1939 of tuberculosis.) Dicky Wells plays trombone on 'I've Got a Date with a Dream', and Lester plays clarinet on two tracks; the best of the four is Ray Noble's 'The Very Thought of You', followed by 'I Can't Get Started', by Ira Gershwin and Vernon Duke.

The stream of pop ballads does seem to become endless at about this point. The last three sessions of 1938, in October and November, are Wilson dates, and feature two brass and no fewer than four reeds: the following year Wilson tried leading a big band for a while, and perhaps this was a rehearsal for it. The Swing Era was ripening: ballrooms did big business and booking agents wanted full-sized bands, so Cootie Williams, Roy Eldridge, Jack Teagarden and many others had a stab at bandleading; but as Lady was to find out a few years later, fronting a big band was a good way to lose a lot of money in a hurry.

The ten vocals recorded by Billie at these sessions were good pop records, but with hindsight are relatively undistinguished in her output. Despite such sidemen as Herschel Evans and Lester Young, Edgar Sampson, Benny Carter, Chu Berry and Bud Freeman (to name the reedmen alone), the rather conventional arrangements did not allow much in the way of jazz; despite such writers and co-writers as Ray Noble ('You're So Desirable'), Mercer and Warren ('Say It with a Kiss') and Hoagy Carmichael ('April in My Heart'), none of the songs turned out to be top-drawer, and even Lady is hard pressed to sound involved. This was a depressing period for her; it was a month later that she left Shaw.

Her spirits at the end of 1938 may have been at an all-time low;

she knew she had lots of fans, and she certainly had many of the best musicians in the country in her corner, but she was denied access to a mass audience. For better or worse, her life and her career took a turn to the left in more ways than one when she opened at Café Society.

Barney Josephson was born in New Jersey, the son of Latvian immigrants. Working for his brother as a shoe buyer in the early 1930s and being a jazz fan, when he was entertained in New York as an out-of-town buyer he asked to be taken to places featuring the music that he liked. Over a period of years he found it frustrating that many of these places were segregated: the artists he liked best were often black, and black people had to sit in the back, or couldn't get in at all. He had also seen political cabaret in Europe and enjoyed satire; he eventually hired iconoclastic entertainers like Zero Mostel, Imogene Coca and Jack Gilford. His brother went broke, and Josephson was working in a shoe store for $40 a week when he threw caution to the winds. Borrowing money from friends, he chose a basement in Sheridan Square that seated 210 people when it was ready, and opened a club where both the entertainment and the audience were integrated, virtually the first of its kind.

The name Café Society was suggested by a gossip column and was intended to be satirical. For a while the club had a doorman who wore a ragged coat and gloves with the fingers cut off; the club's slogan was 'The right place for the wrong people'. Josephson hired artists from the Works Progress Administration, the Roosevelt-era government welfare scheme, to paint surrealistic murals on the walls. He soon ran out of money, but Hammond helped raise some more; after a few months the club was still losing money, so Josephson decided to move to 58th Street between Park and Lexington. He put out a story that the club was doing so well that he was opening another, and the news was so encouraging that business boomed, so that he ended up with two clubs: the first, opened on 18 December 1938, became known as Café Society (Downtown), and Café Society (Uptown) opened on 8 October 1940, seating 350.

These dates are from Whitney Balliett's interviews with Josephson, who died in 1988. The opening was not reported in *down beat* until February 1939; Chilton says, probably quoting *down beat*, that Lady opened there early in January 1939: a few days after New Year's Eve would have been a terrible time to launch a new place. She said in her autobiography that the cabaret licence didn't arrive until the last minute, but she would always mix up the facts for the sake of a good story At any rate, Hammond had helped assemble the band, led by Frankie Newton, and Lady's engagement was a new kind of success for her.

Josephson said in 1971:

> Billie was my first female singer, when I opened Café Society in the winter of '38. She was the star of the show I had, working with Jack Gilford, who was the MC and comic and just starting in show business. I had a band led by Frankie Newton, the trumpet player – died a young man five or six years later. Billy Kyle was his pianist and Billie's accompanist. With Big Joe Turner, and boogie-woogie pianists. John Hammond helped set it up. Billie was not a newcomer, had been around, but nothing had happened for her until she came to Café Society.

Josephson was no doubt relieved by the unexpected success of his operation; he became a legend in his own time and was pleased with himself for the rest of his life. It certainly beat selling shoes. But what can he have meant in saying that nothing had happened to Lady until she worked for him? Nearly two years on the road with Basie and Shaw, to say nothing of dozens of hit records? The quality of the white liberals' mercy is sometimes strained; but his heart was in the right place, and he had good taste. In fact, maybe he had more sense than his friend John Hammond.

> I never suggested a song to Billie, which was quite unusual since I did it with almost everyone who came in, almost constantly. I always felt she was doing the right thing. Her routine with her show, she instinctively knew what was the right thing – how to balance the faster rhythm with the slower . . . I always looked upon Billie as a finished performer, a pro. You don't tell professionals how to work. To me she was established and finished. Mildred too. You'd be out of your mind. But Lena was just starting out.

Josephson said that Hammond thought of her as essentially a blues singer, 'and I do too . . whatever she sang, they were all blues, to me, her singing. To me Billie made a blues out of everything she sang.'

The band would usually come down around three o'clock in the afternoon for rehearsal. The singer would sometimes request a rehearsal; Billie would rehearse every couple of weeks. She was meticulous about her work; she would come down and raise hell with the orchestra. She was tough. The four-letter words you'd hear, well, she'd let out a tirade . . . if Frankie Newton played a note that disturbed her while she was singing, he'd hear about it; if the pianist was one note behind, or too fast, she would pick it up. If she wasn't satisfied she'd let them know, and they'd be scared to death of her. The respect I had for her they had I think even more so, because they were musicians. It was always Lady Day, and when they said Lady, it was like Lady Montgomery of Great Britain . . . they always treated her as a star, as a princess.

Billie drank, but not very much. I was told by the boys that they were all on reefers, and I noticed that most of the boys on the weed didn't drink. But one night I smell the weed and it's coming from a ringside table where a party of six of the highest society people were sitting in the most expensive furs . . and there's Eleanor Walsh McLean smoking one reefer after another. You know, she was the big society party-giver in Washington. The murals were all satires of the social set – the upper 'clahsses' . . . Gilford had material that satirized the upper classes and clubs like the Stork Club, El Morocco – the society clubs – the Lucius Beebes, Brenda Frazier – the deb of that year – and so Brenda Frazier and the Beebes and their sets would come to hear themselves satirized. It was delightful.

Sets were at eight, twelve and two, dancing till four. The show would start with the band coming out, and they would do at least two numbers, then Pete and the other boogie-woogies and Gilford did their thing.

Pete is Pete Johnson; he and Albert Ammons and Meade Lux Lewis and Joe Turner had been among Hammond's stars at his Spirituals to Swing concert in 1938. Newton and Billy Kyle had been among the original personnel of the John Kirby Sextet, first formed in 1937, but Kirby and Newton had fallen out over the singer Maxine Sullivan. Kyle was an underrated stylist who deserves to be better known today, but if he helped open Café

Society he must have been replaced quickly, because the Kirby Sextet, 'the biggest little band in the land', was soon successful on the radio. At another point in his interview, Josephson says Sonny White was the pianist to begin with.

Josephson also met Sadie:

Her mother asked me to ask Billie if she would give her a couple of dollars a week, that she hadn't been getting it for a while, but that I shouldn't tell Billie that she talked to me because Billie would give her hell. But if I ever had an opening where she talked about her mother, you could say, she told me, 'How's your mom?' 'Just say that much and remind her that I'm around and that she should come and see me and that I need help.' Her mother was doing night work as a clean-up woman in office buildings in the city. She was short, chubby, looked a lot like Billie, very poorly dressed, looked like a charwoman. A couple of times after that, when Billie was coming in, I'd say, 'How's your mom, why don't you bring her down some night?' But she'd go right on.

Lady was doing well, evidently living apart from Sadie, and perhaps enjoyed ignoring her mother after years of squabbling. She had a steady job in congenial surroundings, and she was probably as happy as she ever was. Ten years later she said in an interview, 'At Café Society I used to wonder at how quiet – for a nightclub – it was when I sang. I found out later the waiters made a habit of going up to the noisiest characters and saying, "Miss Holiday is afraid you aren't enjoying yourself, pay up and go." Well, that was news to me.' There could be no serious racial problems, because Josephson saw to it that customers were seated and served without discrimination, and the entertainers were treated with equal respect; in fact, between Josephson's two clubs there was eventually a sort of floating pool of acts, and some of these entertainers had more security than they'd ever had before. Kenneth Hollon recalled the job:

We played three sets, seven nights a week. I was making $45 dollars a week, and boy that was a lot of money.
One night Count Basie and Lester Young came in. He came up to the bandstand with his horn and said, 'Man,

move over.' I moved over. Frankie looked at him and said,
'What do you want to play, man?' 'Let's play a little "I Got
Rhythm".' He played the first chorus and then naturally we
just let him blow, and Lester must have taken about ten
choruses, and then Frankie looked at me, and I said, Oh, no
man, not me. But I blew at him and I must have taken about
seven or eight choruses and Lester's eyes got big as half-
dollars, like, Who is this guy blowin' at me? And he yells at
Sonny to go to B natural and it took me three or four
choruses to realize that he was changin' keys – well, to make a
long story short, we played [quite a while], just the two of us,
and you coulda wringed the sweat outta my coat. And when
we finished, he went over to the Count, and they left some
money on the table and went out without even saying
goodbye. And that was the last time I seen Lester. Billie was
there. I surprised myself.

We played her arrangements behind her. We played for
dancing; then at 10.30 the announcer would make a few
cracks and announce Billie, she'd sing three or four songs.
The show would be about an hour . . . She'd sometimes
mingle with the crowd, or we'd sit back in her dressing room
and smoke – you could smell it all over the place.

Hollon says that during the Café Society period Lady was still on
nothing stronger than marijuana; he seems to say that they smoked
it in the dressing room, but Josephson said that he never allowed it
in the club, and that Lady would ride round in a taxi between sets,
smoking joints. Josephson said:

I had very little personal contact with her. Unlike other
people who worked for me, she spent very little time there.
She'd come in before show time, put her gown on, do her
show and often in her gown, put her coat on and up the stairs
and off. Sometimes with someone waiting for her, sometimes
alone. There was a cab waiting for her in Sheridan Square –
there used to be a hack stand there – in the Square in those
days there was Café Society at one end, on the other side
Greenwich Village Inn, there was a typical place with girlie
shows, and around the corner on 4th was the 19th Hall; they
had people like Fats Waller playing there. And El Chico was

in a corner apartment building. So the hackies always had a lot of fares coming from there. Billie got acquainted with one of the hackies and between shows he would drive her around Central Park and then bring her back in time for the next show.
But once she showed her backside to the audience. Well, I gave her hell. Billie comes out and does a song or two early in the show, and she finished her song, and for some reason she didn't like the audience – they were square, noisy, something – so Billie finishes her second song, and you know performers take off all their clothes and put the gown on over, because under the lights it's hot and smoky, and this way they come back to their dressing room and just have to take the gown off, and Billie dressed like that. And so Billie turned her back to the audience and bowed and picked up her gown and showed her ass. They gasped, aghast. I gave the band a cue and they went into a dance. But that was one time a black person said 'kiss my ass' and showed it. I told her never to do that again. She said, 'Fuck 'em.' She was high.
Louise was a second cousin to John Hammond. Louise would come in when Billie was going off and they'd leave together, and at this time nobody else got to Billie, that was it. And at the end of the night, they'd be off again. They had a strong thing going. But she had her boyfriends too.

As Hollon remembered, there was no nonsense about not mingling with the customers; Lady could come and go as she pleased and sometimes amused herself when she was not on stage by playing blackjack with musicians in the band room. But she was effectively turning her back on the mass audience that she was unable to reach anyway Café Society's management and audience were people with a richly political sense of humour who believed in racial brotherhood, and in those days such people were inevitably to be found on the left; later, as the forties wore on and as the Republicans had been kept out of the White House for many years, the left/right divide in American politics began to deepen and become more vicious.
One of the acts Josephson hired later in the forties was folksinger Josh White; born in Mississippi, White had left home working as eyes for street-singers like Blind Lemon Jefferson, and ended up a

top cabaret artist among New York's left-wing fans of cabaret folk. It was Josephson who put him on a high stool with an open-necked shirt to sing his radical songs like 'Jim Crow Train' and 'Bad Housing Blues'. But he also sang at the White House, and Josephson said that the President's wife, Eleanor Roosevelt, a darling of the liberal left, had probably never visited another nightclub in her life, but she came to his.

On Sunday afternoons there were benefits for Spanish relief, and Lady attended some of those; they were later labelled communist fronts. Josephson said the only time Lady ever didn't show up was when she was doing a benefit; this must have been the time he told Whitney Balliett about, when nobody showed up except the band and Jack Gilford, and Gilford did impressions: he was the boogie-woogie pianist, he was Billie, Big Joe Turner, all of them; and the next day he was offered a spot in a revue and his Broadway career had begun. The club lasted until 1950, when the right-wing witch-hunt in the USA was getting well under way; Josephson later had various restaurants called the Cookery, eventually with music, but there was never anything else like Café Society.

On 20 January 1939 Lady was back in the studio with a small group and better songs. Charlie Shavers on trumpet, Tyree Glenn on trombone and Chu Berry on tenor sax played the ensemble writing; the rhythm section was Cozy Cole, John Williams on bass and Al Casey (from Fats Waller's group) on guitar; the pianist was Sonny White. Only two tunes were recorded, but they were better songs, or perhaps the more congenial setting and arrangements make them seem so. 'That's All I Ask of You' was written by someone named Pope, 'Dream of Life' by Carmen McRae; these songs are so obscure they do not appear in the usual reference books, yet they made better Holiday records than those in the immediately previous sessions. Lady seems more involved, and perhaps the fact that she was involved with the pianist had something to do with it.

In August 1941 there would be a record date billed as 'Billie Holiday with Teddy Wilson and his Orchestra', but the date of 30 January 1939 was the last Wilson session to feature Lady. The band was cut back to a septet; Benny Carter's alto sax solos were a highlight, as well as Eldridge's trumpet, and the best of four tunes were 'More Than You Know' and 'Sugar'. On 21 March a session under Lady's name with Ken Kersey on piano featured a three-piece reed section, with old friends Kenneth Hollon and Stanley Payne on tenor sax, and Tab Smith on alto. The records were pretty, but four pop ballads were undistinguished; unusually, there was time left over for an extra side, and the best of the five sides from the date was not released for nearly a decade: 'Long Gone Blues' featured Smith's underrated alto, the muted trumpet of Hot Lips Page and composer credits for Smith and Lady.

Then came the pivotal vehicle of Billie's career, the anti-lynching song called 'Strange Fruit'.

Lewis Allan was a poet then working as a high-school teacher; his real name was Abel Meeropol. His anti-racist credentials did not end with 'Strange Fruit'; he wrote 'The House I Live In', a plea for tolerance recorded by Frank Sinatra for a short film in 1945, and the Meeropols later adopted the sons of Julius and Ethel Rosenberg, who were executed for treason in 1953. In April 1939 Allan brought his poem to Josephson and Robert Gordon, who was responsible for producing the floor shows at the club. They showed it to Lady; Allan played it for her, and later wrote that she didn't know what the word 'pastoral' meant.

> Southern trees bear a strange fruit,
> Blood on the leaves and blood at the root,
> Black bodies swaying in the Southern breeze,
> Strange fruit hanging from the poplar trees.
> Pastoral scene of the gallant South,
> The bulging eyes and the twisted mouth,
> Scent of magnolias, sweet and fresh,
> Then the sudden smell of burning flesh.
> Here is a fruit for the crows to pluck,
> For the rain to gather, for the wind to suck,
> For the sun to rot, for the trees to drop,
> Here is a strange and bitter fruit.

Lady was non-political; when she first looked at 'Strange Fruit' she didn't know what to make of it. She never read anything but comic books – promoter Ernie Anderson once brought her bundles of them – and she was used to learning songs, not reading poetry. At first she had told Allan that she'd have to think it over; she later said that at first, 'I was afraid that people would hate it.' She was an entertainer first of all and shared with her beloved Louis Armstrong the desire to please her audience, albeit in her own way. But after Allan left the club, the story goes, she had made up her mind; when Frankie Newton's band had finished a set, she said to him: 'Some guy's brought me a hell of a damn song that I'm going to do.'

Arthur Herzog had written material for Café Society; he had been introduced to Lady by his close friend, arranger Danny Mendelsohn. Allan had written some music for 'Strange Fruit', and Herzog remembered:

> He wrote something or other alleged to be music and Barney gave it to Danny and Danny rewrote it, put it into shape. What he rewrote or discarded I don't know. And Barney had Billie sing this song. And when she first started singing the song, I really don't believe she knew what she was doing or that the impact hit her . . . My recollection is that the song didn't have much punch at first, when she sang it, and suddenly the impact of it hit her, and she put herself into the song.

Josephson remembered it the same way:

> At first I felt Billie didn't know what the hell the song meant. He brought it to me and played it for her on the piano, and she said she'd sing it, and we rehearsed it with the band. This song came after the opening, maybe she was in four months. Her response was, 'If you think it's okay, man, I'll do it.' . . . I don't think she felt the song [at first] but there came a time when I knew she did. When Allan played it for her she just listened. Billie was very quick on learning lyrics . . . but the time this was, it was the night she sang it and tears came.
>
> The audience responded immediately. When the tears rolled down, it was such an impact from the audience at that time, that I knew Billie knew. And it became such a personal thing with her, so identified with her, that I guess she began to think that she wrote it. She said so in her book. Billie got to the point where, 'This is my song.'
>
> Every time she sang that song it was unforgettable. I listened to it three times a night; she sang it every set. I made her do it as her last number, and no matter how thunderous the applause, she had orders from me not to return for even a bow. I wanted the song to sink in, especially since it closed

every show. The room was completely blacked out, service stopped – at the bar, everywhere. The waiters were not permitted to take a glass to the table, or even take an order. So everything stopped – and everything was dark except for a little pin spot on her face. That was it. When she sang 'Strange Fruit', she never moved. Her hands were down. She didn't even touch the mike. With the little light on her face. The tears never interfered with her voice, but the tears would come and just knock everybody in that house out. The audience would shout for 'Strange Fruit'; those who'd never been down before and didn't know her sets closed with it would shout for it when they felt her set was coming to a close.

Up to that time the national mags did not print black pictures; Marian Anderson could be singing at the opera and she'd be reviewed in the music column of *Time* but not a picture ... Soon after Billie started singing 'Strange Fruit', *Time* came down, and a picture of her appeared, and they printed the lyric. To my knowledge, that was the first time a Negro's photo appeared in *Time/Life*, and from then on others began to appear. But it was the impact of that song that made them print her picture. Gjon Mili – not on assignment from *Life* – would come down and take a million shots.

One evening, Josephson remembered, a woman followed Lady into the powder room crying, 'Don't you dare ever sing that song again. Don't you dare.' She made such a fuss that Josephson got involved, and it turned out that a trauma had been revived:

When she was seven or eight years old she had witnessed a lynching in the South. She saw him tied by the throat to the back fender of an automobile and dragged through the streets and then hung up, and burned. So she'd forgot the whole thing, and she comes into Café to have fun, and Billie sings about burning flesh, and the whole thing came back.

There were people who would walk out on the song, but the protests were mild: 'We don't call this entertainment.' They would just call for their check and leave, said Josephson; usually the trauma of unexpectedly hearing a 'protest' song was less than that of witnessing a brutal racist murder.

John Hammond disliked 'Strange Fruit' and liked to say that it was the worst mistake she ever made, because it made her a *chanteuse* and the freshness went out of her work. But the earlier freshness had already, inevitably, gone out of her work. The mushy ballads she had recorded in the second half of 1938 had been arranged so that Lady sang, there was a tenor sax solo, and Lady sang again: she was now no longer just one of the boys. Instead of her extraordinary contribution happening naturally, like a solo from Lester or Buck – let us not forget Whitney Balliett's description of jazz as 'the sound of surprise' – she was becoming the centrepiece of a jazz-tinged pop record, because there was never room for very long for pure jazz at the centre of the popular music business.

Hammond, Josephson and the others hated racism, but the most they could do was nothing compared to the racist paranoia of the nation and the built-in second-rate nature of the music business, which could not find a way for Lady to be the success she deserved to be. She should have been singing with Basie on the radio every night, but the Swing Era was already half over, a handful of white bands were making the big money, and most of the black ones always struggled. The innocence and freshness of the records that were made in mid-1935 could not have lasted more than a few years; there were no more protest songs, but 'Strange Fruit' did not transform Lady's career by itself. In retrospect it is not surprising that Billie had become a *chanteuse*.

Anyway, it is quite impossible to be an African-American without making political decisions; even the decision to keep your head down is a political decision. In Studs Terkel's oral history collection called *Race* (1992), one of his interviewees described being black in America as like having shoes that are too tight and not being able to change them, so that black people who are militant and those who seek a quiet life all have in common that, metaphorically speaking, their feet hurt. In 1939, nobody knew how many black men were being lynched in the South, because some of these crimes weren't even reported; until well into the 1950s the casual, exceptionally cruel murder of black men was a Saturday-night sport for Southern white trash in the land of the brave and the home of the free, and everybody knew it, including the federal government, which did nothing: the NAACP had been trying to get an anti-lynching federal law for years. Lady also remembered the way her father had died, in a Jim Crow ward of a Dallas hospital.

John White quotes Jack Schiffman at the Apollo, who initially had misgivings about 'Strange Fruit' being performed there. 'If you heard it done elsewhere, you might have been touched and nothing more. But at the Apollo the song took on profound implications.' And after Lady sang it, 'A moment of oppressively heavy silence followed, and then a kind of rustling sound I had never heard before. It was the sound of almost two thousand people sighing.'

Whatever its musical merits or lack of them, it was an even more profoundly moving experience then than it is now. Many years later, in her autobiography, Lady said:

It has a way of separating the straight people from the squares and cripples. One night in Los Angeles, a bitch stood up in the club where I was singing and said, 'Billie, why don't you sing that sexy song you're so famous for? You know, the one about the naked bodies swinging in the trees.'

Needless to say, she reported, she refused to sing it on such occasions. The song obviously had to be recorded, but Columbia wasn't going to touch it. Enter Milt Gabler, of Commodore Records.

In 1926 Gabler had added records to his father's radio parts store. A jazz fan from the beginning, he was the first to reissue jazz records, simply buying a pressing of an out-of-print number from the parent label; then the first to start a mail-order record club, the United Hot Clubs of America. In order to drum up work for musicians and to publicize 52nd Street, he organized free jam sessions, at first in recording studios, then in clubs which were otherwise not being used on Sunday afternoons; John Hammond got Bessie Smith to sing at one of these, and Lady turned up more than once.

Gabler was supplying and delivering records to other dealers and to radio stations; he built WNEW's record library, for many years the best in the country. And then, having attended many a recording session, in 1938 he began producing records for his own Commodore label. By then Gabler had opened a Commodore Music Shop at 46 West 52nd Street, where it stayed open late for the club trade and became a hangout for musicians.

Among the people who worked there, besides Milt, his father

Julius and brothers Barney and Danny, was brother-in-law Jack Crystal, who later took over the jam sessions. The Crystals lived on Long Island, and perhaps Lady visited them there; the legend arose that she babysat with young Billy Crystal, today's popular actor and comedian, who said in 1992, 'That story has gotten way overblown. It's beginning to sound like my parents gave her $3 and told her to stay off the phone.' There must have been a lot of camaraderie in the shop, which was decorated with framed caricatures of musicians by B. Ten Hove.

The complete output of Commodore Records has been reissued by Mosaic Records in Stamford, Connecticut; it fills up sixty-six LPs, including rare material such as eighteen solo tracks by Teddy Wilson, made at the time for a piano school. The set's booklets are priceless for the notes by Dan Morgenstern and an exhaustive interview with Gabler. Morgenstern says that Hammond would have recorded 'Strange Fruit' even though he didn't like it, but Columbia wouldn't let him (by this time ARC had been taken over by CBS and the Columbia label revived). In one interview Hammond's memory failed him at first: he thought that he had got into trouble by recording 'Strange Fruit' and that Gabler had saved his bacon by offering to put the record out, but then he remembered that Brunswick/Columbia had processed and pressed all Gabler's records, which is why the Commodore 10-inch master numbers are in the same numerical sequence. Gabler remembered that Lady came into the store and said, 'Milt, what do you think? Columbia won't let me record "Strange Fruit".' Gabler had an idea:

After all, Columbia was pressing all my records, and I had a good relationship with them. I was a good dealer, and my records weren't jobbed out, they were sold right from the store. A couple of dealers used to buy them, but we didn't sell many records. I says, 'You tell them it's just a little record dealer, has its own label, and see if they'll let you make it for me. Let them give you permission to do one session, which would be four tunes.'

They were at 799 7th Avenue, a block away from my store ... she came right back and said, 'They're afraid to make it. They'll let you make it.'

I picked the tunes. So we did 'Yesterdays'. We did 'I Gotta

Right to Sing the Blues'. We did 'Strange Fruit'. And I said,
'I want you to make a blues.' Because she had a record I
loved called 'Billie's Blues' on Vocalion, her first record with
her own name on it.

The session of 20 April 1939 used the Café Society band:
Newton on trumpet, Hollon, Payne and Tab Smith on reeds,
Johnny McLin on guitar, John Williams on bass, Eddie Dougherty
on drums and Sonny White on piano. Two takes were made of
each tune, except the blues, 'Fine and Mellow', and in each case
it was the first take that was issued. 'Strange Fruit' was the first
recorded, and the performance could hardly be bettered. It sounds
much the way it must have sounded in the club: introduced by
the piano and Newton with a mute, the saxophones moaning the
harmony behind Lady, and Williams's bass notes especially well
placed on the issued take. White refers to the tune in its printed
version, but Lady had already adapted it for herself; all these years
later it is still deeply moving.

For additional intimacy, Jerome Kern's 'Yesterdays' was done
with only one horn: it begins at a slightly faster tempo than
'Strange Fruit', and halfway through the group stops dramatically
and begins again at a somewhat quicker tempo, with Hollon
soloing behind Lady: a change in tempo is often just a hackneyed
way to pad out an uninspired performance with some variety, but
here it is perfectly judged. The song became one of Lady's speciali-
ties: it is said that at first she didn't know what 'sequestered
days' meant in the first verse, but her unerring instinct for a
song that was right for her was working; without singing the
blues, she infused a great show tune (from Roberta, 1933) with
blues feeling.

'Fine and Mellow' came next, and 'I Gotta Right to Sing the
Blues', a sassy song by Ted Koehler and Harold Arlen from 1932,
already made famous by Jack Teagarden, had a fine solo by Tab
Smith and became another Holiday classic.

'Strange Fruit' was the equivalent of a top-twenty hit, despite
being banned by most radio stations. This would have been a
remarkable feat for a record from a tiny label which had a retail
price of a dollar, 25 cents more than most full-price records at the
time, but the sales may have been due to the other side: Gabler
said 'Fine and Mellow' was a juke-box hit.

I asked her if she had gotten her blues lyrics together. She had a little piece of paper, like the side of a bag, and she had written down some standard verses – 'I love my man' – that you find in a lot of blues. I says, 'We need a kicker to make it different than any other blues.' We couldn't just call this 'Billie's Blues No. 2', which is probably what would happen today . . . I came up with the verse 'High-drape pants, stripes are really yellow/Kisses me, makes me really mellow.' And that became the title, the kicker to make it different . . .

I think it was the first modern blues session, really. I had the saxophones play a riff behind her that Tab Smith sketched out, and rambling piano and Frankie Newton's muted trumpet, like Joe Smith would play behind Bessie Smith. An A&R man's stuff is only as good as his memory.

'Strange Fruit' got all the notice when the record came out, but before long Gabler had a call from Decca.

Decca had been launched in 1934 in the USA as a subsidiary of Decca UK by Edward Lewis, who had first tried to buy ARC from Herbert Yates, the film industry buccaneer who was controlling it; Lewis hired Jack Kapp away from Yates to run the new label. Kapp was a very clever record man who had artists under personal contract, so that he could bring Bing Crosby and several others away from Brunswick to the new label, and immediately made Decca a success by selling premium discs at 35 cents each instead of 75 cents. Apart from anything else, this cornered a huge share of the juke-box market, which Decca held until after the Second World War. Gabler continues:

A dealer in Chicago, who used to sell juke boxes a lot of records, called up: do I have any 'Fine and Mellow'? He drove all the way in from Chicago and he cleaned out my whole stock, and drove back with them. He was the only dealer in Chicago that had 'Fine and Mellow', and he put it on his boxes, and that busted it wide open. So now I get this call from Bob Stevens, do I have 'Fine and Mellow'? I know something is happening with that record on coin machines, or they wouldn't have called me from Decca. It wasn't really a commercial record at that point, but I knew if they are calling me, they probably wanted to copy the record. And I said, now how can I sell mine for a dollar if they're going to sell them for 35 cents? So I said, 'Bob, it's selling so well, a guy from Chicago came and cleaned me out. I have none in stock.' I had a few in the back room, but I wasn't going to bring that record over to Decca Records. They were on 50 West 57th Street then.

I collared the next musician that walked into the 52nd Street store. I had four record booths. And I used to sell manuscript paper, sheet music and all, of course. So I said, 'Can you copy music off a record?' He said, 'Sure.' I said, 'Well, what will you charge to me to copy a blues off a Billie Holiday record, with the lyrics?'

The musician went into a booth with the record and made a lead sheet for $15, lyrics and all.

I took it and I wrote on the top of that music, 'Composer: Words and Music, Billie Holiday.' And at the bottom I put 'Commodore Music Shop' and the address. I went over to the post office at 45th and Lex, and I got a registration card. I had an envelope and everything . . . On that registration card it says the fee for registering a song for copyright. I sent it to the Registrar of Copyrights, Washington DC, and I copyrighted that song in Billie's name. When the little card came back with a serial number on it, I called Bob and said, 'Bob, I have the record in stock now You want it?'

Decca covered 'Fine and Mellow' in August 1939 by Alberta Hunter, with a good little band, but it was too late: Lady's record had mopped up the market, and Gabler, who could have taken a co-writing credit or even kept the whole thing for himself, had seen to it that Lady got royalties on that song for the rest of her life.

Ellerton Oswald 'Sonny' White was engaged to Lady for a few months. He was born in Panama City, more than two years younger than Lady; he worked steadily as a reliable sideman until he died in 1971. Cliff Leeman remembered him as a stylist similar to Wilson, but Leeman didn't think Lady and Sonny could have been terribly compatible.

Sonny was a little, meek, beautiful, ingoing person . . . I worked with Sonny, and he got himself off, because he was

boozing too much. They finally took him and put him in the
infantry, I don't know who the hell did that. He was a small
man, chubby-faced. He had beautiful charisma ... he was a
quiet one, very funny. He had a wonderful sense of humour.
He'd get very stoned, but he'd get very quiet. He was with
us, with Ben Webster, a whole bunch of loud-mouthed people,
especially with Ben. We used to tear apartments up, hotel
rooms up, go riding, and shooting guns. Sonny would just sit
and laugh at us. We couldn't get him out to the stables, let
alone get him on a horse.

Sonny White was one of several accompanists who were very close
to Lady. She announced their engagement to a journalist after the
'Strange Fruit' session, and in May *Melody Maker* printed the news,
but nothing came of it. Late in 1939, she told an interviewer that
there had been three men that she had loved: 'One was Marion
Scott, when I was a kid. He works for the post office now The
other was Freddie Green, Basie's guitar man. But Freddie's first
wife is dead, and he has two children and somehow it didn't work
out. The third was Sonny White, the pianist; like me, he lives with
his mother and our plans for marriage didn't gel.' Sonny could just
be the pianist/lover she paid tribute to in her autobiography,
rather than Bobby Henderson; we'll never know.
    Lady's initial engagement at Café Society lasted for nine months.
During the summer of 1939 Coleman Hawkins had returned from
several years in Europe, and the big-toned boss of the tenor sax
played in a cutting contest at Puss Johnson's tavern on St Nicholas
Avenue. Fats Waller's band were there and thought that Hawk
had won; Lady was there too. By the time the account of the battle
was printed in *down beat*, she was working in Chicago, where the
magazine's offices were: she called them to assure them that Lester
had won. But the two great tenor men played such completely
different styles that it was like comparing apples and oranges.
    She was booked again at Café Society to open on 1 October
1940 and didn't show up. Josephson cancelled the contract. Maybe
she was still sore at him for that years later, but there was no
attempt at any accuracy in her autobiography; she said she had
made $75 a week at Café Society. Josephson said it was at least
twice that. She said she left after more than two years because she
needed a vacation; she was there nine months initially and left to

make more money at various other places. She said that she wanted to be replaced by Hazel Scott, the young pianist, composer and singer, but that Josephson didn't want Scott because she wasn't pretty enough and was 'too dark'. 'I had Delores Williams singing,' said Josephson, 'and nobody's blacker than her.'

The actual story of how I took on Hazel is that John Hammond got Ida Cox for me, but she was unable to come in the day after Billie left, so it was arranged for her to come in a week later. Jack Gilford told me he heard a terrific little girl in a small place up in Harlem at a piano that sings . . . so I called her and she said all right. She played a few things for me; Billie wasn't even there. She was only a kid. She would be wearing skirts and sweaters and saddle shoes. She might cover her hair with a bandanna but she didn't look like a mammy.

Born in 1896, Ida Cox was one of Hammond's old favourites and was not a success at Café Society. Hazel Scott came back and stayed over seven years at the club.

Lady's time-keeping had always been unpredictable and would get worse, partly because she liked partying and seeing her friends in various clubs at times of her own choosing, but also because, as many testified, she always lacked self-confidence. Maybe all the liquor and/or marijuana helped her to deal with stage fright; even when she was on the premises she would dawdle in her dressing room long past the time when she was supposed to go on. Once she got on stage she was fine, but in a sense she was unaware of her genius. 'I just have to sing a song my own way, that's all I know,' she would say. But she couldn't figure out why, if everyone thought she was so wonderful, she wasn't more successful outside New York, which did nothing to improve her self-confidence. Nothing in her background had ever given her any reason to regard punctuality as important; in the days when her milieu was more informal, especially during Prohibition, it was not very important at all, but when clubs began to advertise and compete with one another, a non-show reflected on the club itself and hurt her reputation. Arthur Jarwood, whose investments during this period included the Famous Door, said that she could have earned twice as much money if she had been more reliable: club-owners wanted to hire her, but they would only gamble on her at a bargain price.

Her unreliability was probably made worse by a paradoxical combination of lack of self-confidence and a lack of respect for the business, outside her hard-core fans who, she knew, would keep patient. For all the anti-racist activity of Hammond and Josephson, they were still patronizing bosses from her point of view; they hadn't been able to make her the star she wanted to be, and she didn't like being manipulated, by Hammond in particular. Her attitude was a way of helping her to feel that she was still in control. Her relationship with Glaser could be a fiery one, but it lasted a long time because he didn't pretend to be anything but a tough bastard, and she liked having a tough guy in her corner; besides, he usually gave her money when she asked for it. (Josephson said he paid Lady direct.)

There is no doubt that she was an addictive personality. Hollon told a version of the famous story that he told to journalist Johnny Simmen. In the late thirties, on their way to a 'wealthy people's' party on 63rd Street,

> We were comin' from Harlem and drivin' in a little two-seater car and Billie had some pot as big as cigarettes, and she says, 'Try one of these, Kenny. They come all the way from Dakar, Africa, and they're terrific. Try one, anyway.' Well, when I got out of the car, I was dizzy, I couldn't even pick my heels up . . . Frankie and all the boys had the music out, and I took my horn out and blew a few notes and tingled all over. We played the first number, and I couldn't see a note, and Frankie came over and said, 'What the hell are you doin'?' 'Man, I'm blowin'.' He said, 'Well, you ain't.' When he said that, I got tickled and laughed for the next three hours and couldn't play a note, and that was the last time I smoked pot. I slept about two or three days tryin' to get straightened out.

Talking to Simmen, he added, 'I ate like a pig, drank gallons of water, but nothing helped . . . There's no doubt that the stuff Billie gave me that night was the real McCoy.' And he reiterated that he never even saw her drink, let alone shoot heroin. 'All she did was smoke weed.' Soon enough, narcotics would make Billie's life more complicated; John Hammond said that Josephson stopped hiring her because of narcotics, and in his book he bragged about interfering in her career one last time: he said he broke up a relationship with a woman manager who happened to be a friend of his, by warning her family about Lady's drug problem. She always had a lot of men friends. Ben Webster was a sometime escort, and Webster got mean when he drank; on one occasion he beat Lady, and the next time he called for her, the story goes, sitting outside in his car tooting the horn, Sadie followed Lady down the stairs, reached into the car and whacked Webster with an umbrella. Dick Wilson, from Andy Kirk's band, and probably Pha Terrell, Kirk's vocalist, were two more boyfriends, and she is reported to have said about drummer Sid Catlett, 'They don't call him "Big Sid" because he's six foot three, you know.' She didn't go steady with anybody for a while after her engagement to Sonny. But she had always had a weakness for good-looking fellows, and in the summer of 1941, during a gig at the Famous Door, she started going with Jimmy Monroe, whom she described as 'the best-looking man I'd laid eyes on since Buck Clayton'. Harry Edison said, 'She went for the playboy kind – pimps. Like Jimmy Monroe, who had just come back from Europe . . . Jimmy was handsome, and he turned Lady Day onto drugs.' But it wasn't as simple as that.

In the summer of 1941, Billie was twenty-six years old and must have yearned for a normal life; it is clear that she always wanted children. There are any number of stories about how much she loved children and how good she was with them, and she had so many godchildren she couldn't have kept them all straight. She was not very well equipped to lead a normal life, but if she was ever going to try, she had to get away from Sadie.

A few years later, her friend Greer Johnson also knew Sadie:

> She was terribly short, very very fat, and Billie's attitude toward her was alternately tender and very abrupt, a disturbing thing to watch, really. I felt [Sadie] was not awfully bright . . . she functioned on and off as Billie's dresser in clubs, helping her change between numbers or what not . . . Billie was often very impatient with her, and I felt I could not understand what their relationship was. I didn't think she had any feeling for Billie at all. I thought she was a relatively stupid sad little woman who had been caught [by Clarence] and produced a Phoenix, and what do you do with a Phoenix? . . . At no time did I ever have any feeling from Sadie that she

had any inclination whatsoever of the greatness of her daughter.

This may not be fair to Sadie, because Johnson clearly worshipped Lady, who had her own doubts about her greatness; and anyway her talent was not directly relevant to the mother–daughter problem. But here is yet another snapshot of a guilt-ridden relationship. Ruby Helena was an entertainer who first met Lady in a restaurant behind the Apollo Theater at 2 a.m.; Lady asked Ruby to drive her home, and Ruby stayed the night. A couple of years later, Ruby had nowhere to stay and lived with Sadie and Lady for a few months. Lady always called her Helen; she had a car and would drive Lady to recording sessions. The apartment was the one at 99th Street and Central Park West, with two bedrooms; Ruby said that she slept in the living room and that Lady often brought girls home with her, usually white girls. 'Billie even got the name Mister Holiday, because she was seldom seen with fellas . . . And I will always believe that her mother was the cause of it, 'cause she never wanted Billie to get close to any fellas.'

Throughout a long interview, Ruby repeats the litany, the constant factor, of Sadie feeling sorry for herself, telling Lady that 'They're no good – I've heard this about them and that about them –' The mention of Clarence would start Sadie's tears, and of course Lady was a sucker for that; but according to Ruby, Sadie used Clarence to get more than one kind of sympathy: 'She constantly kept in Billie's mind about her father – how her father walked away and left her.' And by constantly reminding Lady of her rejection, Sadie was implicitly warning Lady that she would feel guilty if she left Sadie, rejecting her to have a life of her own.

Ruby had a great many conversations with Sadie, and letters from her over the years – she wished she'd kept them – and her opinion was that Sadie used Lady emotionally. 'Her mother was right under her tail all the time.' Ruby also heard chapter and verse from Sadie about things that had happened earlier, such as Sadie putting the young Eleanora in a brothel when she was no more than a child; Ruby found this hard to understand. (For that matter, Harry Edison stated flatly that Sadie ran a whorehouse, that men used to go there 'to buy a piece of meat'.) Sadie had varicose veins, and would complain about her legs and that she couldn't do this or that. Lady was susceptible to all this; she had given as a reason for the failure of her engagement to Sonny White the fact that they both lived with their mothers. According to Ruby, at least during the several months she stayed in the flat, Lady and Sadie were like sisters, constantly telling each other everything, which Sadie must have liked; and another factor in Lady's bringing girls back to the flat was that she didn't stay out all night with men: she would always call Sadie and let her know where she was. Evidently many years of nagging had had its effect.

Then Monroe came on the scene. Sadie's first complaint, according to Ruby, was that 'she seemed to have thought that Billie was giving him too much of her attention, and neglecting her attentions toward her mother.' And when Sadie first began to worry about drugs, she said, 'Helen, Billie's doing something wrong with that Jimmy. She stays broke all the time. Now, she hasn't given me any money.'

She took Billie to court one time for non-support. But Billie used to give her money. When she started with Jimmy, her mother said she was neglecting her, but she was not, actually, because Billie had put her in business, in this restaurant.

The restaurant was a few doors away at 99th and Amsterdam, according to Ruby, and was a going concern for quite a few years. But Jimmy came to the flat to visit, and Sadie didn't like him.

Her mother used to say that he thought he was cute, because he was fairly nice looking. He was just the opposite of his brother. Clark was a sort of heavy type and upright, and Jimmy was a frail type. She got acquainted with Clark, and Clark started liking her, and people were saying Clark was her boyfriend. All of a sudden Jimmy comes into the picture, with his shrewd self – he had a name for using people. He decided he was going to take over, and get some of the money. Billie was a person who didn't make friends easily, and when she first met him, she didn't like him . . He could be very solemn unless he wanted to charm you . .
He was a person that was always to himself, who didn't talk, one of those persons that you'd have to wonder what they're thinking about   You just couldn't figure him out . .

Ruby decided that the reason Lady started liking Jimmy after all was that Jimmy started supplying her with drugs. Jimmy was an opium smoker, and had already contributed, so people said, to the drug addiction of his first wife. Ruby says that Jimmy made a profit when he obtained drugs with Billie's money, but in the same breath she says she got that information from Sadie: 'I don't think her mother would tell a lie.' At the same time that Ruby watched Sadie taking emotional advantage of Lady, she seems to have taken much of her attitude to Jimmy and the drugs from Sadie.

It has always been assumed that Monroe was the one who introduced Lady to heroin, but some people thought that Monroe was a lot better than some of her later men. Opium is a lesser evil than heroin, and there is no evidence that Monroe used heroin during this period.

According to Ruby, Lady's behaviour changed. Ruby says that she was very young at the time of Lady's first triumph at the Apollo in 1935; her sister had taken her to the show, and later,

> When we met, I was afraid to say something to her about the show, 'cause I didn't want to offend her. But I saw, you know, a different person from the person she was then. I said, 'You were dressed so tacky!' She just screamed! She took it differently than I expected. She took it as a joke. Then I realized she was a nice person.

Lady introduced Ruby Helena to people as her half-sister, and Sadie called her her other daughter. Then there was the matter of the wealthy lady friend:

> There was a wealthy lady who liked her. She had a booking agency, and she even bought her a mink coat. Mrs Crane would drive her, because her chauffeur worked in the theatre. This girl was also Mrs Crane's secretary, worked with me in the theatre. We were in Montreal together a long time . . .

Mrs Crane is probably the 'Brenda' in Lady's autobiography, and the Louise mentioned by Barney Josephson. Louise Crane later became the companion of Elizabeth Bishop, one of the great poets of the century. At any rate, suddenly Lady was 'so nasty' to Mrs Crane and ready to fight with Ruby at the slightest excuse. But Ruby also reveals that, at the request of Sadie, she kept an eye on Lady when they were out together and describes as an example of Lady's changed personality the time she kicked Ruby out of a taxi because she wanted to go somewhere without her: maybe Lady didn't want to have a babysitter at the age of twenty-six.

Sadie and Ruby blamed the change in Lady on drugs, but it seems just as likely that Lady was getting fed up: if she was thinking of trying marriage, she would have had to give up her girlfriends and her babysitter. And meanwhile, Sadie said to Jimmy, according to Ruby, 'You're no good, and I don't want you coming around here. If Billie's going to hang out with you against my will, she'll have to go someplace else and stay.'

Sadie liked the hopelessly square white man John Hammond, and a few years later she approved of John Simmons, another of Lady's boyfriends, because, he said, 'I kept myself sharp.' But she did not perceive Hammond or Simmons as threats. Jimmy Monroe was sharp and considered himself an operator; Sadie immediately spotted him as someone who was never going to take any nonsense from her and didn't give a damn what she thought. So she hated him. Joe Glaser didn't approve of him either; but Jimmy was sharp in an understated way, one suspects, and may have had better manners than Glaser; furthermore, he had been to Europe, had been married to a movie star and probably fancied himself as an entrepreneur: Glaser didn't need this complication in his relationship with Lady, who was trouble enough by herself.

Without any discernible talent of his own, Jimmy Monroe survived over eighty years on his wits and his charm; when one operation seemed to dry up, he found another. His neighbours in New York say that in his old age he has still had women squabbling over him. He was in Europe in 1938 because his then wife was working in London; according to Bill Coleman (in his memoir, *Trumpet Story*, 1990) Monroe could not get permission to stay in England, able only to visit his wife a few days at a time, so he opened a club in Paris in the Cité Pigalle, with a partner called Bob Grier. 'The club featured the latest jazz records and became a rendezvous for American Negro artists and their French friends.' (Jimmy said that the reason for this was that the Americans liked to pick up French girls, and Bricktop, the famous expatriate who ran a club in Paris, didn't want them doing it in her place.) As for Nina Mae McKinney, she survived being married to Jimmy well enough to make several more films, including a good supporting role in *Pinky* in 1949, yet another movie about a black girl passing for white, before she died in 1968. Jimmy could have dumped

Nina Mae for any number of reasons, or maybe she dumped him. At any rate, Lady said in her autobiography many years later that she thought that the reason Sadie and Joe Glaser disapproved of Monroe was that they thought he would never marry her; this rings psychologically true, and would have been like waving a red flag at a bull.

They were married on 25 August 1941, in Elkton, Maryland. 'When she came in that morning,' said Ruby, 'her mother was angry, because she'd been out all day and all night, and she hadn't called her. She threw the marriage licence on the table; she said, "We're married, so can he come in *now*?"' This marriage didn't do her much good in the end, but it seems equally clear that Sadie had lost yet another battle with life.

From the 'Strange Fruit' session to mid-1942, there were ten more recording sessions at Columbia, and a single one-off recording at Capitol; then the musicians' union ban on recordings intervened, and Billie did not enter the studio again until March 1944, recording again for Commodore. During this period she became one of the biggest attractions on 52nd Street, but she would henceforth remain a cult attraction, more famous among the public at large for her problems than for her talent. In every respect, the second half of her life had begun.

10

The War Years

At the end of the 1930s, one of Lady's closest friends was Irene Wilson.

Born Irene Armstrong in Ohio, Irene had moved to Detroit, then to Chicago as a teenager, and by 1930 was a well-known bandleader in the Windy City. Al Capone was a fan of hers, so she had plenty of work; her sidemen were mostly male, including such well-known names as Walter Fuller and Budd Johnson, who had respect for her because she was a well-rounded musician as well as a good pianist. When the Vogue was raided and closed, Irene worked for Joe Glaser at the Sunset, leading a trio called Three Classy Misses, that included Kathryn Perry on violin and dancer/singer Eloise Bennett; the act finished with all three girls singing and dancing. When the Vogue reopened she formed what she later said was her best band ever.

In 1932 Irene married Teddy Wilson and continued working as a bandleader until they moved to New York in 1934: her mother-in-law disapproved of her career, and Teddy's seemed more important.

The first time I saw Billie was in a little club called the Hot-Cha, and there was a little balcony up there where she used to sing. Benny Carter had told Teddy about Billie, so we went by there to see her. She was robust, carefree, just like a big kid. She was young. He asked her up to the house where we were staying to rehearse, and when she first came up, there was nobody there but me, and we just became friendly right there. She called me Renie. She was the first to call me that,

182

and then everybody called me Renie. And she told me right
there, 'Renie, I've met a lot of wives – Duke's wife and that
one's wife, but you're the first wife I've met that seems real.
You're just a top chick. I can dig you, 'cause you are a real
person.'
And I used to go to all Teddy's recording sessions. Well,
you know she didn't have too much schooling; so one day she
called me over and asked me, 'Renie, how do you pronounce
this word?' I put on my glasses and told her. Well, she had to
feel close and comfortable with me to ask me something like
that. We just went on from there.

But not long after Teddy hit the big time, he left Irene. She was
broken-hearted; but in self-defence she had to tell John Hammond
where to get off, and provides more evidence of Hammond's
attempts to manipulate his artists. Irene had no personal knowledge
of why Lady had left the Basie band, but did not doubt that
Hammond had something to do with it; she said Basie 'let John
Hammond run his life almost, for a long time'.

She – Lady – didn't like John for nothin'. Not much. She
didn't want him to run her life. He wanted to run everybody's
life. Lady was smokin' that pot around there and drinkin' a
lot, but she was still doin' her work. He was a square guy, oh
yes . . . but it was funny. He wanted to tell everybody what to
do, yes indeed. He took me out first thing when Ted and I
separated; he wanted to know what I was going to do. Couple
of times John took me to the Savoy, and out to dinner once
out of town to hear a trio . . .
When he found out he couldn't run Teddy's life, he was
around there tryin' to cut Ted's work out. And I wasn't even
with Ted, but that was still my bread and butter because he
was still supporting me. And I made an appointment and met
John one night at Café Society, and I said, 'Now listen, you
and me's supposed to be friends, and when Ted and me
separated, you was the first one come to my house' – Ted ran
off with another woman, and he didn't like her because she
wasn't nothing but a tramp. So anyway, John was so mad – I
told him, 'Ted is still giving me money, so unless you want to
support me, you stop cutting him out of work. Let him alone

and let him get some work, 'cause when you're cuttin' him out, you're cuttin' me out.' And Lady said, 'Yeah, Renie, you go right in there and tell him, yeah, that's what you should do.'

Irene later fell ill and went back to Cleveland, where an aunt looked after her; she recovered and met an Ohio State Youth Commissioner named Elden Kitchings. They were married in 1946; she was losing her sight when she was interviewed in 1971 and died a few years later, but she had three happy decades as Mrs Kitchings.

Back in New York, Benny Carter had helped her through the crisis of her failed marriage by persuading her to return to writing. She had written music for her bands in Chicago, and Carter knew she had a unique skill with harmony. Now she turned out a handful of beautiful songs. In the aftermath of her separation from Wilson, as her cousin Callye Arter put it, 'That music was just pouring from her heart.'

Lady had introduced Irene to Arthur Herzog, who was quoted in Sally Placksin's valuable book *American Women in Jazz: 1900 to the Present*, saying that he never had to make any changes to Irene's music. 'This is very unusual among collaborators, but I don't think I ever asked her to change a note. Anything she wrote, I could put words to, and that doesn't happen very often.' In turn, Irene told Helen Oakley, she never had to ask Herzog to change a word. 'He and Billie were tight. The way she felt about race was never nasty, you know. If you were all right, that was it, and never mind colour.'

Lady and Irene grew even closer after Irene split up with Ted. Irene said:

Lady knew that she could sing. That's all she knew how to do; that's all that made her real happy was to sing. I know how she talked. 'Oh, Renie, I really did that. Oh, Renie, I really felt it that time.' And I mean she knew that I was a musician too and I really admired her singing. She may in later years have compared her singing then with how she sounded earlier, and she couldn't have liked that. But that's all she knew how to do. It was a means of livelihood. Yes, I'll tell you that all she wanted to *do* was sing. And she used to slip off and go into those sporting houses in Baltimore just to ask them could she sing, and pick up money doing that. She told me that, oh yeah.

She took me down to meet Arthur – 'He's a pretty nice cat, Renie. I want you to meet him, and he writes lyrics. I want you to hear some lyrics he wrote for your song. He named it and everything.' I played it and Lady sang those lyrics – No! Here's how it went: Lady told me about this and I went down to Arthur's – he lived on 12th Street then and I went down with Carmen McRae, and when Helen Oakley had us for dinner, I said, 'Lady, I have this song and I want you to hear it.' And Carmen sang it. Carmen was with me all the time up there; I played it for Carmen. And they said when they looked up Lady was sitting there with tears in her eyes, and she said, 'Renie, I want to make that song.' And I said, 'Lady, you know it's yours.'

I knew nothing about songwriting. 'Some Other Spring'. I went with her on that date when she made that – we got a cab from her house, I picked her up – Sonny played piano on that date – she was going with him . . . she said, 'Renie, don't worry about these songs, you just write 'em and bring 'em to me and I'll make 'em.' Because she made what she wanted to. Nobody dictated to her what to record.

Canadian-born Helen Oakley was a publicist for jazz and an A&R director for Irving Mills's Variety label; she gave Teddy Wilson the fare to go back to Chicago to appear with Goodman at the Congress Hotel in 1935, the beginning of the Goodman trio. She married Stanley Dance, an English-born writer whose interviews and oral histories of the era are priceless; and she wrote a chapter about Irene for his book *The World of Earl Hines* (1977). As Helen Oakley Dance she has continued to this day as a music journalist, both helping with her husband's work and in her own right (she published *Stormy Monday*, a biography of T-Bone Walker, in 1987). She told Placksin, 'I had the best of influences, because Irene Kitchings and Billie Holiday were my closest friends.'

Lady's first recording session after 'Strange Fruit', back with Columbia on the Vocalion/Okeh labels, carried on the change from her earlier work. The personnel was almost the same as in the 'Strange Fruit' session, except that Bernard Addison replaced

McLin on guitar and Charlie Shavers replaced Newton on trumpet; so she was more or less recording with her regular backing group from Café Society, following the Commodore precedent. The tunes are heavily arranged, but the ensemble plays effectively behind her, and they all sound as though they belong together, as befits a working band. True, the spontaneity of the best earlier sides is gone, but what we are hearing is a new act, with a different kind of integrity. Billie herself remained an interpretative artist – a jazz singer – whatever she did, but the context in which she did it changed with the rest of the popular music of the time. As the Swing Era wore on, the jazz content in mainstream pop music was being watered down, yet it was still infused with jazz values.

Whether or not anyone understood it as early as 1939, in retrospect it is easy to see that the new era of pop singers was beginning. It takes many years of hard work to learn to play a musical instrument well, and young people fed a steady diet of romantic love in films and songs found it easier to identify with the vocalists than with a trumpet player or a saxophonist. The economic imperative entered into it, long before the post-war baby boom; as the USA climbed out of the Depression and entered the Second World War, in 1940 the percentage of records being sold to the juke-box operators had fallen below 40 per cent, because the retail side was recovering (hence the introduction of the *Billboard* chart that year). More and more records were being sold to the young people who followed the vocalists. In 1919, when Paul Whiteman hired Morton Downey to sing with his band, the other leaders thought he was mad; but by the early 1940s, Perry Como, Frank Sinatra, Dick Haymes, Jo Stafford, Margaret Whiting, Peggy Lee and many others were becoming more popular than the bands they sang with, and during that decade they went solo, remaining hit-makers (and heart-throbs) for many years.

When Lady turned from the improvised small-group jazz session towards a more central role as a vocalist, she and the record producers were aiming at the centre of what were becoming pop records. Of course, as the young fans of the era were mostly white, they didn't relate to African-American heart-throbs, or in any case didn't get a chance to do so, given the way the records were marketed. Significantly, it is at this point, according to *Pop Memories*, that Lady's 'hits' fell off: with more records being sold to the white retail trade, her sales became a smaller percentage of the total. Once again, her records were the best of their kind; and once again, she could not achieve the success that white artists did.

The first tune recorded on 5 July 1939 was 'Some Other Spring'. Lady said in her book that she had shown it to Benny Goodman, who agreed that it was a beautiful song; in fact he said it was too beautiful: it would never sell. 'He was right,' said Lady. 'It didn't sell.' Yet the song has stayed alive: later that year Teddy Wilson recorded it with his big band, Jean Eldridge singing; since then, singers ranging from Ella Fitzgerald, Anita O'Day, Carmen McRae and Dakota Staton to Anthony Newley and Marianne Faithfull have recorded it, as well as musicians like Art Tatum, Jimmy Rowles, Tommy Flanagan, George Shearing, Charlie Byrd and Benny Carter. It is a yearning story, the sort of ballad that doesn't need much in the way of obvious jazzation, and some people know a good song when they hear one.

'Our Love Is Different' is a lesser song, and an obscure one, but an affecting performance. Next was 'Them There Eyes', a song that remained in Lady's repertoire for the rest of her life; the arrangement begins with a rocking riff voiced for the reeds that is reminiscent of Duke Ellington charts of several years earlier. The song was co-written in 1930 by Maceo Pinkard, who also helped with 'Sugar' and 'Sweet Georgia Brown'; the quicker tempo allows solos by Tab Smith, Shavers and Hollon. 'Swing, Brother, Swing!', credited in part to Clarence Williams, the most successful black music publisher, is not as effective as in the version with Basie, but it's still fun, the solos including a few bars from Sonny White.

Lady's next session, on 15 December, is even more of a concession to the coming era. The band is entirely Basie's except for pianist Joe Sullivan: two trumpets (Clayton and Edison), three reeds (Earle Warren, Lester Young and Jack Washington) and that nonpareil rhythm section, but the arrangements are uninspired: the records are well done, but any competent bunch could have done them. Cole Porter's 'Night and Day' is all Lady's; she breaks the lines where she likes, so that for a change 'making love to you night and day' is all one thought, instead of a pair of unrelated phrases. George and Ira Gershwin's 'The Man I Love' is right up Lady's alley, but the arrangement seems to drag it down: if you just listen to Lady, the understated pathos is there, but the Goodman Quartet played a more dramatic version in the 1938 Carnegie

Hall concert. Still, at least there's a solo by Lester. 'You're Just a No Account', by Gershwin and Sammy Cahn, raises the tempo a bit, and there are short solos by Buck and Lester; 'You're a Lucky Guy', by Cahn and Saul Chaplin, raises the tempo still more, so that the rhythm section gets a chance to walk, and there's another pair of short solos.

On the whole, this session perhaps provides a paradigm for the future of popular music: given a roomful of geniuses, all you need is an open mike, but it is easy to spend money on production that gets in the way. Lady's arrangements improved, but the record business will always spend the maximum amount of money available, chasing what it perceives as the hit-making formula. It was as though the Swing Era was already tired; Shaw and Tommy Dorsey added unnecessary and impractical string sections to their bands, a lot of boring pop music was to come in the 1950s, and the same thing happened when the rock era became overripe: the industry never learns that records made with less self-consciousness date less quickly than those that are over-produced.

On 29 February 1940 Lady's personnel was completely different and perfectly competent, with Sonny on piano and slightly less lugubrious accompaniment, but again Lady did not need three reeds simply moaning behind her. There are two more tunes from Irene Wilson and Herzog: 'Ghost of Yesterday' and 'What Is This Going to Get Us?'. There's lovely muted horn from Roy Eldridge on the first, a solo from Sonny on the second, and the songs themselves are compelling listening. Johnny Green's 'Body and Soul' had been a top-ten hit in an instrumental recording by Coleman Hawkins, who did not play the tune at all, but strings of gorgeous arpeggios on it; Lady recomposes it her way. 'Falling in Love Again' is a German song by Frederick Hollander, sung in the film *The Blue Angel* by Marlene Dietrich in 1930, here with English words by Sammy Lenner; the tempo has picked up and Lady's laconic delivery is almost self-consciously amusing: her engagement to Sonny over, she may have been wondering if true romance would be as elusive as commercial success. There's a nice sax solo, and the writing for the reeds actually aspires to some commentary on the song in the last chorus.

From the session of 7 June 1940, Eldridge is on trumpet, Teddy Wilson on piano, Freddie Green on guitar and Walter Page on bass, with J. C. Heard on drums. There are two alto saxes and two tenors, including Lester Young, and the arrangements do not get in the way. Maybe they are by Wilson; he said years later that he always loved to write, which may be one reason why he was talked into fronting a big band; at any rate, with this session Bernie Hanighen (or Morty Palitz, Billie's other producer) seems to have come to grips with the problem of how to make this kind of record. Irene had sent 'I'm Pulling Through' to Arthur Herzog from Cleveland; it was their last collaboration, and there are solos from Eldridge and Lester Young. 'Tell Me More' is credited to Lady herself, and on the subject of this song Herzog was grumpily funny in 1971. One evening Danny Mendelsohn was at his house:

The house was two blocks below 14th and 8th Avenue, and we were four or five blocks away from Café Society – she used to come over sometimes Monday nights which were her nights off – I forget where she was living at the time; it made no difference to her because she lived all over the place. She popped up once living a floor under my younger son; he had an apartment on the West 80s and discovered one day he was living above Billie.

She came rushing in to Danny. She was a great artist, but creative – no. She said to Danny, 'Danny, I've got a great tune, take it down for me.' And she sings, da-daing, 'St James Infirmary'. So Danny says, 'Yes, Billie, it's a great tune, but it's "St James Infirmary".' 'Oh, Danny, bend it a little for me, bend it.' So Danny took out his pencil, put it in blues time, four/four, attached a bridge to it and said, 'All right Arthur, give me some words.' So I popped the first thing that came into my mind: 'Tell me more and more and then some', inane kind of thing, so we scratched this underneath and forgot about it completely.

Six months went by, and there's a record out – 'Tell Me More', words and music by Billie Holiday, sung by Billie Holiday, accompanied by the Billie Holiday Orchestra – of which there was no such thing, of course. There it was. 'Danny, what are we going to do about this? This idiot friend has done this to us and the song isn't worth a goddam.' I mean, 'St James Infirmary'.

After she died, Herbie Marks called me up and said, 'I seem to remember that you had something to do with this song, and I'd like to do something with it,' and I said, 'Herbie, I can't prove anything, but this song was written by yours truly and the late Danny Mendelsohn.' That's how it happened. It never made any money.

Herzog is being unfair to their own hackwork, to say nothing of using the word 'creative' in a very limited sense. Lady had commissioned the song and even told them how to write it; of course they should have got some credit. The song has a strong blues feeling, and its lingering resemblance to 'St James Infirmary' doesn't hurt a bit, so that it sounds as though you've heard it before but can't remember where. The way the words fall is pleasing, and with the arrangement's stop-time moments and a solo from Teddy, it's an unusual love song and a nice record.

'Laughing at Life', co-written by Charles and Nick Kenny, who were partly responsible for Wilson's big hit on 'Carelessly', almost recaptures the old days: the tempo is up a bit and the song is unpretentious; Lady sits out for some nice solos, and the reeds play a rhythmic riff behind her on the last chorus. She resurrects her dying fall in pitch on the ends of phrases, making more of the words: we might be only pretending to laugh. 'Time on My Hands' is a fine song by Vincent Youmans, a good record for romantic dancing, with lots of lovely muted Eldridge, alternating with Lester in the background.

On 12 September 1940, Wilson and Eldridge were again present. The four reeds included Jimmy Hamilton and Don Byas, who were up-and-comers; Don Redman, the influential bandleader who had recently disbanded; and Georgie Auld, a friend of Billie's from 52nd Street: Auld was one of the best white musicians of the era, a member of a later edition of Shaw's band, and at this time was playing on Goodman's sextet records with Charlie Christian, among the best Goodman ever made. 'I Hear Music', by Burton Lane and Frank Loesser, is the happiest tune from the date, with solos from Eldridge and Auld; 'I'm All for You' and 'It's the Same Old Story' are smoochers, and Al Hall on bass is particularly fine at this slow tempo for dancers. There were hit recordings by two obscure dance bands of 'Practice Makes Perfect'; Lady's record picks up the tempo a bit, making room for the two soloists again, and the arrangements must be by Redman, they're so good of their kind: the reeds actually have some fun.

On 15 October 1940, Leonard Feather and John Hammond were making a tribute to W.C. Handy, with 'Benny Carter and his All Star Orchestra'. They intended to record eight tunes for an album of four 78s, but never finished the project; two tunes were recorded by Joe Turner, and 'St Louis Blues' and 'Loveless Love' (also called 'Careless Love') by Billie Holiday. Sonny White played piano, Bill Coleman was there on trumpet; there's a clarinet solo by Carter on the first and a tenor solo by Auld on the second. Lady does a fine job, but as with many tributes, the results are well-meant rather than inspired.

Lady's next two sessions marked her first recordings with pianist Eddie Heywood, who had worked with Carter and later led the band at Café Society. On 21 March another journeyman, trumpeter Shad Collins, had returned from Europe for the duration; three reeds included Lester Young, and the young Kenny Clarke played drums. All four tracks were thoroughly arranged, the trumpet, two alto saxes and a tenor yielding a pastel sound like that of John Kirby's small group, then at the height of its success. Cole Porter's 'Let's Do It' is thoroughly recomposed; one wonders what Porter thought of it. It's an easy, informal outing on its own terms, with solos from Heywood and Lester. Hoagy Carmichael's 'Georgia on My Mind' gets a laid-back, yearning Holiday treatment, though one doubts that she wanted to spend much time in that state, then one of the most viciously segregated; the arrangement has an ill-judged big finish, with two loud chords. 'All of Me' is a marvellously successful version of the torch song by Seymour Simons and Gerald Marks that had three hit recordings in 1932, including Louis Armstrong's; as usual with Lady, she is torchy without yielding integrity.

'Romance in the Dark', also known as 'In the Dark', had been a hit at the end of 1940 by Lil Green, who wrote it. Green was a cabaret artist who wrote other songs, but she died of bronchial pneumonia at the age of thirty-four, and modern record labels credit 'Costow–Niesen' with writing 'Romance in the Dark', whoever they were. Lady's version of it is bouncy fun.

The American Society of Composers, Authors and Publishers had struck the broadcasters at the end of 1940, demanding an unrealistic royalty rate for ASCAP songs played on the radio: the strike backfired horribly, Broadcast Music Inc. (BMI) was formed and ASCAP settled for less than it had been getting before the strike. Meanwhile, bandleaders and songwriters were not fools; during the strike they registered their work with BMI if they could, so that it was played on the radio: Charlie Barnet's 'Redskin Rhumba' was merely a sequel to his big hit with Billy May's arrangement of Ray Noble's 'Cherokee', but it was a BMI tune and a hit during the strike. Arthur Herzog had the same idea.

In those days the only things that got on the air were things like 'Jeanie with the Light Brown Hair', things in the public domain. I figured, if I don't belong to ASCAP maybe I can get a song on radio. One night I met Holiday when she was off from work and Danny came up, and I said to Billie, this is the idea that I've got, and I want you to give me an old-fashioned Southern expression that we can turn into a song, like 'Water Boy'. She scratched her head and came up with nothing . .

We turned to conversation about her mother, Sadie, and about how she was opening up an after-hours illicit joint, and wanted money from Billie, and how Billie didn't want to give it to her, didn't have it, and in a moment of exasperation she said, 'God bless the child.' And I said, 'Billie, what does that mean?' She said, 'You know. That's what we used to say – your mother's got money, your father's got money, your sister's got money, your cousin's got money, but if you haven't got it yourself, God bless the child that's got his own.' And I said, 'This is it, Billie.' And the song took twenty minutes to do as it stands today. Danny took it down – we made one change: Billie said, 'I want to do it this way,' and we changed one note a half a tone. I wrote the words and the music and Danny took it down, and we took it down the next day to a publisher, and the publisher snapped it up because Billie had the authority to record it. I said, 'Billie, I'll give you half the song if you make the record.' She uttered the words and I picked it up. She has never written a line of words or music.

This version of the story is different from the one in Lady's book, where she said that she wanted money from her mother, rather than the other way round; not only is her book hopelessly unreliable, but when William Dufty was writing it for her, ten years after Sadie's death, her usual lack of concern about details was made worse by guilt. At any rate, 'God Bless the Child' was almost her last hit record (she never had a hit in the *Billboard* retail chart). 'God Bless the Child' was recorded at the second date with Eddie Heywood, on 9 May 1941, and reckoned to be a hit in October. It was a very similar session to the last one, with Eldridge on trumpet and three reeds (no Lester). All four tracks were slow ones, but not too slow; 'God Bless the Child' is philosophical rather than torchy, immediately and uniquely appealing. 'I'm in a Low Down Groove' remains an obscure tune, but a nice torchy one, with a fine muted solo from Eldridge. Lady's version of Duke Ellington's 'Solitude' is lovely: she changes a few notes, but Duke couldn't have minded; the song's beauty is intact. 'Am I Blue?', by Grant Clarke and Harry Akst, had six hit versions in 1929, including those of Libby Holman, Annette Hanshaw and Ethel Waters, who introduced it in a film. It's a great song and a great record; Grachan Moncur is back on bass, and has improved: he is particularly fine on 'Am I Blue?', his accents adding to Lady's laid-back angst.

On 7 August Teddy Wilson was back on piano, but the musically successful formula continued, with identical instrumentation, Emmett Berry providing the muted trumpet commentary, John Williams on bass providing an accurate undercurrent of just a touch of anxiety. 'I Cover the Waterfront', by Edward Heyman and Johnny Green, began in 1933 as a promotional song for a film of a novel of the same name; unusually, Lady sings the introduction, and the song remained associated with her.

'Love Me or Leave Me' is by Gus Kahn and Walter Donaldson, made famous by Ruth Etting in 1929; Lady sings the introduction here too, and when she gets to the familiar melody, her recomposition is simple but classic: in the first two lines of the song as written – 'Love me or leave me, and let me be lonely/you won't believe me, I love you only' – there is a drop of an octave between 'or' and 'leave', and an identical drop between the two syllables of 'believe'. In the first line Lady ignores the drop in pitch, but lets us have it on 'believe', and it is the more effective because we're waiting for it. But of course, the reason we're waiting for it is that we're familiar with the tune: part of the mystery of the artist's interpretation is that the reason it is done is not necessarily what we hear.

'Gloomy Sunday' was a Hungarian torch song by Rezso Seress, with English words by Sam Lewis; it was first sung in the USA by Paul Robeson and was promoted as 'the Hungarian suicide song', banned by some radio stations (the composer took his own life in 1968). It has a distinctive Continental melody and an even more effective bridge, and remained one of Lady's best-known numbers. 'Jim' was a pop song which had two hit versions in 1941; one of its co-authors was said to be James C. Petrillo, a hack pianist and bandleader from Chicago who had risen to become president of the American Federation of Musicians.

On 10 February 1942 the same group backed Lady on 'Mandy Is Two', a sweet song written by Johnny Mercer for his daughter; the music is by Fulton ('Fiji') McGrath. Lady loved children, and the song brought out her tenderness, which never became sentimentality. Billy Mayhew's 'It's a Sin to Tell a Lie' and 'Until the Real Thing Comes Along' had both been hits for Fats Waller in 1936; the latter had been written by Mann Holiner and Alberta Nichols in 1931, but became a hit after being reworked by Sammy Cahn and Saul Chaplin. Lady does a fine job on both, slightly uptempo on the first and on the second torchier, employing her terminal vibrato to excellent effect. 'Wherever You Are' from this session remains obscure.

And having started recording for Columbia in late 1933, and continuing with ARC from July 1935, after less than nine years her relationship with what had once again become Columbia had come to an end. After a shaky start with recording sessions immediately before and after 'Strange Fruit', Columbia had made two dozen fine Holiday sides, placing her at the centre of classic pop records backed by good studio bands with decent arrangements; her voice and her style were fully mature, while she still sounded young and confident. But fate put an end to the momentum of this period; Petrillo ordered his American Federation of Musicians to go on strike, and recording stopped on 1 August 1942.

The first AFM recording ban was opposed by many members and was a disaster for the music business, because the big-name singers, such as Sinatra, Crosby and many others, not being allowed to belong to the union, continued recording and had hit records with *a cappella* backing, and another nail was driven into the coffin of the Swing Era. The bandleaders and their sidemen never recovered the income they lost during the strike, and a lot of records were never made during a critical time in the evolution of popular music. Except for one more side for Capitol (as 'Lady

Day'), Billie did not enter the studio again for over two years; and her marriage wasn't doing so well, either.

Before the marriage had a chance, there was more trouble with Sadie. Lady told Irene Wilson that she thought a lot of things would have been different if Clarence had 'done right' by Sadie; she knew that her mother had been 'just a child' when she was born, but this understanding didn't help much twenty-five years later. 'Her mother was a staunch Catholic,' said Irene,

and Lady being the only child and they always being together – and Sadie wanted Lady to do things that was right. I remember one night we were riding around the Village and she was sayin', 'Mama so and so and so, and Mama so and so.' And I said, 'But Lady, this is how it is, so and so.' 'Aw Renie,' she said, 'you make me sick too, because you're just like Mom.' Sadie was just a mother. The hours Lady would come in. 'Lady, you shouldn't drink so much.' 'Oh, Mom.' She objected to her and Freddie because he was married and she didn't want her to waste her life on him. Lady would slam the door and say, 'Aw, Mom.' They would fuss like two sisters.

Sadie and Irene were happy when Lady was engaged to Sonny White: 'We thought they were going to make it, you know.' She thought Monroe had helped to break it up: 'Lady went for that flashy kind. She was kiddish, childish ...' During this period, Irene continues,

When I was breaking things up to go to Cleveland, I stayed with Billie and her mother .. Sadie told me, 'Renie, I'm worried about Billie.' Because she hated Monroe, her mother did. She didn't think he was any good. But he was a nice lookin' fella, sharp. So Lady would come in in the morning – see, it was he who hooked her good – she would come in and put something in her coffee – hashish, that's what they get out of hop once it's been smoked – they dig it out. Well, this stuff he was giving her, and she was putting it in her coffee. And then one morning Sadie said, 'She's strange. She comes here after he kicks her out, and I know she has got to work and he must not be right, he don't want to come up here, he don't want to face me.' I told Lady, 'What you put in that coffee?

What you puttin' in there?' And she said, 'Aw, Renie, this is just somethin'. Don't pay it no mind.' So I said, 'No, what is it?' 'Aw, it's not gonna hurt you.' Next thing I know, Lady's in the bathroom just as sick as a dog. It made you sick when you started. She wasn't mainlining yet, no, no; she was just using this hop in her coffee. Next thing I knew he had her smokin' hop. And the next thing I knew he had her using coke . . .

Lady was not a stranger to cocaine, and whatever she was putting in her coffee was not hashish. If only she had stuck to hash, which is only a form of marijuana. But in any case opium, while addictive, is not as addictive as heroin, and nothing smoked is as addictive as mainlining (injecting directly into the bloodstream). Lady's book also says that she began smoking with Monroe in an attempt to save her marriage, which was rocky from the start. 'And it was during this time that I got hooked.'

But one had no more to do with the other, really, and Jimmy was no more the cause of my doing what I did than my mother was. That goes for any man I ever knew. I was as strong, if not stronger, than any of them. And when it's that way, you can't blame anybody but yourself.

The book says that Monroe had been sick at her mother's flat on 99th Street, and a violent scene followed that led to Monroe and Lady getting a place of their own. Apparently opium can make you nauseous, and it also makes your throat sore, hardly good news for a singer. Lady had always been fond of alcohol, and it may be now that she began using it to loosen her throat; soon she had the habit of priming herself with liquor at a recording session. In any case, an ability to handle opium may have led her to believe that she could keep anything under control, but she had embarked on a slippery slope.

Her book indicated that she and Monroe lived with Sadie for a while, but the chronology of their movements will never be clear. After their marriage, at the end of a six-week engagement at the Famous Door, they left for Chicago, where Lady appeared with Lionel Hampton's newly formed big band at the Hotel Sherman. Then she went to California, where trombonist turned comedian Jerry Colonna had invested in a club which called itself Café

Society and claimed to be the West Coast version of Josephson's concept (Josephson objected to Colonna's use of the name). Lady knew Colonna from New York, and she loved the ambience of the movie colony: John Chilton says that at some point Ginger Rogers was reported as saying that she wished her mouth was shaped like Lady's, and this meant as much to her childlike nature as any amount of praise for her singing. At any rate, the trip to Tinseltown was not successful: the club opened on 1 October 1941 and lasted only a few weeks. Lady and her husband were broke, and she went back East alone while Monroe stayed on the West Coast.

The marriage was soon effectively over, but not before Lady got a song out of it. Her book says that Monroe had brought a 'big beautiful Cockney chick' back from England with him, that he had taught her to sing and was managing her and was still involved with her during their marriage, and that this girl had called Sadie and tried to convince her that Monroe would never marry Lady. Irene said that Sadie complained about calls from Nina Mae McKinney, who was neither Cockney nor English.

> This girl – it was pitiful – Nina Mae – called Sadie and told her that [Monroe] told her that if she tried to give him any trouble about Lady Day – 'cause he was trying to make Lady then – he was going to see that she was deported.

Nina Mae was an American, and there was no way Monroe could have got her 'deported' back to England, but by all accounts Nina Mae was not too bright. (Ruby Helena described her as 'temperamental'.) In any case, whoever he fooled around with, he came home one night with lipstick on his collar; he began to defend himself, but Lady wasn't having any. According to her book,

> Lying to me was worse than anything he could have done with any bitch. I cut him off, just like that. 'Take a bath, man,' I said, 'don't explain.'

Maybe it gestated for a while; given the inexactitude of her book, it may have been one of her other men who inspired it. 'Don't Explain' was not recorded until 1945. It was published the, next year (with words by Herzog and music by Lady, according to the reference books), and it became one of her best-known tunes.

Meanwhile, in 1942 she appeared at the Club Congo in Detroit, then at the Boogie Woogie, a new racially integrated club in

Cleveland. The Cleveland engagement was cut short because business was poor, and as Chilton points out, the fact that she could not yet afford to hire a permanent accompanist indicates that outside New York she was not yet a big draw. But in May 1942 she made another trip to Hollywood, to appear at Billy Berg's Trouville Club, with a septet that was co-led by Lester and Lee Young. Lester had left Basie at the end of 1941, allegedly unwilling to turn up for a recording date on the 13th of the month; a second tenor sax was played by Hubert 'Bumps' Myers, and Red Callender was on bass. This was a happier engagement and lasted for two months.

Lady's ghost-writer tells several stories about her encounters with movie stars such as Clark Gable; whether or not they are true we shall never know. Certainly the film world included Holiday fans; she met Orson Welles, who planned to make a movie about jazz that never happened. She also met a young college student named Norman Granz: Callender says in his autobiography (*Unfinished Dream*, with Elaine Cohen, 1985) that Granz worked during the day as a film cutter at MGM and was organizing Sunday afternoon jam sessions, just as Milt Gabler had done in New York.

It was during the Trouville engagement that Lady met pianist Jimmy Rowles, who became a life-long friend. For that previously mentioned rehearsal tape from the mid-fifties, Rowles says that Artie Shapiro had switched on the tape deck without telling anyone; with Rowles listening, she recalled that she had been suspicious of Rowles at first because he was white, 'and Lester says, "I don't know . . . this cat can blow".'

Again, we shall never get the details straight. Chilton says that the trumpet player during the Trouville engagement was a Red Mack; Red Callender writes that Berg's business was so good at the Capri that he opened a bigger place; Rowles's version goes like this:

We were in the other club before Lady Day showed up and it was a different kind of band. That's the first time I met Billy Berg – he calls me to say they're going to do a combination of Lady Day and Lester Young. Lester Young! Shit. So I go out there and I'm writing music and carrying on and we're a group of Lee and Prez and me and Bumps and a trumpet player named Jake Porter. Paul Campbell didn't show up until later. Now something happens; Berg's lost his liquor licence. Boom, we come to work, juke box. We're through, nothing. 'Okay, fellas, anything comes through, I'll call you.' We're all washed up. Started looking for a gig. Phone rings, boom: he bought another club, the Trouville.

The arrangers included Rowles, Dudley Brooks and Gerald Wilson, according to Lee Young. Lee said that Paul Campbell was the trumpeter and Louis Gonzalez played guitar. They played half an hour at a time; the gimmick to make them different from other groups was that they all memorized the music and played standing, except Lee at the drums and Rowles at the piano. Rowles said they broadcast every night at eleven, and airchecks of 'I Hear Music' and 'Solitude' with Lady are rumoured to exist.

In 1945, when Berg brought Dizzy Gillespie and Charlie Parker to the West Coast, that historic gig was not a success, partly because all the patrons got was music; they wanted jokes and variety as well. A few years earlier the emphasis was still on entertainment: while Rowles was at the Trouville, he says, the bill included at various times Slim & Slam, the Spirits of Rhythm and Joe Turner:

> I couldn't wait for Billie to get here. Couldn't believe she was coming out. The only reason she was coming out was because Lester Young was here. Used to rehearse every morning, came to every rehearsal. She and Prez were brother and sister; she was going with Bumps Myers . . . Bumps and Billie lived together. A nice cat, sweet guy. Never got mad. They got along well together; he handled her very nicely.

Talking about her men in general, Rowles said, 'I knew Jimmy Monroe. I have nothing to say about him. Maybe I was a little disappointed . . . He was slick, Monroe, is what he was. Slick.' But compared to the others, 'Monroe wasn't too bad. I'm glad I wasn't around for when the shit hit the fan,' perhaps a reference to her even more disastrous later relationships. Leo Watson sang with the Spirits of Rhythm; he had been a hit on 52nd Street as an unusual and inventive scat singer, but without enough discipline to make himself a lasting career. Rowles describes a party in Lady's room:

And she had her records on, and Monroe had showed up. (Bumps was on his way out.) And she was dancing around, sne was fairly happy. Monroe's a sleek, pimpy cat, high collar, real conk, all that shit, greasy little motherfucker is what he really was. I don't want to put him down. Little teeny cat. Slick. Bumps was like a football player.

She's just jumpin' around, in slacks, dancin', everything's happening in this tiny room. The door opens and it's Leo Watson. Leo Watson's a wild one. Pretty soon Leo gets loud; after a couple more drinks he starts swearing. There are three or four white girls there. So she looks at Monroe and says, 'You get that son of a bitch out of here.' So he went over and tried to talk to Leo which is like trying to talk to Gargantua, and he didn't get nowhere. So she's dancing and swinging and gettin' high and all this shit, and she's picking up on what's gonna happen, that Monroe couldn't get to first base with Leo Watson. So she picked up a batch of her best records and she landed them on Leo's head and busted the whole thing – almost knocked him through the floor. Then she grabbed him, and the blood is comin' out of his head, and his hair was stickin' up and everything, and he's screamin' and he's bleedin' and she picked him up like this and she said, 'Open the door.' And they threw open the door, and she threw him clear across the hall, and he hit the wall, boom, and he went down and out, and she slammed the door and came back and put another record on.

And for three weeks that guy worked in the same club and you should have seen him come to work every night and stick his head through the door and say, 'Where is Lady Day?' He was hiding from her all the time. He was a powerful little cat, like a gorilla, strong. But he was scared to death of her, petrified. Monroe couldn't handle that one, so she did. This was when we were at the Trouville.

On 12 June Lady made a record for the brand-new Capitol label, where a Paul Whiteman recording session, with arranger Jimmy Mundy, included vocals by Johnny Mercer, Jack Teagarden and Lady (billed on her record as 'Lady Day' to evade her Columbia contract); Whiteman is said to have asked for her specifically. The band was a full-sized one, including unnecessary strings; the tune was 'Trav'lin' Light', which may have been spelled that way because there already was a song 'Travelin' Light', from 1937. The new tune had been written by trombonist Trummy Young while he was with the Earl Hines band, but hadn't been copyrighted; the words were by Mercer, who was one of the founders of Capitol. At first Young didn't get a credit, but Mercer, who was from Young's home town of Savannah, put his name on it.

Lady said in her book that she happened to be on the West Coast, chumming with Trummy, and that they got $75 each for the record; she thought it happened in 1944: one wonders again why nobody checked such elementary facts. It's a nice record, her last before the musicians went on strike, but of little consequence in her output. Rowles says she came back from the date raving about lead trombonist Skip Layton, who plays a nice solo on the record. Trummy corroborated Lady's book, saying that they had got $75 each for the Capitol record date, and that when they had celebrated they were broke: Sadie had to wire them money for a bus ride all the way back to New York. Young said, 'Can you imagine riding a bus for 3,000 miles?'

Singer and dancer Marie Bryant followed Lady at the Trouville, *down beat* reported; Bryant had appeared in Duke Ellington's revue *Jump for Joy* in Los Angeles the year before, playing Katharine Hepburn in a skit called 'Garbo and Hepburn'. Marie was a popular entertainer, particularly well known as a singer for two tunes: 'My Man' in Lady's style and 'On the Sunny Side of the Street' *à la* Louis Armstrong. In 1944 she sang the latter in the famous short film by Gjon Mili, *Jammin' the Blues* with Lester Young.

Lady had performed on the West Coast before, said Marie, in 1935 or 1936; she played all the places on Central Avenue in Los Angeles – these were the days when a viable black community had a ghetto which at least functioned, before it was destroyed by local politics and commerce – and she appeared at the Lincoln Theater. She and Marie became life-long friends. Marie's memory may have been playing tricks in the early seventies; the 1941 visit to California is thought to have been her first. Marie said she introduced Lady to Norman Granz. They were friends to the point that Lady would listen to Marie's advice. She didn't necessarily take it – 'she went her own way' – but she would listen and weigh it up. To begin with, Marie thought, Lady had got her attitude towards men from her mother.

Marie was talking about managers taking advantage of their clients, and gave Pearl Bailey credit for the fact that the law had been changed so that people could not be got under contract for longer than three years, because of the way entertainers had been cheated; and went on to say that whether it was Joe Glaser, Norman Granz or her boyfriends and husbands, Lady was 'looking for the father image. I don't think you can be that simple about it, but that's what's mixed up with it.'

She watched her mother going through this or that, but her mother loved Billie's father. No matter what happened, 'How dare you, this is my man.' And she's following her mother, who got one guy that – you know – Fanny Bryce, Helen Morgan, Billie Holiday. To the day of her death, Billie was the most loyal person I knew. I mean in the face of whatever happened. And this is the way her mother was. I didn't know Sadie, but I knew her from what Billie told me. When you got one guy in your corner, then you've got the whole world. Clarence wasn't in Sadie's corner, but she thought he was. He could always tell her a story about why he was doing this and why he was doing that, and she wanted to believe it, so it's the easiest thing to believe. And Billie was that type of person.

Marie knew most of Lady's men and she had some sympathy for Jimmy Monroe. He'd lived up to his classy image, she thought, in that he taught Lady things about how to dress and comport herself; and he'd certainly started out as a pimp.

She knew what to expect . . . but I still think Jimmy was the best one for her. She knew he had other other women which of course hurt, but his number one thing in life was Billie. Originally it was for what he could get. He was going to do what a pimp does, and this is going to be his dame, and so she sings a little bit and so I'll use her, you know, and do the whole thing. But I think pretty soon her vulnerability began to get to him, and he was sincere.

I didn't think of Jimmy as weak at all, except where Billie was concerned, because I think Billie took the balls out of him as a pimp. A pimp isn't supposed to be soft – it's against his very success in his business to be soft on anybody . . . I don't think she loved anybody – but almost loved Jimmy. Because at the time she met Jimmy, he was older than she was, he was beautiful to look at, he had just been to Paris, he was the complete man.

The word 'pimp' will often be heard in the context of Lady's men, but it seems to refer to a man who lives off a woman's earnings, as though it were unnatural for a woman to earn more money than a man. Louis Armstrong said that King Oliver had advised him to find a white man who would put his hand on Louis's shoulder and say, 'This is my nigger.' Joe Glaser played that role for Armstrong; the more specific problem of a black female artist was that she needed a boyfriend or a husband who was capable of earning his keep by serving as a road manager, helping to make her life easier. But as Lady became better known and toured first the USA and then Europe, she also needed a man who could negotiate with the white world, and in the 1940s that was still very difficult for a black man, while Lady's dysfunctional relationships with men made it virtually impossible.

Monroe was doomed before he began. No doubt he realized how talented and special she was, but his role had changed and he couldn't deal with it: she had disarmed him, perhaps without meaning to, but in the end he did not have whatever she needed. 'Billie Holiday stood apart,' Marie went on:

She may have had fifty million men – she never had one man, if you know what I'm saying. You talk about the vestal virgin; Billie was the vestal virgin, with fifty million scars. Her doosey might have been just as wide as, you know, but Billie Holiday until the day she died was completely intact. She never found that key that would have opened her – I just don't think she ever loved anybody, or knew what love was. She just suffered. She got to love suffering because she didn't know what love was. She thought she had it several times but it just wasn't there, and without knowing that you can never be a complete person.

This woman was only feelings. Billie was only quivering nerves, quivering emotions. That's why she couldn't make it in this world, she could never make it. She was just too gentle, too honest, too emotional – you know there wasn't a conniving bone in her body. She was shrewd, but like an urchin is shrewd who's going up on the street and has to get some food, etcetera, do the whole thing. But inside you're vulnerable. It's a role you assume . . . There are certain people who cannot take it. She couldn't take it. Marilyn Monroe couldn't take it – Joe Guy, John Simmons, Bumps Myers, Lester – my God, Lester; how Billie and I loved Lester . . . But he couldn't make it; he couldn't understand these people . . . They couldn't play the game, couldn't make it on the terms of the world. They were pure: they were the real people, and the rest of the world were not. I think they were unconscious of it. All they wanted to do was their thing, and God had given them this pure way of expressing themselves, but they'd be appalled, if they were here now [in 1971], by the crassness. They did everything to get out of the crassness. Today they'd be gone even faster.

If a pattern emerges through Marie's grief at the memory of her lost friends, she alludes to part of the puzzle when she mentions the informal nationwide phenomenon of the vipers' club.

You didn't drink liquor or do anything else at all. But whenever you went to different cities, soon enough a guy would knock on your hotel door with a phonograph and Louis's and Billie's records, and other records he thought you'd like, and a little thing of pot; and then if you'd like to buy some more pot from him, it was fine; if not, you were just as welcome to this. And this happened all over the country, a society of people who just loved Billie, loved Pops. Anywhere in this country. This was before it became a federal offence. We were against liquor – nix on the lush-heads. And Louis was the king, and Billie was the queen. You didn't know these people before, who knocked on your door, but you could count on them. They knew you, who was where, who dug Pops, who dug Billie, and it was just really beautiful. And they collected the records and phonograph back when you left town. You could buy pot from them, or they would let you know the other people in town who had good pot. But that first bit was given to you gratis. I could be in Detroit – I don't know about Iowa or places like that – I'm talking about any decent city – Chicago, Detroit, L.A., New Orleans. It was connected with being in show business; practically nobody smoked pot except people that were in show business, or Mexicans or Indians. It was like a nickel a stick. And it was a rule: you never put anybody else on. If somebody had made up their minds to smoke, they were welcome, but nobody turned anybody else on.

Having recently abandoned one sort of prohibition, in 1937 America enacted another, this time without an amendment to the Constitution. By that time, under the urging of puritan bureaucrats, thirty-six of the forty-eight states had adopted anti-marijuana laws, many of them adding it to their list of narcotics, although marijuana is not a narcotic. Harry J. Anslinger had been appointed in 1930 to the newly created post of Commissioner of Narcotic Drugs, and his campaign against marijuana had been so successful that it was reasoned that if the stuff was so dangerous there ought to be a federal law against it, especially at a time when federal agencies were having their budgets cut. Thus Anslinger's agency had its budget restored, and middle America made criminals out of entertainers using a recreational drug that is probably the least dangerous of all.

California had been one of the first to enact an anti-marijuana law, in 1915, probably in a subliminally racist attempt to keep its Spanish-speaking population under control, and Louis Armstrong had already been arrested there, in a parking lot in 1931. When it became a federal offence, Marie went on,

For protection, we started drinking, 'cause before, if you were smoking pot you weren't drinking. Even Pops let it be put out that he didn't smoke pot any more, I let it be put out, because it was federal, and we were the first people who were going to be picked on. I had an FBI man come here and said that he knew I was smokin' and in with Louis and Billie, and that he knew I wasn't selling it or nothing, but he advised me to cool it. During that time – about 1945 or so – I was doing a number in a Hollywood club called Cigarettes and Cigars, so I would go out into the audience and sell cigarettes, to make it dramatic, and under the cigarettes I had pot, and

I'm selling it to John Garfield, and Errol Flynn, to everybody.
Then it had gone up to a dollar.

The reason the price of a marijuana cigarette had gone up from
five cents to a dollar was that it was illegal. This could be called a
value-added tax, since the people who were selling it were now
taking a risk, and soon some of them were willing to take a bigger
risk selling worse stuff for more profit. It cannot be entirely a
coincidence that the heroin plague hit during the 1940s, only a few
years after smoking marijuana became a federal offence.

Although Lady seems to have gone back to New York after the
engagement at the Trouville, she spent much of the rest of 1942 in
Chicago. The three months starting in mid-August at Joe Sherman's Garrick Showbar, on a bill with a sextet led by Red Allen,
were a success, and they were followed by a week at the Regal
Theater. During this period she was arrested and briefly incarcer-
ated when a car she was riding in collided with an ambulance.
Nobody was seriously hurt, but Lady is said to have had cuts on
her knees, and her instinctive reaction to trouble was to leave the
scene: she was arrested even though she hadn't been driving at all,
but the charges were dropped.

In January 1943 she began an engagement at Kelly's Stable,
leaving after two months on a train to Los Angeles, perhaps in an
unsuccessful attempt at a reconciliation with Monroe. (Maybe this
was when the party Rowles described took place; he said it was a
birthday party, which would make it April.) She came back to
New York and went to work at the Onyx; at the end of the
following year Monroe was sentenced to nine months in jail for
smuggling marijuana from Mexico to California.

Lady made more trips to the West Coast, and indeed toured the
USA and Europe in the following decade, and made more money.
But she could never hang onto money anyway, and it was in the
1940s that her reputation was made as one of the biggest stars of
52nd Street, along with Art Tatum, Nat Cole and Coleman
Hawkins. These must have been among the happiest years of her
life; she was surrounded by people who loved her and working
with musicians who were her equals and whom she loved. She also
did as she pleased, and for some time got away with it.

For all her bad habits, she was an aristocrat. Her act began to follow a ritual: when she finally emerged from her dressing room, she would take her time getting to the stage, stopping and greeting people and even having drinks at the bar while her accompanists vamped. Something might happen to change her mood on the way, so that she might cut a set short or she might sing several encores. Josephson's stage-managing of 'Strange Fruit' had had its effect: she liked working with a single spotlight on her, because not being able to see the audience kept down her stage fright. On stage she was almost motionless, her face and her hair providing more elegance than other entertainers could get up with the most expensive gowns and hairdressers; it all worked to command the rapt attention of her audiences.

One of Lady's fans was Harold Cromer, 'Big Stump', of the black comedy team Stump & Stumpy (the other guy was James Cross, 'Little Stump'). Big Stump described her on the Street:

Lady became an ulterior thing, a real thing. A potentatress. This is a face that dressed itself. Lady Day was handsome. And all of a sudden she would come out and be this other glamorous thing . . . but Lady was always part of the band – she was a *band* singer that spread her thing around; she had little dribbles that she'd give to each musician – here you are, here you are, here's part of it, now come on sing with me. And it was so pretty and so beautiful, like it would send out sparks.

Going off – she'd nod just to the side to the right, just a nod and a pretty smile – she walked off regal – Rosalind Russell stole Lady Day's walk – that tall regal sweep thing. Oh, she didn't do it fast, because she'd be in tempo with the music, always.

Sylvia Syms also had her memories. She began hanging around the Street when she was little more than a child, unafraid of the night life: 'Who wanted to make passes at a fat Jewish girl from Brooklyn?' She wore her hair in braids and parted in the middle; Art Tatum called her Moonbeam Moscowitz, the Jewish Indian. She told Whitney Balliett:

Billie Holiday became my mentor, and I copied everything she did, excluding the drugs and the booze. She said to me once, 'You know what's wrong with you, Sugar? You love me.' She was a beautiful, dignified lady with an innate sense of good taste. She was drawn to singing songs you knew she understood. She had a kind of animal relativity to the songs she sang . . .

Once I saved twenty-five dollars and bought her a print gown for her birthday, and she was so pleased you'd have thought I'd given her the moon on a stick. I can remember her in the gown at the Onyx Club, coming down those little stairs in the back and the lights softening and the room becoming silent and her moving onto the stage and looking just like a panther. She began wearing gardenias in her hair because of me. One night when she was working at Kelly's Stable, she burned her hair with a curling iron just before show time, and I ran down the street to the Three Deuces, where Ada Kurtz had the checkroom. Checkroom girls sold flowers then, and I bought a gardenia and Billie put it in her hair to hide the burned place.

This is a famous story, and may be true in its details (the need to cover up the burned hair), but Jean Bach, attending a dance at the University of Virginia, saw Lady singing with Basie and says that she was wearing flowers in her hair in 1937, years before Syms appeared on the scene. A music business insider all her life, Bach also says that Syms named Mildred Bailey as her mentor until Mildred's star began to wane, but that's showbiz.

Jimmy Rowles, full of love for Lady and not the sort of fellow to grind axes, is probably as reliable as anybody:

When I first met that girl, she was one of the most beautiful women I had ever seen. She was big, but she didn't seem big. She was just strong, you know Her skin was like satin, like the tune 'Satin Doll'. Her skin was flawless. And she was very graceful. Watching her was like watching a dream walk through the room, even if she was jumping around with slacks on. After hours she'd say, 'I want to change my clothes,' and she'd put the record machine on and start dancing around snapping her fingers. She was just adorable. Every night I saw her body — every inch of her — and I was only a kid, twenty years old. And she'd call me in there — 'I want the chords to this tune, I want to sing that tune' — and I'd write out the chords ... when I worked with her in 1942, she had her hair dyed red, and she had this dyed red [pubic hair], and she'd stand there with just a pair of shoes on, and I loved her all the more because she was so gorgeous, so beautiful.

So now this is a long time later [recording for Norman Granz in about 1956]. She's still coy. She's in there trying to get dressed, and she's got this corset she's trying to get on, and she calls me in to tie her up while she's holding herself together, and she says to me, 'Don't *peeeek!*' And she's loaded, and I'm laughing ...

Lady Day was like one of the cats. She had no complexes, no personality problems. She was open from the beginning. She was always the same. But Sarah [was] not always the same, very moody, shy, introspective, and a lot of things, plus being beautiful. And she's constantly different. Lady Day's very outspoken, like she'd say, 'That bitch! I'll fix her ass; who she think *she* is?' And Sass over there might be thinkin', 'Ain't she *great?*' But if Lady Day ever got to know her they'd be thick as thieves. Carmen is more like Lady Day; Sarah and Carmen are very close ... Lady Day was always involved with the cats and always up on this level.

Stump describes the first time he met her:

In 1936 I had just come to New York, and it was my good fortune to run into this cab with this lady standing up through the top. The cabs in those days had this slide-open roof. I'm late getting to the Cotton Club, and this cab was standing in front of the Alhambra Grill, 126th and 7th, and I get in this cab and this lady's standing there happily smoking a cigarette – and at that time there was no cigarette I knew of could make you *that* happy – and I said, 'I'm late, man; I've got to get to the Cotton Club, the show is in seven minutes.' So he says, 'All right, Lady; can I take him?' And she says, 'Yeah, take him – take him, baby.' And Billy Wood was the cab driver's name. He said, 'Come on, Stump. This is Stump from Stump and Stumpy, Lady; Stump, this is Lady Day – Billie Holiday.' And she looked down and grinned at me the prettiest smile – oh, the smile melts ya – ya gotta go when the smile comes – and she says, 'Stump Daddy,' and that was my name to her from then on.

Stump's memories tumble out of him, drenched in love; but he is also a name-dropper, and we can't always be sure that he isn't getting the memories mixed up. Nevertheless the feelings are warm. Lady was in California in October 1941, Ellington's revue had opened in July, and Stump says it was the '*Jump for Joy* era'; he was working on *Ship Ahoy*, an MGM musical completed in early 1942. His impressionism is valuable.

Such nobles such as Orson Welles would come in every night and kneel on one knee – well, this was the Duke. The Bogarts, they would be there, every night. Orson Welles was our air raid warden, on the street. Lena Horne lived on the top, Lady and I lived on the bottom, and Humphrey Bogart lived on one side and Orson Welles lived on the other side. A block in Hollywood, just up the Strip. Bobby Short used to play on the corner. Humphrey Bogart was our boy, our thing . . . Lady had some respect for Lena Horne, and Lena Horne dug her, they had a thing going, not a personal thing, but vocally. And they became good friends, and we all lived in the Clarke Annex Hotel, and Lena was getting introduced to pictures . . . We used to have a love thing that we all had then that doesn't happen now.

Young Lena Horne had sung 'Fine and Mellow' at Carnegie Hall in 1941 and heard that Lady was upset about it, so she did exactly the right thing: she called at the Stable and asked Lady's permission. Lady may have recalled getting in trouble a few years earlier for singing one of Ethel Waters' songs; Waters' subsequent opinion of the young Billie Holiday was reportedly that her voice 'sounded like her feet hurt'. Now Lady had an acolyte of her own, and she proved to be a better judge than Waters. 'That gal really knows her business,' Lady would say, and Lena's admiration became mutual.

Tallulah Bankhead was a nationally famous personality; born in Alabama in a prominent family (her father was a Congressman), as an actress she was the talk of London's West End in the 1920s, and her role in Lillian Hellman's *The Little Foxes* in 1939 has been described as 'one of the great performances of the American theatre'. (But her films were usually flops.) Even more than Lady, both her rages and her wit could be spectacular; and like Lady she was startlingly honest. According to one story, Louis B. Mayer at MGM asked her about her lesbianism; instead of denying it or changing the subject, she said 'You mean like so-and-so?' naming one of the studio's biggest stars.

Tallulah was a fan of Lady's, and Stump says he saw them together:

> Tallu and Lady were like sisters. Lady called her Lula. She'd say, 'Here come Lula, Stump Daddy.' Because you could hear this thundering thing down the stoop − 'LADY!' 'Here she comes, here comes that lady again.' 'STUMP DAHLING WILL YOU PLEASE ANNOUNCE ME?' I say, 'Miss Day, here comes Tallu.' 'Lula, come here,' with her little cute voice. She sang as she talked, Lady. Her voice was always a melody. Her favourite tune was Claude Thornhill's 'Snowfall', it was so pretty and we used to play it all the time, except for Lester Young, who loved Lady like he loved spring summer winter fall and every day that broke at dawn. It wasn't a love thing − she inspired his playing or something . . .
>
> She inspired anybody when she was around, because Lady had a knack with a lyric. She'd look at the music sheet, put it down, walk away, have a blast and come back to sing the tune. Between where she went to that drink and who brought her those lyrics I don't know; there must have been a lyric angel that came down from the clouds and said, 'Here they are, Lady, you got 'em,' cause she'd come back in about three minutes and sing the whole thing down . . . To Lady, to sing was a wonderful time: playing records in her room and having friends around − that was a wonderful time . . . I don't think Lady ever found a musician that she didn't love . . . she always found something in them she loved. No great knowledge on paper of music or reading things or reading musical notes. She just knew it. From somewhere it came . . .
>
> They'd be in the middle of Harlem or somewhere, and somebody'd say it: 'Mabel Mercer time.' And they'd go straight to hear Mabel, on the East Side, or 52nd Street at Spivey's Reef. And Mabel sang the written word for ever − the lyric, the melody, the whole thing. And Lady adored her.

Lady knows the verse to every song that everybody ever sings, before you get to the chorus or the melody ... And Tallu would be amazed at her knowing all the lyrics Mabel knew. And they'd throw it at one another ... Oh, Cole Porter, Jerome Kern – 'Bill', from *Show Boat*. Oh, we'd do that for Lady Day, you know, 'He's just my Bill, ladaladede,' and Tallu would say, 'She's just my Willie – Willie dahling' ... Mabel would sing all night, then Lady would sing, then Tallu would do an act of some sort with anything, with the waiter in the club, waiters cleaning up doing their thing, or the stragglers who didn't belong.

Lady would be in Kelly's or the Onyx or wherever; we'd go to the White Rose – 6th Avenue and 52nd, this is where at the break all the musicians would be, where a chair especially for Lady – no one sat in the seat – this was Lady's seat. At the bar, dead centre, where she surveys it all. She's the Lady, you know, everyone knows, the Lady. Lady Day.

Mabel Mercer became one of Lady's influences; Thelma Carpenter says she was the one who took Lady to go and hear Mabel, when Mabel was singing at Tony's, which was across the street from the Onyx. Mercer, born in England of an American father, had worked in Paris and went to the USA in 1938; her small voice was an acquired taste, but she was a great interpreter and a storehouse of good songs.

Stump also talks about his own act and segues into the other reigning monarch of jazz:

Sing a song, intro ourselves – 'How do you do, I'm Stump, I'm Stumpy' – then we go onto this thing, my partner would do his versions of Ronald Colman, James Cagney, Barry Fitzgerald, and I had two imitations – I would only do people I love – and that was Jimmy Durante and Louis Armstrong.

He was the landlord – like he owned jazz, and any room he's in, that's jazz, so he's the landlord. 'Stump Daddy, let's go see the landlord.' 'Landlord? What landlord?' 'Stump Daddy, let's go see the landlord. Let's go see Louis Armstrong.' He would make her day. Anywhere, just to hear him play, and she would interpret what he played on trumpet into her thing, and in turn he would love her rendition of whatever she did. She said Pops had more soul than any singer.

Louis Armstrong would sing it or record it first. Like 'Darn That Dream'. 'Stump Daddy, let's get it.' 'Okay, Lady, we'll get it.' So we go out, 'Pops, gotta have it, Lady wants it.' 'Okay, Jack, if Lady Day . . . take the song sheet, take the music.' They loved each other.

A lot of people, including Stump, remark on the fact that the 'gay boys', the homosexual community, were Holiday fans: it was not only her consummate artistry, but the way she escaped completely into her art, free of persecution and self-consciousness, free of everything except beauty.

Why did I love her? As I was telling you, about soul. I loved her because of the way she said 'Good mornin', Stump Daddy.' She could sit so grand; and Tallulah would always tell her, 'Sit, Lady.' She was Queen Bess. Her face, I don't know, a sculptor could tell you more than I could, because it was such a beautiful thing – pure little face, little turned-up nose, beautiful features, beautiful eyes, luscious mouth, chin and neckline was very regal; she was a Lady. Like Lady Peel, this was Lady Day. And Lester would say – he was the only one who would say, 'Miss Day, how do you do Miss Day?' To Count Basie she was William. Now this is a thing I used to love, because he was William Basie and he would call her William. At rehearsal [at the Strand Theater in 1948] she'd say, 'Bill,' he'd say, 'Yeah, William,' 'Let's run through this,' and they run through a tune and the whole band would rouse itself for Lady Day.

Lady worked at Kelly's Stable off and on for five years; the original Stable, perhaps named after a place in Chicago (nobody knew who Kelly was), had been on 51st, but it soon moved to a bigger location on 52nd. Ralph Watkins said:

For the five years that Billie Holiday worked for me, she was a doll. I never had a bit of trouble with her. When I came back from overseas, she was a changed girl. Before that, the worst thing she ever did was smoke pot. But everyone did. It wasn't a crime, as it now is . . . When I saw her after the war, she was on a very expensive habit.

By the time Watkins went into the army, she had a new boyfriend. She already knew Joe Guy from the Uptown, if not earlier.

Clark Monroe, the more substantial brother, gave a boost to the young turks of modern jazz at his Uptown House, but the other place where bop was being midwifed was Minton's Playhouse, at 210 West 118th Street. Henry Minton was a saxophonist; his club had become a hangout for the older generation, but in 1940 another saxophonist took over the room. Teddy Hill had led a successful band, employing people like Roy Eldridge, Dizzy Gillespie and Kenny Clarke; now he started jam sessions on Monday nights. He hired Clarke to put together a house band, 'even though he had fired me from his band several years before because I was beginning to play modern drums even then'.

Anyway, when Teddy took over, Minton's changed its music policy. Teddy wanted to do something for the guys who had worked with him. He turned out to be sort of a benefactor since work was very scarce at that time. Teddy never tried to tell us how to play. We played just as we felt.

The first band, around the beginning of 1941, had Joe Guy, [Thelonious] Monk, Nick Fenton [on bass] and myself . . .

Minton's was an exciting place. Only the best could keep up with Monk's exploration of harmony; given Lady's ear and her love of music, she soon became a regular visitor. Jam sessions were against union rules, because people played for nothing, but the young jammers were protected to some extent because Minton, who still owned the place, had been the first black delegate of Local 802, the New York musicians' union. Bassist Milt Hinton lived across the street; among the visitors, he said, 'kids from downtown, kids that couldn't blow, would come in and they would interrupt'.

So Diz told me on the roof one night at the Cotton Club, 'Now look, when we go down to the jam session, we're gonna say we're gonna play "I Got Rhythm", but we're gonna use these changes' . . . all these kids would be up there . . . and they couldn't get in because they didn't know what changes we were using, and eventually they would put their horns away, and we could go on and blow in peace and get our little exercise.

And so the new music developed. Joe Guy was not one of the biggest stars of it, but a good trumpeter who had played with Coleman Hawkins and Fats Waller, and in 1941 was one of the black musicians hired by Charlie Barnet, who hired whomever he liked. Guy became a heroin addict, but it would be pointless to blame Lady for his addiction, or him for hers: she had plenty of friends who had bad habits, and anyway a heroin plague was under way. John Simmons thinks that saxophonist Don Byas was the one who gave Guy the affliction. At any rate, she was already on the stuff by the beginning of 1942, according to Stump:

We started opium up in Monroe's in the back room with Dickie Wells. Cocaine. George Raft and them used to do it; happy dust it was called . . .
    I don't think opium thrilled her too much. She didn't like laying on your side and hugging this thing – there must be some echelon of highness, you know. You lay on your ear, on a pillow, and you take a drawer and you puff it and it smells like burnt pork chops and you have to cover your doors with wet towels and she dug it, she did it, but she wanted to get high *fast*. This is like a relaxed ritual, when you have nothing else to do tomorrow . . . After this, Lady and I strayed . . .
    Lady poured me on the train – out of the bottle on the train. Oh my God I didn't want to go to Fort Something Alabama, and I had never seen dee South? Oh my goodness, oh, such tears. Like when my sister told me there was no Santa Claus and I hated her for two years. I was a Philadelphia boy . . . I went in the army January 29, 1942, when I just made *Ship Ahoy*. She was on heroin . . .

Lady certainly made more money than Guy, and as her friends repeatedly pointed out, there was nothing she wouldn't do for people she loved. It was an expensive habit in more ways than one, but she had never looked after her money anyway.
    And soon there were the dogs. Irene Kitchings started that:

I had a Dane named Gypsy . . . She and Jimmy used to fight
a lot. As I said, Lady had this terrific temper. I had Gypsy
with me, and she said, 'Go on, Gypsy, get 'im!' And Gypsy
weighed 180 pounds. And Gypsy ran in there on Monroe
and pushed him up on the bed. I had to get Gypsy off him
and tell her to stop, but she just kept on saying, 'Get 'im,
Gypsy!' But I didn't see too much of them after they were
married . . .
  Lady loved Gypsy so much that when her doctor gave her
a dog she named hers Gypsy. It was just a dog, like a he-
blackish brown dog.

In Lady's book, the dog the doctor gave her was named Rajah
Ravoy, a fancy name because he was so smart. The dog was never
on a lead, but knew his way around town, and always evaded the
dog catcher (the Man might give Lady all kinds of trouble, but her
dogs never took any nonsense). Rajah ended up keeping Sadie
company, and Sadie was heartbroken when he died. This must
have been in 1944, when Lady was singing in an East Side club,
the Ruban Bleu; harpist Daphne Hellman remembered her crying
over the dog. Hellman had reason to remember the gig: according
to Chilton, the pianist on the gig reported that Lady complained
about 'a society bitch that plays harp, says she won't share a
dressing room with me'. Hellman was astonished to hear this,
saying that they were all thrilled to be working with her, but they
all became friends in the end; she remembered that Lady disliked
working on the East Side, and was nervous about opening nights.
And she was suspicious of people she didn't know, especially white
people.
  Sylvia Syms and Thelma Carpenter talked about a wire-haired
terrier that Lady got from Prez, who was called Moochie. This was
short for Bessie Mae Moocho, or 'Besame Mucho' ('Kiss me a lot'),
a Mexican song that was a big hit in 1943. They said that the dog
would sit outside the club and wag its tail like a metronome, in
time to the music.
  Soon Lady's inseparable companion was a boxer, Mister. Chilton
quotes Lena Horne: 'She was just too sensitive to survive. The
thing I remember talking to her about most were her dogs; her
animals were really her only trusted friends.' Big Stump
remembered Mister:

Mister was the best hang-out dog on earth, you know, Mister could take it, poor thing, I don't know how he did it, and in between bartenders and whatever would feed Mister. Mister would sit backstage near where he could hear Lady's voice. As long as he heard her voice, he's happy. He was a comfortable boxer, gentle boxer, he didn't believe in playing around, all he believed in was Lady, you know, not a thing with the paws. He was always high. They'd feed him while she was sitting at the bar. Or maybe Lady would leave him in the dressing room if she was coming out to the bar, which he detested. But he couldn't do anything about it and he'd wait patiently till Lady got back and he heard her footsteps . .

Lady would trip over herself because she was so stoned, till she got herself together in her dressing room. Oh no, she didn't get herself together before she got to the club.

It began to take her longer and longer to get out of her dressing room, often because she was looking for a vein; again, perhaps the dope helped her to overcome her stage fright and her lack of confidence. John Simmons says that Mister knew when she was supposed to go on, and sometimes she'd be swearing as the dog dragged her down the bar towards the stage. Hard as it may be to believe, both Stump and Simmons say separately that Mister was a junkie: that Billie and her friends used to shoot him up. 'She would hit Mister,' Simmons said, 'and Mister would get so high and he would scratch behind his ear and flop right down . . .'

John Simmons was one of the best and most reliable bassists of the Swing Era and also understood the new music: he was one of those who hung around at Minton's. He thought there was a similarity between Jimmy Monroe and Joe Guy, 'so far as being leeches, yes. Jimmy tried to be a pimp I think to prove his manhood, and Joe tried to prove he was a man through his instrument.'

Another bassist, Al Lucas, shared an apartment with Joe Guy and his brother, Lee. 'They used to wear each others' pants – when one went out, the other couldn't go out. He'd have to wait for his brother to come back. Joe Guy was a nice quiet guy, nice to be around until he got hooked. Then you couldn't trust him. He got hooked when he met her.' Whether or not this means that Lucas blamed her for Guy's drug addiction, all we know for sure is that they were both victims of the heroin plague at about the same time.

In 1945 Lady announced that she had got a Mexican divorce from Monroe and married Joe Guy, but this is not true. Her relationship with Simmons may have been as important as that with Guy: Simmons and Billie lived together for a while and got back together now and then, but Guy stuck closer to her over several years, while Simmons was a proud man, who liked to work freelance rather than in a steady job. He played on countless recording sessions, recording with Billie as late as 1955, and he was her friend and her lover, but apparently not her partner in heroin until later.

Marie Bryant thought that it might have been Simmons that got her hooked. 'John Simmons and Billie had music, sex and drugs. He always was a junky, always . . ' She says that Billie was probably impressed by his musicianship, the way she, Marie, had 'flipped' over Ray Nance's violin playing (Marie had a daughter in the early 1940s by Nance, who played trumpet and violin and sang with Duke Ellington). Then she adds,

> I'm figuring he had to be great in bed. He probably did something good for her. Anybody that does anything good for her, now you have to go out and have a few drinks with her, or you can get high, [or she'll] take you to dinner – she's got to pay you back for any marvellous thing you did for her, anything you were in her corner for.

And then Marie qualifies her earlier statement: 'Sim wasn't always a junky. When I knew him in Chicago he wasn't, around 1940. But he was a very weak, very gentle, very strange guy . . . John was standoffish.' Talking about his own life in 1972, Simmons doesn't come across as weak at all, but confirms the standoffishness:

> When I was with her I didn't want for anything, because I was working and making a good salary – not the salary that *she* was makin', but for a musician I was making top money. If I was on a record date I might get a hundred, hundred and a half, if they wanted *me* on the date. If they just wanted a bass player, they could get somebody else. And I got a lot of recordings, a hell of a lot of recordings . . . Although Billie

had used bass players on her dates, she just thought of bass players as supposed to be there, but after she met me, well, she got an interest in a bass ... I never worked a regular job with her, just record dates. I wouldn't work with her because we would conflict on things, like if she wasn't on the stand, they would come to me and tell me to get her on. So I wouldn't go for it.

I had experienced drugs early, when I was a teenager – fifteen – an older cousin introduced me to it. At that time you could just go to the drug store and get a prescription for it. He ended up going to the penitentiary . . so I went to bed for three months trying to kick it, and when I got over it I didn't have no desire for it.

Simmons was born in Oklahoma, turned pro in Los Angeles, worked in Chicago and went to New York. He played in Louis Armstrong's big band and then was 'the first Negro to be hired over at NBC on the staff – me and Eddie Barefield, sax player – and this was more or less a token during the war to show they were liberal and whatnot' John Hammond had started a music magazine, *Music and Rhythm*, and had shamed NBC into hiring a few black musicians during 1942; he wrote that when he was drafted they were all fired. Simmons was there twelve weeks, he said, and then 'went to CBS with Raymond Scott, Perry Como and Dorothy Collins, Charlie Shavers, Benny Morton, Ben Webster, Specs Powell – eighteen-piece band'. Raymond Scott was music director of CBS radio; he was not a jazzman, but apart from his radio duties, he wrote intricate charts with titles like 'Dinner Music for a Pack of Hungry Cannibals', which required good musicians to play them. Scott hired black musicians by choice, but true to himself, Simmons never stayed anywhere long. He also played with Duke Ellington, and often with Stuff Smith on 52nd Street, and in between all this with Heywood.

At that time Eddie was wearing, uh, Howard clothes and Thom McAn shoes, his socks rolled down, he wasn't combing his hair, and people came up to me with requests because they thought I was the leader. And she'd come down there one night to see Eddie, because he'd been her accompanist, and she asked me who I was, and I told her.

I liked her, yep. I had admired her for so long, just listening to her records, like when I was a school kid, when I was just learning *how* to play bass, I dropped into school one day and hit the road the next playin' music. A lot of times I was mistaking her voice for Putney Dandridge, their voices were something alike, but I finally got straight on that, and from then on I was listening to Billie Holiday records from 1937 . . .

Dandridge was a pianist and singer known for a series of combo records made in 1935–6. It was in 1937 that Simmons, about nineteen years old, recorded in Los Angeles on a beautiful and unusual Teddy Wilson instrumental date, with no drums: just a quartet of Wilson, Simmons, Red Norvo on xylophone and Harry James on trumpet. He said he hit New York in 1941, and met Lady in 1942.

Simmons spoke at length about his close friend Sid Catlett; they often worked together:

Sid was as much of a comedian as you wanna see – he could have been a dancer, could sing a little bit, play beautiful drums – during my time, he was the greatest . . . He had this heart attack and the doctors told him to stop smoking cigarettes, but he said that they didn't tell him to stop smoking weed . . . 'Really,' I told him, I said, 'You gonna crumble into little small pieces.' He finally had a heart attack from overdoing it. His thing was just as bad as Billie's. His sex drive was like her dope drive . . . he actually fucked himself to death.

Catlett had another, fatal heart attack at a theatre date in Chicago in 1953.

Musicians have a thing to try to see how many chicks they can make in the course of a night, see which one they can get, and they would be makin' eyes and try to send messages, and I didn't dig this. I felt as though if it was for me they would say something to me, and then I would know it was real. As far as one-night stands and things like that, I never had the desire.

When she saw something she wanted, Lady was not the one to hold back or play games.

Even from the beginning there was nothing I could say – she chose me. That night, after I met her, she said, 'Well, pick me up tonight, this is when I get off.' So I went up and she was walking out the door with a chick, and she dropped her head. I said, 'There's other nights.' So the next night she didn't do the last show and she came down after me and we went to her mother's apartment; her mother had a restaurant down the street from where they lived. Billie didn't have anything, just a sitting room with double glass doors and a three-quarter bed in it. And she told me that what I had when I was with her was, I had sex, I had money, I had blah blah blah, you know, I didn't have to go away from her for anything. So we proceeded to try to make it that night but her mama was in the next room, and I said, 'I can't do nothing with your mama in there. No good.' So the next day she went out and got an apartment, a gift to me so we could be together. We started from there. Somethin' else . . .

She wanted to be dominated – yes and no She couldn't understand me not taking orders and being spoken down to, but I felt that I was just as much of a musician as she was a singer. And this is the point I tried to stress – that I'm the man, not her. She stayed with me because .   [laughs] She was more of a woman than any woman I knew – beautiful, she knew how to act for a man At least for me she did. I don't know how she acted for the others; she recognized me as a man.

When her marriage to Jimmy Monroe was over, Ruby Helena said, Lady cried about it, and she also felt guilty and cried because of the way she'd treated Sadie at the time. And of course Sadie had been right, hadn't she? But apparently Lady no longer hesitated to bring men home if she felt like it; Sadie had lost another battle. Simmons was frank about his own drug habits and didn't seem to have anything to hide. His interview is less discursive than some, and he says quite clearly that he didn't get back on hard drugs, having kicked it when he was a teenager, until after their steady time together was over. It also appears that if Lady was using heroin earlier, she wasn't mainlining at first.

She didn't start shooting up until latter part of '42, '43. When she started shooting up there was no time for sex . . . heroin is a depressant and you don't have any desire. But before she was a sex machine.

When we first started going together there was nothing but weed involved. We would smoke it all day and all night. When we got off at night, we'd walk down the block to Fifth Avenue and have smoked a joint, and then stop off at the White Rose and have a drink at 51st and then go back to work . . . before she started fixing we had good times . . . maybe go downtown and catch a stage show, something like that; New York at that time was twenty-four hours a day you could find something. Then we'd go up to Clark Monroe's place, Uptown House . . . [at home] we were always swamped with visitors, people comin' by . . .

Billie didn't read. If she wasn't asleep, she was getting high. Wake up, 11, 12; get off work at 4 a.m., come home and clean the house till 6 or 7, get four to five hours' sleep. Every night she'd come home from work and clean. This was her thing, time to think. Cleanin' the house and cookin'. Sit down and eat and have food strokes – so good, so much. We would eat, and someone come by and they was hungry, she wouldn't serve them or cater to them . . . If you wanted something you go ahead and warm it up and serve yourself.

During this period they had a sort of social life, perhaps as close as Lady ever came to ordinary domesticity. Greer Johnson, a young white man from Lexington, Kentucky, shared a flat with novelist Elizabeth Hardwick, his close friend from home; they had become her friends, and Billie invited them to dinner:

The property had been raided because of drugs and there was a white policeman standing out front. He asked where we were going, and I said, 'We're going in here. We have a dinner date with Miss Holiday.' And the policeman said, 'You don't really want to go in there.' I said, 'Yes, we do. We're invited to dinner with Miss Holiday.' And he said, 'I think the best thing for you two to do is turn around and go back downtown.' We refused and he said, 'Well, this is raided property,' and we said, 'We're not here to buy drugs or get drugs or sell drugs so if you don't mind' – and we did.

Lady wasn't ready, as usual, and Johnson describes how she curled her hair, which was short at that time, heating a curling iron with a can of Sterno and curling her hair

to the point where the scalp sizzled. Of course, when she was finished, she was more beautiful than anybody in the world could possibly be .. Billie had the most fabulous dinner you could imagine. It was a little late, but it was there ... some sort of braised meat with onions and rice. That's all I remember except it was fabulous.

On another occasion Billie said to me, 'Baby, you never have me to dinner.' This was when Elizabeth and I lived at the Hotel Schuyler; and I said, 'Well, we will,' and we did. That night I waited outside the hotel (which was a tacky place on 45th Street that's torn down now) just to make sure she was not in any way embarrassed or insulted. She showed up with John Simmons, the bass player, and we served them dinner.

Simmons was a sort of man's man in his way, and Johnson was gay; they didn't care much for each other. Johnson said Simmons was 'mean to Billie', and he was going to tell a story about Simmons, but wandered off the subject. In any case, this period of domesticity didn't last long; Simmons says that her addictive personality got out of hand:

All of a sudden she started fixin' and everything, and buying opium ... [John] Levy and Dickie Wells knew how to cook opium . if it's in a pure form it can be smoked several times – the ashes that fall in the pipe, you save those, and when it's all smoked up you put it back in the container that it came in, put some alcohol in it and mix it up, it goes back into its original form, and you can smoke it two or three times. It's a pretty cheap high, but a most beautiful high ... because you can dream, sleep and hold a conversation at the same time, and you never lose your presence of mind. First time I smoked it, I took one draw, and I was off the floor this high, the next draw I was in the middle of the room, and the third draw I was bouncing off the ceiling . suspended, levitated ... then I started to getting a nervous stomach from it. I'd go on the subway and have to ride between the trains to dump, you know, and I couldn't take that.

She could consume more stimulants than any ten men and still perform. She would smoke opium when we got home from work at night, and she'd light up a joint, and she had a ten-pound candy box full of pills – she'd grab a fistful of them – all kinds of pills – and chase it with a big tumbler of ale. And she would drink scotch behind that. *And* she would go in the bathroom and fix. She could barely whisper . . . Anybody else would have been dead in six months doin' what she did. Never sick. No voice trouble or anything. She'd wake up hoarse and she'd take a drink and she was in fine voice . . .

I never heard her practise a tune, or even get off with an arranger, person composing a tune or something, never saw her get with them once, never saw her listen to a record or anything so far as learning a tune, but when she got to the studio, she knew the tune. When she had time I don't know [laughs]. She didn't know anything about music. They play it for her and she learn the lyrics and listen to the melody two or three times, and she knew it. I think she was satisfied doing her version. It never dawned on her whether she was in tune or anything else. She didn't have a voice. It was just her version of lyrics, singing from within, from her soul, her heart. The way it came out, that's the way it came out.

Simmons mentions a whip in two places in his interview. Somebody named Jesse went downtown with him when he bought the whip . . .

What we had goin' was nothing but understanding after she started shooting, 'cause I would constantly see a white boy from Texas, a white boy named Specs – he was the one that started her [not drummer Specs Powell, who was a black New Yorker]. He was just known by Specs. I could never catch him, because I had a good whipping stored up for him. He would slip in while I was on the bandstand, and he would go next door and slip it to her. And she was adventuresome. Anything to get high she was for. She was a sitting duck. Just her attraction – she was attracted to drugs. Whisky didn't make her high enough. She was usin' heroin *and* cocaine at the same time. And after a while a speedball. Start to keeping her broke; never had any money, had to draw all the time to keep her habit up. Whereas before that she'd draw and get $2,000 or $3,000 any time she wanted it, but after she got hooked she'd have to look in the drawer for a dollar. I said, 'What is this?' This is a $2,000 a week job trying to keep her out of fights and things. And I'm being fronted off on the streets – 52nd Street – people she would insult and things. Someone would say, 'Hello Billie' – 'Kiss my ass, I don't know you.' You know, then she'd turn to me and say, 'Am I crazy?'

No, she wasn't crazy, but she wanted to be. In her earlier years she was used extremely, so she got to the point where she thought everyone was trying to use her, so she said, 'Fuck the world!'

Greer Johnson thought Sadie was stupid, but that Lady was 'extremely bright, as bright and sharp and intelligent as anyone I have ever known . . .' Johnson was prejudiced; he was clearly crazy about her. There is a persistent story, unverifiable now, that the great harpsichordist Ralph Kirkpatrick took her home with him one evening and played Bach for her, and she was enchanted: her understanding of music would not have depended on education. She was perfectly bright; her lack of education contributed to her lack of confidence. But few people are smarter than a great musician; on that sort of plateau, the word 'smart' loses its meaning. Simmons was a slightly cynical man; he took a narrower view.

I don't think she was smart. She was cunning, she wasn't smart. She had mother wit, common sense, plenty of that to get by on . . . She knew how to cut corners, like situations would arise in Joe Glaser's office, and she might want certain things that he wouldn't give to her, and she'd say, 'Well, all right, remember that at contract time.' She usually got what she wanted from Glaser. It was a business with them . . . there wouldn't be any formalities with them; they would be down in the dirt, they would curse back and forth . . .

She knew how to conceal things from people – they would see her and they would never know she was on dope. They'd think maybe she smoked weed, but people in the business – they knew, and finally it got around to the public. Word of mouth, grapevine, that's the greatest message-carrier in the world. She might miss a show sometime if she didn't feel like it, but she didn't make a habit of doing it ..

In clubs she was all right. She catered to the public. She'd go over and have drinks with them, sit down and laugh and talk, although she didn't know what they was talking about – her education didn't leave her where she could converse with people on different subjects and things. It was mostly like interviews where people would ask her about her life, and when she started singing, and what does she think about when she was singing and things like that, and that would wear her down and she would run upstairs to her dressing room to fix, and get this nervous condition away from her, because it was like they'd inflicted real pain on her just from holding a conversation .. I saw it happen . . .

If someone introduced her to a woman and she had eyes, 'I'm William' – she'd introduce herself as a man, 'I'm William.' In fact she wasn't as notorious on that side as people thought she was. Like she would go off with a chick or something like that and she would probably make them perform like a three-ring circus, and she wouldn't do anything. And after that she would probably go off and get a prostitute and give her $5 for a French job. That was her. Why? Who knows? I don't know.

All this is a description of a frenetic flight from feelings of failure. She talked about her father's death, said Simmons, and blamed it on racism; she was nervous, lacked confidence, and many of her fans were sophisticated people indeed. Frank Sinatra was the biggest sensation in show business at the time, foreshadowing the hysteria over Elvis Presley and then the Beatles; she told columnist Earl Wilson, apparently in 1944,

Listen darling, I didn't teach Frank anything. I was at the Chicago Three Deuces and Frank was with Harry James. So me like a dope, I didn't know, I went over to where he was and they wouldn't let me in. But Frank and the others saw me, so four of us, we just went out and had a ball. I told him he didn't phrase right. He should bend certain notes. He says, 'Lady, you're not commercial.' But I told him about notes at the end he should bend, and later he said I inspired him.

226

Bending those notes – that's all I helped Frankie with.

Sinatra was with James in 1939, and was already praised that year in *Metronome* for his 'easy phrasing'. Another of her fans a few years later was Dick Haymes, Simmons said, who was a rival to Sinatra at the time.

He'd come by and see her, but I didn't dig him, because he appeared effeminate to me at times. He was some kind of knick-knack, I don't know, but he wasn't all man. He thought he was the prettiest thing that walked. He was a real egotist. I couldn't stand him.

Haymes was not gay, but was probably a narcissist and a sometime alcoholic; he was also a very good pop singer, and no doubt genuinely her fan. In any case, attention from a star like Haymes, with about forty big hit records in the 1940s, would have meant gratification for her fragile ego. She was supposed to be a great singer, but had been fired from the Basie band, had to leave the Shaw band and wasn't wanted by the sponsors on the radio; Jimmy Monroe had failed as a pimp on the West Coast, Simmons said, and Joe Guy was an errand boy sent to find dope for her. Men didn't amount to much, and perhaps Lady's experience had taught her to keep sex separate from love. And what was love? She was learning that she couldn't buy love with sex after all, so perhaps gobbling pills and shooting dope was a way of keeping everything at bay.

The time came when she wanted to get off heroin. She was doing so much that her feet swelled so that she couldn't get her shoes on, and she had more and more trouble finding a vein.

She would wear thongs, and she had like these duck socks cut out around the toes where she could wear these socks with her shoes . . . And she would end up trying to hit in her vagina, and she did it. I couldn't have done that kind of thing. I knew men who hit in their genitals – wheew – I couldn't even start in that direction.

Simmons says he was tired of the pushers waiting for her when she got off work, and one night during a thunderstorm it all came to a head.

She got scared and landed straight up in the bed on her feet, and she ran straight into the bathroom to fix. She had broke out in hot and cold sweat and I jumped right down and whipped it all out of her. It was rather sadistic on my part, but I had told her to stop and it all hinged on our staying together and everything . . . she didn't like me whipping her, not when she started into fixing, because this took everything out of her. She had to go and fix again.

Simmons seems to be saying that he yanked the needle out of her; anyway, he packed his bags and left, not without a violent struggle as she tried to stop him. And then Simmons was arrested; he doesn't say what for.

I got busted in New York, and they took my cabaret card away from me just like they did her. So it seemed like the end of the world to me. Couldn't work. I was like an employment agency – someone gave me a job that I couldn't take, I gave it to someone else, and they go and play the job and they wouldn't even come back and say here's $5, thanks for the job, or anything. So I was just on my ass. So I started usin'
She found out . . . I had walked into a pad – Freddie Jacobs' house – a dancer, she was his son's godmother – Freddie was dealing, and she was sitting there when I walked in. She started laughing – 'oh, no, oh no, not you!' So Freddie and I went into the bathroom trying to transact business, and she came in the bathroom – 'I know you're gonna give me some' – so we got high together . . .
After we split, yeah, we would slip off, and have a drink together, and go to bed together, and eventually we started fixing together. '47, '48, '49, '50, on up until the end.

Like Charlie Parker, she was a heroin addict for years without getting into trouble; she had friends who'd hold her stuff for her. Big Stump remembered all that:

Lady had this thing, anxiety, like, Make 'em wait, I'm Lady, here I come. 'Stump Daddy, I'm from Baltimore, Green Willow Street, and if they can't wait fifteen minutes' – this would be her thing . . . all the Baltimoreans I knew used to say, 'I'm from Baltimore, and they can make it.' Snakehips Tucker said it.

The Chinaman at the Onyx Club – she loved the China-man. He was just a cook, but he got the opium for Jimmy Monroe. 'Chin Fu,' she'd say, 'my man, he's sick and he needs some stuff,' and she'd say, 'No flucky round, kicky ass too good.' Chin Fu cooked Chinese food; she loved it. Egg fu yung and pepper steak. He made a whole Chinese thing for her one time, the whole dinner thing as he would do in Peking or Canton, nothing like the thing he'd do ordinary . . .

And by the time she got to the end of the bar, she copped. He held everything for Lady.

Down there when she strolled through the street, the Lady, and the doormen, 'Here you are Lady, I got it here.' They had her thing . . . And from the White Rose a couple of soldiers would take her back to the club, a teeny short guy and a big guy, and hold her shit, hold it for her. Her favourite doorman was Chick, a big doorman . . . They'd hold the shit for her that somebody gave them. They'd say, 'Lady, somebody left something for you.' They'd come back; she wouldn't have to come out. They'd come backstage, 'Lady, here's something for you,' and she knew where it came from. Lady Day never *went* to anybody; they came to her.

On 52nd Street we were in our own domain, like nobody could touch us. Like if something happened to Lady – 'Who? What? What happened to Lady?' and we'd come to her rescue. If somebody'd steal her squirrel mink or one of her coats, we'd have it back for her in ten minutes.

Greer Johnson knew Lady for many years. He became a theatri-cal press agent and later a dance critic; he eventually died a lonely alcoholic. But he was a twenty-three-year-old greenhorn when he came to New York from Kentucky in early 1943 and he was amazed when she accepted his friendship. The first night he met her, he held her jewelled coin-purse for her while she did a set; years later, perhaps he realized that he might have been holding her stash.

She used him, Johnson said, but he didn't mind; he knew a great artist when he saw one, and he sometimes came in handy because a lot of her other friends weren't up during the day. In particular she used him when she needed an escort, as when she wanted to see the Katherine Dunham dance group: 'I want to know what the Negroes are doing, baby; would you take me?'

I was penniless and really struggling for a livelihood. It was very hard for me to buy two beers on 52nd Street to hear Billie – not that I minded. But I said I would take her and I did. I took everything I had, went to the Martin Beck Theater and bought two tickets in the orchestra for the opening night . . . She had on a sweater and skirt with a turban around her hair and large hooped brass earrings, and she looked incredibly beautiful and believe me I looked like nothing. I mean, I had a suit and tie on, but believe me I looked like nothing.

People in the theatre kept turning round and staring at them, and Lady thought it was because she was a black woman with a white boy, but Johnson thought it was because she was so beautiful. Afterwards she took him to a club in Harlem where his was the only white face, and everybody stared at *him*. (Neither of them thought much of Katherine Dunham.) Finally she sent him home in a taxi.

He had become a Holiday fan through listening to her records; the record shop on Main Street in Lexington had given him strange looks because he was ordering what was then called 'race music'. He said that there was never any discrimination at any of the places where he saw her; she mixed with the customers and drank at the bar. But some of the customers and the cops were occasionally a problem.

This was a long time after I had gotten established on that street and they knew who I was. I can tell you about somebody coming up behind me, and literally feeling a sharp pain in my behind. Somebody had kicked me right smack in the ass and said, 'What are you waiting for the black bitch for?' . . . I'd been told by the police, 'You don't *really* want to do this.' . . . I laugh when I hear about today's liberated youth. They don't know what we did without any kind of banners . . It's such a screaming joke.

Not long after a racial incident in a club, pianist Joe Springer remembered, they were walking down 52nd Street when a black friend greeted her: 'How are you doing, Lady Day?' She replied, 'Well, you know, I'm still a nigger.' This was the other side of an old joke in the black community, about a white man who complained to a black friend that he had lost his job, his wife had left him, his car had been repossessed and so forth; his friend replied, 'What are you worried about? You're still *white*, aren't you?'

The incidents in the clubs often upset her, but never got the best of her (except in so far as they must have worn her down cumulatively: it was in this metaphorical sense that her feet hurt). Frank Sinatra floored a wise guy one night. Usually somebody came to her rescue, and a troublemaker would be hustled out fast, but sometimes the troublemaker got into trouble. There are countless stories, different in each version: Bobby Tucker said that one New Year's Eve a merchant marine turned to the bartender and asked, 'Since when did you start serving nigger bitches?' 'She was drinking brandy and white crème de menthe – those big long shot glasses – and she just worked his face all over with the end of that glass until he looked like a three-ring Ballantine thing' (the beer company's logo of intersecting circles).

In John Jeremy's 1984 film, Thelma Carpenter told the famous story about her coat. They were standing at the bar

> During the war, soldiers and sailors around, a bit on the prejudiced side – not too cool . . . These guys are stickin' cigarettes on her *coat* .   She says, 'Something's burning.' 'Yeah, it's your *coat. They* did it ' She says [sultry, pouting voice], '*Hey*, mister . . .'

They all went outside; the sailors thought they were going to beat her up, but she'd learned how to fight in Baltimore.

> She gave me that coat to *hold*. And I wanna tell ya, she'd laid 'em *flat* – and I threw a few milk bottles at 'em – When the cops came, she got very feminine, and she says, 'They *attacked* me ' And the cops cracked up. Two sailors layin' out on the street, and she says, they *attacked* her. She put on her coat and went back into the club

It was the musicians, male and female, who knew who she really was. Johnson said that he thought a lot of big names in show business resented her because she was far ahead of them musically,

but he wouldn't name them. Big Stump said, 'Musicians would
flock – Lady, can I make it Lady, Lady can I do it? And they
would crack up because they didn't know the riffs.' Stump is
talking about scat-singing here.

Lady Day didn't like to riff. But Lady Day could cut Ella's
teeth in riffing, I'm telling you, Lady Day knew more music
. . . How she learned it I don't know, but she could crack
your skull with a riff. She'd come out of the sky with somethin',
and I'd be in the wings, you know, 'cause I always led her to
the wings – 'This is my stick, Stump Daddy' – and she'd
'Shadadadee, shadadado,' and I'd cry. She'd leave me like
this. [Then she went out into the spotlight] . . . she'd go right
into that with her finger snappin', and she'd look back at me
and she knew what she did, 'cause she's such a doll, she was,
ahhhh Lady Day . . .
    Musicians who played for her – you see all the pimps in the
front, there was a musician behind with his heart broken. The
guy that accompanied her loved her, but this big pimp
parasite was in the front, like Jimmy Monroe, John Levy –
they're sittin' there collecting all the glory, but these guys are
crying to Lady, 'Please come with me Lady,' it's like an echo
in the night from Valhalla somewhere. Oh, there were so
many musicians that loved her . . .
    Piano players like Sonny White, like Ellis Larkins, and like
Eddie Heywood, who used to cry when she sang; so did
Sonny. Sonny was so beautiful, he loved her so badly, I think
she threw him a curve. He was a very, very dear boy, he was
a cherub . . . I've seen him come off the stage and break
down; when she went off with the big man parasite this used
to drive him mad, and I could see the tears in his eyes. She'd
just sang a song like 'You're My Thrill' or something, and he
would just go in a corner and cry.
    But Lady had a knack for picking a piano player – she'd
say, 'C'mon, baby, you're gonna play for me.' And there
was another guy, Clyde Hart – these were people that loved
Lady so . . . Because they didn't have nowhere to go but
just – she'd just go her way and he'd just play the melody,
and she's got him in her magic bag. Eddie Heywood cried
too – 'Low Down Mood' – You sort of got acquainted with

Lady Day's style and you all of a sudden joined the Lady Day league.

Joe Springer was playing for her one night on the Street when she was so stoned she could hardly stand up for the last set. This didn't happen often to Lady on stage (though Johnson saw her sink to the floor once, saying to the audience, 'Folks, I'm really drunk'). On this occasion she fell so far behind the beat that Springer was afraid he would have to skip a few bars, which would give the game away. Then suddenly, 'Billie skipped a half a dozen words and meshed perfectly with the music. Part of her befuddled brain kept track of the music, even though her vocalizing was like an old-time phonograph that needed to be wound up.'

Another time Johnny Guarnieri led a trio for her at the Onyx. He told Arnold Shaw:

> The first night she handed me some tattered lead sheets and said, 'Give me four bars.' I played four bars. But she didn't come in. Figuring she hadn't heard me, or just missed her cue, I started over again. Suddenly I felt a tap on the back of my head and I heard her say, 'Don't worry 'bout me – I'll be there.'

He discovered that she liked to come in behind the beat, and that he didn't have to make her look good. 'Few performers had such solid judgement about tempi as she did . . . Billie Holiday was the greatest tempo singer that ever lived.'

Greer Johnson told a story about an occasion when she was drunk and depressed and 'fell, literally flat on the floor, and said, "Baby, fuck it! I'll never sing again."' He harangued her: 'What the hell then do you think you can do if you don't sing? "I don't give a fuck!" Fine. Then what *will* you do? She finally got up, dusted herself off and said, "I'll sing again."'

Eddie Heywood had already recorded with Lady and he was at the centre of the next phase of her recording career. The musicians' strike against the record companies dragged on until the end of 1944 for the major labels; the federal government's labour department didn't like the strike, but finally it was clear that they weren't going to get tough with Petrillo, so smaller operators settled with the union, being less able to wait out the strike and also seeing an opportunity to make records ahead of the competition. One of these was Dave Kapp at Decca, who always had an eye for the main chance; another was Milt Gabler at Commodore, who resumed recording in November 1943. He did sessions with Eddie Heywood in February 1944; by then Heywood was the leader at, Café Society, and by then, Josephson told Whitney Balliett, the bandleader at the club was also the emcee.

Heywood stammered. He told me he was afraid people would laugh at him, and I told him not to worry. The first night was pretty bad, the next night better, and in a week there was hardly a trace. It must have had something to do with the intimacy of a microphone, and possibly also my confidence in him. Anyway, a couple of weeks later he explained that he was classified 4-F on account of his stammering and that he was due for a medical review and could he quit emceeing for a few days until his stammer returned? He did, his 4-F status was renewed, and that night he announced shows again.

Heywood's poppish Commodore recording of 'Begin the Beguine' created something of a sensation on a 12-inch 78, and meanwhile Gabler had gone to work for Decca (in 1941, the year the Commodore Music Shop on 52nd Street closed; the 42nd Street store lasted until 1958). Kapp had said to Gabler, 'I don't mind you making Commodores every Saturday and after work, but don't you ever make a hit on Commodore!' So Heywood went to Decca as a leader, and a new 10-inch version of 'Begin the Beguine' was a top-twenty hit (according to *Pop Memories*, though it did not appear in the *Billboard* chart at the time).

Meanwhile, *Esquire* magazine had set up the first jazz poll to be decided by critics rather than readers, and Lady won her first poll as number one female vocalist. It was also connected to the USA's fourth and last war-bond drive, and a lot of money was raised; in January 1944 a concert by the Esquire All-American All-Stars was recorded from the Metropolitan Opera House, Lady singing three tunes with a band including Roy Eldridge, Art Tatum, Coleman Hawkins and Sid Catlett (her beloved Louis Armstrong was also on the bill, but they did not perform together.) She also won a *Metronome* poll in 1945.

John Hammond said that the reason why Columbia didn't renew Lady's contract was that he didn't like the way her style had changed, but in March 1944 Columbia wasn't making any records at all. Gabler wanted more sides by her so that he could put out albums of 78s with four discs (eight sides). He offered Joe Glaser $1,000 a recording session, which was more than Columbia had ever paid her; and at three sessions in March and April, twelve tunes were recorded, plus alternate takes.

Most of the takes included a septet of Heywood, Catlett, Simmons, Teddy Walters on guitar, Doc Cheatham on trumpet, Vic Dickenson on trombone and Lem Davis on alto sax. On four tunes Walters was not present, and on several takes at the last session, everybody sat out except a trio of Heywood, Simmons and Catlett. The tunes, chosen by Gabler, were all top drawer: 'How Am I to Know', 'My Old Flame', 'I'll Get By', 'I Cover the Waterfront', 'I'll Be Seeing You', 'I'm Yours', 'Embraceable You', 'As Time Goes By', 'He's Funny That Way' and 'Lover Come Back to Me'; and a remake of Gabler's old favourite 'Billie's Blues' was added at the end. 'I Cover the Waterfront' had been recorded for Columbia, but was not released until after the Commodore recording; this was the first time Lady remade something she had already recorded. All the Commodores are beautiful, and all are classics.

On her earlier records for Brunswick and then Columbia, she had often sung only one chorus, but as we have seen, she had begun to be presented more as a pop star than as a jazz musician on her later records; Gabler carried on in this way quite purposefully

> She wanted to really be a pop singer. To me, she used to sing in clubs for losers. I would go any time she was working . . . I'd go in and catch a set. But she would sing for the lovelorn, you know. And that's what she liked to sing, that stuff, too. So this was the start of her having a non-jazz background. Like, I caught hell in *down beat* on these and from a lot of critics, because I did it with a smooth orchestra behind her on ballads and all. But I wanted to project these ballads as songs. I was always a song man . . She wanted to sell the songs like she did in a room!

Then one night in a club he heard her singing 'Lover Man'. He thought, 'Oh my gosh! That's a natural hit!'

> In those days the elevators had elevator operators. If you were singing that song in the elevator going up to the 14th

floor at Decca, the elevator operator said, 'Gee, that's a great song' . . . You know, it can't miss. It's a natural. You just put it in the groove, walk around the bases, and that's all.
So I said, 'I can't make that for Commodore. I'll get fired!'
So I went up to Joe . . . and I signed her for Decca and I gave her the same $1,000 plus a 5 per cent royalty on that, and Joe grabbed it.

She wanted strings, so Gabler gave them to her, along with five horns and rhythm. The arranger and director was Salvador Tutti 'Toots' Camarata, a trumpeter and former arranger for Jimmy Dorsey. 'Lover Man (Oh, Where Can You Be?)', based on a tune by Roger 'Ram' Ramirez, was recorded in October 1944, and was the equivalent of a top-twenty hit in May 1945 (though again not listed in the *Billboard* retail chart); it was also a number five on the black chart that *Billboard* had started in 1942 (it was her first and last hit on that chart, which had begun as 'Harlem Hit Parade' and was changed in early 1945 to 'Most-Played Juke Box Race Records') Furthermore, this was a hit in a revived business: the juke-box trade had encouraged the retail end, which was now recovering from the Depression, so that to get a hit in any chart she must have been selling quite a few retail copies. The other side of the hit was 'That Ole Devil Called Love', co-written by Camarata and Bob Russell, from her second Decca session, in November 1944. Her next session in August 1945 was led by bassist Bob Haggart, with friends including Tiny Grimes on guitar, Specs Powell on drums, and Joe Guy.
Haggart describes first meeting her at a club in 52nd Street to get the keys for the tunes 'She was very cordial and friendly, and put me completely at ease immediately. She had all four song copies in front of her and knew just what she wanted '
Before any more Decca records were released, her one-year contract was renewed. Decca had to be considered a major label by this time; it still had a big share of the juke-box trade, and had become an independent American company (UK Decca, like other British companies, cashed in overseas investments during the war, in Decca's case to help pay for the development of radar) Lady was now not only a legend among musicians and critics and a bona fide poll-winner, but had a major-label contract, on the

same label as Bing Crosby, Dick Haymes and Ella Fitzgerald; she was getting royalties and had a national hit. She was thirty years old and at the commercial peak of her career.

11

Triumph and Trouble

In the second half of the 1940s the decay of the Swing Era was complete. For a variety of reasons, including wartime fuel rationing and entertainment taxes (taxes not lifted until well into the 1950s), ballrooms and dance halls all over the country had closed, and in any case keeping a big band on the road had become uneconomic. On top of that, returning soldiers were starting families, and the first result of the baby boom was that families soon stayed at home to watch television instead of going out dancing.

In January 1947 nine big-name bands folded all at once, and by then a great many hit records were coming from new, small independent labels. The music business knew that a new era had begun, but had no idea what to do about it. In 1948, just to make sure of doing as much damage as possible, James Petrillo called another musicians' union strike against the record companies, and by then it was becoming obvious that radio play would be the main impetus to record sales: the era of the deejay and the pop singer was well under way and top-forty radio was not far in the future.

In retrospect, it is obvious that black music and hillbilly sounds were bubbling under American popular music with a vigour that would not go away; the dominance of Broadway, Hollywood and Tin Pan Alley was almost over as far as hit records were concerned, but ingrained racist and classist methods of marketing and distribution kept the so-called 'minority musics' away from the mainstream. An Armed Forces Radio poll saw Roy Acuff beat Frank Sinatra as the most popular vocalist among American servicemen, but Acuff's records never appeared in the pop chart;

jazz was once again a small-group genre, and great records were made, but they were not much heard on the radio either. Of America's black female singers, Ella Fitzgerald and Dinah Washington were the most successful, Dinah appearing mostly in the black chart but Ella easily crossing over. Dinah Shore, rumoured to be a mulatto but performing white-oriented material, was a huge star in the 1940s; Sarah Vaughan's amazing voice and technique, together with ritzy production and often performing material that had little to do with jazz, earned her twenty hits in the 1950s in the *Billboard* retail chart. Lena Horne, enjoying a long and stable Hollywood marriage to Lennie Hayton, did not spend a lot of time in the recording studio, but even so had a couple of hits. With the possible exception of Ella, they had all been influenced by Billie Holiday, who had no hits at all after 'Lover Man'.

Lady's erratic reliability was well known (though her fans always forgave her), and rumours circulated about her bad habits. She seemed to confound it all when she opened at the Downbeat Club in May 1945, doing good business and making the shows on time, but by July she was 'not appearing regularly', according to *down beat* magazine. Then she took an unnecessary burden on herself: in August she and Joe Guy organized a sixteen-piece band to go on tour.

A lot of bands were sponsored by booking agents or publishers, such as Willard Alexander or Irving Mills; some of the most successful leaders, like Goodman and Dorsey, were experienced businessmen by the time they formed their bands; keeping a band on the road requires a lot of coordination of bookings, publicity, transport and lodging. Lady and Joe hit the road without any experience at all at a time when the big-band business was about to collapse. It was a disaster; Lady's autobiography says that she lost $35,000 in a few months. And right in the middle of it, on 6 October, Sadie died, at the age of forty-nine.

Lady's book says that she and Guy were working in Washington and that she'd had a premonition. In fact, according to the death certificate, Sadie had spent thirteen days in Wadsworth Hospital, Manhattan; no cause of death is named. Ruby Helena said that Sadie had given up her restaurant and moved to the Bronx and didn't live long after that. Detroit Red said that Lady was in Baltimore, near Washington; Red was working in another theatre and went to see Lady backstage. Lady asked about Red's children, and Red asked after Sadie, and Lady said that her mother wasn't well. Red was there when she got the telegram, and said that she took it very hard.

Joe Glaser helped with the funeral details. Lady is listed as the informant on the death certificate, which gives their addresses as 1293 Union Avenue and says that Sadie had been living in New York City for thirty years; it describes Sadie as the widow of Clarence, Sadie's father's name as Julian Fagan and her mother's name as Julia.

Lady's book says that she warned Joe Guy that 'You better be good to me because you're all I've got now.' Several people repeat a story that Lady tried to commit suicide by jumping off a train after Sadie's death, but there is no first-hand testimony of this; Greer Johnson said that he was with her and some other people in a bar after the funeral, and she seemed quite normal. While Glaser had announced that Lady might take some time off, she went straight back to work, which was probably the best thing to do, but she must have felt bereft. Whatever Sadie's shortcomings may have been, she had been the one person who was central in Lady's life, sharing the poverty and the squabbles, the ups as well as the downs.

Discipline in the band was erratic, the usual problems of shepherding musicians made worse by lack of experience; just getting them on the bus was difficult. As usual, the musicians loved her: Chilton quotes trombonist Floyd Brady, who ruefully recalled that he had been drinking with Lady one moment, missed a high note in a solo the next and was fired on the spot, in a small town in Georgia. Clyde Bernhardt was asked to join the band for a booking at the Apollo.

> Billie heard Joe Guy talking to me, she butted in and said to me, 'Don't you like my band?' I said, 'Yes,' then she said, 'Well why in the hell don't you just join the damn band if you like it? Don't bullshit man, just shit or get off the pot.' I began to laugh, then she began to laugh, and said to me, 'Now, what in the hell is funny?' She was really something. I liked to talk to her when she was in a good mood, and she would talk her trash.

By the end of the year the band had run out of bookings, and Lady's accompaniment was reduced to Guy, Springer, Tiny Grimes on guitar, Lloyd Trotman on bass and Eddie Nicholson on drums. It was with this group that she had one of her greatest triumphs, in a concert at New York's Town Hall on 16 February 1946, which was not recorded.

Greer Johnson thought that she ought to have become a singer of art songs, that what she was doing was so far ahead of anyone else that she should have been able to establish once and for all the best American songs as an art form to stand next to the greatest of nineteenth-century German lieder. And maybe, in the end, that is what she helped to do; but this was never to be obvious or useful to the music business.

The distinction between 'popular' and 'classical' music had been discussed in the American music press since the 1840s, but the impetus towards commercialism always kept the genres distinct: a successful popular song was first of all a commercial product, no matter how good or bad it was. Perhaps Johnson and others realized already in the 1940s that a golden age in American song was coming to an end. Gershwin's *Porgy & Bess* had been a flop; it did not emerge as the first great American opera until the 1980s, long after two or three of its songs had become pop standards. *Oklahoma* in 1943 and *South Pacific* in 1949 were seen as marking progress in the musical theatre, with the songs advancing the plot, as in an opera, instead of dropped into a fluffy story-line; but the songs of Richard Rodgers and Oscar Hammerstein II were never as 'popular' as those of Rodgers and Lorenz Hart had been, because Hammerstein's lyrics, good as they are, are somehow less obviously American, a move away from the demotic style that had been the strength of the golden age. And recitals by singers of American popular songs are still mostly found in places where booze is sold.

Nevertheless, by 1946 Johnson had something of a career as a press agent and was the promoter of Lady's Town Hall concert. In fact, according to Ernie Anderson she had already proved that she could be a draw at Town Hall, but that was splitting a bill. This was to be her own recital. Apart from her club work, Johnson said in 1971,

> She had done a couple of Eddie Condon jam sessions and she had appeared briefly here and there, and I said to her, 'I think it's time for a jazz artist to do a recital the way Lotte

Lehmann does it. The way anybody in classical music does a recital. That is, it is programmed and you do these numbers. You may do any number of encores, depending on how it goes, but that is it. It is structured, and it is so billed.' Billie said, 'All right.'

Columnist Robert Coleman printed this item in a New York paper, along with others about Igor Stravinsky and producer Mike Todd:

To correct any misapprehension about Billie Holiday's concert in Town Hall Saturday afternoon, Greer Johnson writes: 'In a sense, it is a jazz lieder programme and not a jam session.' So that's that, you jitterbuggers.

'Again, I had very little money,' continues Johnson, 'but at least I had an income as a press agent.'

It was very hard. The other fellow's name was Robert Snyder; I was afraid to do it alone and the way it was done – the way we got it on was barely barely. But as it happened, we turned away 1,000 people and we could have done it three times over. It was an absolute triumph ... I went after the first-string critics on the papers ... I got Paul Bowles of the *Tribune*. Believe me that was hard to do; those people didn't go to jazz concerts in those days ... Mark Schubert of *The Times* and so on ... it was a great success, and it's never quite been done that way since ...

I had to get Billie up a full hour-and-a-half before, get her dressed, which wasn't easy, come downtown through the mob scene that had grown outside the Town Hall – and on the way down, Billie suddenly decided she wanted another dress, that she wanted to wear a second dress for the second half. I said she didn't have to, that one doesn't at a recital. But she insisted, and we stopped at – I think it was W.R. Burnett ... it wasn't a particularly elegant dress shop. Billie bought another dress ... by the time we got to the hall I was hysterical, but she still went on on time.

At intermission, Billie was elated, as she should have been. She was kicking up her heels and grabbing me, kissing people and carrying on. I was in her dressing room when the brother of one of the musicians came running in to tell me that Billie's apartment had just been robbed. I said, for God's sake, don't tell her for another thirty-five or forty minutes. Her reputation was such that she would not show up for the first show, that she might make the second show possibly, and with luck she might make the third show – and I thought, seeing the way this was going, if anything happens now, it really would be pretty bad. So I asked him not to tell Billie because nothing more could be done, and to let her finish the concert. And she did.

She sang eighteen songs in a concert lasting only an hour and ten minutes, according to Chilton, who quotes two critics: John Hammond described it as 'a triumph long overdue', saying that 'She sang with far more apparent pleasure and ease than on West 52nd Street.' Leonard Feather said that 'her dignified bearing and her wonderful poise helped to keep the large, quiet, intelligent audience enthralled.' Both men were no doubt happy to see her presented in such a setting rather than in a nightclub for a change, and it is heart-breaking to wonder how the rest of her life would have gone if such jazz concerts had become the norm: there were fewer dope pushers hanging around concert halls. But the great *chanteuse* never completely broke through to the status of recitalist; many decades later, some of our foremost jazz musicians still cannot make a living at playing concerts, to say nothing of all those who don't even get the opportunity.

Perhaps Lady's Decca records are a case in point. They did well enough without making any charts; her first four sessions, between October 1944 and January 1946, all included strings, with arrangements by Camarata, Bob Haggart and possibly alto saxist Bill Stegmeyer, who is listed as director on the last one. Joe Guy played on the last two sessions, and the last of the four included Sid Catlett and John Simmons as well. It is interesting that the number of fiddles dropped from six on the first two sessions to five and then four, yielding a thinner sound. There were some felicitous touches, such as reedmen doubling on clarinets and bass clarinets here and there, but by and large the overall effect of the arrangements was slushy. Lady herself delivered classic performances of such tunes as her own 'Don't Explain', Cole Porter's 'What Is This Thing Called Love?' and Irene's 'Good Morning Heartache' and

'No Good Man' (collaborating with wordsmiths other than Herzog). But the settings amounted to run-of-the-mill pop records. These sessions included no fewer than four attempts at 'Big Stuff', an American art song by the young Leonard Bernstein. Significantly, a month after her triumph at Town Hall, the successful recording was finally done with only five musicians: Guy, Springer, Grimes, Billy Taylor on bass and Kelly Martin on drums. There were no strings, much less in the way of arrangement, and it was the only track recorded at the March 1946 session. The song was associated with Bernstein's successful ballet *Fancy Free*, which had its première in April 1944; the ballet takes place in a tavern, and subsequent performances of it began with Billie's record played on a juke box on stage. Whatever one thinks of Bernstein's song, it was an attempt at the sort of thing that Greer Johnson and others would have had in mind: a talent like Lady's used at the centre of indigenous American art, rather than simply shining out of a pop record or a booze parlour. But the relentless American economic imperative has rarely allowed a marriage of art and commerce to be consummated.

The year 1946 also saw a new friendship with folksinger Josh White. Lady had known him for some time; Ruby says he was a regular customer at Sadie's restaurant. When she heard that he was performing 'Strange Fruit' at Café Society, she called on him at the club, ready to 'cut my throat', according to an interview White gave in 1959, but the result was that she gave him permission to sing the song his way, and they did some club-crawling together for a few months. She also sang for the first time in the Jazz at the Philharmonic touring concerts that Norman Granz was organizing; fifteen tunes were recorded on five dates in 1945–7 with various lineups, often including Lester Young.

It was probably also in 1946 that her friendship with Roy Harte included a trip to Cuba. Harte later went to the West Coast and operated a drum shop; it was a $500 loan from him to Richard Bock that got the Pacific Jazz label started in 1952. But he began working as a relief drummer on 52nd Street as a teenager; one evening he found himself playing for Lady:

She heard the difference and turned around and said, 'Who's the white kid?' I played my heart out for her. The second or third week I worked there she took me home with her. It was the Downbeat Club, most likely. She was pretty healthy at the time, so it was a kick to hear her sing for me alone. So I dug her. I'd run for food, and do the thing. There was a lot of grass smoked at the time. It was plentiful and good . . . And there were some little cubes that came down from Columbia University. This was acid. And we used to feed 'em to the horses and take a ride in Central Park. There was a cabby, who couldn't figure out what was wrong with the horse. We'd be breaking up.

Harte was too young to be drafted during the early part of the war, which is one reason he got work on the Street; but his relationship with Lady lasted until after the war. Lysergic acid diethylamide (LSD) had been synthesized in Switzerland in 1943, and after the war research continued at Columbia, probably financed by the CIA.

She was singing all the time, and that's all I really wanted her to do . . . I even took certain jobs because I knew she was going to be in town.

She was aggressive, until we got to bed. We found ourselves there, then it was up to me. 'Come home with me; pat my ass . . .' She'd almost break my hand, she'd hold it so tight. I just figured she was very horny. She used to say, 'Let's get out of here. I'm only gonna do four tunes on the second show tonight. Start your hard-on!' When we'd get to the bedroom, and she'd get high and start to swim a little in her head – the bennies were on top of her, chopping at her. She'd fix before her shows, not after.

They never lived together – 'Here or there a weekend, maybe.' They spent only about a hundred days together over a period of three years or so, Harte said; 'The most time I ever spent with her was in Cuba.' When he went on tour with Lucky Millinder's band, there were various bills, sometimes with Fats Waller, later the Slam Stewart Trio.

The big shots in the coloured neighbourhoods were honorary mayors. When coloured bands came to town, there'd be two dances – a white one from eight to twelve and a coloured one from one to 5 a.m. And we'd stay in the coloured section, they would house us. We'd stay with the richer coloured people rather than stay in a hotel that was really bad. Lucky Millinder used to call them the Mayors of Harlem.

In Jacksonville, Florida, where Lady was on the bill, a crazy fan stuck Millinder with a knife because he got tired of playing his 'Shorty's Got to Go', which was his hit in mid-1946. Harte packed his bag and went to the hospital to see Millinder; Lady was there, and she said, 'You've got ten days off.' They'd lost three days' work, then a week off before he had to be at the Savoy in New York, and she had to be in Chicago. They went to Miami for a couple of days; she found them a place to stay, but they couldn't go anywhere together: 'It was lily-white. Restaurants and everything.' They went to Cuba and hung out on the beach:

At the end of the ten days I was as black as she was. She didn't have a bathing suit. She wore culottes. She didn't swim. We just walked to the beach, day and night. I was playing a little flute at the time, too. She'd sing, we'd get juiced, go to bed and pass out.

She sang whatever I asked her to sing. It would be whatever was popular . . . I asked her to sing 'Dinah' or 'Sweet Sue'; I was putting her on, asking her to sing tunes with girls' names, because she was a les and everybody knew it . . . She had a good sense of humour.

John Simmons and now Roy Harte say that the drugs got in the way of Billie's sex life – not that sex with men had ever brought her any lasting benefit. 'She dug all the holes she had. She was pretty strong . . . There were times when I'd start at her, and she was too far away from the bedroom . . . Plus she had no shit left. No ovaries. They'd gotten fucked up. She'd say, "Go ahead, don't worry about it."' At first Harte thought they were having a baby; of course he was leaving it up to her to take precautions. The transcription of the interview is not complete; she may have told Harte a story about why she could not have children, something about an accident: perhaps she had had a botched abortion when she was younger.

We laughed constantly, because we didn't understand why we were there. She'd say, 'What am I doing here with you?'

or 'What are you doing here with me?' I'd say, 'I like the way you taste; I like the way you sing. That's two good reasons.' She used to yell, instead of 'Fuck me fuck me,' like a chick who doesn't get a chance to curse, she'd say, 'Use me, use me.' I never heard that from anybody else. She didn't mind being used; it was one of the things we once talked about seriously. Being used was part of the theory of life . . . To be used well all your life was the thing to do. Those were Hobson's words. I was reading a lot at the time, and I'd read to her; on the bus, I'd read. I used to steal books from the libraries of colleges where we worked, and drop them off at a college in the next town . . . She'd read newspapers, down South. She'd point out racial things I wasn't aware of.

The only time we were really together was in Cuba. At other times it was three hours, five hours. It was just another experience for me, young as I was. I didn't learn anything. I wish I could say I did.

Asked if she was a 'good ball', Harte replied:

I don't know. I just know I was out first . . . She always seemed pretty satisfied with it, but there was a hole in it somewhere. There was something missing. It was more like an aunt with a nephew . . . She was my first black broad; I wanted the experience. She was no better than any white chick.

Many years later, an older and wiser Harte observed about the myth of black sexual potency, 'It's killing the black men.'

In September Lady was on the West Coast to start work on her first and last feature film.

Having decided many years earlier that she would do anything to avoid domestic service, she was of course put in that very role: she was not about to turn down the chance to appear in a movie, but there is a deep, brave sadness in her remark to Leonard Feather that 'I'll be playing a maid, but she's really a cute maid.' *New Orleans*, billed as 'the story of the odyssey of jazz', was nothing of the kind, and has to rank as one of the worst pictures ever made, despite having Louis Armstrong, Meade Lux Lewis, the Woody Herman band and other jazz luminaries in the cast. At a time when the armed forces and major league sports were being integrated, Hollywood was still afraid to make a film that might not play well in the South, so they made a turkey instead.

Lady's poor punctuality on the set caused a few problems, but the musicians didn't mind; clarinettist Barney Bigard recalled that in fact they appreciated the overtime pay. Lady's book says that the film's 'star', Dorothy Patrick, had objected to Lady's scene-stealing, but she was just being herself; she told Greer Johnson that director Arthur Lubin told her that she had made Patrick look like 'a hole in the screen'. The quickly made film opened to lukewarm reviews in early 1947; Patrick had risen without trace.

Lady went back to work in New York. Eddie Heywood's career had been going well; his hit record of 'Begin the Beguine' was still selling and his little band, which often accompanied Lady, had appeared in a couple of films. Heywood had been appearing at the Downbeat and he was supposed to accompany Lady, but on her opening night in November, 'the big star's sign went up and Eddie's comes down,' said pianist Bobby Tucker. 'The club-owner counts Eddie as a filler, but Eddie thinks he's bigger; he says, "Put my sign up or I don't play for her." But on the Street only three signs count: Art Tatum, Nat King Cole and Billie Holiday.'

Tucker was about twenty-six years old, living in his home town of Morristown, New Jersey, and 'sweating out his card', waiting a statutory period before being admitted to New York's Local 802 of the musicians' union. He had a few private students in town, and was walking down the Street when he was accosted by his friend, clarinettist Tony Scott, also a friend of Lady's. 'I just happened to be passing by. Full house – show in ten minutes – no music – no pianist.' Scott and Tucker walked into the club just as John Simmons was punching Eddie Heywood in the eye; Tucker was familiar with Billie's repertoire because he had been a long-time fan of Teddy Wilson's. 'Tony introduced me to Lady and she picked a show.' He played for her for several years, and they remained friends until she died.

Later Tucker worked for Billy Eckstine for many years; before Lady he had played for Mildred Bailey. Bailey had made a mistake on stage and blamed it on Tucker; 'I closed up the piano, picked up the music and walked off the stage, and, well, it's a longer story than that, but when she got ready to go somewhere else I told her, "I won't go to the *zoo* with you."' When Scott introduced him to Lady, she said, 'I've heard of you; will you play for me? ... I heard what happened between you and Bail. Don't worry, you ain't gonna have no trouble with me.'

I was scared that first time, yes. There was no bass, no drums, just me; and I wasn't dressed. But for the next four or five weeks I played for her at the Downbeat, and I felt like I was stealing her money. Wherever I put the tune, she found the groove and made it happen. She could swing in the hardest tempo and float on top of it like it was made for her; when I put it slow, she sang it slow – but the most beautiful slow you ever heard.

To her fans, Lady could do no wrong; but Lady was getting very unreliable. First off, we never did a show before midnight. I would take my train out of Morristown, the tube out of Hoboken, the D train out of 34th Street and walk into the Downbeat every night at exactly twenty-eight minutes to ten. The show was supposed to go on between 9.30 and ten, but what's wrong? Where's Lady? They're knocking on her door, and she's saying, 'Just a minute, just a minute.' For two and a half hours.

It was during this period – both Tucker and Billy Eckstine tell the story – that she made a three-ring circus in a racist's face with a tall shot glass. 'If she got bugged she might walk out, and that's the end of the show.' There were even occasions when she didn't come out at all and Tucker worked alone.

But it was mostly the drugs. 'Lady knew people all over the place,' Tucker said. 'She could be in Durham, North Carolina, and she could find stuff. Ninety per cent of the towns would be square as a block, but there would be one or two people who knew what was going on.' On one occasion in New York, she sent somebody out who disappeared with her money; this meant that the 9.30 show, which didn't go on until midnight anyway, didn't go on until 2 a.m. because she had to go uptown to make the connection herself.

About two months later, someone comes and tells Lady that the cat that swung with her bread was out on the Street. She just had her panties on; she put a coat on, grabbed a butcher knife from the kitchen, and caught up with the guy. He was a junkie, and he told her that some cats threatened to throw him in the East River if he didn't give them the bread, that he didn't intend to sting her, and he'd make it good. She ushered him into a little alcove off the Three Deuces, which was a couple of doors away from the Downbeat; she handed the butcher knife to Eddie Nicholson, who was our drummer, and she told Eddie, 'Don't stop us. Just make sure he fights fair.' And she beat the mess out of him with her fists.

On the Street she could do no wrong. Outside of New York they could get pretty bugged, but it's a funny thing about the money guys – as long as the tills were filled – on the Street in '46 she was getting $1,500 [a week], but that was absolute tops. Wherever we worked she would get them to take my salary out in front so I would get paid on payday.

Lady sometimes didn't get paid at all, because she'd be drawing money out to buy dope, and she would have no idea how much she had coming. Nobody was looking after her; Joe Guy was still there, but Tucker said, 'Joe was a weakling – like dishwater.' And by that time the writing was on the wall for 52nd Street; *down beat* reported in February 1947 that Lady and Art Tatum had their salaries cut at the Downbeat Club, and it didn't help. The club soon closed its doors.

She no doubt had some time on her hands at that point, and Joe Glaser gave her an ultimatum, insisting that she try to break her drug habit; in fact, the heat was on from the law, because Glaser had seen to it. She went in for a 'check up' according to *down beat*, but it was an open secret that she was paying $2,000 for a three-week 'cold turkey' cure in a New York clinic. Tucker said:

Word had gotten around and nobody wanted to take a chance. It was beginning to be written in her contract that if she didn't go on on time she'd be docked; it had got to that point.

She wasn't taking a cure. They had glucose to clean out her system, they had great big bottles of that stuff – jugs – it's like purifying the system and those kinds of things don't work, all it does is make her a virgin when she comes out. I remember visiting her in hospital; in fact there were only three people that could visit her and they were Louis

Armstrong, Joe Glaser and me. And it ended up that she was getting stuff from the nurse.

Meanwhile, between April 1946 and February 1947 Lady had recorded eight tunes at three Decca sessions, plus alternate takes, without strings. The first date used a quintet, the next a sextet and the last a ten-piece band. On the first session, Billy Kyle played piano; on the others Tucker had taken over. The tunes were nearly all torch songs – 'Baby, I Don't Cry Over You', 'I'll Look Around', 'The Blues Are Brewin'', 'Guilty', 'Deep Song' and 'There Is No Greater Love'. Sometimes Decca had songs written for her; Gabler remembered that Douglass Cross and George Cory, who wrote 'Deep Song', were fond of Lady. (They later wrote 'I Left My Heart in San Francisco'.)

The arrangements on the last of these sessions were by Haggart, who played bass, and the sound of the larger band is very nice indeed. The last session also included remakes of two of her earlier records – Ralph Rainger's 'Easy Living' and Duke Ellington's 'Solitude'. The tempos are uniformly slow on all these tracks; it is tempting to ascribe the extreme languor here to Lady's deep involvement with heroin, and one might have preferred to hear 'Easy Living' and 'There Is No Greater Love' done slightly quicker, but on their own terms these sides are a big improvement on the earlier sessions with strings. As far as Lady's art is concerned, as Haggart put it, 'The release to the tune "There Is No Greater Love" is an excellent example of how Billie could take a standard tune and add her Midas touch to the existing melody – giving the song a whole new value.' Tucker remembered the difficulty of getting her to the session:

> She was living on LaSalle Street off 125th Street – it's not even a street any more; there's a big project there now – and I couldn't get her downtown. The band's been there since 12 o'clock, and they're ready to pack up but the company's taken the place till 3, so they sit there . . . So we walk in at 20 minutes after 2 and she goes to the ladies' room. And she came in at 20 minutes to 3 and we were done at 10 minutes to 3. And those are the records you hear now.

Ten minutes for the whole session is an exaggeration, for five tracks were recorded, including two takes of 'Solitude', and Tucker has the time of day wrong, according to Decca's files; but the point is that she was always on top of the music. Milt Gabler said that the band would rehearse while they waited for Lady to arrive or to loosen up her voice with liquor; Jack Kapp had a button he could push any time he wanted to hear what was going on in the studio, so Gabler was careful not to be wasting any time. But once Lady was ready, the work was finished quickly.

Joe Guy played on the first of these three sessions, but on the other two is absent; his career was on the wane because of his drug habit. John Simmons, who played bass and was music director on the second session, recalled that Guy would obtain drugs for her, and that he and his brother would sit on a couch in the living room waiting for her to fix, in case she left some for them. Once they accidentally set fire to the couch, a landlady threw them out and they spent the night sleeping on the subway. At any rate, as soon as Lady was out of the clinic and back in the jazz-club subculture, she resumed her old habits.

It must have been very soon that they played at Colossimo's, because that was when Tucker first met Jimmy Ascendio, Lady's new road manager. Tucker said he thought it was a nightclub for gangsters, 'where Al Capone supposedly shot old man Colossimo. Anyway I got a call at my hotel room about 9 a.m. and a voice said, "You better get up here right away."' He went to Lady's room and met Ascendio, the owner of the voice.

He told me that she'd got ahold of some bad stuff; a guy named Boss Moss made the connection for her, and she and two other guys are 'dead' The valet's out in the street, walking one of the guys, and we can't let her fall asleep because she'll never wake up.

We filled a tub with water and threw her in, and she was fighting. We walked her, and slapped her, and all she wanted to do was sleep. It took four hours; she was strong as a bull. We left there and had a day off, because we were going to Philadelphia.

When they went to Philadelphia, Ascendio came too. He wasn't a user himself; Tucker thought he had been a trainer for fighters, and when he had nothing doing in the fight business, he turned to junk. Most of Lady's road managers were connections: 'They want to sell, she wants to buy ...' In Philadelphia, Ascendio was making trips back and forth to New York, buying dope. It was only a matter of time before she was arrested. For the rest of her life she complained that she never had any problem when she was shooting heroin, and as soon as she tried to stop, the law picked on her; but in May 1947 she was not trying to stop, and the truth is more interesting than that.

To begin with, there was rivalry between the narcotics squad of the New York Police Department and Anslinger's Federal Bureau of Narcotics, and between the police and the FBI, partly because when a cop made an arrest the feds often got the credit. Then there were ill-feelings on the part of the little people who were involved with drugs towards the more famous people, who had more money and better lawyers, and whose habits were common knowledge, but who seemed to get away with it.

Then there were more and more heroin users in the jazz world at the time, but most of them were men; Lady's flamboyant behaviour, born of her combination of honesty and naïvety, attracted attention to her partly because she was a woman, as well as a solo star with a major-label contract. Racism was an added attraction for some of the cops: drummer Roy Porter remembered his own arrest in San Francisco a few years later. Stopped in the street, he threw two 'papers' of heroin in the gutter, the cop shined a flashlight on them and said, 'Okay, now run, you black junkie son-of-a-bitch, so I can blow your nigger brains out. Run, go on, try it!' Norman Granz tells a story about having to face down some cops in a Southern venue because he was afraid they were going to plant dope in Ella Fitzgerald's dressing room. As for Lady, 'It wasn't until she went to Philadelphia that she started getting surveillance by the narco people,' said Tucker. 'But Philadelphia's known for that. Very rough city.' In fact she had already been watched for years.

Jimmy Fletcher, a black narcotics agent who had attended Howard University and worked for the government in Kansas City and Chicago from the mid-1930s, knew Joe Glaser and John Levy from that period. He had transferred to New York in 1945, where he ran informers and kept an eye on the scene. He became friends with Lady – years later she gave him an autographed copy of her book – and he had plenty of sympathy for the people on the scene. But he hated narcotics.

Fletcher is interesting on the details of running an informer who is usually a junkie himself, and trying to get the junkie/informer to work himself up the ladder so that the law could get closer to the worst criminals. A dope peddler would not even be seized for only one sale: the law wanted at least three sales, because one might look like entrapment, especially with a good lawyer playing on the jury's sympathy. Fletcher seems to use the word 'pimp' for a drug runner as well as one who lives off prostitution; in this sense, Joe Guy was Billie's pimp. Fletcher also points out that the law protects the criminal, and since there have to be such rules, sometimes they are broken.

There is a libertarian argument that drugs should not be illegal, because that would take the profit out of it and put the pushers out of business; and anti-drug education would be more effective than wars against drugs. But one of Fletcher's stories will suffice to illustrate the sort of horror that he fought against. On a New Year's Day in Chicago, with search warrants,

We went in a place on Michigan Avenue; on holidays they never expected you, but the man wasn't there. A big marijuana peddler, third floor. Bill Fry and I found these sixteen mason jars full of manicured marijuana, and we seized it. On our way down [past] one of those Pullman flat places, we walked right by that door, wide open. Fry stepped in and stepped back out. He didn't see anybody – I'm coming down the steps with him, Fry has this great big box of stuff, sixteen mason jars, and I stepped in. Following him, he was down that first flight, on his way. I looked in, and I walked in further, and I just saw over the rocking-chair back, the head of a man ... I went down and said, 'My God, Fry, put that stuff down and come on up! Here's a guy in an act!'

So we went back up. Now he heard us. He came up and a girl looked around the rocking chair ... This woman, when we were coming around to look at her, put her head down and started to cry. A little bit of a person. Then we realized she was just a girl ... She started crying like hell and screaming. There were three little rooms; Fry took this guy, hauled him and handcuffed him to a bed in the next room.

I'd heard about these things but it was the first time I'd seen it. I sat at the chair, asking her what was wrong; there she was, her legs closed, and finally she started to calm down.

I closed both doors and asked her. She said that he was shooting her up with heroin; he was her sister's man. 'How old are you?' 'Fourteen.' 'What is it?' Then she opened up and showed us the needle hanging in one side of her vagina. The needle hanging. She opened her legs and started crying again. She just sat back and cried.

Well, my first feeling is, Kill the guy. That's your first feeling.

The fourteen-year-old's sister had been a prostitute for some years; the forty-two-year-old pimp was trying to enslave the younger girl. The case was widely reported at the time; the courtroom was full and the pimp was sent to prison for twenty years. A decade later, in New York, Fletcher had seen little over the years to inspire him with libertarianism.

I never knew a victim. There's no way I could even try to bring that about, because [Lady] made herself a victim. They're not victims when the law in general is trying to get the source of the lowest kind of trade in the world: the narcotics traffic. You victimize yourself by becoming a junkie.

Lady's surveillance had begun before she knew Fletcher. He is a good interviewee, perhaps because of his training as a lawman; he makes clear what is conjecture, what he does not know first-hand, and what he knows beyond doubt. And Joe Glaser was trying to get Billie arrested.

I knew Glaser in Chicago, when he was out there messing around with the big underworld, Al Capone's set. But he wasn't in it, he was just messing around ... He did have whorehouses, that was in Chicago. He was banned from Chicago ... During those days, police departments were permitted to tell you to leave town and don't come back.

One day I was called in the office, a confidential conversation with Col. Williams and the supervisor, and he said, 'I just got a call from Anslinger, and he said, "You send down Jimmy Fletcher, Joe Glaser wants a coloured agent," and it's all about Billie Holiday. He wants to work with you on getting a case on Billie Holiday, because of the fact that her mother is starving to death' – I think that was the exact expression — 'while Billie Holiday is making $750 a week and spending it all on narcotics.'

Matt gave me permission to set up an appointment with Joe Glaser. I called and made the appointment, and he said, 'Tomorrow, meet me at the Palm Tavern, and we'll have lunch there.' That's what we did . . . He confided in me, about Billie being his girl, how he'd like to save her, and the only way to save her is to have her knocked out by the government. He asked the commissioner, according to the teletype, if he would be violating the law in any respect, because on several occasions he had given her money for buying an ounce of heroin right down there. He'd advance money from her salary, knowing that it was for heroin. Technically there is a conspiracy factor there. Anslinger gave him enough answer about it, let him know that it would all depend upon how I made the case. So I spent quite a lot of talk on that that afternoon, how I'd write it up, and miss the point about telling the history for it, in my case report.

So the law was already targeting Lady before Sadie died in October 1945. How much did Sadie have to do with it? Was she complaining to Glaser about Lady not paying enough attention to her, and blaming it on drugs? The relationship between mother and daughter was not any business of Anslinger or Glaser, but Anslinger's motives are clear enough. He was a crackpot who finally had to be forced into retirement in the early 1960s; meanwhile, bagging a high-profile drug user like Lady could only be good for his bureau. Glaser's motives must have been more complicated, but Fletcher was convinced that Glaser had Lady's welfare at heart, though Fletcher did not believe there was a cure for heroin addiction.

Fletcher says that Lady never informed on anybody and was not known for sharing her dope with other musicians; but of course the pushers would take advantage of her.

She was buying two ounces a week from Sam, $400. They'd sell a half-ounce then, at street price, for $150. Many did ask her for $500 [for half an ounce] . . she has to go on, she's sick and all, what she really wants is a couple of fixes or something, but they wouldn't think of letting her have it that small.

They'd take advantage of her; she's making money, let her go
in the office and get it. They're mean, that's all. Nothing but
meanness. All of them are potential stoolpigeons, no way out
of it . . . you can make a stoolpigeon out of them by getting a
case on them. Tell them if they want to cooperate – I've
never seen any of them that would turn down that offer.

Fletcher had confronted Lady in the Braddock Hotel, a well-
known shooting gallery; during a raid, he knew the room was full
of junkies and that Lady had been waiting for a supplier, but she
said, 'All I want to say is will you search me and let me go?' 'So I
pulled a sort of casual search and, because you form a rapport
with the defendants previously and after an arrest, you've given
them a lot of confidence. And she wanted to open up, show
everything. Wouldn't let her do that.' She was clean, and he let
her go; besides, in order to do a proper search he would have
needed a policewoman, and he didn't trust the police.

Agents were already watching Joe Guy, who was known to be a
junkie and known to be supplying Lady; no doubt part of Glaser's
plan was to get rid of Guy. Fletcher said:

He always furnished her. He bought an ounce every day from
somebody there in New York. Our office was trying to make a
case against him. The day that Cohen and I ran in on him,
our lead was that every day Joe Guy walked up Eighth
Avenue and picked up an ounce from some connection, with it
tied or in the collar of Billie Holiday's boxer dog . . . he
walked the dog from way down on Morningside Drive up to
125th on Eighth and told the dog to go ahead. The dog
would go right in the Braddock Hotel, on the side, about
128th Street I think, and the elevator operator was waiting
for him, and he would carry the dog up in the elevator . . .
The elevator operator was in collusion, was trying to protect
Billie Holiday. He wanted the entertainers in there that made
big money; they tipped him like the devil . . .

But on the day they were watching, the dog did not appear,

and I said, 'I'll go up and pull the old telegram thing.'
Whatever it was I said, she said, 'Stick it under the door,' and
I said (in dialect), 'Too big to go under the door. I'll take it

on back if you don't' – and she opened the door. Then Cohen and I went in. That was the first close contact that ever happened. We found the syringe and all. She reached out the window. Got the syringe out of the side, on the street side of the window. Gave it to me.

We didn't prosecute for that. There was about a quarter of an ounce of solution in there, and a needle, which was particularly against the law, the two of them together; our reputation was at stake, in that we never brought in a petty case like that. Too small a case. After all, when a defence attorney gets you up there on that stand, I don't care what entertainer it is, they always have a slew of people who love them. They fill up a court and you're up there testifying, and the defence attorney gets on you about, 'And that's the kind of agent you are. Poor little girl and you come in – Lemme show you the evidence,' he's showing it to the audience of course, and to the jury, and all you're doing is sitting there, it looks bad. After a lot of years, it doesn't bother you . . .

The bigger the reputation as an entertainer, the less chance [they take]. That's what their pimps are for. I talked it over with the United States Commissioner, and he approved of it, and said, 'No, I wouldn't want to go in and prosecute that.' But you have to get permission to drop things like that from your prosecutor. So that's what I got.

Maybe they were also trying to go easy because they were getting cooperation from Glaser, who probably did not want Lady to get into big trouble. Glaser's plotting was successful in getting Lady into a clinic in April, but it didn't do her much good in the end, and the whole thing backfired, because finally she was convicted of a felony, which meant that she could no longer obtain the precious New York cabaret card which allowed her to work in places where liquor was sold. For in May events took over from the participants.

Lady and Tucker were playing the Royale Theater in Philadelphia on a bill with Armstrong when the Attucks Hotel, where they were staying, was raided. Clarence Holiday's boyhood friend Elmer Snowden, Lady's putative godfather, said he was also in town:

When I went where she was working, she would jump off the

bandstand and hug and kiss me and call me daddy; see, her daddy was gone. In 1947, I was working in the Club Calistic on Juniper and Race ... I had invited Nat King Cole and Louis and Billie, and they sat in and jammed.

I went into her dressing room and she was sitting and combing her hair, and she didn't even look at me. I was lookin' at her in the mirror. I said, 'I came over to invite you to an affair tonight where I'm working.' And she said, 'Can't make it.' And I said, 'Do you know who this is?' And she said, 'Yeah, Elmer Snowden.' So I figured, if that's the way she felt, okay. But the first person in the place that night was Billie. She had got herself together and she was herself, not like she was in her dressing room. See, I wasn't familiar with the hard stuff at that time. And her manager, he was a great big fella, like a prize-fighter ...

Tucker says that Lady had bought herself a new set of luggage in Philadelphia. After the last night of the engagement at the Royale, she went to the hotel to pick up her things; when she got there, Lady told *down beat* magazine, they could see that something was up. She said that her driver got out of the car to see what was going on and came back to the car in a hurry because, she thought, he already had a police record and was afraid of losing his car. (Fletcher said, 'They had already found two ounces in that car ...') The driver tore away from the kerb, hitting another car, and the police shot at them. Thelma Carpenter repeated the story Billie later printed in her book, that Billie drove all the way back to New York, although she had never driven before, but we don't have to believe that; there was also a story that she had climbed out of a window to escape. Newspapers at the time reported that one of the things the law wanted to charge her with was ordering her driver to run down a cop. At any rate, Tucker said years later,

Like I told all her managers *and* all her boyfriends as they came along, 'Lady never asked me to hold nothing for her, she never asked me to get nothing for her. So I'm not accusing you of doing it now, but if you do, I don't want to know about it.' The thing that I dug about Lady was that she made an issue, if something was about to happen, to send me on an errand, and when I came back I wouldn't be able to get in her dressing room. She told people, 'He may *think* a lot of things, but he don't know *for sure.*' She never let me see her take off.

Ascendio and I were sharing a room in the same hotel in Philly when Lady got arrested, and Jimmy threw the drugs under the bed. Before the hearing, he admitted the whole thing and asked me to get a story. I said, 'Look, man, I told you before — no stories!' I didn't even have a hearing. Lady took care of that.

Ascendio did some time (and died about 1949, Tucker said, killed in an accident with a horse). Tucker had been arrested at the scene, but was soon released; Lady said that 'the strongest thing he ever had in his life was a Camel cigarette.' But Lady was clearly worried; she also told *down beat*, 'Sure I know about Gene Krupa but don't forget he's white and I'm a Negro. I've got two strikes against me and don't you forget it.' (The famous drummer and bandleader had served time for possession of marijuana; Krupa is not thought to have used drugs; it is believed that he was framed because he refused to take the hint and bribe a crooked cop.)

Glaser wanted Lady to come clean, hoping to get her off with another cure, this time compulsory; but meanwhile, on a Friday night, Fletcher was on his way to Washington for the weekend. He didn't make it.

She had sailed along without getting caught until that shootout in Philly . . . but during that period, she was brought in to New York State Commissioner, to our office, by Max R—, who did the shooting down in Philly.

Washington had wired our New York office and told them about the shootout; they got away and were heading for the Grampion Hotel, right up the street from the Braddock. They knew that because Joe Guy had been heard to say to the band, 'You can get me at the Grampion Hotel . . .'

I was getting ready to take my regular train out of New York, at 5 o'clock. I was locking up. I'd stayed in the office too long and was the only agent there. I had picked up my little overnight bag and walked out to the elevator. I heard Col. Williams holler, 'Reeny, John, Phillip, who's back there?

Any agents back there?' If I'd just got on that elevator, I'd have had my weekend, I wouldn't have gotten involved with Billie Holiday. I was reluctant; after all, when you form a sort of a friendship with anybody, it's not pleasant to get involved with criminal activity against that person. I hollered, 'Yes, Mr Williams?' He was coming into the hall and I was going to meet him. 'Where were you on your way?' I said, mumbled, 'Well, I was on my way to Washington.' 'Like hell you are. You find some agent, call their homes and find somebody, and the two of you get to Newark, under that viaduct, and pick up Billie Holiday and her group, blah blah blah . . . Stick with her till Monday morning.'

I couldn't get anybody. Everybody was smart enough; you're just not home to be working all night and all. So I went to Newark, and the police had been notified there too, but Billie Holiday had circumvented Newark and went around and came up over the George Washington Bridge. I went up to the Grampion Hotel and saw the Cadillac, all shot up. Well, they had fixed the back fender that they had caught in another car; it said in the teletype it was standing up, but they had pushed it down. The only way I knew it was the Cadillac was when I went around and I didn't have a flashlight which I should have, I just felt around. Then I got my matches or lighter or whatever, looked around and there were bullet holes, .45 bullet holes.

I went and asked for Joe Guy's room, at the desk clerk. I didn't want the desk clerk to know, so you ask in a dumb manner, 'Hey, hey, what room Joe Guy got?' They'll tell you. They have no reason to suspicion anything and they don't care, even. He noticed that I don't go right up, you see? So he told me.

Fletcher staked out the room until a musician 'carrying this big old tuba horn' came to call; 'Joe Guy came out of his room, they spoke and went on in. So that was my clue to the fact that it *was* his room. Then I quit and went to my apartment . . . Started out again at 8 or 9.' He followed Lady to a club on 52nd Street and spent some money there, and complained that sometimes the office would refuse to honour such items on an expense account. He was supposed to keep an eye on her, but not do anything, because they didn't want to arrest Billie until Monday or Tuesday, because they couldn't get any warrants to make a clean-cut arrest until Monday morning. They had nothing against Billie Holiday, had no possession, but of course she had been shooting it up there in that hotel. Jimmy Ascendio and a chauffeur, and it was three of them. They didn't get anything on them down in Philly, they knew the top echelon peddler from whom Jimmy bought stuff for her, that was found in the car, and they had him under observation; they wanted to get all the warrants at the right time. They didn't want to blow it, that's the word. Glaser's set-up with me ended in New York. But my files went on down. Just like we had previous files about her from the beginning, by other agents who had tried to make cases against her several years before I was even in New York.

There was no cases against her at all . . .

But after Fletcher had staked her out, the rooms at the Grampion were raided and heroin was found, and Lady and Joe Guy were arrested. Fletcher was not involved in the raid, no doubt to his relief; she was freed on bail and went back to work, but now she acceded to Glaser's request that she face the music: she asked for the proceedings to begin as soon as possible, and her trial certainly took place long before Guy's, in a federal building in Philadelphia before Judge J. Cullen Gancy on 27 May 1947.

She was apparently driven to Philadelphia by one of Glaser's drivers, yet appeared in court without a lawyer. Assistant US Attorney Joseph Hildenburger described the 'parasites' who preyed on her, 'charging her a hundred dollars for dosages of narcotics costing five dollars'. All she wanted was a cure, but if the idea was to throw herself on the mercy of the court, it didn't work; she pleaded guilty, was convicted of possession of narcotics, sentenced to a year and a day in the Federal Reformatory for Women at Alderson, West Virginia, and taken there almost immediately.

It is reported that she was given a shot of something to keep her comfortable on the way to Alderson. The admission documents are interesting: she had $6.34 in her possession; she was 5ft 5ins tall, weighed 172 pounds, described her own build as 'large' and gave her address as 142 West 44th Street, New York. Her 'psychometric testing report USPHS classification' gave her IQ as 81, and she was described as of 'low average intelligence'. The fact that there is no such thing as a low average will tell us something about the bureaucracy we are dealing with here; she was given an SAT test, which generations of Americans have taken in high school: it is a general knowledge test designed for the middle class. The documents say that she claimed completion of the 6th grade, though she had been locked up for not going to school in the 4th, and added 'rates best in language and vocabulary, poor in factual knowledge'. It hardly needs to be said that the random sort of factual knowledge available to middle-class high-school kids could not have been obtained in the streets on the Point in Baltimore.

Her stay at Alderson was uneventful and no doubt boring, after the first period of withdrawal from drugs; she was not supposed to be allowed visitors, but she received mail.

In September she was taken to court in Philadelphia again to testify at Guy's trial; she was supposed to be a government witness and had already told the court in May that Guy was responsible for her drug addiction, but once again she was loyal to a boyfriend: she no doubt reasoned that she could not get into worse trouble than she was in already, and testified that the heroin found in their New York apartment was for her use and that Guy had nothing to do with it. Guy was released. He had had enough, and faded back down South where he was born, leaving Lady's life completely.

Guy had wrecked his life and his career with heroin, a junkie and a peddler as well; when he didn't have any money, he came back to Lady, reduced to a drug-runner. Her bail is said to have been $1,000, while his was $3,000; it seems that the law was not harassing Billie: Guy was the one they wanted, as well as the next supplier up the ladder.

But in a *down beat* interview, she pointed out that Glaser blamed Guy, and added, 'Don't you believe it. I'm a grown-up. I knew what I was doing. Joe may have done things he shouldn't, but I did them of my own accord too . . . Joe didn't make it any easier for me at times – but then I haven't been any easy gal either.' Jimmy Monroe, Greer Johnson, Roy Harte, Guy and Tucker and others ended up mothered by Lady, who could not have children; this addictive personality, so ill-equipped to cope with her own ups and downs, once again refused to blame anybody else for her troubles.

Norman Granz organized a benefit concert for her at Carnegie

Hall on 29 November, but Glaser did his best to spoil it, saying that he had a letter from her saying that she didn't want any benefit. Granz's JATP troupe performed, and the Nat Cole Trio had agreed to appear, but couldn't because of a contract conflict. The concert was poorly attended and only about $500 was raised; Glaser refused to accept it on Lady's behalf and Granz gave the money to charity

Lady behaved herself perfectly at Alderson, taking up knitting and getting along with everyone. It is fair to suppose that the government was not pleased that she did not help them to convict Guy, but she got the standard time off for good behaviour and was released on 16 March 1948. She said later that she had been worried that her dog, Mister, would have forgotten her, and was relieved when he was overjoyed to see her; John Simmons told a different story:

> When she had to go to Virginia, she left Mister with Bobby Tucker in Morristown, and Mister went under the house and stayed under the house for a week without coming out, and he woke up one morning and said, 'I'm alive!' and started running across the field; he ran, he ran, he ran. When Billie got out Mister ran back under the house. 'Take her away; I don't wanna see her.'

This account reflects Simmons's disgust either with the absolute nature of Billie's addiction, or with her mistreatment of the dog if it is true that she shot Mister with heroin. As she had done after her stay in the clinic, she rested at Tucker's mother's house, this time on probation. Tucker met her train in Newark, taking the dog with him, and confirms that her story is true: the dog was so glad to see her he nearly knocked her over.

'When she got off the train, she came up and grabbed me, and I could see that she was completely out of it.' She had changed trains in Washington and already made a connection. 'I said, "Lady, how *could* you?" That's all I said.'

12

The Jailbird

Now Lady was a famous junkie, and she knew that people who came ostensibly to hear her sing were coming, some of them, just to gawp. Yet it was a role she chose willingly. She had been on the wrong side of the fence all her life, and that was where she felt she belonged, or where she felt the least uncomfortable. Heroin was an escape, as marijuana and alcohol were an escape. When he met her at the train, Bobby Tucker was disappointed to see that she was already stoned; and he added that he had seen her three or four times when she was 'in' (referring to the earlier stay in a clinic) and 'she looked great – big and fat, healthy and happy'. Later she told him, 'There's chicks down there [in Alderson] for stealing welfare checks or murder or whatever. Some are doing fifteen years, some twenty. You know how they do that time? Counting the years, months and days until they can get high.' 'That was the driving force, to get high,' added Tucker.

And as she grew older it is fair to speculate that she found it more and more difficult to set herself free. The music business was difficult enough for a man; for a woman the insults were more profound and more personal, and for a black woman from Lady's sort of background who happened to be a great artist, there was no escape.

The heroin plague hit the black community at the time bop was being invented. Lady and Lester had been part of a vanguard, but during the 1940s a great many musicians, especially black ones, were furiously innovating. Ira Gitler has asked the vexing question about the relationship between drugs and music in his books (*Jazz Masters of the Forties*, 1966, and the invaluable oral history *Swing to*

Bop, 1985): the music wouldn't have been what it was without everything that went into it. The people who made it were different, and being different is always lonely.

At least the druggies of the era rarely lost sight of the music. Thirty or forty years later the young black jazz musicians coming up were too busy to take lope: they were getting college degrees and becoming businessmen as well as musicians, the better to manage their own careers; meanwhile, rock'n'rollers had been fed a media-fostered image of a somehow dangerous and revolutionary music which was nothing of the kind. As the image became more important than the music, which was not innovatory at all, in the 1970s and 1980s it was the rockers who died of drugs.

Big Stump, Greer Johnson and others hint that there were people who resented Lady, especially singers, because they didn't understand what she was doing, or because they couldn't do it. To be sure, she was already doing it long before she became a junkie, but she had always sought the escape of stimulants. Lady did not fully understand her talent, but she knew that she remained a cult figure. More people buy Volkswagens than Rolls-Royces, said Tucker, and that doesn't mean that Volkswagens are more 'popular'; but Lady was full of childlike yearnings that her background kept for ever out of reach. Glamour, adulation and true love may seem like banal and immature things to yearn for, but all they amount to is approval, in psychological terms, and there is no human being alive who does not need that.

It is not possible to be a better musician when stoned, for the same reason as it is dangerous to operate heavy machinery under the influence. Paradoxically, though, drugs can facilitate concentration, to the extent that they shut out noise and worries and allow musicians to get on with their work. Gerry Mulligan said that for years he could write tunes and arrangements for eighteen hours at a stretch while he was on heroin. The noise and worries may be caused by the meanness and stupidity of the music business, or by racism, or by the immaturity of the individual – 'I think I managed to not be an adult in just about every imaginable area,' said Mulligan many years later – but approval is still the bottom line. Jazz people of the 1940s, and especially the black ones, were working in a society largely controlled by people who were prejudiced against them in every possible way; to get high, especially in such an illegal, exotic and dangerous way, helped in coping with racism, allowing the necessary metaphorical genuflexion to be made with some other part of the mind, so that the insults could effectively be ignored. But most of the musicians did *not* take to the needle, after all; John Simmons, as we have seen, was disgusted with the degree of Lady's addiction, even though he later became an addict himself, while Roy Harte said that he could faint at the sight of a needle. Record producer Phil Schaap wrote in the extensive notes to a major Holiday reissue in 1992:

Lester Young had introduced Billie Holiday to tenor saxophonist Buddy Tate, Hèrschel Evans's replacement in the Basie band [in early 1939]. Lady Day and Lady Tate became close for a time. Buddy had no problem with Billie's involvement with booze and marijuana until he realized it was an addiction. 'Lady,' he told her, 'you can't get high all the time, not every day.' Buddy's advice went unheeded.

Buck Clayton phased himself out of her circle at a later point. Billie leaned on Buck to try heroin, which he refused to do . . .

Lady and Lester fell out for a while in the early 1950s. According to Schaap, Clayton thought that the issue was heroin: Lester's alcoholism worsened after the war, but he would have been the last person to stick a needle in himself. Clayton said surprisingly little about Lady in his memoirs in 1986, apart from admiring her as a musician, and when interviewed in about 1971 he distanced himself from her at first, saying 'I didn't know Billie.' But he told a story about Lady going off to see an artist, a painter, about 'a new kind of stuff – not pot.' He refused to go with her. Later, Clayton said, the needle marks on her arm became so infected that a doctor warned her that it would be amputated if she didn't stop, so she began shooting in her fingertips. Clayton blamed Lady for getting Joe Guy addicted.

And Clayton told a horrifying story about an incident 'in the Douglas House Hotel, on St Nicholas Avenue':

The maid went in to clean Billie's room. Billie didn't answer her knock. When she opened the door, Billie had a little girl in the room. The little girl had been coming home from school, she had school books. Billie had put a [tourniquet] around this little girl's arm and was about to use the needle when the maid stopped her. Then she had trouble, 'cause the maid went back and reported it, and they made Billie leave. It cost Glaser a lot of money . . .

We do not have to believe all of this story. It is second-hand, and nobody else mentions it; even if something like it actually happened, maybe the other girl was just another junkie. But Clayton was familiar with the hotel, because he used it himself, and implies that a lot of people knew the story because 'everyone was kind of mad at her'. This was before Alderson, and people do say that Glaser spent money keeping Lady out of trouble, without specifying what kind of trouble. Clayton also says he saw her beat up a girl in a jealous lesbian rage; his point is that her personality changed when she went on heroin: 'When she smoked pot, she was happy all the time.'

Clayton was clearly disgusted by her habit, and says that the heroin caused rifts with some of the best friends she ever had. Harry Edison said, 'After she got on horse, everybody she had around her were people affiliated with it. That left a lot of us out, 'cause I never dug it. But we were still good buddies, 'cause I didn't give a damn what she did, and she didn't give a damn what I did.' But Sweets seems also to allow that the gulf with some of her friends was greater.

In a conversation with Thelma Carpenter, I got the impression that Thelma was disgusted by the needle; she said that the manager of a club where Mabel Mercer was singing didn't want Billie around when she was out of her head. I asked Thelma if Lady's personality had changed, and she said, 'How are you gonna be happy when you're on that stuff?' But she did not abandon Lady. 'I thought, I don't need to be around that stuff. But my mother said to me, "Now's the time she needs a friend." So I used to go around and see her.' And Thelma added that she never saw Lady shoot up; she wouldn't have done that in front of a non-user, and Thelma never knew Lady to try to turn other people on to drugs. 'All these people who say they were her best friends, where were they later on, when she was alone? She didn't *have* anybody to say "Don't do that."' But the bottom line is that she wouldn't have listened; there never was a more addictive personality.

Clayton makes clear in his memoirs that he came from a large, warm family in Kansas and stayed close to them even when he was touring the world; this of course was the opposite of Lady's experience. Clayton had approval, and she did not; there is often an element of self-hatred in the use of the needle which others completely lacked.

Then there was Lady's lack of confidence; it may be significant, as Schaap speculates, that her heroin addiction began just as her star was rising, as though she couldn't cope with success. Again and again Tucker makes the point:

> The lyric meant most to her; she would tell a story. But she really didn't think she was a good singer . . . I really don't think she was in love with the way she sounded. She didn't like it . . . She was always amazed that people would want to come and see her . . . I don't think she ever once had the feeling that she was a good singer . . . She'd be more interested in what was going on *around* her, in the recording session, or in some soloist than in her own performance . . .

But also:

> She wasn't trying to prove anything to anybody. She was just being herself. Yes, she'd be nervous . . . She'd practically be 'out of it' during the show. When she was ready, I'd play the introduction, and she'd sing. When she finished, I'd play another introduction, and she'd sing the next number. When she got tired, you could applaud until tomorrow, but she was *through.*

She must have been more nervous before a concert in a large hall; in a smaller room it was easier to get a spotlight on her, so that she couldn't see the audience. One year she won an award, Tucker said, that was to be presented on the Arthur Godfrey radio show; he said it was a *down beat* award, but she never won a *down beat* poll.

> We were in Cleveland at the Tijuana Club, and it was a coast-to-coast hookup broadcast, and she was to receive the award at the Majestic Theater, where Lionel Hampton was playing. We went down in the daytime to do a couple of numbers and they were going to present her with the award, and when they announced her and they turned up the house

lights – it was a big theatre – it was like broad daylight, and she froze. When she saw the people she literally froze, her voice was shaking, she was trembling; she couldn't stand to look at the people.

An aircheck exists of Lady doing 'I Cover the Waterfront' with members of the Hampton band in July 1948; they wouldn't have had an arrangement, so it was just Tucker, probably Charles Mingus on bass and Ben Kynard on clarinet, with a big chord from the band at the end. It is a good performance, but Lady's vibrato is unusually fast, as though she were nervous.

Tucker also tells the story quoted by Chilton of the time in Boston when a club filled up with Shriners from a nearby convention, who chattered all the way through her act. They didn't mean anything by it; they didn't even know who she was, but afterwards she was heart-broken. This was by contrast with her usual hold on an audience, for Tucker says in another context:

> It was never a matter of playing an intro until the audience quieted down. She had the whole thing. Before she opened her mouth, she had them. She would walk out on a stage and just stand there until everyone was quiet. She wasn't punishing them. When she went into her first tune – small joint or a concert thing – she had everybody in the place.
>
> This is one thing I think kids are missing today. They're playing to 25,000, and it's the first thing they've ever done musically; it's like the audience is part of their programme. Not with us. We were it, and everything revolved around her . . . I've only seen two or three people who have that. Marian Anderson . . . maybe one or two others.

About the voice itself, Tucker added:

> It's a quality that's not trained . . . A person like Tony Bennett really doesn't have a quality sound, but to me, Tony's like a male Billie Holiday. You couldn't compare him voice-wise to any of the great singers, yet he's a great singer. Ray Charles is a stylist, but Lady had more than that. She had your attention, from right now.

Martin Williams described her, in his *The Jazz Tradition* (1983), as 'an actress without an act':

Through it all she maintained artistic distance; she was not merely indulging her feelings in public. In a sense, she was an actress, a great natural actress who had learned to draw on her own feelings and convey them with honest directness to a listener. And like a great actress, she did not entirely become what she portrayed, but in some secret way she also stood aside from it, and gave us the double image of character and an implied criticism.

Williams does not exactly say that she was an actress, but is merely comparing her to an actress. Lady didn't know how she did it, and she needed to hide from the mystery of it; and one of her ways of hiding from it was to have many identities. Her dressing room would be 'a cubby hole', said Tucker:

> She'd be fixin' her face or her hair or whatever . . . Did you look at those early pictures? And on every one she looks different. Well, that's how she'd do – one time she'd come out lookin' like this, and another time – no two of them looked alike – and that's how she'd look. Lady could look like any one of her pictures.

There are lots of stories about her relationships with other singers, but Tucker, who travelled with her for several years, was a witness:

> Mabel Mercer – *that* was Lady's favourite singer. Mabel sang by herself with a pianist. She was in one club for a thousand years, a little East Side joint, one of those chic joints, where she would look for a story that would fit how she felt, and most of them were very rarely happy-type tunes. Lady used to go by and sit, a lot of times. Mabel didn't even know she was there. But she got an awful lot of tunes from Mabel – even though they didn't do them in the same way.
>
> And there were other singers, like Margaret Whiting . . . In Billie's book, I think it says she spoke less than nicely about Sarah Vaughan, and she *loved* Sarah. When Sarah started getting big, I kind of felt that Lady felt envy . . . She thought that Sarah probably had the greatest sound in the world. She loved it.

Lady complained in her autobiography that after her time at

Alderson, Sarah snubbed her backstage somewhere; but Sarah told Max Jones that she was nearsighted and all that could have happened was that maybe she didn't see Lady. Tucker was there, as Lady said in the book, and he says there was no snub. 'Can you imagine anyone in any field – someone you admire – somebody snubbing Frank Sinatra today? It doesn't make sense. Lady was really the symbol among musicians and jazz singers. She was like the uncrowned . . .'

Lady was also conscious that she was now a jailbird, an ex-prisoner, and more sensitive than ever to a snub, real or imagined. Tucker tells a story about a benefit for the *Pittsburgh Courier*: 'She was still on probation – that ninety-day period. A bunch of chicks planned a big dinner for her after the benefit.' She refused to go unless Tucker came too, then paid her complete attention to him, until he realized what she was doing: 'The whole thing was planned. I said, "Lady, if you start this, I'm gonna leave." She said, "The minute you leave, I'm leaving." Everybody was asking questions, and I said, "Don't you hear them?"'

Tucker went to the juke box and went to the men's room and Lady followed him:

I said, 'Don't you realize you're embarrassing me?' And she came up with an appropriate remark about these people: she called them a bunch of cocksuckers, but she still hadn't said anything to *them*. So we go back to the table and one of the girls says, 'After all, Billie, he's not the only one at the table.' And this was what it was all about: she had a tirade that she had rehearsed, about the whole time she was in prison the only way she knew there was a world outside was because *I* wrote to her, and my mother took her into her house, 'And *you* so-and-so's . . .' It was set up, it was ridiculous.

She felt that they were using her, that they didn't care except that she was a big celebrity and a star . . she blew it out of proportion. They felt, she'd been in jail, so – there were a lot of people in jail, but she took it personally. She felt nobody cared, nobody really gives a damn, so whatever happened – 'It's nobody's business what I do.'

But she could be generous and understanding with younger people. During this period, young Ruth Brown did a residency at Café Society, after being fired from the Lucky Millinder band, and

Lady came to hear her, so Ruth threw everything out of her act that wasn't Billie Holiday, put extra flowers in her hair and did 'Gloomy Sunday', 'Strange Fruit' and 'Miss Brown to You'. She told Michael Bourne that Lady got up and left her table in a huff; afterwards she found Lady waiting for her in the dressing room, and got a lecture:

> Every time you open your mouth and do that it makes it better for me. I think what you need to do is find out who you are, because as long as you sound like me, nobody is ever gonna try to sound like you . . . You have great possibilities. You don't need to copy me.

It was the best lesson she ever got, Ruth said, and it must have done some good, because she soon became the first female vocalist signed to the new Atlantic label, and she had over twenty big hits in the black chart in the fifties, most of them in the top ten, several at number one, and a few crossing over to the white chart. When she stopped being a copycat, Ruth Brown had white artists covering *her* hits.

Lady refused to play the Chez Paree in Chicago, according to Tucker, one of the most famous nightclubs of the era:

> One of the owners was a Billie Holiday fan; he wanted her to come into the Chez Paree. She didn't care about going into that club. These are the qualities which put her up there as a human being, and she was a gorgeous human being. She wasn't intimidated by the money. She wasn't intimidated by the glory of being the first black person to work the Chez Paree. She said, 'Stick it!'

She was willing to try to be a trail-blazer when she wanted a decent hotel room in 1938, but why should she lend a white club-owner glory for finally hiring a black act, ten years later? Billy Eckstine said flatly that she didn't care whether she got along with people or not:

> She didn't give a shit about that. No sir. If you didn't like her, it didn't mean a goddam thing to her; she couldn't care less. And Lady would *make* herself not like certain people. Lady said she couldn't stand Ella's singing, and I *know* she had to *love* Ella's singing. I'd say, 'Bullshit; you know the girl

can sing, don't give me that shit.' And she'd say, 'William, goddam it, that bitch can't sing at all, man.' I say, 'You're wrong, Lady; you know damn well that girl can sing.' 'Oh, bullshit. I don't understand how you can think that shit. That's horrible.' And I know good and well that any singer has got to love Ella Fitzgerald, just for what she does. And Ella used to love Lady's voice. But Ella's a different person; she's a calm person. But Lady is never gonna admit that in her life – and she died that way. She wouldn't adhere to nothing to make you happy. No way.

'Billie was so honest that sometimes she had to tell a lie to be honest,' said Tucker. 'You could ask her a question, and twenty minutes later she'd give you a different answer, but it was still *her*.' Some of this was an instinctive front; she constantly changed her identity, afraid that people were trying to pin her down. Tucker tells a story about a big shot in a club, 'a screenwriter on *Gone with the Wind*' (which would make him a Hollywood big shot), who adored her and who brought big parties to a club on the Street every night of her engagement, spending a lot of money. The club-owner pestered her to be nice to the guy; all he wanted to do was meet her. She did her best, but essentially 'fluffed him off', said Tucker, nervous about a stranger trying to capture a piece of her. 'It would have been the same thing if it was the President.' Incidents like this could be embarrassing, but 'it was the kind of embarrassment that gives you a glow after it's over.' Again, this was also black pride before it was fashionable: people who have been taught to be defensive need to practise pride in order to find out how to be themselves.

She occasionally mentioned Sadie, Tucker said; 'She had gotten to the place where she was melodramatically romantic about her mother.' The feelings of guilt would re-surface, too, but for all the old difficulties with Sadie, she never forgot or forgave the way her mother had been ground down by lack of approval.

She was one of the first to 'up the establishment'. It's just that the things that were important to her were *really* important. What*ever* it was. Some of her friends might be attendants in the ladies' room. This would *really* be a friend, and this friend wouldn't take a back seat to the First Lady, or the Queen of

England. If she was with you, then she's not impressed by this
or that.

She occasionally worked in Baltimore, and even if she had
written off the Fagans, she always visited old friends; she never put
on airs. Freddie Green had been buying her records, not knowing
it was Eleanora he was listening to, and 'the first time I knew it
was Eleanora was when Miss Sadie came to town to my mother's
house.' Apparently Lady was touring with Basie, but she came to
visit her old neighbourhood.

She said, 'Billie's in town over at the Royale.' It shocked me.
My mother says, 'You know who Billie is — Eleanora!' . . .
They had an affair for her and she did her last show at the
Royale and came over to the Savoy Grille, down on Bond
and Monument Street, and it was mobbed, they had
tablecloths and everything. They had a three-piece band —
with Charlie King, who played trumpet and piano at that
time — and she did four or five numbers that night . . . And
I'm sittin' back at the table thinkin', 'Billie Holiday.' Beautiful. Hilda was there. The bar was loaded — it was a small bar
— and she saw me and said, 'Freddie! Hey, Freddie!' And I
had my seat there right next to her and her mother, and I
said, 'Oh girl, you're fabulous!' and she said, 'Sit down and
shut up' . . .
    She was regular people. Whenever she came into town she
would say, 'Let's go see Hilda.' We went down to a bar on Pratt
Street and Bethel, Rosie's bar. She's a Polish lady, Miss Rosie . . .

Evelyn Randolph, an ex-show girl who was associated with
Lloyal Randolph, a local politician who owned or operated some
of these places, was a chum when Lady came to Baltimore. 'I went
backstage with Evelyn at the Royale,' Freddie said. Hilda, like
Freddie, was a friend from the old days. Lady had no side to her,
no secrets from her old friends. She was careless about her dope
(this was long before Alderson); on one of her visits to Baltimore,
Freddie came to pick her up and take her to Rosie's, 'and I saw
this powder in this glassine bag and she said, "You want some
horse?" Oh, no; I never could do anything but smoke. I never saw
her take it, but she was negligent. She'd have grass on her dresser
and some powder over there and people could come in and see it.'

Another time:

She saw two girls in a club one night that she wanted to entertain – we was at the downstairs room in the York Bar – the chicks were together, one was brownskin, the other was light – yeah – and I knew these girls. I said I was going to my room, and she said, 'Invite them too, Freddie.' And I did, and they was yellin' too when they knew it was Billie Holiday – wow, Billie Holiday. And definitely I left. And she winked at me when I walked out the door.

But she never changed, no matter how much of a star she was. She'd go down in the slums, in the bars, and she'd have her mink, you know, and she'd just throw it on a chair, then sit down with a little booze and buy for everybody else, and she would tell jokes in different voices . . . There'd be little kids, dirty and all, and she'd grab 'em up in her arms and not care and hold 'em, and 'How you feel?', and they'd have molasses on them. She wouldn't care. She loved people.

But as she entered the last phase of her career, perhaps she was losing touch with her oldest friends; Freddie said that the last time he saw her was 'in 1948 at the Club Astoria bar'.

Lady remained vulnerable, and could show it. She and Eckstine were not lovers, but buddies;

She'd seek me out and say, 'William, you and I are gonna hang out. You gonna be with me, baby.' She was soft inside. She was definitely like a little girl; she could lay her head on me and be just the little girl she was. She could be like that with Bobby Tucker, too.

And she mothered Tucker: once she raised hell in a hotel because she thought he had a girl in his room when he wasn't even there.

In our relationship, I couldn't talk to any girls. We'd been finished at 2 a.m.; at 5 in the morning I'd been in one of the musicians' homes, and when I came back she stormed into the room. She'd been standing at the door, watching it; she's looking in the bathroom and under the bed. She had called the house detective . . . So when I came in she said, 'I'm not going to call your wife; I'm going to call your mother.' And she did. From Vancouver! She's protecting me.

Bassist John Levy said:

She was always trying to keep a hard front, but she was a beautiful person. Like with us: I was married, Bobby was married, and she was like a mother hen on the road; if some chicks came around she'd come on, 'Oh, no, they're married, I don't want you hanging around' . . . She always had respect for me and Bobby Tucker; we were pals, and she always tried to protect us from this other shit, because we were so damn square . . .
And yet she'd turn us on to somebody that she has – you know what her story was. 'I don't want this chick; you can have her. Give her what she wants, give it to her.' But it would be like a masculine thing, just out of spite, like if you were a hanger-on, trying to get next to her . . .
I've seen women that were millionaires, bringing their husbands, and when they get there they say to them, 'Why don't you go?' And he'd leave, and I couldn't understand that. He'd be pretty damn dumb not to know. And yet there had to be a man in her life – a man had to be there.

She was professionally jealous. Eckstine said that he first met Tucker, and Tucker first played for him, while Lady was at Alderson; Tucker was working at the Onyx, with Babs Gonzales and his group, 3 Bips and a Bop. But Tucker didn't accept long-term work and didn't play for any women singers. Lady never forgot that loyalty.

She didn't want me to play for anybody. Once, when we were working in the Ebony Club, she lost her voice for two or three days. Different people came in – Billy Daniels, Sarah Vaughan – she didn't want me to play. I said, 'Lady, this is *your* gig; the girl is working your gig to save *you*.' She said, 'Well, all right; play pretty for her.'

(Note that Sarah did this favour for her – Lady mentioned it to *Ebony* magazine in 1949 – during the period when Sarah was supposed to have snubbed her.)
She was always full of mischief: she certainly would not have

been above teasing Eckstine about his love of Ella's work. Tucker said she would tell stories and jokes, 'and get them all screwed up and *that* would be funny'

> I would stop her from doing things, like if she wanted to get bad with somebody, I'd say, 'Cool it.' She was strong as a mule, but I'd tilt her to one side, so she couldn't plant both feet. She'd finally break up laughing. Joe Louis came to see her one night when he was still champ, and he said something to me, and she told him, 'Don't let Bobby get you down, you'll never get loose!'

Sometimes she did not give Tucker a set list before they went to work, and he would just start playing a tune; if she didn't feel like doing that one, she would say, 'Uh, uh.' And sometimes they would play a little game: he would refuse to change to another tune, and she would just keep smiling and refusing to sing until he did.

Even before Alderson, she stole a song from Tucker:

> I can show you the original transcript. But my name isn't on the music. I used to play this tune; she said, 'Why don't we write a song?' So we put it together, and she said she'd call it 'Somebody's on My Mind'. The idea at the time was not to write a great tune; we would write it, take it to a publisher and get an advance – enough to get high on, this was the general idea. She got in trouble with the lyric and Arthur Herzog ended up doing about twenty-six or twenty-seven different sets of lyrics; they played one publisher against the other, saying she'd record it, trying to get the largest advance.
>
> After she was arrested and went away, she asked me to go through her things and see if there was anything that might involve somebody else and get rid of it . . . I found a letter from E.B. Marks which said, 'Dear Miss Holiday, Here is the advance of $400, as per request we have removed Bobby Tucker's name.' But I didn't really get angry about it. Many years later, they were playing the record, and she said, 'Well, *we* know, don't we?' I do often wonder – suppose it was a big hit. I'd probably want to kill her!

Lady and Mabel Mercer did the songs differently, but they had one important thing in common. 'Lady was vain about how she *felt,*' said Tucker. When he first met her at the Downbeat Club in November 1946, he had told Tony Scott that he was not a big fan of hers.

Lady didn't kill me. Tony asked, 'What is it you don't like?' I said, she's got no sound; it's like a flat thing. He said, 'Then who *do* you like?' I named Ella and some other singers. He said, 'But with a singer like Ella, when she sings "my man has left me", you think the guy's going down the street for a loaf of bread. But when Lady sings it, man, you see the bags are packed, the cat's going down the street and you *know* he ain't *never* coming back.' The next set I started listening to what Lady was saying and *how* she was saying it.

What really got to her fans was the meaning she could give a lyric; the lyric meant most to her . . . a tune like 'That Ole Devil Called Love' – there's a line about 'rocks in my heart', and when she sang it you said to yourself, 'How cold can it *get?*'

It would get very cold indeed for Lady in the next decade, but not until the end, as her health gave out. Despite being a jailbird and without a cabaret card, and with even worse men trouble to come, she still had a lot of good work ahead of her, and a lot of laughter.

She played concerts in New York that did not require the cabaret card, and gigs in other parts of the country which were occasionally broadcast; at this time in her career the airchecks and 'bootleg' recordings become more common. Before and after Alderson she played at Carnegie Hall, and Tucker said that 'as a matter of fact, those Carnegie things were the best things I've ever done, musically.' On 24 May 1947, a few days before her trial, she and Tucker did a solo spot in a Jazz at the Philharmonic concert; 'You'd Better Go Now', 'You're Driving Me Crazy', 'There Is No Greater Love' and 'I Cover the Waterfront' were recorded, and Tucker's accompaniment is exquisite. His debt to Teddy Wilson is apparent, but his choice of what he plays – adding to the beauty without getting in the way – and his placing of the notes reminds us that accompaniment on this level is a special art all its own. If Lady could swing at any tempo, Tucker was as perfect a partner as any others had been.

As for Lady, her live recordings were always somehow special, the audience – even if she didn't want to see it – helping her to reach another level: in the studio, she was always a great jazz singer; in concert, the subtlety of her art was beyond category. Again and again, as on the phrase 'Oh, how I yearn' in 'I Cover the Waterfront', she seems to be throwing away the words, yet wrings more emotion out of them than the most emotive 'artiste': living the words, yet, as Martin Williams wrote, somehow in some secret way also standing outside them.

And after her eight months in jail and still on probation, she was a greater singer than ever. In March 1948 she played her own Carnegie Hall concert, the first of two. 'I think she was so glad to get back,' Tucker said, 'and she was so amazed that people hadn't forgotten her, that she did one helluva show.'

> It was fantastic. It was unbelievable. There were seats in the aisles, and there were about six hundred people sitting on the stage. Nowadays that's against every fire law in New York. The musicians – and there were only four – had to carry their instruments above the crowd to get on stage. There were people sitting around the piano, and it was like a living room. Everybody was scared to death until the introduction to the first tune. It never was a contest; it was just pure fun.

She wrote in her book that she was frightened at first to have an audience *behind* her on stage. She thought, 'What the hell is that big choir out there for?' The musicians in addition to Tucker were Remo Palmieri on guitar, Levy on bass and Denzil Best on drums; Ernie Anderson produced the concert just because he was a Billie Holiday fan, according to Tucker. 'To show you how uncommercial it was, they didn't even tape it. They didn't record it. And I don't know a thing she'd recorded that she sung as well.'

Ernie Anderson promoted her Carnegie Hall concerts; he already knew Lady's drawing power. Around 1945 he had booked Town Hall for a concert by cornettist Bobby Hackett, who was one of the best jazzmen of the era, admired by Louis Armstrong among others, but who never achieved the fame he should have had.

> I put ads in the papers and paid disc jockeys on the key Manhattan stations to plug Bobby's concert. Every day I'd call the box office; I was shocked to learn that there was virtually no sale. Three days before the concert I called Billie

and asked her if she would split the bill with Bobby; Billie also
loved Bobby Hackett. She agreed; I ran one small ad and we
sold out.

So Carnegie Hall was not regarded by Anderson as a non-com-
mercial gamble. After she got out of Alderson, Anderson wrote,

When she arrived in Manhattan she wanted to be in a hotel
in midtown. She asked for a hotel on Dream Street, West
47th Street, so called because of all the drug busts. I put her
in there and I got the impression that she was clean and was
going to stay off drugs, that she was trying to stay away from
Harlem and drug pushers and ex-husbands, who sometimes
provided drugs to keep her in line. She did ask for comic
books; I went out to a news-stand and bought her a huge
stack. She was terribly grateful.

Anderson had met Joe Guy once, introduced as Billie's husband,
and was shocked to realize that Guy was high as a kite.

Meanwhile at Carnegie Hall the box office was going crazy.
The five Heck brothers who ran the box office said it was an
enormous draw. The senior Heck said we could sell more
concerts by Billie that night. He even asked, 'Why not? She
could do another concert at 2 a.m. and another at 5 a.m. . . . '
He seriously proposed this but I wouldn't think of it . . .
Well, the gross we racked up set a new house record for
Carnegie Hall. Moreover, I later discovered the Heck brothers
had made a private killing on seats sold that weren't ever on
the floor plan. A few years later they were all arrested for a
similar scam.

She sang twenty-one songs and, to everyone's surprise, half a
dozen encores as well; the music magazines printed glowing
reviews. 'So I booked the hall for a second concert three weeks
later,' wrote Anderson, 'and that sold out on announcement. This
time Billie broke her own Carnegie Hall record.'

At one of these concerts she was wearing her hair in a bun, said
Tucker (in her book she said it was a gardenia; maybe it was
both), and somehow Billie got stuck in the scalp with a hatpin.
'She bled like a son of a gun, and it was gory, but she didn't faint.'
In her book she later said that she'd passed out, as though her life

wasn't dramatic enough as it was. Lady could have originated the saying, 'If the truth and the legend conflict, print the legend.' In her case she made up legends, almost as though she suspected that she herself would become a living legend and needed to try to beat that game, too.

It would be interesting to know how much she suspected that Joe Glaser had set the law on her, and if so how much she resented it, because when she came out of Alderson she had agent trouble. Anderson says that Ed Fishman had somehow got in to see her at Alderson. 'He said, "I've even promised her that from now on she'll have a French maid travelling with her." Naturally I was telling Glaser everything. After all, I had played her several times and always through him . . . so I tried to pacify both agents.' He paid both Glaser and Fishman, to be sure that Lady would show up for the first Carnegie Hall concert.

While Lady was in Alderson, Glaser got divorced, and it was a messy, acrimonious split. Anderson heard all about it:

> Joe Glaser only got married once in his life, and that was to the madame of the whorehouse; the place was called the Astor Hotel, in Cleveland, Ohio. When Joe Bushkin played a three-month stand with the Bunny Berigan band at the Aragon ballroom there, he practically lived there, because the madame had a cook who made terrific yiddische food for him.
>   Later Mrs Glaser moved with Joe to Beverly Hills, where he had purchased a mansion directly across the street from the Beverly Hills Hotel. Joe Glaser was always a Chicagoan; Joey Bushkin was staying across the street, and he had married the Chicago department-store heiress Francese Netcher, who was a regular item in the Chicago society pages, so Glaser decided that he had to have Joey and Francese at his housewarming. 'When Joe Glaser introduced me to his wife, she and I both smiled and looked blank. It was a bizarre moment I can tell you,' recalled Bushkin.

Glaser's California residence didn't last too long, said Anderson, because he was soon back in his Manhattan apartment and working out of his New York office. Some years later he ran into Fishman at the Embers, where Bushkin had a quartet with Buck Clayton, Milt Hinton and Jo Jones. Anderson asked Fishman, 'Are you handling this act?' 'No,' was the answer, 'Joe Glaser got here first.' Then Fishman took great pleasure in telling Anderson his version of the details of Glaser's marital bust-up. Glaser and his wife had a huge fight. Joe had a safe deposit box in Beverly Hills where he kept a vast amount of cash safe from the taxman; Mrs Glaser had a key to the stash, they both raced for it, and Joe won. Maybe that was when Glaser's wife called Ed Fishman, Tucker said, and told him that Billie's contract with him was about to run out, causing trouble for Glaser at Lady's expense.

Joe told me later that he and Ed Fishman had worked in the same office, and Fishman had stolen from him. They had AGVA meetings because Lady was supposed to be under Joe Glaser and was with Ed Fishman. I had to go with her to the meetings. Joe Glaser and Ed Fishman literally didn't want to walk on the same street; it was ridiculous.

Ed Fishman promised her the moon, when she was away. Joe had a lot of things lined up, but she'd been nickeling and diming him to death, and it wasn't a pleasant relationship – plus the violent scenes they'd have in his office. She felt she was being done in, that Joe was selling her down the river.

Lady soon decided that she'd made a mistake with Fishman, and in any case the American Guild of Variety Artists decided that Associated Booking, Glaser's company, still had the right to represent her. Fishman sued her for breach of contract, but Levy thought that Fishman backed out without too much trouble because of Glaser's gangster connections: 'He didn't want to be found in an alley somewhere.'

Glaser saw his income shrinking because Billie couldn't work in New York clubs, but he also saw more money coming in from Louis Armstrong, who had embarked on a new phase of his career: having given up his big band, Louis was playing concerts and theatres very successfully with his All-Stars, which meant larger audiences. So Glaser tried to steer Lady in that direction. A show called 'Holiday on Broadway' at the Mansfield Theater in June 1948, which included Slam Stewart's trio and other acts, was musically satisfying, according to Tucker, but lasted less than a week; the theatre had never presented jazz before.

Another gig beginning in July harked back to the Swing Era. At the Strand movie theatre, Count Basie's band with Lady supported the hit Humphrey Bogart movie *Key Largo*, and it was the longest theatre engagement of her career, almost six weeks of ovations and good reviews. But she complained to Barry Ulanov for *Metronome* magazine that she thought the audiences there came to see her 'get all fouled up'. 'I'm tired of fighting,' she told Ulanov, and claimed to be off drugs for good; she was fighting against her own lack of confidence as well as the ever-present temptation of drugs, which she went on and off, having withdrawal symptoms each time. But it is also true that she simply liked to complain. It was natural for her to feel misused, but she was also long past working as a maid or a prostitute, and many of her friends thought that she wasn't happy unless she was miserable, and misery was good for business: even as she resented the people who came to gawp at a jailbird, she must have been pleased at the number of paying customers. During this period some of the club-owners who hired her did record-breaking business.

She also told Ulanov that Bobby Tucker and John Levy teased her about her lack of education, asking her questions about 'history and geography. They made me count. They insisted I was too smart. They asked me what I was trying to pull.' But there were now two John Levys: one was the bass player in Tucker's trio, but she was referring to a would-be gangster, her new boyfriend. She had contined her pattern of choosing a man each time who was worse than the last one. 'I believe if they had a whole battalion and they picked every first-class quality that a woman would want in a man,' said Tucker, 'and they put a rotten egg in with the battalion, she'd find it. She laughed and she admitted it.'

13

The Gangster and the Bassist

John H. Levy had begun with a string of candy stores. Nothing was ever in his own name, and all his operations included the whole family; as a boy, nephew Ron Levy sold candy out in front while the book-making went on in the back room. In 1942 Levy married Wilhelmina Gray, whose professional name was Tondaleyo; she had been dancing since she was a child and first appeared on Broadway in *Flying Colours*, the show that featured Monette Moore. In 1943 they opened Tondaleyo's on 52nd Street, and the club was successful for about eighteen months, until the bank that owned the land kicked them out; Erroll Garner got his start there. Tonda left Levy in 1945 and they were divorced in 1947, because, she said,

> He was a miserable bastard, a terrible man. He gave me everything I wanted; I had furs, diamonds, clothes, a Cadillac. But I was in prison, I couldn't move. Every morning he'd be on the adding machine; if I wanted pocket money I had to steal it from him, and he'd yell, 'I'm a hundred short!' He'd beat me, and if he was frustrated he'd pound his head on the wall. He was crazy

Tonda finally took her baby and sneaked out on him; the only clothes she kept were the ones that were at the cleaners. He cut up the rest, and threatened to cut up her face.

In 1948 Levy was a partner in the Ebony Club, at 1687 Broadway, which later became Birdland. One of the other managers at the Ebony was Dickie Wells; Lady had known them both for years.

Although she did not have a cabaret card, and although the following year she was turned down when she applied for one, she appeared at the Ebony Club. In her 1949 appeal, a judge commended the police department for refusing to give her the card, as though making it hard for her to earn a living would stop her from shooting dope if she felt like it; meanwhile, a small-time gangster pulled a few strings and the law apparently looked the other way. Though Tonda and Ron say that she did not in fact get away with working at the Ebony, forced out by the law after one or two nights, *down beat* reported that she worked there twice, in June 1948 between the two theatre engagements and again in October. At any rate, Levy's attempts at string-pulling were as good a reason as any for her to get involved with him, so that the self-righteous law of the puritans had even helped her to screw up her private life.

Sometimes Lady had not had anybody looking after her; Joe Glaser was a booking agent, not a manager, and he had other clients to take care of. Lady's managers, such as they were, were always her boyfriends, and even if they did a poor job of it at least she had someone to fight with. Levy was light enough to pass for white – he once decribed himself as half Jewish and half Negro – so now she had a man on her side who could pound the table on an equal basis with the white man. Some people were impressed that Levy immediately spent a lot of money on her, renting her a nice apartment and providing gowns, fur coats and a green Cadillac convertible, but this was an investment, and Levy wanted a big pay-off: she was paid very well at the Strand, but had to ask him for pocket money.

Ron Levy, a teenager in 1948, often travelled with Lady, because his Uncle John was claustrophobic and could not ride on an aeroplane. 'One time he tried it. He got on an airplane in Boston, when he wanted to get to her birthday party or something, and he was so ill they had to take him off even before the plane took off.' When Lady asked John for money, Ron said, the reply was, 'You got accounts at all the department stores, you got a room full of clothes, you got a Cadillac with a driver out there waiting for you; what do you need money for?' And Ron adds that when they were together he looked after the money. 'If we went out to eat or something, I'd have to pay. She couldn't count. If you gave her five hundred-dollar bills she'd be happy, but as soon as she changed one she didn't know how much money she had.' Ron also says that although John Levy's fair skin may have been an advantage, he never tried to pass. 'Lots of times we'd be going to a baseball game with Joe Glaser or somebody and he'd always introduce me as his nephew.'

Before her return to the Ebony in October she worked in Philadelphia and at the Blue Note in Chicago; afterwards she returned to Chicago, this time to the Silhouette Club.

In 1947 and 1948 on Musicraft, and from 1949 on Columbia, Sarah Vaughan's records were selling well, she had a lovely, rich vocal colour and her range was extraordinary. It is no disrespect to Sarah to say that her material and her interpretations were simply easier to take, whereas Lady required closer listening. Sarah also won the jazz polls during this period. Lady was envious, and one wonders if this did not reinforce in some way her decision to turn down offers from the Chez Paree: why shouldn't the all-white club break the colour barrier with a singer who obviously appealed to a wider white audience? Lady's stubbornness and capacity for taking umbrage reinforced themselves; she was acknowledging her status as a cult favourite.

She did good business wherever she went, after all; there was no lack of offers. There were not enough theatre and concert opportunities, but perhaps there were not enough promoters like Ernie Anderson thinking in that direction. Plans for a tour with Lady's own backing group, including a chorus, came to nothing; perhaps the plans were only her pipe dream, a fantasy about approaching the flash of a big-time pop star, but in any case Levy would have been opposed to risking that kind of money, and so would Glaser, for less selfish reasons: she was never entirely reliable, and cancelled engagements would have meant having to pay the entourage regardless.

The three weeks at the Silhouette in November 1948 were not happy ones: Lady hated openings anyway, and if an engagement started badly it was sure to be a bumpy one. She had a cold to begin with; then the owner was impressed, Tucker remembered, because Joey Jacobson (apparently her fan from the Chez Paree management) was coming to hear her, and she refused to go on: 'She said, "I don't care nothing about it."' For most of the engagement she sang only four songs a set, and Jimmy

McPartland's band had to carry more than its share of the load. The reviews were not good either; under the circumstances, Lady was not singing her best.

There followed a short gig in Philadelphia, and on 10 December she was in New York, where she resumed her series of Decca recordings. The personnel was just Tucker, John Levy on bass, Denzil Best on drums and Mundell Lowe on acoustic rhythm guitar, and the Stardusters, a vocal backing group of about six voices, who sang only on the first two selections: 'Weep No More' is a nice tune co-written by Gordon Jenkins and Tom Adair, and the Stardusters' contribution is apposite, but they become wearisome on Ralph Blane's somewhat syrupy 'Girls Were Made to Take Care of Boys'. Without the chorus, 'I Loves You Porgy' was beautifully and intimately done. (Greer Johnson liked it very much and asked Billie why she didn't do it in clubs; she told him that 'she didn't think Gershwin's *Porgy & Bess* had done much for the race,' but he may have been projecting his white liberal correctness on her.) The verse on her remake of 'My Man (Mon Homme)' now includes the words 'He isn't true/He beats me, too/ What can I do?', perhaps reflecting the quality of her life with the other Levy, the pimp.

Everyone was looking forward to the next engagement, at Billy Berg's in Hollywood. Business would surely be good during the holiday season, and it would be nice to spend a large part of the winter in California. She opened successfully on 15 December, but New Year's Eve turned into a violent fracas and got her in the headlines again. Her friend Mike Gould was looking forward to a New Year's Day dinner: 'She said she would do all the cooking – and she had a baked ham, turkey, sweet potato pie, and I picked up the food and brought it out to the house, and we waited and waited.' Lady was busy getting arrested.

The usual straightforward account as related by John Chilton is accurate, but Jimmy Rowles and Bobby Tucker were there, and their accounts add verisimilitude. 'It was New Year's Eve, about a minute to 12,' said Rowles.

I was playing with Red Norvo, Neal Hefti, Herbie Steward – about a six-piece band, playing the alternative set from hers – and the place was packed hand over fist. So where the piano was on the right side of the stage, there's a curtain there closing off the kitchen, and Lady spent a lot of time in there with this peg-legged cat, he's the chef, and Red Norvo's saying, 'Any minute now, Auld Lang Syne.' And John Levy – Al Capone – he was out there countin' the bread because he wants his taste, and he goes in the kitchen, and all of a sudden I hear this terrifying noise and this cursing and screaming, and she's throwing plates and tearing the kitchen apart and it's a big rumpus. Shit, that bitch is at it again. Redesign the club tonight. And from behind the curtain comes this ofay cat I've never seen before, and he's got a white shirt on, no tie, and in this hand he's got a basket of biscuits and he's got a twelve-inch butcher knife buried in his left shoulder just above his heart, and the blood is gushing out and his eyes are glazed and he's coming at me: he's in shock and he's two feet from me and he's gah-gah-gah, and I look at this cat and I say 'Holy Christ!' and I went right under the piano backwards clear across the stage, and the bass player looks up and says 'Jesus!' and the next thing you know we were all over in the corner.

And the police came. And we went on the next night, and we finished the engagement. But I never thought I'd see anything like that.

Drummer Chico Hamilton was there too, but all he could remember over twenty years later was that there was blood all over the place, and he was astonished afterwards that his good suit hadn't got messed up.

Rowles didn't know Levy well. 'I had heard John Levy was mean. Those kinds of guys, you don't know what they're gonna do, so I stayed away from him.' Tucker knew Levy, and he puts a new spin on it; the incident was certainly Levy's fault, but not exactly because he was as tough as he looked. Lady was in the kitchen, which was crowded with the usual hangers-on, one of whom, Tucker says, was Johnny Stompanato, another small-time gangster, whose violence against women eventually cost him his life in 1958, when he was stabbed to death by Lana Turner's daughter. Something happened in the kitchen; Billie was unpredictable, and suddenly Levy was there. 'That incident should never have happened,' said Tucker.

Lady's always been one of the guys, *until* John is there. Then she's Lady Ashley. Most of the time, John's not around. It was two or three guys back there; we were just talking; one guy might have said, 'Hey baby,' you know, and might have patted her on the can or something. But because *John* is there, he got very 'WHAT ARE YOU DOING?' She went into her act, so that John could go into *his* act; they're trying to explain, and John is really trying to pursue it more. They're saying, 'We love her; we wouldn't think of getting out of line.' John's getting scared, because there are three guys . .

Tucker, a perceptive observer, is saying here that Lady was already getting the better of Levy. They had only been together a few months, and she had already got his number: she cannot mother him, but she can get him to make a fool of himself; if he is going to be the tough guy and live off her money, one way or another he is going to have to earn it.

He snatched a butcher knife – to keep them off him It just snowballed and got all out of proportion, and a guy standing on the sidelines got it in the shoulder. He wasn't even involved! Well, Lady started throwing bottles, and the guy takes his jacket off and walked up on the stage; he realized he's been cut, but he doesn't know by who or what for, and he's all bloody He walked on stage and everybody walked out It just shouldn't have happened.

Tucker repeats, 'she went into an act, because John was there. He was going to do what she wanted him to do ' To act the man? 'Yes, but he really wasn't. What made me mad was, I had to spend the whole night trying to keep this bum out of jail, and I was hoping they'd keep him there for ever . . . he would *like* to have been a gangster. He was all mouth.'

The violence with Levy was endemic and mutual. Eddie Beal, a pianist who put together a show for Lady in San Francisco in 1949, saw Levy drag her across a room by her hair; Bobby Tucker saw him beating her up. 'I'd go to get her for work, and she's on the floor and he's standing up in her stomach – kicking her. We're due on stage, and she could have avoided it.' But she provoked Levy. 'Oh, yeah, anything. Almost like a child will do things to make you blow your top. Once you blow your top they're satisfied, they feel like they've beaten you.' Levy the bassist said that he and Tucker had to tape up her ribs once before a show, because she had been beaten and complained that she couldn't breathe (the next day she went to a doctor, but nothing was seriously wrong). Levy the pimp took his lumps, too; Lady was tough enough, and often gave as good as she got.

Why did she choose men like this, and why did they get worse over the years? Having been rejected by the Fagans and by her father and abandoned by Philip Gough, she had little self-esteem, and Sadie was not the one to instil it into her. Lady avoided the possibility of deeper disappointment by choosing unsuitable men. She was also a masochist; the violence had become part of her love life. Men who were tough, or at least behaved as though they were tough, seemed to be the only ones who could do anything for her; paradoxically, she kept herself safe by not risking the vulnerable part of herself. It was a game, and pain was part of the prize; and there was also economic determinism.

As Milt Hinton put it, young musicians in the 1930s and early 1940s, even if they had a steady job in those days, could not compete with the 'sportsmen' in terms of flashy cars and clothes and presents for the women; so the musicians played their hearts out for her and shed tears over her and watched her go off with a pimp. Perhaps this comes directly from our biology: in prehistoric times the most desirable man was the man who could lead the successful hunt, bag the biggest prey and keep the predators away, because he was the man who would ensure the survival of the woman's children; this translates today into the man who can get the promotion at the office, so that he can afford to buy new furniture for the living room. For much of the working class there has never been any worthwhile promotion to hope for: Carl Perkins's masterpiece, 'Blue Suede Shoes', is about a hillbilly who knows that he is going to live from paycheck to paycheck for the rest of his life, but at least he's got a new pair of shoes to cheer him up on a certain Saturday night; he knows that even the shoes are ephemeral, to be worn out in a few weeks, but he looks ahead no further than that. And in the African-American sub-culture that Lady came from, there was not even a weekly paycheck, and no security at all; the pimp with money in the pocket of his flashy suit was a one-eyed king in the land of those who'd had both eyes poked out by the racism in the American economy.

And the pimp at least needed Lady; no one else seemed to. Bobby Henderson, Sonny White and even Jimmy Monroe would not fight, could not project the sort of masculinity that Billie recognized as need of her. The pattern of self-debasement of girl singers was not unique to her: even Ella and Sarah put up with a certain amount of it. At one gig at the Apollo in the forties, Tucker said, Ella played the venue with sunglasses, owing to a black eye bestowed by her man of the moment; Billie followed her into the same place, wearing sunglasses for the same reason.

Levy the bassist later got into management, handling pianist George Shearing, but mostly singers such as Nancy Wilson and Roberta Flack. Talking about the girl singer,

. . . [She] does everything to hurt herself, little things. Why do that? Why would you punish yourself, put yourself in that position? You don't have to do that! I think they feel that with this god-given talent, they feel like they got lucky and they think they gotta pay for it in some kind of a way, so they punish themselves.

One of his girls told him:

'I knew it was wrong, but I just had to let K. do how he say, and there was conflicts, and I just wanted him to be the big man, and I just be under him.' Which was awful, because he had nothing to offer her. She was the star, the performer, but she just let him keep her right down until it got to the point where she had to get away from him or be destroyed. He wasn't even a good businessman, he got investments screwed up, and there he was in the latest suits driving that Cadillac being the big shot, walking in and talking loud and making everybody hate her and not wanting to be around her. [She] learned, but in the meantime she's constantly searching – he's gotta be *the* man, and he's gotta be the whole thing and the whole bit . . . Men who really are great and straight people, men who got their own thing – she don't want them. She wants the kind of man that's gotta need her, that she's gonna feel that she's gonna be able to give him the money and things . . .

Even Doris Day, white as the driven snow and one of the biggest box-office stars of the century, had a first husband who was a violent alcoholic musician, and later stuck with her third husband until he died, although Marty Melcher was a second-rate con-man who squandered millions of dollars of her money and turned down the best film parts she was ever offered without even telling her. Levy the bassist remembered Levy the pimp driving his car through the Loop in Chicago at 80 miles an hour, running all the red lights, knowing that he'd get pulled over and all he had to do was pass a $20 bill out the window. First the pimp could confirm his manhood by buying off cops, and then the singers were caught in a double bind, because of their position: they were earning the money, but they thought they had to support the man emotionally, allow him to believe that he was doing something necessary, that he was the boss. Levy the pimp bought property with Billie's money, and he didn't even know anything about artist management.

Some of the women were tough, too. Levy the bassist said he didn't think anybody could manage Sarah Vaughan; she was selfish compared to Lady, and Ella would scold a musician on the stand, whereas Nancy Wilson would wait until later, and neither Tucker nor Levy ever heard a harsh word from Lady. 'Even in those days, even though I was just a musician, I could see how she was being exploited,' Levy said. 'The places she played, it was just a matter of getting the money. Like he would phone and say, "She won't play for you unless you give me two weeks in advance." So he'd pick up the money and fly back to New York . . .' (Is it possible that the reason she didn't play the Chez Paree is that the management of such a posh place would have nothing to do with Levy the pimp?)

Levy the bassist said to himself, 'Why do some people take misuse and abuse from another human being?' One of his clients 'didn't have the beatings but she had the verbal things and the misuse of her talents and her money and she could sit there and see it and know it and allow it to happen – females call that love – I don't understand it.'

That's when the bug began to get in my head about management, because I said, I know that's wrong, it shouldn't be that way. Billie would never have let me manage her even if it had come up; they have to have that man that once in a while beat on them – the Frankie and Johnny syndrome, I call it. There's no simple answer but I see it as another thing I disagree with: it's like, 'I've gotta have a man that keeps reminding me that I'm making more money than he can make, that I'm more famous than he is, so in order for him to assert his masculinity he knocks me down.' I was with Ike & Tina Turner, and although he was a performer along with her, had his own talent and abilities, without her he was just another guitar player – she was the act – but that same kind of male dominance existed that doesn't allow her to express herself except in what he allows her to say – she's completely dominated. But I always felt that a woman deserves the same feelings as I do.

And the irony was that as a manager the bassist had to live down having the same name as the pimp.

I was managing George Shearing, and we did a thing, we had Bing Crosby, Frank Sinatra and Peggy Lee, and George played for Peggy, and Paul Smith played for Sinatra, and – can't think of his name – played for Crosby. And Peggy Lee told somebody, 'I don't like John Levy because of what he did to Billie Holiday.' And I met her one day at Capitol Records and I said, 'I've gotta straighten something out; you think I'm John Levy that managed Billie, but I just played bass for her for less than a year, before I went with George.' And everything was cool.

Orchids had been sent to Billie, and this guy walks up to me and says, 'You John Levy, you're a manager?' 'Yeah, I manage Nancy Wilson, George Shearing.' 'Did you ever manage Billie Holiday?' 'I just played for her.' 'You sure? Because there's a bill at the florist shop downstairs where we sent the orchids up every night –' The bill was about $75, and I know how Levy operated; he would order it and never pay for it. But I said that I would like to straighten this out, so I went to the florist shop and he said, 'That's not the man. Big fellow, looked like an Italian, big Italian-looking man.'

He always paid her hotel bills; as far as I know she was never strung that way, because just like any pimp or hustler, he makes sure a woman's taken care of so far as her *needs* –

after that, forget it. I think he was supplying her [with drugs].
He was halfway hooked himself, on opium.
    But they never tried to turn us on; Bobby and me, we were
just working musicians, $200 at the most a week. In those
days they wouldn't bother with people like us.

Lady soon lost two of the best musicians she ever had because
they couldn't stand her pimp, but the bassist never forgot the
experience. Like all the others, he loved her. So *many* people loved
her.

She never had an entourage, like most female singers would
have an entourage of females who are there with the dresses
and the hair doer, the this and that and the valet. The only
people I would see were the people who came around to sell
her some shit. We used to dress her, Bobby and me, go into
the dressing room before a concert and button her up,
because there was nothing between us that way. She'd just
walk in, take off her clothes, sit and talk to you, rappin',
and at first I was so prudish, such a square − squaaare! −
and she said, 'Sit down, motherfucker, where you goin'?' I
wasn't that young, but just to have somebody be so deliber-
ate with it, you know.
    I thought she was beautiful. Very few people are beautiful
sitting up there with no clothes on, because very few of us
have bodies that are that beautiful, but it was done in such a
way that you really thought about the inside of the person, of
who she was and the whole thing, and she really looked good
. . . Her skin − beautiful, yeah. Her complexion when she
came out of Alderson was just great. Later on she began to
get the bumps and scars and droops and sags. But in speaking
about her with her clothes off, it was never done in a vulgar
way.
    Even that 'motherfucker'. We did that thing on Broadway
at the Mansfield, and she bought Denzil and me tuxedos;
after we worked there for a week or so and we had some other
dates coming up, I said to her, 'I got paid, but you didn't
take out for the suit.' She said, 'You've got a wife and three
children; you give them the money. Give it to your old lady,
she needs it more than me.' But I said, 'You paid for it −' And

she said, 'So what, motherfucker?' Even saying something like that, it was meant in a completely different way.

I'd been out there and done a lot of things, so it wasn't that, I'd been around, but I could never adapt to that way of life completely, it was always on the outside. Those people were coming around — we knew why they were coming around — they were spoiling her career — and here you love somebody and you workin' with her every night, and when that chick was right and she walked out to sing — I just couldn't wait. You know, Bobby and I used to rehearse together and figure out a lot of things to do behind her, and when she was right, and you walk out there, and she started singin' gooood! It's just something you can't ever forget.

I've had three experiences you couldn't buy from me. I came to New York in 1944 with Stuff Smith, the violinist, a trio of violin, bass and Jimmy Jones on piano, and some of the things that happened with him — I remember one night I was playing and crying, it was just that emotional. Well, I'm emotional anyway. And Billie Holiday and her Carnegie Hall concert and some of the other nights when she was really together, and you got such a thing. And then Erroll Garner, a couple of times there.

And the one thing in the management thing was when Nancy Wilson opened at the Coconut Grove, and the show that Luther Henderson and I had to fight with her to put together; and how she came off and all the people stood up and started applauding, opening night, and I sat down and cried again. (And I got fired three or four months later.) Even with George Shearing all those years, and we were making a lot of money and we were playing some great music together, and I felt very good with Roberta on occasions, but I never reached that emotional peak that I did with Stuff or Billie . . .

The show was supposed to start at 9 o'clock and she wouldn't be there until 11, and then she'd walk in with Mister and she'd sit him on a stool and they'd have to give him some milk and he'd lap that up, and then she'd take a couple of drinks and talk to everybody at the bar, and then walk on down to the stage — and people would be lined up around the block to see her. That day is gone; nobody's gonna wait to see anybody now. The younger generation, they don't understand, they weren't around – Billie Holiday wasn't a singer in the sense of a Nancy Wilson, or even an Ella or a Sarah – she was a complete stylist. When you listened to Billie Holiday sing, you felt that she had lived that experience and she was telling a story about it . . .

She was a great woman; she had more feeling for everything and for people than anybody I've been in touch with.

There were two John Levys, Bobby Tucker often had to explain, and the one who played bass, 'He's a beautiful human being.'

But there was still the other one to deal with. Following on the New Year's Eve at Billy Berg's, Levy the pimp and Lady were arrested and freed on bail of $2,500 each, charged with assault with a deadly weapon. On 13 January 1949 Lady opened to standing room only at Joe Tenner's Café Society in San Francisco; on 22 January their hotel room was raided and, the federal narcotics agency's superintendent Colonel George H. White said, an amount of opium worth less than $50 and a pipe were found. They were arrested again and freed on $500 bail each.

There has always been gossip about this arrest to the effect that Levy helped to frame Lady. He would certainly have been capable of it; she was making a lot of money and he had been stealing as much of it as he could for nearly a year, he had his business interests and his family in New York, and by this time he may have decided that he couldn't control her even with violence. He may even have understood that she was capable of manipulating him, and from his point of view, especially after that New Year's Eve, she may have become more trouble than she was worth. But there is no evidence of a frame-up; Bobby Tucker never believed it (and nobody despised Levy more than Tucker), and if Levy had wanted to get rid of Lady all he would have had to do was walk away. It was more in character for him to do what he in fact did, which was to continue to steal her money as long as he could. In any case, whatever was supposed to be happening, the law made a complete mess of it.

'It just happened that while she was in town,' White said, 'we had picked up four or five little coloured prostitutes on drug charges; they were involved in some minor conspiracy, but they complained in effect, why do you pick on poor little people like us and then let Billie Holiday run around and use drugs?' White saw their point, he said in a 1971 interview, but he contradicted himself. He pointed out that she had a very ostentatious life-style, and that it was right to arrest richer people as well as the poorer; but he also said that Holiday to them was nothing, and was only hurting herself by taking drugs, and that they didn't make a habit of arresting addicts unless there were other circumstances involved. He said that it was Levy they wanted, because they knew he had connections.

One Saturday morning, at any rate, I got together a couple of police officers – in those days search warrants were required in federal court but not in state court, so if we found anything it would have gone to state court because we didn't have warrants – and I found out somewhere that they were staying at the Mark Twain in the Tenderloin district, and went down there and asked the desk clerk what room they were in, and went up and knocked on the door . . 'Just a minute, just a minute' . . . finally we kicked it open. It doesn't matter who makes the arrest; I made it, and we took them into state court.

Apparently Levy had gathered up the paraphernalia and a small quantity of opium and told her to get rid of it. She was up against the door in the other room – I think she slammed the door and I opened it – and she ran into the bathroom of the other room to try to flush the stuff down the toilet, though the smoking paraphernalia was such that I don't think it would have readily flushed; there was an improvised pipe with a little glass bottle, and a little lamp of some kind, and a little bit of opium . . We both reached the bathroom at the same time, and she tried to throw the stuff into the open toilet and sort of fell into the bathtub, without hurting herself.

They were both in their pyjamas and cold sober; there was no smell of opium in the room, so no recent smoking; there was not even a gin bottle in the room, said White. There was no resistance after the goods were nabbed, and Lady was calm. White had worked in New York and knew 'Jake' Levy by reputation: that he was an opium smoker, had a police record and had been an informer. Before they even got them booked it was established that they were both opium smokers and that the amount found was for their own use only. White said (over twenty years later) that he had formed the impression that Levy was the actual owner of the opium, although Levy hadn't said so in so many words. Levy had immediately mentioned the names of some officers in New York he'd worked for, and offered to 'turn the tricks on some very important people in the narcotics traffic.'

I wanted to know who the people were, and he was very vague on it, though I was pretty sure that if he wanted to he could give us some pretty good people. But we learned early in the game not to rely on promises, so I told him he would have to make bail, and if they wanted to do something of any importance, we would try to recommend that they not be prosecuted. Levy said, 'If you come on down to the club tonight, I'll be able to tell you who these people are I deal with, and I'll get on the phone and see if my connection is still intact.' So I went there, and we were sitting at a table, and Billie was performing on stage, and Levy kept saying, 'It takes time, give it a chance.'

If White ever got any firm offers out of Levy, he doesn't say so.

The procedure in state court then and now is that if you have a case you want to prosecute you have a preliminary hearing, which appears before a judge to determine whether there's evidence to go to trial, and they can take this evidence before the Grand Jury and indict, and that will take you directly to trial in Superior Court .. However, much to my surprise, the Grand Jury did not indict Levy but Billie Holiday ... I was very curious about the reason Levy was not indicted, and I asked the Assistant District Attorney, because of course the Grand Jury did whatever the DA told them, and he said, we could have indicted Levy, but Billie Holiday is the name and we want to get some publicity, or something like that. 'Levy to us is a nothing guy.' I said at the time, this leaves it open for Holiday to claim later that it was Levy's stuff, and the jury might acquit her. In the meantime Levy would be gone ... oh, I forgot to say that while I was at the nightclub that evening, a photographer snapped a photograph of Levy and myself at a table, which is commonplace. The photograph

turned out to be a serious piece of evidence. I don't think it
was planned at the time . . .

Lady completed her engagement at Tenner's Club, playing to
capacity audiences until 9 February; ten days later she was
indicted, Levy was not, and he immediately left the state, so as not
to be called as a witness. In March Lady went on a tour of
Northern California with a trio led by Red Norvo; it was a flop
and she walked away before it was finished. She then went back to
New York and was reunited with the pimp who was supposed to
be framing her. It was during this period that she applied for a
cabaret card and was turned down. In May she returned to
California as the date of her trial approached.

She was acquitted, 'which was not disappointing to me,' White
said. 'I was disappointed that Levy got away, because I knew that
if I got a charge against him he would turn informer. Now it was
neither Levy nor Holiday nor the information I sought. The only
thing I did achieve was to convince the little prostitutes that we
could move with equal spirit against the rich . . .' White was also
immediately aware that the case gave rise to the story that there
had been a conspiracy of Levy and himself against Billie.

On the one hand, if White wanted Levy, why did he not make
this clear to the court before the preliminary hearing? Jimmy
Fletcher said that the one thing White was famous for throughout
the federal agency was being a drunk; maybe he forgot. And on
the other hand, if Levy wanted to frame Lady, why did he, a
known opium smoker, plant opium on her instead of heroin?
Couldn't he have arranged for her to be alone in the suite when
the door was kicked in? And if there was a conspiracy, would
White have been dumb enough to allow himself to be photographed in the club, either before or after the arrest?

Meanwhile, Tenner had contacted Jack Ehrlich, who acted as
Billie's lawyer.

She had to be got out on bail, and that took a little bit of
doing, because of her record as a user. I didn't know at the
time I was getting Levy out just exactly what their relationship
was. As she told me later, he cleaned her out; I thought they
were sweethearts, and so getting one out I should get the
other out . . . Then I suggested that she go and get her

personal physician to put her in and dry her out so to speak,
because when we went to court I didn't want to have that
facing me, or her for that matter. I assumed she was using
opium; he handed it to her to throw away. I'm a lawyer, I
play safe; I wouldn't walk into a courtroom and have
something happen that would reflect the use of it and I
couldn't win ...
I asked whether she knew this man White. She didn't know
him. I said, 'You think back; take your time. Did Levy meet
anybody in that club, have drinks with anybody?' That was
quite a place out there in those days, you know; we had no
trouble like we do now. There were nice spots out on Fillmore
there ... Anyhow, she finally said yes − this was a couple of
days later − well, I know human nature; all you have to do is
go someplace with a camera and every son of a bitch wants to
be photographed. So I went there one night and [met] a
woman who took pictures there, and we took her films, boxes
of them, put them up on an x-ray machine, and sure enough
here's my old friend George White *and* Mr Levy sitting at a
table, each with a drink in front of them. And I said, 'Print
that.'
And when I got to court, I started examining George
White − a friend of mine, oh yes, and a man for whom I have
great respect. He's one of the limited few who won't stretch a
testimony a hair; he's an honourable man. I tried other cases
with him. I was asking him about whether he'd made a deal
with Levy, about planting this girl and so forth, and I said,
'Well, you know Levy, don't you?' And he said, 'No, not
particularly. I knew that he was an informer in New York.'
And I said, 'Well, you knew him well enough to have drinks
with him,' and I whipped out the picture. At the trial. Of
course the District Attorney checked it, and of course it
wasn't admissible but the jury saw it. It was inadmissible
because there were no foundations made for introducing it; I
would have had to prove that I went there, and how it was
done, who took the picture and all that, and it wouldn't have
had the effect.

White was shocked when he saw the picture, and the courtroom
broke up when he blurted, 'That's not a good picture of me.'

Ehrlich joined the laughter in spite of himself. He was convinced
the picture had been taken before the arrest, but his reasoning was
circular: White wouldn't have gone there after the arrest, because
he wouldn't have wanted to be seen in public with Levy if he was
going to let him go; but there is no evidence that White ever
intended to let Levy go, and no reason why White should have
been afraid to go to the club unless he was conspiring with Levy to
frame Billie, which Ehrlich refused to believe.

When Linda Kuehl was interviewing Ehrlich, she wanted
desperately to believe that White and Levy were working a frame-
up together, and Ehrlich patronized her – 'Young lady, you're
missing the point' – but finally had to say, 'I'm sorry you can't see
it, I can't explain it.' He was a good and clever lawyer, and he
convinced himself that Levy was framing Billie because he was
more likely to succeed with that defence if he believed it himself.
The young District Attorney certainly needed the advice he hadn't
got from White; he was hopelessly outclassed by the opposition.

'Levy was a minor pimp and opium user. I only wanted him as
an informer,' White said, and in fact, in a grudging way, White
almost admired him:

> I thought he was a smart man who'd do anything he could to
> extricate himself from trouble. He was awfully smooth,
> persuasive, not charming, not crude; he would give you more
> the impression of being a shrewd businessman. As pimps go,
> on a scale of ten, I'd give him possibly seven ... I wouldn't
> have pegged him as a pimp if I hadn't known, any more than
> I could tag a high-class prostitute. No 'P' on his forehead.

Ehrlich thought that Levy had 'cleaned her out' and that she was
'on her way down', which is silly. She was making plenty of
money. Ehrlich thought that perhaps Levy wanted to get rid of
Lady because he had a guilty conscience about stealing from her, a
risible notion. 'He called me from New York after the verdict. He
wanted Mrs Ehrlich and me to come to New York and see his kids.
For a victory celebration. Can you see me doing that?' He despised
Levy, which is all very well, but clearly Lady had Ehrlich wrapped
round her finger.

Ehrlich says that Lady's doctor's name was Henderson; the
accepted version of events is that she and Levy had known Herbert
B. Henderson for years, and that after the arrest he put them up in

his home, because no hotels would have them. Whatever the truth of this, the psychiatrist involved, Dr James Hamilton, tells a fuller story. As Billie's trial date approached, her defence went into action. 'My contact with her was through George White,' said Hamilton.

As soon as he arrested her he sort of felt from the other side that he would like to help, so he got me onto the case. I felt that as long as there was any allegation that this woman was hooked on dope, it would be a helluva job to get her off . . . She came to me, and I said that the only way I could help her was to know if she was on the hop, and the only way to know that was to lock her up, and she demurred, and I said, 'Then, tough.' And she said, 'Okay, how?' So I plunked her into Twin Pines, which was a psychiatric sanatorium, eighty-five miles down the road in Belmont, and the only thing they didn't give her was dope. She felt that in order to get by in confinement she had to have ample quantities of booze, and as I remember she had a mixture of crème de menthe and brandy which amounted to nine ounces a day . . .

Now actually if she had been addicted to heroin, she would have had diarrhoea and withdrawal symptoms, but she didn't; after five days it was perfectly apparent to me that she was not addicted. I put her under full psychiatric controls except with booze. I had one piece of information: she was not addicted to narcotics. If it was opium, this was a different range of magnitude from the stuff that you shoot . . . I don't know what her use was because she didn't tell me. [There would have been blood and urine tests as well; probably she was completely clean in May, several months after the arrest.] But we were still faced with a charge of possession, and George White got the dope right out of her hand. And working this over with Ehrlich, I was primed with the idea that I had to make my point with one gust of wind, so to speak.

So when I was put on the stand I was qualified and then Ehrlich said, 'Are you acquainted with this lady?' I said, 'Yes, this is Miss Holiday. She came under my care a week ago and I immediately put her under full psychiatric controls and proved that she was not addicted.' And the prosecution jumped up and said, 'Object, object, object, this is not the issue – the issue is possession.' And the judge banged his gavel and yelled at me, 'You can't say that.' And then the two attorneys and the judge left the courtroom with me on the stand and the jury were kicked out too; and there was a lapse of maybe forty-five minutes, and everybody came back in and I was given some very firm instructions, as though I had exposed the worst thing in the world, the fact that this woman was not an addict. I was given the sermon and asked one or two minor questions and dismissed.

But it just happened that I knew somebody on the jury, and so I heard the full story afterward: in talking it over they said, 'Well, it was a funny thing that they shut up that guy Hamilton when he had been her doctor; why didn't they let him testify? We think there's something funny about this whole case, and we think the real culprit is Mr Levy, who went out of town.'

As for Lady, she famously testified that when Levy gave her something to get rid of, she was just doing what her man told her. White said she did everything but sit on a piano and sing 'My Man'. Hamilton thought that Levy's departure from the scene was due to Ehrlich, who thus saw to it that he could blame Levy, and it worked.

The reason for doing this kind of thing was that she was royalty, we thought – I thought, and I think George White thought. He did bust her, but why else did George get me, a really tough person to have? I can tell you why, because George is all cop, a cop with a tough exterior but with a heart of gold, so he got me, and this whole thing was done – not with his connivance, because he wouldn't connive, but putting me with Jake Ehrlich – that's as far as he could go as a cop to stack the case against himself. So that's what happened there.

Informed that Ehrlich had said that he could be a heavy-handed cop, White said:

That meant that when I was arresting somebody I would be firm, and if they showed any resistance I would lock the guy in such a way that – the theory being that it would be better to punch them in the stomach than to shoot them. I was one of the best narcotics agents in the business; this was one of the few cases I lost ... I told Ehrlich that he was a conniving shyster lawyer of the first order, and he would laugh and he'd think that was a compliment.

Hamilton said:

We whipped her down to Twin Pines the first day I met her. She took command of that hospital. She set the hours that she would eat, and she had her drinks when she wanted them, fixed when she wanted them, I mean a psychiatric hospital cook doesn't usually act as a bartender ... She went to Henderson's place afterwards.

All this was long after Levy had left the state. Hamilton went to see Billie at Henderson's on a Saturday night, and there were about forty people there and 'it was a high-class, swinging party ... What Henderson has,' Hamilton added in 1971, 'is a big, pretty swinging black practice, and these are the guys that take $100,000 out of Medicare and all this crap. I guess they see 200 patients a day to make them happy.'

Perhaps the story is true that Henderson and his wife drove her to Twin Pines and that on the way there she bought a chihuahua and asked Henderson to look after it for her while she was there. 'She had a little dog when she got out of Twin Pines,' said Hamilton, 'and she came to my apartment at 11 in the morning and said, "I'm going shopping. This little dog isn't going to hurt you to have in your office," and I said, "Of course not."' They put the dog on a table where he played for two hours while Lady shopped. On the whole, this does not sound like a woman who was worried about going back to jail any time soon.

What drove Billie? I don't like to use this word – it's not a good word – but she's really a psychopath. An impulse-driven, strong, talented but undependable woman ... The impulse-ridden thing. I think those of us who are not so impulse-ridden go through a long learning process in which we learn control, or if we want to discharge our impulses, we go to Las Vegas and gamble, or we do some other odd things, but we do them without having them reflected in society's eyes, because we're thinking of tomorrow, and the next year, when they're going to be thrown up on us. Billie didn't have this training.

In other words, as Pony Kane had understood without any education or big words, she was just don't care-ish.

Lady complained that she was often bothered by crew-cut agent types visiting her dressing room, warning her that they were watching her; in fact when she was caught with dope in her hand the law couldn't convict her. Twice the law had wanted her boyfriend/suppliers, and twice they had got away unscathed. After her acquittal in June, she played to full houses at a theatre in Los Angeles, while a booking agent was suing her for non-appearance at some March engagements upstate; then she went back to New York to a tumultuous reception at the Apollo: she was doing as she pleased, and not doing badly for a jailbird. On 17 August there was a Decca recording session, and the first tune she recorded became for ever hers: languorously slow, yet rhythmically inflected so that it became sassy in a new way, it was 'Tain't Nobody's Business If I Do'.

14

The Last Decade Begins

The world that Lady grew up in was disappearing. Most of the Harlem clubs were gone, 52nd Street was dying, and there was less work for the musicians who had always been her best friends. Everybody was copying Lady, who effectively acknowledged that she was a cult item, because she had no choice. She continued to do as she pleased, but within the limits imposed by a world that was passing her by.

The 1950s were not kind to Lester Young, either. Dexter Gordon, Sonny Rollins and others followed the big-toned tenor sax tradition of Coleman Hawkins, but Stan Getz, Zoot Sims, Al Cohn, Paul Quinichette (who was called 'Little Prez') and others were inspired by Lester, and some of them (especially the white ones) worked more and made more money. There is a story about Lester approaching a bandstand and shouting at one of them, 'You're not you, you're *me!*' Of Quinichette he said, 'I don't know whether to play like myself or Lady Q, 'cos he's playing just like I play.' On another occasion he is supposed to have said, 'It's kind of bitter when all your disciples are working and you get a job once in a while.'

His experience of a US Army stockade in Georgia hadn't done his gentle spirit any good; only the Army knows why, having diagnosed his physical condition, it then kept him until months after the war was over, only to give him a dishonourable discharge. The orthodoxy that Lester was so damaged by the military that his music had suffered is not true; he knew what he was doing on his horn until the end: his talent had evolved and taken in all his experience, but if an artist complains that 'you can't keep doing the same stuff over and over again', the critics often don't want to listen, and the critics of the 1950s were no exception. Jimmy Rowles said, 'Hammond was in another world . . . But those guys sound out the musicians and then wrap up their opinions. It all goes back to when they missed the boat on Charlie Parker. If they had taken the time to listen, they would have known. But they didn't.'

All this was also true for Lady. Roy Harte said that in 1946 she would imitate other singers imitating her: 'She'd say, "Did you hear that record? I sound like Dinah Shore!"' She made problems of her own with her unreliability, but most people never got a chance to see her anyway, and even her records often received polite, lukewarm reviews during her last decade, because few were really listening. Yet every scrap she recorded is now selling around the world on compact disc over thirty years after her death, and where is Dinah Shore? Where is Patti Page? But Lady's last decade was not as bad as it looks to us in retrospect; there continued to be ups as well as downs.

Drummer Denzil Best and bassist John Levy had jumped ship to go with pianist George Shearing by the end of 1948; the faithful Bobby Tucker stuck it out a few months longer, but by the turn of the decade he was gone, too. 'As close as we were, I couldn't stand John Levy any more. It got completely ridiculous. He was accusing me of having affairs with her, and he insulted me, but I knew that that was her man.' Ralph J. Gleason wrote in *down beat* that she had turned up for the trial in San Francisco with a black eye and complained that Levy had taken her mink coat away, probably in case she went to jail; if this is true, perhaps she had gone all the way to New York between Twin Pines and the trial for a quick beating. She told everyone that he was her man, he was looking after her: 'He knows what I want.' Jimmy Rowles avoided Levy, but he witnessed it all, too, at Billy Berg's:

> That motherfucker Levy comes over and says [Jimmy does a stone imitation of a gangster]: 'You don't mind going up there and filling in on the piano till Lady Day gets up there, do you? I gotta go down there and stomp on her tummy a little, wrestle her around a little bit, beat the shit out of her so she sings good.' 'Right away, John, sir,' 'cause I'm scared of him and I'd rather play piano than have him after me. So

308

I'm at the piano, and people are saying, 'Jesus Christ, where's —' and he's got her down there on the floor and he's jumping up and down on her stomach, getting her in trim for the show, and she's not even made up yet, and Billy Berg's saying, 'You better go down there and get that motherfucker off her so she can make it up here to sing a tune.' And people are saying, 'Where the hell is Lady Day?' And Tucker says *he's* not going down there: 'John Levy's down there; if you think you're gonna get my ass down there, you're crazy.' Tucker wouldn't go down there and I wouldn't go down there; nobody would. So we all had to sit up there and wait.

And then she came up. Now she's pulling herself together. And she says, 'Hey, motherfucker, am I all right? Look at me.' Go ahead, it's right over there, and you'd point her. She's got up the stairs; now she's gotta get from there to the bandstand, so there's another problem, because if you know Lady, the minute she shows up, everybody was there, her friends, fans, they all loved her. She didn't start no trouble; she sometimes just *caused* trouble. Right away someone would call her, 'Lady Day,' and she'd say, 'Hi baby,' and she's off into a party scene. Okay, that's another forty-five minutes. She sits and they start bringing drinks. All of a sudden she gets into an argument with a cat, and boom, she curses the son of a bitch out and stamps away, 'You motherfucker.' She gets about ten more feet and she's at the end of the bar and someone says 'Lady Day,' and again, 'Oh, hi, baby,' so it's show time any minute if we can get her past the next twelve seats. On her way down the bar she'd have like twelve drinks, and then she'd come up, and I get off and Tucker gets on.

('I'll show these sons of bitches.' 'You think you can accompany a singer; you ain't shit.' 'Wait until you hear this shit. Wait'll this bitch gets up here, I'm gonna play some shit. I'm gonna wipe you out.' 'You can't play for that woman.' 'Fuck you.' 'Fuck *you*,' and Tucker and I are arguing till she's at about the last two, and we're buddies, we're putting each other down. We got into this from hanging around with Art Tatum; he tipped us into this and it was great fun. 'Play that change for her, you son of a bitch.' 'I was playing changes when your head was that big around.' That's the way it was. Non-malicious medicine.)

Now she finally gets up there. The last guy she talked to got her mad and now she hates the world. She started out as an angel, got herself together, got her tits lined up, and was all ready to go out there and gas everybody, and John just got through kicking the shit out of her so she aches and burns and her crotch hurts which is great 'cause that's where she sings from. If she aches, it's great, she's happy; if he kicks her good, then she can sing. So she's starting to think about what she's gonna sing, and she thinks she's gonna sing 'My Man', but by the time she gets there, she's had it twelve times; it's like the atomic bomb that destroyed Hiroshima, and she doesn't like it. She gets up there, she's out of her skull. She looks out and there's all these people who've waited for her in their fur coats and their Beverly Hills bullshit; and she gets up, and Tucker's waiting for her, and she's madder than a bitch and she turns to him and says, 'Strange Fruit'. But that's the end of her show, the last tune she sings. And he says, 'But Lady,' and she turns around and slams the thing down, bam, and he just gets his hands out in time, he could have lost his hands at the wrist. He looks at me and says 'Whew' and he's mopping his brow, and she has one hand on the edge of the piano and she says, 'Strange Fruit'. And he says 'Okay,' and she does 'Strange Fruit' and gets off, with just one fuckin' tune. And these money motherfuckers have waited three hours for her . . .

I just had to look at Levy to know he was a hood. She was unfortunate enough to be mentally arranged that she had to have a cat that beat the shit out of her three times a week to keep her happy. That's the downfall of too many girl singers. They come from a bag.

In order to show how tough he was, Levy the pimp made mistakes. He was too dumb to know that he should have treated Tucker better; Bobby lasted until the summer of 1949.

I came in from Milwaukee, and I told them I was not going to make it any more. I was building my house, on the road, things were going wrong with the contract, so I told them I gotta look out for my house, and he says okay. He's in New York; he told her to go to Chicago, he'd meet her there.

Our last night in Milwaukee, she said, 'Don't get lost. We've got a dinner date tomorrow night.' I said, 'Not me. I got a reservation on that 2 o'clock plane.' She says, 'You're gonna leave me here?' I said, 'No, just go make your reservation.' She said, 'I can't go, 'cause my daddy told me to meet him in Chicago.' I said, 'I gotta take the bread to him.' I was handling the money if he wasn't there. We were on a percentage plus a guarantee, the door tapes against the bar tapes, and I gotta bring him the bread. And he'd hold the bread for a week before he'd pay me, all that nasty kind of stuff.

I couldn't take it any more. I really liked her and I couldn't stand the way he was treating her. If she asked him for fifty dollars, he'd knock her down. He said, 'Don't ask me for money in public.' He'd knock her down literally – with his fist in her face, in her stomach, anywhere.

He'd once told me piano players are a dime a dozen. Well, he went to Chicago; she said, 'Where's Bobby?' He says, 'He's not going to make it.' And she hit the ceiling; she screamed bloody murder. He called me up and he said, 'I guess we were a little hasty, and she doesn't want you to leave.' I said, 'Look, I explained it to you . . .' and he went into his gangster bag. He said, 'I'm sending the bread to you, a plane – I'll have some guys – you'll never play the piano again!' I wrote her a letter and she wrote me back that she understood.

I got a letter from Joe Glaser telling me she wanted me to come back. She knew how I felt about John. Glaser guaranteed that John wasn't in the picture any more; but every night I heard that I'd had a long distance call from Washington, and it turns out to be John Levy. He finally got on to me and he said, 'Hey buddy, believe me she's straight, and I told her if she stayed straight I'd get you back.' In his mind, the reason I left was because she's a junkie. I said, 'John, I can't leave; I'm working for Billy Eckstine now.' He says, 'I don't care how much you're making; we'll double it.' He told me piano players are a dime a dozen, and he doesn't even know what my salary is, and I'm a musical director now. I just said 'Later,' and hung up.

She was living in her usual dream world; in 1949 she announced that she had finally divorced Monroe and married Levy the next day. But she and Monroe were still married, and still friendly from time to time. Her next accompanist was Carl Drinkard.

Round the corner from the Howard Theater in Washington DC, where all the big bands and shows appeared, was the Club Little Harlem, upstairs from a restaurant, a typical small place of the era that seated only about fifty people. Late in the summer of 1949 Carl Drinkard, who was playing there, got a phone call from Al Suter, the maître d' of the Club Bali, then the most lavish jazz club in Washington, where Lady was playing. Owner Benny Caldwell had engaged Coolridge Davis to play for her, but he played 'that big fat piano in that Fats Waller bag,' Carl said, and Lady didn't want it.

So Al says Lady Day was in town, and she had heard me play once before on her way through (although I didn't know it) and suggested that he call me. Well, I was getting ready to go back to Howard University, and I had never played Lady's music, and she was the sort of person that was worshipped by every musician, but I told Al, 'Thank you very much, I'm very flattered blah blah blah, but I really don't think I can make it.' Actually I was scared to death.

I hung up the phone and went back to the piano, and about twenty minutes later I hear a commotion, and there was Lady Day at the top of the steps.

Now when you first saw her, even if you didn't know who she was, you would say to yourself, 'Truly I don't know who this woman is, but she must be *some*body.' She had a way of walking without looking to right or left, but straight ahead, which gave everybody the impression that she was independent, though I later learned that she was anything but that. She wore a white sequined gown, sequined from top to toe like the suits the warriors wore to the Crusades. She was without a doubt the most beautiful woman I've ever seen in an evening gown; the woman and the gown sort of melted into each other, and the way the gown fell over her hips was in*sane*, and she knew how to walk with just enough movement to be seductive without being gaudy or vulgar. So she walks over to the piano, and thank God we were getting ready to break anyway; she points at me and she says, 'YOU — YOU'RE COMING WITH ME!'

Well! Submissively, I went with her, thinking, I'm going to have to try, anyway, although I really don't think I can make her music, but if I do goof it up I can get back to the Harlem in time to salvage my job. So instead of going right back to the Club Bali, she takes me to a place called the Crystal Cavern Club and orders some drinks.

She was drinking her infamous combination of brandy and white crème de menthe which, Carl said later, John Levy tried to keep away from her; in some contracts it was written that the management would not serve her that drink. She bought a double gin for Carl, who was not much of a drinker; it went to his head, he said, so that soon he began to believe what she was telling him: 'You don't have to worry about my music. If you can play "The Man I Love", you can play for me. I'm the eeeaaasiest thing in the *world* to play for!' They sat and had their drink while back at the Club Bali a huge crowd was waiting to hear Lady.

Finally we get back in the car, and on the way I'm thinking, surely she's going to talk these tunes over with me *now*. But we went to her dressing room, and she pulled the first five numbers off the top of her book, handed them to me and said, 'Let's go on.' Just like that, she says '*Let's go on.*' I was ready to drop dead.

The Club Bali was a big room, with tables spread all over the place, the bandstand raised about four feet off the floor with several steps leading up to it and surrounded by a huge horseshoe-shaped bar.

Now seated at the bar, would you believe, was none other than the great Art Tatum. When I looked up and saw Art, I'm ready to walk out of the place. Art was the idol of every pianist, and although we weren't playing in Art's bag, he was the one you put on the shelf and then considered everyone else. But Art said to me – this was the other miraculous thing that happened that evening – 'Carl, look, just do your best. Nobody can expect any more than that.' And I needed that more than anything else, because I knew that even if I messed up, at least Art would understand.

That first set included 'My Man', 'Waterfront', 'Them

There Eyes', and 'My Kind of Man', which she never sang again, and never recorded; Dinah Washington ended up recording it. This song was supposed to be dedicated to her man, John Levy; she used to tell everybody she was going to record this tune, because of him. But they had so many ups and downs, she never got around to recording it . . . Much to my surprise, those first numbers I cut to her complete satisfaction, so that when we walked off she said, 'From now on, you belong to me! You're going to be my piano player!' Can you imagine how I felt?

It is tempting to speculate that Lady had begun to see that if Levy was screwing up the musical side, she needed to find a new tough guy; but it was quite a while after she lost Bobby Tucker that Levy's time ran out. She was doing very good business wherever she worked; back in San Francisco in early 1950, she had to commute to Los Angeles Superior Court to clear up some lawsuits. On a Monday she flew down only to find out that it was a holiday and the courthouse was closed; on Tuesday she was late, but on Wednesday she made it on time. She told the *Los Angeles Times*, 'The pilot asked me if it would be cheaper for me to buy my own plane.' Ed Fishman lost his suit for $75,000 because he had no licence as a promoter in California, but she had to pay him a little over $2,000. Two people had been stabbed at Berg's on that New Year's Eve, but a Marian Epstein got $1,540 in damages because her ankle had been cut by a flying plate. And Jake Ehrlich was suing her: she found out about stacks of unpaid bills; Levy kept telling her he was paying the bills, but she owed money everywhere.

Her spirits were not improved by her chauffeur's arrest for possession of narcotics and the impounding of her new blue Lincoln. The following October Cottrell Cortez Amos was sentenced to one to six years in San Quentin.

But the main thing was the music. Impresario Jimmy Lyons first heard Lady in about 1950, when he was still a broadcaster. It was a downstairs club, possibly the Club Alabam, in the Fillmore district of San Francisco.

The place was pretty full, and I was waiting and waiting to see her, and it was the strangest thing – all of a sudden, everybody in the place stopped talking. Behind everybody through the front door came Miss Holiday with a dog, and nobody knew, but it was just electric. The back of your head tingled. She just walked right in and came on up and sang and did a perfect set, but never in my life had I witnessed such electricity You've seen a million shows, but . .

Trumpeter Chlora Bryant remembered an engagement at the Club Alabam during this period, with Wardell Gray in the band:

One night backstage she autographed a picture for one of my kids, and she wrote, 'Stay happy'. I never saw anybody autograph like that, and she explained it, and I never heard anybody do that – explain what was behind the autograph. We talked about kids comin' up, and she said, 'Try to see that your kids stay happy.' What she meant was, they're gonna have their problems, but try to see that they smile through it all, or something like that.

She wasn't like the papers described her. I was expecting her to act loud, like a monster. To me she was always a Lady; she was on top. Dinah [Washington] was the one I was around a lot, and she would pick on women just because she didn't like them. But the two of them were a contrast there, because Dinah was acting the way I had heard Billie acted. But just playing there in the band behind her – that was a thrill.

In August 1950 Lady made a short film with a Count Basie septet, directed by Will Cowan for Universal International; the white clarinettist Buddy DeFranco was a member of the group and played on the soundtrack, but on screen Marshal Royal was substituted. In June she went on the road with a big band led by Gerald Wilson, and the tour was a disaster, either because Levy simply helped himself to all the money he could get, perhaps anticipating his departure from Lady's life, or at best he finally proved that he couldn't manage a drunken party in a brewery: the tour wasn't promoted at all, and the band was stranded in South Carolina.

Gerald Wilson is a trumpeter, composer, arranger and bandleader who has been successful with critics and the public on the West Coast for decades, but without a lot of recognition from the media or the national music business; when he was interviewed in 1971 he had just done an album with Ella Fitzgerald. He had a track record since leading his first bands in the mid-forties; in 1949 he worked for both Dizzy Gillespie and Count Basie, but both these leaders had slimmed down to combos in 1950.

I was walking down 125th Street one evening and a fella named Earl Dancer accosted me. He was a producer at one time at the Cotton Club; I think maybe he was married to Ethel Waters . . . Billie Holiday was planning a Southern tour and Dancer knew that I had a successful band at the Apollo in 1946, and also I had played a week's engagement with Billie here in Los Angeles back in '46, I think it was, at the Plantation Club. What happened there was, Sarah Vaughan and Billy Eckstine's band were appearing there and something happened and they had to leave and we filled in for them for a week . . . So anyway I talked it over with her manager, who was John Levy at the time; he had a bar on Eighth Avenue I think it was, called Poor John's. I had admired Billie Holiday ever since before I left school in Detroit.

Poor John's was at Eighth and 122nd Avenue, said Carl Drinkard, and Lady thought that she owned part of it, but she never owned anything that Levy bought with her money. The band was a good one, including Johnny Coles and Willie Cook on trumpets, both of whom went on to play with Duke Ellington; Coles, the younger of the two, has also worked with Ray Charles, Charles Mingus, Herbie Hancock and many others. Gerald Wilson had written arrangements for Lee and Lester Young earlier, but he never wrote any arrangements for Lady because she had her own; on the 1950 tour he played his music when she wasn't singing.

The band rehearsed in Philadelphia, opened in Baltimore, where there was 'a very big crowd out at the park, at some kind of ballroom and beach out there', and from then on it was downhill, through Delaware, Norfolk, Virginia and into the Carolinas, where the tour ground to a halt, 'finally stranded in Greenville, South Carolina, or Greensboro, one of those Greens. They made us get off the bus because they hadn't paid the bus company. Nobody got paid. I knew all these places, having played them with Jimmie Lunceford and Basie and even Dizzy, and we would get there and no one would know that Billie Holiday was going to be in town. It was very bad promotion.'

Melba Liston, twenty-four years old at the time, was the trombone player:

> Levy would have me stay with Lady in her room, see that nothing happens to her. She would get nervous. She'd wake up and have her coffee and sit up in bed and have her bourbon with it, and talk a while and get dressed and walk around the restaurants . . . not irritable, generally pleasant. Like she'd dance, get out by the juke box and stuff; I thought she was really great. I just loved her.

Melba would ride with her on the bus, when she wasn't travelling with Levy in their car. Sometimes they stayed in hotels and once Melba remembered staying in the home, of a schoolteacher:

> and Billie stayed somewhere like that . . . After the show we'd stay around together. We were all strangers down South and the people didn't really take to us too well, so it kind of kept us together as a family, and we stayed together and played records and jammed. We were playing black places, but we were foreign to them. It's a territorial thing – Northern blacks were something else to the Southern blacks, at least to people we were playing for. We didn't talk the same language, we were outsiders.
>
> We played the beaches, with the sort of ballrooms – more like a barn, rather crude. Didn't sell much liquor, though once in a while a place would have a bar. A summer tour; people would bring picnics. We stayed on the ferry a lot – back and forth across Chesapeake Bay, that area. The bus would be on a ferry.

The further South they went the worse it got. 'The money wasn't coming in,' Melba said; 'the ads and publicity and the radio weren't taken care of, so very few people came.' Levy wasn't there much, and when he was there he was trouble.

> I was a timid child; I didn't like any fighting. I stayed as far from Levy as I could; I just read my book. Stayed in a corner. Billie was strong, because they used to fight .. One I heard about happened in a hotel and they both had to go to a hospital; she split his head open with a coke bottle or

something – and he cut her – but they were okay that night. We worked that night; it didn't show on her.

One started on the bus and I had to get under a seat. They were in the front of the bus, and there was a sign, a roller sign with a guard over it on the inside – said 'The Lady Day Orchestra' or something like that – and she said she was sick of it, didn't want her name on it; she ripped the sign down and ripped it up . . .

We were at a hotel, and we checked out, and the bus driver hadn't gotten his money; they didn't pay him and he stranded us in South Carolina, and we spent a few nights on the bus waitin' for him to come back. She and John pulled out with the promise to send money back for us . . . while we were on the bus it was terrible. The cops used to come by every night with the sticks and threaten us that if anything went wrong in town the guys were responsible, and we got frightened, and I was going to pieces until I got out of there.

They waited in vain. 'In fact I lost all my savings, giving it to the orchestra,' said Gerald Wilson. Wilson and Melba headed back to the West Coast; when they had got as far as Kansas City, Wilson said, 'luckily a friend of mine who was with Bull Moose Jackson's group at the time came through and loaned me some money.' Everybody knew it wasn't Wilson's fault, or even Lady's, but there were complaints to the musicians' union.

Wilson said that he thought a man named Dewey Shewey had been responsible for the publicity on the tour: 'I guess that was his real name.' Carl Drinkard said that he was lucky he hadn't gone on that tour and that Dewey was an associate of Levy's, a chauffeur whose primary occupation was as a second-storey man, a burglar, and who had got arrested during the tour. If the promotion had been in the charge of someone like that, who may also have been responsible for paying the bus driver, Levy had screwed up pretty badly. He was taking Lady's money, but he wasn't pulling his weight.

A letter survives from this period, undated but written on notepaper from a hotel in Norfolk, Virginia, and clearly from the disastrous tour. Maely, to whom the letter was addressed, was a Russian Jewish woman, a refugee who had got to New York and evidently had a gift for getting into people's lives. She and Lady were both orphans; they first met in 1947, when Maely was married to Freddie Bartholomew, an English-born actor who had been a child star, playing the lead in *Little Lord Fauntleroy* in 1936. Carl Drinkard described Maely as 'one of Lady's most intimate friends until the day she died'.

Hi Mailey Honey

I know you will be surprised hearing from me and from me and from this godforsaken coutry Well Mr John Levy has lived up to everything that you said he would he won't give me a fucking penny to come home with and I have to wait until he gets ready for me to eat I have wrote to Joe asking him for money to come to New York with When I insisted he pay me the other night for my work he beat me in the head with a bottle I now have five stitches so baby if you receive this please look for me any day give my love to Freddie Will wire you before I get there

Billie Holiday

PS Darling Please excuse bad writing but I am so fucking upset

Lady was used to violence and even expected it, but Levy's violence was overdone and not balanced by any other redeeming qualities. And Drinkard gives another reason why Levy soon left. The important thing by now was to keep Lady supplied with whatever she wanted, and what she wanted was dope. According to her autobiography, 'I had the white gowns and the white shoes. And every night they'd bring me the white gardenias and the white junk.' But that's the way Lady wanted it.

Lady could not kick any habit. Lady did not *want* to kick any habit. So often she would tell me, 'Carl, if I had to live my life without drugs, life wouldn't be worth living.' Lady was a very simple person to understand; all she wanted was to wake up in the morning feeling beautiful, and to feel beautiful to Lady meant waking up knowing that she had enough drugs to feel beautiful. She couldn't remember anything except whether she had stuff or didn't have stuff.

We know that Jimmy Monroe did not have what it took to look after Lady. Drinkard felt sorry for Monroe; he had heard about him for years, and Monroe had done things that few black men ever get a chance to do, but meeting him was a disappointment. Levy told Carl that he had helped to get Lady arrested in 1947 in order to get her when she came out, and he was devious enough to have done that if he'd thought of it; Joe Guy had disappeared for good, and suddenly she was working at Levy's Ebony Club even though she didn't have a cabaret card. Joe Glaser may have sent for Monroe to help keep an eye on Lady; at any rate, she told Carl, one night Levy walked into her dressing room and told Monroe 'to get the hell out of the way'.

So I asked Lady, 'What did you do?' And she says, 'I looked at Jimmy to see what *he* was gonna do.' I said, 'What did Jimmy do?' She said: 'Jimmy got the hell out of there. So I went with John after that, because I couldn't stand the punk.'

Drinkard had thought that Levy was Jewish at first, but he was black, on the old American drop-of-blood principle. 'Her favourite word was "motherfucker". She could say it like no one else – except John Levy. I'd never heard a white man say "motherfucker" like that, and I thought, "My God, we have another brother here."' But Levy's downfall, according to Drinkard, was that he got between Lady and her heroin.

Levy was 'scared to death' of heroin, because he knew it would bring the law quicker than anything else, and she already had a conviction for possession. Besides, heroin was frowned upon by the gangsters Levy admired; cocaine and especially opium were the drugs for gentlemen gangsters, while heroin was for junkies. Opium cost so much in those days that most druggies never came into contact with it, said Drinkard (although later, when it became scarce, some of the gangsters turned to what they called 'white stuff'). Levy and his pals used to go to Hot Springs, Arkansas, to take the rest cure that they thought would enable them to continue their opium binges; but Levy didn't like heroin. He made *his* drug available – which further contradicts the case for a Levy frame-up in San Francisco in 1949 – but opium wasn't what she wanted.

Yet one thing puzzled Drinkard:

One of John's best friends was Pensicola. Pensicola was Lady's New York connection when I first went with her; he was the type of drug dealer that was dap. He was the pimp type; he was hooked up with a rock on his finger; he wore Chesterfields when pimps wore Chesterfields, wore a wide-brimmed hat which was fashionable, 'gator shoes – the whole bit.

And it seemed to Drinkard that 'John knew that Pensicola was supplying Lady, because there couldn't be any way that he did *not* know.' And as devious and greedy as Levy was, Drinkard even found himself wondering if Levy wasn't making a profit on Lady's dope even though he hated it. At any rate, 'He underestimated her, or at least he underestimated the power of heroin. That contributed to John's demise.'

There were also questions about money. 'Lady didn't care about money for money's sake, but every so often she'd bring it up,' said Drinkard. 'One example was in the Earle Theater in Philadelphia.' This must have been in April 1950; last on a bill that included George Shearing, on the 14th she was so smashed on stage that she got a terrible review: a scandalized local critic reported that she was 'scarcely intelligible'. But otherwise it must have been a good week.

John had been messing up an awful lot of money all week; I would hear John betting on the telephone, and evidently he'd been losing. Closing day, I see these two goons – very well dressed, but you could tell they were hardened goons – standing just inside the stage door. So I went up to the dressing room, and I said, 'Listen John, I don't want to get into your business, but there's a couple of guys down at the stage door . . .' Well, John turned beet red, and I knew I had hit it on the head. What John had intended was to get to the office, collect the money, split to New York and have Lady join him later. John went down to the office, came back, talked with the guys and they left. Evidently, he paid them the money.

Well, Lady had worked for a pretty good salary that week, and it was to go into percentage above a certain amount. We'd had a very good week – George Shearing was on the bill, and it was generally understood that we'd gone into percentage; she knew that she'd made a lot of money. She didn't even know how much the percentage was, but the guarantee alone was substantial. Lady asked John about her money, and the next thing I knew there was this screaming in her dressing room; Lady had hit John in the head with a television set. It was one of the first portable sets I'd ever seen. Every time she and John got into those fights, he'd be huffing and puffing because he'd gotten the worst of the battle; he'd knock her down, but she'd manage to hurt him in some way. The time she hit him with the TV set he had a criss-cross patch on his bald spot, and it looked so funny, because he was a real proud guy, and he wanted to appear to be so bad, and to find out that a woman had succeeded in hurting him . . .

Levy was fat and was on the vulgar side, said Drinkard; Marie Bryant also says that there was nothing attractive about him. Lady told Drinkard that they weren't even sleeping together any more; she told him all about the 1949 opium arrest, and if she is to be believed, when she was doing her 'My Man' act in the courtroom, Levy was no longer her man in that sense. 'He gorilla'd her mind. He was so forceful that John made Lady believe whatever he wanted her to believe. He didn't frighten her, but he made her believe that he couldn't say anything that was wrong . . . John always put her in the position of being a child.'

Levy had bought a house in St Albans on Long Island. In 1950 Drinkard stayed there with Lady and Levy; they all had separate bedrooms. 'It was decorated by a little guy in the village, whose name was Jay. He was the innovator of this nylon fabric flock, for walls; he would apply a two-foot square of adhesive and blow nylon fabric onto the walls.' Lady had a twelve-foot round bed; the flocked wall, the carpet and the coverlet on the bed were all chartreuse. When Lady wasn't working she would get up between 10 and noon and start drinking gin, said Drinkard; she didn't eat much, but she loved to cook for others, and there were no servants, because she enjoyed housework. The furnishings in the house were good but minimal, and Levy was rarely there; it was a place where Lady could relax, but she got cheated out of that, too. It was supposed to be in her name as well as Levy's, but of course it wasn't. 'The fact that she didn't sign anything didn't occur to her.'

His ability to gorilla her mind may have convinced Levy that he would be able to get Lady off heroin and onto opium; but suddenly none of his act worked any more. Whatever the reason, he finally left her life, yet his power was such that she had to sneak out on him, just as Tonda had had to do a few years earlier. It must have been late in 1950; Drinkard had a combo at the Brown Derby on Connecticut Avenue in Washington, and he must have been trying to stay out of Lady's clutches, for he had told his band that no matter what happened he was going to stick with them, and warned them just how tricky she could be. Lady and Levy were staying at the Charles Hotel:

> Lady went down the fire escape with nothing but her dog, her fur coat and something like $17,000, which had been stashed in the hotel safe where John couldn't get to it. Lady and I hadn't seen each other for a while; she was so happy to see me, and to tell the truth I was happy to see her. That was how she loused my band up. On closing night, she waved a contract in my face; she had signed my whole band up. I had promised that I wasn't going to leave them, and they were getting ready to leave me.

Levy the pimp died in 1957 of a brain haemorrhage. Bobby Tucker complained to Jimmy Rowles that 'he didn't even have the courtesy to let somebody shoot him'.

Monroe then returned to the scene. Lady must have been fond of him, and it is poignant that she probably retained that fondness from the time she married him, when she thought that she was taking charge of her life and had found a man she could depend on. But Monroe was used to getting what he wanted from women on his looks alone, as Drinkard pointed out, and could not contribute to the violence she seemed to need; she had long since lost all respect for him. Her men always looked after her money, said Drinkard, except for Monroe: 'She was making $4,500 a week, and her husband didn't have as much as $50 in his pocket.'

Drug addicts play games, and Drinkard saw all the games and participated in them, for he was a heroin user, and so, by now, was Monroe. 'On many occasions, she would give me money to cop for her; then Jimmy would creep up behind her and hand me his little money to cop for him.' Lady told Drinkard that she had to sleep with one eye open: he asked her why. 'Because when Jimmy thinks I'm asleep, he creeps into the bathroom and sits there all fuckin' night shooting up my shit. I've gotta get rid of that motherfucker or I'm gonna die from lack of rest.' 'She must have told Jimmy something pretty strong,' added Drinkard, because suddenly he wasn't there any more.

Lady went on and off the needle, but she was almost never without heroin; yet although a slave to the drug, she preached against it, the way Charlie Parker did. Drinkard was hip to the scene:

I have been accused so many times of having an affair with Lady Day that I can't begin to keep count. This is a hundred per cent lie. When people say to me, 'I know you've been making it with Lady Day,' I tell them, 'Would you think of having something to do with your own mother?' God knows, to me, when I first joined Lady, she was the greatest jazz singer the world had ever known, not a sex machine.

And Lady Day has been accused so goddam many times of getting me hooked on drugs ... The first time I ever took stuff was a long time before I even met Lady. Well, for me it was a long time, because any time before I met Lady was a long time.

I already knew what heroin was. I already had a connection; I was in a position to cop for her. But Lady was an ironical person. Lady was the first to say that no one *else* should use stuff. She was very emphatic about this; she could not endorse the use of heroin, *except* by herself. She told the world she could not stand a dope fiend; she took the attitude that '*I'm* the only one strong enough to use stuff and everyone else is a low-life.' She would say, 'Now look, Carl, now don't you use no shit. Don't you go near it. Don't you end up like me.'

The first time I knew Lady was an addict was the very first week I was working for her; she made no pretence of hiding it. Every time John went out of the room, she reached into the stash that she kept at the top of her stocking, rolled a match-book cover and snorted, leaving traces sometimes around the tip of her nose. Lady was a snorter; she was sniffing. Every time she wanted to convince somebody that she kicked the habit, any time she wanted to fool her man or almost any time after she got busted, Lady went back to snorting. Lady didn't get back to the needle regularly until after we got to San Francisco in 1950, and John went to New York to attend his sister's funeral.

John warned me when we hit Frisco, he said, 'Now look,

Carl, you're crazy if you start fucking around with Lady in this goddam town, because they have this internal possession law out here, and you can go to jail just for having marks. Don't let Billie talk you into no bullshit about getting any stuff or they'll lock you both up!'

She was also jealous, and mothered Carl like she did everyone else:

I had two girls, Elissa and Jeanette, who were living with me, and Lady wanted to break up this affair. She couldn't get up to my room; I had left orders with everyone in the hotel not to allow Lady up to my room, so she decided if she couldn't get up to my room to put my girls out, she would keep me out all day long. She called a rehearsal early in the morning, and she took me with Jarbooty in his raggedy-ass little car to his dingy little pad where he kept his stash. Jarbooty took out a needle and cooker and cooked up some stuff and hit Lady in her right hand; that's the first time I saw Lady use a needle. Then Lady said to Jarbooty, 'Fix Carl up, too.' So Jarbooty gave me stuff to snort. I got pretty tore up and Lady got pretty tore up and kept me out all day, though somehow I didn't seem to mind.

When she warned Drinkard against getting hooked, she was warning him against the needle, and he understood that, but still the warning didn't sink in.

Along with her stash and her cash, Lady carried her double-edged 'widdle wazor blade' in the top of her stocking. This was Lady being tough, but she never cut anybody with her blade; rather it was a matter of lashing out with the nearest thing at hand when she lost her temper. She cut Levy with knives, and once across the chest with a piece of glass ('She was aiming for his throat,' said Drinkard); at the Club Blue Mirror in Washington DC she waved a butcher knife at him, and 'he screamed like a bitch'. Another time the nearest weapon was the television set. Later, Louis McKay thought he had been cut with the 'widdle wazor', but that was because he was so drunk at the time, said Drinkard; in fact Lady had stabbed him with a fork.

It was in San Francisco, Drinkard said, and it must have been after Levy returned from New York, that she had a package delivered to Carl without telling him beforehand.

A bellhop brought it to my room and said, 'Give this to Billie.' Well, I was scared to death behind what John told me about this internal possession bullshit. I never saw the inside of a jail up to that time, and here was this package of what they now call pure heroin – about two ounces of it, I should imagine.

I brought it to a rehearsal. Lady knew it was coming, but she just couldn't cool it in the club. No, Lady had to go running down the steps like a goddam chicken without her head on while John was following right behind her, wondering, 'She's been sick all night, so what the hell has she got to be so happy about?' But Lady pranced around, giving the whole thing away. John said to her – and John only had to say a few words to her – 'Billie, get into that fuckin' bar,' and she went into the fuckin' bar. Which is when John shoved a gun in my ribs and backed me into the men's room, saying, 'Carl, I should kill you' – he was trying to impress me with his gangster bag – he said, 'I should kill you. You're supposed to be like a son to me. You shouldn't allow yourself to be used by Lady. Lady uses everyone.'

So Drinkard was immediately *au fait* with the antics junkies get up to. Meanwhile, Lady's Decca recording contract came to an end.

The recording session in August 1949 had included, besides the Porter Grainger song 'Tain't Nobody's Business If I Do', a sassy Leonard Feather tune, 'Baby Get Lost'. An excellent fourteen-piece band was led by Buster Harding, and included Clayton, Lester and other old friends, but there were no solos. The next two dates, in late August and early September, used similar bands led by ex-Lunceford and Tommy Dorsey arranger Sy Oliver, this time with solo room here and there (but no Lester). The tunes were 'Them There Eyes' (with Oliver's patented two-beat treatment behind the vocal, perfect for the tune), and three more Bessie Smith numbers: 'Tain't Nobody's Business' had been made famous by Bessie in 1923; now 'Keeps On a Rainin', 'Do Your Duty' and 'Gimme a Pigfoot and a Bottle of Beer' were added (on the latter, 'shim-sham-shimmy' was replaced by 'oo-bop-a-dop', and Bessie's reference to reefers had disappeared).

On the last day of September, with a slightly smaller band and Oliver still in charge, Lady recorded 'Now or Never', her own

326

tune written with Curtis Lewis, and two duets with her beloved Louis Armstrong. Both tunes had been co-written by James P. Johnson for *Sugar Hill*, a flop Broadway show in 1931: 'You Can't Lose a Broken Heart' and 'My Sweet Hunk o' Trash'. The last is particularly delightful; Louis's broad humour has him sounding like Moms Mabley at one point, and he's having such a good time that he seems to blurt out 'Fuck 'em, baby'. The record came out that way, but there were complaints – Walter Winchell didn't approve – and Gabler had to splice a reissued master with 'Come on, baby'.

Her last two Decca sessions were in October 1949 and March 1950, both directed by Gordon Jenkins with strings and a flute. The tunes were 'You're My Thrill' (memorably recorded by Lena Horne with Charlie Barnet in 1941), 'Crazy He Calls Me', 'Please Tell Me Now', 'Somebody's on My Mind' and 'God Bless the Child' (both credited to Lady and Herzog), and 'This Is Heaven to Me'. The first four of these have much better arrangements and recorded sound than Lady's earliest Decca records: the strings don't sound scrawny and don't get in the way, while the jazz feeling is preserved. The last two sides, however, came from Lady's only Decca session done in Hollywood rather than New York, and which Gabler did not produce; and it included backing by a vocal chorus, which sang the introduction to 'God Bless the Child'. Gabler said:

I would have killed that introduction. I would have just had the left-handed piano intro right into 'God Bless the Child' . . . Gordon was crazy about Billie. He loved the singers, and all the singers loved him. It's like having Tchaikovsky and half a symphony orchestra behind you when you sang in front of Gordon Jenkins. He had such taste. The only thing he didn't have was a black taste for that intro – and it doesn't belong there.

The other side of the record, 'This Is Heaven to Me', was a quasi-religious epic (on the other side of a song with 'God' in the title), which with the chorus ends up sounding a lot like 'That Lucky Old Sun', of which there were six hit recordings the year before, among them Louis Armstrong's on Decca. The groups on Lady's last records with Jenkins were relatively small, twelve pieces in October 1949 and only nine plus the chorus in March 1950, but his arrangements made them sound bigger. The big ballad with strings was becoming common in pop, because everything in post-war America had to be bigger and better than ever; the conventional dance band of around sixteen pieces was no longer economic on the road, yet studio accompaniments grew in the 1950s until they became symphony orchestras. And if Lady's last Decca record had equalled the success of 'That Lucky Old Sun', her contract no doubt would have been renewed, but it didn't, and her major label career ended on a rather damp note.

Although none of her Decca records after 'Lover Man' appeared in any charts, Gabler said that 'one of the new ballads, "Crazy He Calls Me", was pretty big'; but the *Billboard* chart only listed the top thirty in those years anyway, and a lot of records made a profit without charting. Gabler also described how he would manage the recording session, having the band rehearsed, and brandy, honey and tea on hand for Lady if she needed it, and also said, 'Don't forget, a performer who works at night in clubs, when you make records at two in the afternoon it's like before breakfast.' He speculated, twenty years later, that there might have been a problem setting dates for recording sessions, because not having a cabaret card she was often working out of town; but this could not have been much of a problem: she had made her last fifteen Decca sides at six sessions in less than eight months.

Furthermore, not only did she sound good on the records, but she was using some of the best recording technology in the industry. Bing Crosby, the biggest star on Decca, had begun taping his radio shows as early as 1946, to make his own life easier, and was a founder of Ampex, who made much of the studio equipment of the era; he helped see to it that Decca's studios were up to date. On the whole, these last fifteen Decca records of Lady's have to be included among the best pop records of the period.

Perhaps they got less airplay than they might have got because of her bad reputation, and that is certainly the reason her Decca contract was not renewed. Jack Kapp might have done as he pleased, but he had died in 1947; his brother Dave Kapp was still there, but did not have Jack's flair. Gabler said, 'Just say the top echelon didn't want to risk it. She was getting a lot of notoriety . . . They figured there would be problems.'

A short-lived contract with Aladdin resulted in four sides made in April 1951, with a band led by guitarist Tiny Grimes, including

Heywood Henry on reeds. The discographies say it was Bobby Tucker on the Aladdin session, but Bobby says no, and Carl remembered the date quite clearly. He said that Grimes's pianist was also included, so that he could get some money, but he didn't remember the man's name, and the bassist and the drummer also remain unknown.

The tunes were 'Blue Turning Grey over You', by Fats Waller and Andy Razaf, done in a more laid-back way than Louis Armstrong's or Waller's much earlier versions; 'Be Fair with Me Baby' and 'Rocky Mountain Blues', both blues, and a ballad, 'Detour Ahead'. Drinkard said that Lady got 'Detour Ahead' from Jeri Southern (and Southern, a superior cabaret singer of that era, said that she got 'You Better Go Now' from Lady). Unsurprisingly, given the period and the label, which catered to the black community, the sides have a strong rhythm & blues flavour. On 'Be Fair to Me Baby' Drinkard sounds a bit like Avery Parrish on his 1940 hit 'After Hours', with Erskine Hawkins. It was on 'Rocky Mountain Blues', Drinkard said, that there were two pianists; the sound is a bit muddy, but somebody plays a slow kling-kling-kling style, like Fats Domino.

It may have seemed to Lady's faithful fans that she was on the skids. Since beating the opium charge in San Francisco, it had been a difficult period: in the autumn of that year there had been an upsetting incident in Detroit, when she met trumpeter Chuck Peterson, an old friend from the Shaw band; he tried to protect her from racist remarks and got knocked down (his attackers were described as 'hillbillies' in the press). A few months later there was the disaster of the Southern tour, and there had been the occasional problems with club-owners, too; then she finally had to get rid of Levy. Yet over the holiday season at the end of 1950 a gig at the Hi-Note in Chicago, on a bill with Miles Davis, was a complete success, the club's manager praising her to the skies.

Lady was always a hit in Chicago, but she complained that the winters were so cold there that she had to get everything lined with fur, 'including my douche bag'. She played the Hi-Note several times, and it is unclear exactly when the next part of our story took place, but it was there that Carl Drinkard became a slave to the needle:

From that California date on, I had been dibbing and dabbing more and more, which takes us to our engagement in the Hi-Note in Chicago, when the Hi-Note just moved to the north side of the Loop. The morning we arrived was the time a chemical plant blew up and there was a big traffic jam and it was something like fifteen degrees below zero. Miles Davis happened to have the band opposite us, and Miles had no piano player, so he asked Lady would she mind if I work with him the term of our mutual engagement.

And it's a strange thing, because Miles was the only one Lady seemed to like sufficiently to allow me to work with. Anyone else she'd be quick to say, 'Carl's *my* piano player; he's not gonna play for nobody else and that's where it's at.' I recall when we were working Providence, Rhode Island, with Stan Getz and his band, and Lady was the finale. King Pleasure was in the house that night. He had just cut a record called 'Moody's Mood for Love', and it was doing pretty good and somebody asked Lady would she make the announcement that King Pleasure was in the house, and she was friendly that way. She would pretend to know somebody she never saw in her life; if they were in show business and she was in show business she was not going to let them down. So Lady announced him: 'Ladies and gentlemen let's give him a big round of applause and get him up on the stage,' and King Pleasure walked up smiling at everybody, feeling very proud. I was playing Lady's chaser, and when Lady ran off the stage, Pleasure signalled for me to go into 'Moody's Mood'. I played the intro and he started singing. 'There I go, there I go, theeeere IIII go, pret-ty ba-by, da-da-da-da-dada,' and he has his lungs filled up with this pretty unique song, he's going great guns, when Lady returned to the stand. I thought she was gonna join him, but she grabbed me by the arm, lifted me from the piano stool and trotted me off to her dressing room and left poor Pleasure there in front of all those people wailing his head off and I'm sure he felt like dropping dead.

So at the Hi-Note it was a most unusual thing that Lady allowed me to work with Miles, and it was a gas, because I dug Miles, and I rarely got the chance to work with a band any more as opposed to accompanying, and I was using the money from Miles to support my habit and letting my money from Lady pile up. We did several weeks there, and dope was much cheaper then. Miles had Israel Crosby on bass, and a little drummer from Chicago named Jimmy Green, and every night Miles would draw the money for the band, and Miles, Jimmy and I – we were the dope fiends in the band, Israel was the only clean one – would go down to Judson Boulevard to cop. Then we'd go over to Green's house and split the stuff three ways. We'd get high and sit there and write all night, and whatever we wrote we'd play the next night.

They were shooting and I was snorting, and one night Miles said to Green, 'If Carl doesn't stop wasting this stuff, we're gonna take it away from him.' And he was only kidding, but this particular night I began to wonder, how could shooting be that different from snorting? So just to satisfy my curiosity, you understand, I let him hit me in my right arm and wreck my life right there. Although I can't blame anybody, because I was supposed to be a mature individual, and he had suggested something I already had in my mind, namely to see what all these fucking fools found so special in shooting shit. I felt too strong; I felt I could shoot once and never get hooked, the famous last words of anyone who ever got addicted to heroin. That's absolutely true, and I'm the living proof.

Because I found out all right; the difference was so amazing that the next night I snorted as usual, only it didn't do anything ... Then I got to thinking, how silly to go clear across Chicago when I know a girl down the hall in my hotel who uses a needle. That night I asked her could she loan me one, and she pulled out a box and said, 'Pick yourself out a set.' And that's how I got my first set of works.

Weeeell, when Lady discovered I was using the spike she said, 'Goddamn it Carl, I've warned you and warned you, and now you're hooked, and there's nothing I can do but try to help you.' So Lady cooked up some stuff, and what Lady put into the cooker was fantastic. She had a tablespoon that she would fill up so it hardly cooked clear. I was afraid to shoot so Lady shot me, and that first shot I got from Lady should have killed me, but it only served to get me straight, and by getting straight I mean exactly that – getting normal. There's no such thing as 'getting high'. After that first fix you can throw the fucking 'high' out the window.

Thus began the relationship between Lady and me and our two sets of works.

Asked about Miles's habit, Drinkard said, 'He'd shoot up just as often as his money would allow him. You space it according to how much your money will allow you. Nobody ever really has as much as they want.' Lady shot up before she went to the club, or sometimes she took it with her to her dressing room, but she shot up so much that she didn't have to shoot up afterwards; she had a reputation as someone who didn't want to party with fans after the show, but it wasn't because she was in a hurry to go home and shoot. She just liked that time to herself.

By this time she was also an alcoholic. Drinkard said she was drinking at least a quart of Gordon's gin every day. She also table-hopped, schmoozing with fans and making some work for the club's photographer, and drank doubles at each table, although she left unfinished drinks all over the place. 'She thought she was fooling the public, and the police. At that time, people thought that anyone who drank heavily couldn't possibly be using drugs.' They reckoned without Lady. 'She used to say to me, especially in California, where they have that internal possession law, where you can be arrested merely for being addicted – "Well, they can't say I'm using drugs, not the way I'm drinking." Lady would shoot up, then she'd drink up.'

Miles kicked his heroin habit by the mid-fifties. Stan Getz had asked Drinkard to cop for him, but soon kicked his habit. Duke Ellington had junkies and juice-heads in his band from time to time, but refused to be their guardian, knowing that either they would grow up, or they wouldn't. But Lady never quit doing anything for long.

15

The Last Merry-Go-Round: Fun, Fights and Fame

In early 1951 Lady met Lester Young in Philadelphia, and thereafter did not see him for three years, as she wallowed in drugs and he withdrew into alcohol, each seeking release from several kinds of pain. That year she had no manager, no regular accompanist and no more studio recordings after the Aladdin date; but Maely Bartholomew wanted to look after her. Drinkard described the friendship:

> Every time we were in New York, she'd drop by her house; whenever she was running away from [a man], Lady would run up and seek shelter at Maely's house. And Maely was smart enough to figure she would outlast Lady Day, and if she did she would have a very good thing in her grasp. Maely always struck me as the sort of woman who could always take advantage of any situation – give her an inch and she'll take a mile. At least this is the way Lady used to describe her . . . Lady used to speak so harshly about Maely. She used to talk about what a fat, funky, jive bitch Maely was, and how she couldn't stand her. I can hear her: 'BIL–LIE' with that phoney accent of hers; she used to put on this Dahling and blah, blah, blah, and Lady would say, 'Bitch, why don't you stop that bullshit? You weren't so dicty when Hitler marched your ass out of Poland with no fuckin' shoes on.' Lady used to talk about Maely like a dog.

Levy the bassist said Lady would call Maely 'a fat funky slob, right to her face. She'd sit there and look at her and take it' Drinkard goes on about the short period between Levy the pimp and Louis (Louie) McKay:

Well, Maely really had eyes, and she thought she was going to seek the road managership of Lady ... one time we were going to Detroit, and we were getting in the taxi in New York to go to the airport, and Lady hands her case to Billy Sharpe that contained her dope — poor Billy, God bless him, he's gone now, he never knew how many times he carried Lady's dope — all the way to the airport, Maely was talking her ass off, but I didn't realize it was so drastic. It was no secret that Maely would have liked to take over the managership of Lady. She went all the way to the airport with us, and she talks Lady into buying her a ticket and she gets on the plane, no luggage, no nothing. All the time she was there with us she was wearing Lady's half-slip, and she wore it like a whole slip.

A lot of people describe Maely as an opportunist; Drinkard said, 'I don't know what would have happened if Louis hadn't turned up.' That's an interesting point. Maely had reason to believe that Lady was tired of violence, but it was in Detroit that she ran into McKay and finally got involved with him. McKay had a wife and two kids, Drinkard said, and McKay and his wife agreed that it would be a good thing if he went with Lady, and McKay's end of the bargain was that he would continue looking after them. Drinkard remembered riding in a car with all of them, and Lady making amorous advances to McKay in the presence of the wife.

Drinkard remembered playing at the High Hat in Boston, and George Wein coming to the club and asking Lady to come over to his new club, Storyville, to help celebrate opening night, in the basement of the Buckminster Hotel. They had to get back for their own next set at the High Hat, and the crowd wanted Lady to sing a song; 'The place was packed to the rafters, and Lady turns to me and says, "We're gonna have to do something to get out of here." I went up to the piano and instead of singing one song, I can't tell you how many tunes it took for her to be able to get off that stage.'

At the end of October 1951 she went to the Storyville for the first of several legendary gigs there, with Harding on piano, John Fields and Marquis Foster on bass and drums; they were playing opposite Stan Getz, who played on a few tunes with Lady. She paid Harding nice compliments, saying that 'Buster not only plays for me, writes for me — he feels how I feel. Some nights I'm tired, and I don't feel too good, and I don't want the tempo too fast; he knows and sets exactly the right tempo and mood.'

George Wein soon became producer of the Newport Jazz Festival; the pianist and budding impresario had just turned twenty-six years old in October 1951, but he already knew a thing or two about publicity: some of the Storyville gigs were broadcast, so there are legendary airchecks made over a period of three days from Lady's first appearance there. Two different versions of 'Miss Brown to You' are particularly interesting: on one she is relaxed, almost slurring, perfectly in time although she was clearly feeling no pain. But on the other she is flying over the beat, furiously chanting the words, as though they were a warning: it's less than two minutes long, and it's hair-raising: all her identities were still intact and in balance.

During this engagement she gave an unusually upbeat interview to Nat Hentoff for *down beat*, for she was married again, she said, to Louis McKay. She had known him for many years; he was five years older than she was and had two children; she at least had someone to look after her, and wanted to make a last stab at a normal life. But she was still talking off the top of her head; McKay and Lady got married, but not just yet.

In the same interview, she praised the singing of Jo Stafford, saying, 'I've been listening to her for six or seven years. She sounds like an instrument.' Stafford was in the middle of a long run of hit records then; during the war she had been called 'G.I. Jo'; she had virtually perfect pitch, with a beautifully clear and cool style, and a unique vocal colour to warm it up.

In the spring of 1952 Lady began recording for Norman Granz, at first on Mercury and the following year on Granz's own Clef label. Her recording career was in good hands for the next five years, but her life didn't change much.

Levy the bassist later knew McKay:

He was an idiot, a poor kind of pimp, not a classy one or one that ever really made it. Compared to the rest of them he was a sweet cat up to that point, and he went down with her all the way; he wasn't like John Levy, who was just out-and-out cruel and it was so obvious, but Louis was hanging on for dear life because that's all he had. He tried to get into management – called me up – 'How do you go about doing this? Can I work for you?' Forget it. He was just another pimp and she was on her way down.

Anybody was a sweet cat compared to Levy the pimp. The violence continued; Billie regularly appeared with black eyes and other bruises. Yet Jimmy Rowles, Drinkard and others thought she really loved McKay, and more to the point, she thought she did. Some thought that she still wanted to start a family, but surely she knew by this time that she was not going to have any children of her own; she talked about adoption, but that wasn't very likely, either. That McKay beat her is not surprising; Drinkard said that she respected him because he was the only man who was tougher than she was, and could beat her without leaving a mark on her. They were all playing roles: McKay was not as violent for its own sake as Levy had been, and she mothered him in her way, manipulating him and letting him do the best he could, hanging onto him the way he hung onto her.

She stayed on the West Coast in early 1952, earning money to pay her bills. In March 1952 her car turned over three times after a tyre blew out; Lady was thrown out of the car (which is incredibly dangerous) but escaped with cuts and bruises, and went on to sing for 300 servicemen at Fort Ord hospital. In an interview printed in the *Melody Maker* in April, she exercised a new identity, saying, 'I don't dig all this modern stuff . . . Jazz is not what it used to be. For me, Benny Goodman is still the greatest.' At the time, at Tiffany's in Hollywood, she was being backed by Wardell Gray, Hampton Hawes and Chico Hamilton, all modernists; but in 1952 'modern jazz' was not a commercial proposition, swamped by the typical hit records of the time. Big orchestras, big sound and multi-mike technology were in and intimacy was out, but Benny Goodman was still a big name, and maybe Lady was trying to curry favour with the public, the better to pay those bills.

And as Alvin Stoller put it on behalf of the musicians:

People would want to do what *she* wanted to do, because it was *her*. They weren't trying to look for a hit record. She was more into music . . . I don't care if I'm playing for Gene Autry, I'll play the best I can; but if you play for someone like Billie Holiday, why, that's up there, that's good and personal. When you're finished playing it leaves you with a feeling of accomplishment.

Stoller was talking about the Norman Granz sessions. Billie had already known Granz for a dozen years, and had performed in his Jazz at the Philharmonic touring roadshow (fifteen of her tunes were recorded live between 1945 and 1947). Granz was certainly not in the pop chart business. He said, 'Billie was a great artist and she needed recordings, so you did them.' He was referring to Lady's later years, when recording her was a gamble, but that is effectively the attitude he took towards every record he ever made. 'Granz was not a commercial recorder,' Stoller said. 'You could go in to record fifteen minutes with Oscar Peterson and just record for hours; if it fell into a groove, he'd get it. He never locked it up.'

Granz started the Clef and Norgran labels, combined into Verve in 1956, and had built an important jazz catalogue by the time he sold it to MGM in 1960; then he started all over again with Pablo, sold to Fantasy in 1987. Many years after he first recorded Lady, at a time when the mainstream record industry wanted million-selling rock albums, Granz said that if he only made $9,000 on an album that was still a profit, and what was wrong with that? Even more to the point, from the first recorded JATP concert in 1944, issued on Asch 78s in 1946, he made records which are still selling today.

At two sessions in Los Angeles in the spring of 1952, Lady recorded fifteen tunes for Granz and she was back in the milieu where her fans wanted her: the sextet of first-class musicians included Oscar Peterson on piano, Charlie Shavers on trumpet, Flip Phillips on tenor sax, Barney Kessel on guitar, Ray Brown on bass and Stoller on drums. Six more tunes were recorded in July in New York, with Peterson and Brown, Joe Newman on trumpet, Paul Quinichette on tenor, Gus Johnson on drums, and her old sweetheart Freddie Green on guitar.

The tunes included a few remakes, such as the third studio recording of 'My Man' (the line 'He beats me too' firmly in place); Duke Ellington's 'Solitude' is very fine. The new tunes included first-class fare such as 'Autumn in New York', and she finally recorded 'If the Moon Turns Green', which she'd first sung nearly twenty years earlier. Shavers plays a lot of open horn, and as with

Red Allen in 1937, some thought that he was overpowering in this context, but I don't think so, and Lady certainly didn't. (He is lovely, and muted, on 'Solitude' and others.) A mid-tempo 'I Only Have Eyes 'for You' is a delight. 'Love for Sale' was a duet, with just Peterson and Lady. Peterson must have enjoyed playing for her: Shirley Horn, the wonderful pianist/singer who has become better known in recent years, said, 'Oscar spread flowers beneath her.' Peterson told Joel E. Siegel recently:

I was worried about being extra busy – something I've always been charged with – so at first I sort of held back, but she didn't want that. She wanted everybody to just play. Billie wasn't even aware that there were four beats going on behind her, she'd just sing her own time and somehow it happened to match. It was unbelievable. She could go way out there and then she'd come back in a way that you wouldn't expect. Suddenly, she'd just be standing there beside you . . .

As with the Teddy Wilson sessions of the 1930s, there was no rehearsal and little in the way of arrangements; that's the way Granz wanted it. She was as responsible for her arrangements as anybody, said Peterson: 'She'd let us know the way she wanted a tune to take a certain shape, and then she'd call for whomever she wanted to play the solos.' She was as on top of the music as ever, and the records are proof. Linda Kuehl wrote the sleeve note for a 1976 reissue of these tracks: 'When she sings the final syllables of "Yesterdays", she is piercing, and one knows what Imamu Baraka (LeRoi Jones) meant when he wrote, "Sometimes you are afraid to listen to this lady."' But one never needs to be afraid to listen to Lady; in the very next sentence Linda wrote about 'an undercurrent of laughter that complements the darkness . . . always the teasing endearing playfulness . . '

These were and are beautiful records. Her voice is grainier and has lost its youth, leaving the artistry burnished and even more visible. The voice was always an acquired taste, and no doubt there are many who never liked it, but they're not listening to the songs: again and again, as in the phrase 'can't saaave a cent' in 'He's Funny That Way', the story becomes hers, no matter how many times we think we've heard it before.

'Lover, Come Back to Me' is uptempo, and even here it's the band that does the work, while Lady swings on the time, as she always did in this sort of context, and as she must have been able to do with Basie among the big bands. She's not hogging the limelight, no longer obliged to try to be a pop star, but just one of the boys again. Linda Kuehl wrote that Oscar played too many notes for her, and that Lady didn't like him, but there is no evidence of this; Shirley Horn's opinion seems more reliable. Peterson's swinging solo, both hot and cool, on 'Lover, Come Back to Me' is not to be missed, and I cannot believe that Lady did not dig the hell out of it.

In fact, the critics always wanted her back in this context, but they never like it when they get what they say they want. As Granz put it, it's not a question of different standards, but different values. Miles Davis said, 'I'd rather hear her now. She's become much more mature. Sometimes you can sing words every night for five years, and all of a sudden it dawns on you what the song means.' Granz thought that she was making as much money as Sarah Vaughan or Ella Fitzgerald; if she complained that she was short of cash, she spent a lot of it on dope and booze, and McKay, like all her men, was stealing it.

An overseas tour was planned in 1952 with her friend and fan, Dick Haymes. But he had been born in Argentina, of an English father and an Irish mother (a concert singer); despite being resident in the USA since childhood and having trouble with the Internal Revenue Service in the early fifties, he was threatened with deportation and at the same time forbidden to leave the country. The tour fell through, and both singers lost income from overseas on which they would have paid taxes in the USA.

In November 1952 she sang at Carnegie Hall in the Duke Ellington Twenty-Fifth Anniversary Concerts; her accompanists, apart from Jimmy Hamilton and Ray Nance from the Ellington band, were the same she had worked with at Boston's Storyville more than a year earlier, including Buster Harding; she was one of the biggest stars in a star-studded show. Then Drinkard was working for her again, and in August they were to play on a bill with Ellington at the Apollo, a place that was always close to her heart; but her face was badly swollen, and the story of an abscess was given out, although insiders thought she looked as though she had been beaten. Annie Ross sang the show instead.

Born into a show-business family, she had known Duke Ellington since she was a child, but she had never met Lady, who was her idol: the first record she ever had was one of Lady's. Before she met Lady she experienced Joe Glaser's gangster act:

> I went downtown to meet Glaser, and he scared me to death – he was a very forceful, loud, uncouth, rough kind of character. So he said, 'Okay, we'll see what we can do for ya. Whattaya do, honey?' I said, 'I sing.' The next morning I get a phone call from him; he said, 'You gotta dress?' 'Yes.' 'You got any music?' 'Yes.' 'Can you get a pianist?' 'Yes.' 'All right, I wantcha to get up to the Apollo Theater by 10.30.' So I said, 'Tonight?' He said, 'No, now.' I say, 'What am I doing there?' 'You're replacing somebody.' I said 'Who?' He said, 'Billie Holiday.'

'So after I picked myself off the floor,' she said, she went to the Apollo to find that Ellington was also on the bill.

> And the first show on Monday was like the heavy show, 'cause all the cats come to see what's happening. Duke came into my dressing room and he was extremely kind and gentle and calm and sweet as he always was, and he said, 'Why are you so nervous?' I said, 'Well, you know, because it's Billie Holiday,' and he said, 'Have you ever met her?' I said, 'No, and I don't want to.' 'Why?' I said, 'Because I heard that if she doesn't like you she could really put you down.' 'No, she's not like that at all,' said Duke, 'she's really a *lovely* lady.' And he took me down to her dressing room, and Lady was there, and her story was that she had an infected tooth and her jaw was out like that.

Lady asked Annie if she had a dress and a pianist and so forth, 'and she was just great'. They had announced that Lady wouldn't appear, and some people had walked out.

> But I did my thing, and when I walked off, Lady was there, and she opened up her arms to me, and I started crying, and she started crying, and Duke came over and said, 'What are you ladies doing standing here crying? Come out and take a bow.' So the three of us went out and took a bow.

In 1953 the first annual *down beat* critics' poll tied Lady in second place with Sarah Vaughan; in the readers' poll the same year, she came seventh. (Ella was always first.) In October that year she did the third TV show in a series hosted by George Jessell called *The Comeback Story*; the first programme had featured Bobby Breen, the child singer and actor of the 1930s, and the second was about a blind baseball player. For Lady to take part in this was absurd on the face of it, because she hadn't been anywhere lately to come back from, but it was interesting publicity in more ways than one. Some of Lady's former friends refused to appear, or wanted too much money, but Mae Barnes, Artie Shaw, Pod Hollingsworth (who died a few months later), Arthur Herzog, Leonard Feather and Louis Armstrong took part; Jessel introduces someone 'as one of the great personalities of our time', but doesn't name her: it was probably Tallulah Bankhead. (Some of the voices sounded as though they were pre-recorded.)

Perhaps Lady was nervous; she sounded as though she was only half there. But the remarkable thing about this half-hour of coast-to-coast TV in 1953 was that it talked about narcotics addiction and presented a brave black woman, together with her friends both white and black, to audiences everywhere, including the South, whether they liked it or not. It was an example of the effect television was beginning to have on the world: only four years later, Armstrong made headlines by exploding with wrath at the sight of black children being spat on by white trash in Little Rock, and the Civil Rights Era began in earnest.

In 1952 and again in 1953 Lady returned to the Storyville in Boston; Chilton says that her opening-night jitters in September 1953 earned her a bad review, and of course the critic didn't come back for any of the twelve succeeding nights. In 1953 her pianist at Storyville was Drinkard.

He said that he went to work for Lady full time at the end of 1949, some months after first meeting her, but subsequently he came and went. Later, after he got married, Drinkard and his wife were both voluntary patients at the federal hospital in Lexington, Kentucky; he checked himself out early and went straight back to Lady, who had a parcel of heroin sitting on her dressing table: Carl was soon back on the white stuff. Lady, Drinkard and McKay were all heroin users and played all the little games that druggies play, adding a few more just for themselves. Carl knew them well and had plenty of sympathy for them both.

Louis McKay was an African-American who was doing the best he could, and like Jimmy Monroe before him, did things that most black Americans did not get to do. He bought himself one of the first Cadillac El Dorados, said Drinkard, and had it driven from Chicago so that he was the first in Los Angeles to have one. Drinkard thought that he may have done that with the profit from selling heroin, but it takes money to make money, and McKay had Lady's. All Lady seemed to want was to be beaten, to have her money stolen and to be supplied with drugs; McKay seems to have been the only man she ever had who gave her exactly what she wanted, at least for a while. McKay played his role and took the rewards; as far as we know he did not throw away money on horses, nor hit her any more often or any harder than she wanted.

The games they played were precise and according to unspoken rules. She would goad McKay just like a naughty child (as she did all her men) until it was time for him to hit her. Drinkard once looked up in a hotel lounge to see her softly mouthing the word at McKay: 'mo–ther–fuck–er'. He understood immediately that McKay had just told her not to call him that, so she did it again, and he hit her with his fist, knocking her out and catching her before she hit the floor. No one else but Carl had seen the blow; McKay then carried her away, and a short time later,

> here comes Lady, prancing from the dressing room, looking fresh as a daisy, as though nothing had happened. Now, that was Lady. That's about as clear a picture as I can give of her. Knocked out one minute and prancing from the dressing room the next, looking as though she'd just stepped out of the shower.

She was happy.

She always had her more domestic side. At the house in St Albans, Drinkard said, she had a selection of expensive, comfortable dressing gowns. She would turn the radio on, not to listen to anything in particular, but just for background. She enjoyed crocheting and knitting, and sometimes travelled with knitting needles as well as the other kind. Once she wanted to knit a sweater for Drinkard and asked him what colour he wanted; he chose tomato red, and she didn't like that, so she made a sweater for her dog instead. She never went anywhere without her dog, and all her friends agree that this was not simply image: she really loved the dogs. She eventually gave Mister to Bobby Tucker and his kids; the first chihuahua's name was Chiquita, and then she acquired another one called Pepe (through Ava Gardner, Drinkard said) and until Chiquita died there were two of them.

Lady never lost touch with her childhood self. She enjoyed getting away with things; if she went in a shop she would steal something small and unimportant, such as a pair of scissors. Drinkard said that sometimes McKay followed along in Lady's wake, paying for things as though he were worried about embarrassing trouble with the law, but he was careful not to let her see him, because that would have spoiled it for her. (A few years later, in Paris, Annie Ross said, they visited a high-class jewellery shop and Lady boosted two or three items of rather more value.)

But as she grew older perhaps she got harder to get along with; or perhaps it was simply that she was almost constantly on the road, living in hotel rooms and singing in saloons. By now she had been on dope for so long that the dope may have allowed her to behave any way she liked, metaphorically thumbing her nose while her essential spirituality became more and more private. And as we shall see, the emotional and psychological stand-off with McKay eventually became burdensome. Once she even got Drinkard to hit her.

He testifies, like others, that Lady was always gracious on stage, 'unlike other singers I could name'. She would never chastise a musician in front of the fans, but he would hear about it later. When he knew she was sore at him he would go to his room and stay there, trying to avoid her, but she might send somebody after him, and then it would not be Carl, but 'Mr Drinkard'.

'I suppose you know you've ruined my career, Mr Drinkard.' And I'd know it was going to be a lengthy thing from then on, because Lady didn't start right off full of fury; she'd start signifying. 'I don't know how it is that every time I walk out on that goddam stage, you do just the opposite of what I want you to do. I don't know what it is. I've been training you for years, Carl.' (She's been training me for years: now I know she's working herself up.) 'I thought by now you might know that the tempo is too fast for me.' Now, I know it wasn't too fast, because some nights she comes out and does it twice as fast; Lady was inconsistent about tempos. But she has to get all this off her chest before I try to leave. If I try to leave right then, she'll really snap; all she wants me to do is listen to all this shit she wants to talk. I'm trying to let it go in one ear and out the other . . .

One night at the Senator Hotel in Philadelphia, we were playing in the Rendezvous Lounge opposite Barbara Carroll; that was the front bar where people got dressed up and spent money, and the Pioneer Bar in the back was where they served draught beer and people didn't dress up. She'd go into the back bar between every show; she liked to hang out with the common people. She liked to talk loud, and she liked to think that people were dwelling on every word. So she's running the bar, and they're drinking her whisky. She had a maid, a faggot called Grady; she had trouble keeping a female maid, so now she's trying it with a male maid, and she and Grady were juicing it up; they'd been doing this all night and they're really getting soused. Some guy comes into the bar and asks her where her accompanist is. Lady says, 'Carl's around here someplace.' And the guy says, 'I want to see him, because he owes me some money.' And she snaps.

You have to understand: looking at me as the son she never had, and being a pathological liar — she could tell herself something enough times so she'd believe it — she was extremely possessive. Anybody that belonged to her, belonged strictly to her. She didn't want them to make a move — to breathe — without her permission. So she snapped at the idea that I would borrow money from some dirty sonofabitch who would go around telling everybody about it. If I needed money, why didn't I come to her? So she sends Billy Sharpe to get me, our road manager, who worked for Glaser. He comes to my room and says, 'Lady wants to see you.' I'm thinking she wants to get the next set down; it's a little early, but I'll get it over with. So I go down to the bar with my pen and a pad.

Lady looked up when I came in, and I heard a guy say, 'Oh no, he's not the one,' and she reached out with her right hand, took my glasses off and threw them across the bar, and I'm looking to see where my glasses went and she hit me with her left. I'm blind without my glasses, and somebody's hitting me, and before I could stop myself, I hit her in the jaw and knocked her down! Then Grady's running over and Billy Sharpe's running over to pick Lady up off the floor.

Well, now I'm really mad. Lady's broken my glasses and

the whole thing was a drag. I was just sick and tired of being dominated by Lady, so I go upstairs and start packing my bags, and about fifteen minutes later, here comes Billy Sharpe saying, 'Oh Carl, Lady's really sorry; she knows she did wrong, please don't hold it against her.' I told him I was tired of her shit and she could play the last set herself; I knew she couldn't play a note. And he keeps saying, 'Carl, will you let Lady apologize and everything?' And then I started thinking rationally; it's the end of the week and I haven't got a dime and I can't even check out of the hotel.

Drinkard said that, contrary to popular belief, neither her ear nor her time were faultless; maybe this means that her hard living was beginning to catch up with her. He would beg her to stick to the same tempo through a tune: 'Slowing down during a tune tears the heart out of it. Sometimes you can speed up a little without hurting it, but it's not good to do either one.' Often they hired a bassist and a drummer who were thrilled to play with Lady but were unfamiliar with her habits; he remembered one occasion at Carnegie Hall when the bassist was George Duvivier. He couldn't remember the name of the drummer, 'but he was that good too'.

Lady used to wear wedgies to make her look taller, and when she wanted to slow the beat she'd kick the floor with the wedgie. I had told the bassist and the drummer to watch me and I'd watch Lady, and she started stomping with that wedgie in the middle of a tune. And they were watching me and I knew what Lady was doing but they didn't, and here we were in Carnegie Hall of all places, and she's getting slower and slower, so I had to slow down, and the other two are wailing away having a ball playing for Lady, and she didn't care where any of us were. I used to beg her to stick to a tempo, and she'd promise not to change it, but the next night she'd do it again.

Of course, I'm talking now about some of the bad nights. There were lots of good ones.

Playing for Lady was a musical highlight of Drinkard's career, as it was with Bobby Tucker and John Levy the bassist. He remembered one tune and one night in particular. He couldn't explain what was so special about these events: it was a matter, he said, of finding exactly the right tempo for the mood she was in. Russ Freeman, who was playing piano for Chet Baker during the early fifties, described these magic moments like this: '. . . I seem to be behind my right shoulder watching myself play, literally watching my hands on the keyboard . . . you're just creating music, and it's like pouring water out of a pitcher.' The tune Drinkard remembered was a tune that she sometimes used as a closer, but not always, so that he didn't get tired of playing it, and anyway, he liked the tune. It was 'I'll Be Seeing You'.

Drinkard thought that Lady was always a 'faggot heart'. That was her dismissive phrase for someone who allowed his or her heart to show, but he thought she was more like that than most of the people she said it about: she talked tough, but she was basically a little girl who behaved like a spoiled brat. Drinkard thought that she had wanted to be one of the boys when she was travelling on a bus, as with Basie or Shaw, but now she was Lady Day, with an image to live up to; she behaved like a brat because she could get away with it and because it was expected of her, and she was also distancing herself, protecting herself with another layer of identity.

Yet as difficult as Lady could be, Drinkard had found out almost immediately that she was also absolutely straight. The very first week, in 1949, a man had come into the dressing room and said, 'Lady, guess what. Odessa just got busted.'

She said, 'Odessa? You mean Big *black* Odessa?' Big Odessa was a cocaine dealer in Washington, and Lady turns around to the guy as if to say how in the world did they ever get Odessa, because she never kept any stuff around. He said, 'Well, look, she had a man who was a dope fiend, and she had to keep stuff around to keep him straight.' So then Lady said, 'What? Odessa with a *man*?' Because Odessa was known as a fabulous les in Washington. He says yes. She says, 'A real live man, with a *dick*?' And I said to myself, Oh my God, I never heard a woman talk like that before. That was when my education began. From that time on I realized that Lady spoke straight – I mean to everyone, to anybody.

As an example of one of the roles the public had assigned to her, Drinkard tells a story about Lady pulling a couple of white women who looked like money:

They were really out of sight, both of them. They were both
wearing silver blue mink jackets, beautiful girls, American
beauty types – Madison Avenue grooming. One had reddish
hair, and the other was a brunette. Well, they wanted very
much to meet Lady. The maître d' comes over and says
they've been there all evening and spent a baby fortune and
would she mind having a drink with them. Everybody in the
club is watching Lady, because she has this reputation of
being a fabulous les, and anything Lady is, has to be fabulous.
Then we have to go do the last set, and she says, 'Don't go
away girls, I'll be right back,' and when we get to the
dressing room she says, 'You want these bitches, Carl?' Lady
pulled a lot of broads for me, but then again, she would cross
me up so much, spoil it at the last minute by insulting them
or something.

Carl found it hard to describe how Lady did it, but she could
act the way the girls expected her to act, lead them to believe that
she was going to take them home with her. She also said things
like, 'These people expect me to take these broads out of here, and
I'm not going to disappoint them.' But sure enough, when the
quartet got to the Sherman Hotel, Carl unlocked Lady's door and
was about to hand her the key as he always did, wondering
whether the girls would come with him to his room if Lady didn't
queer the whole thing. 'And this time, Lady pulled me by the wrist
into her room and said, "Good night, girls," and slammed the
door.'

'Lady told me, "Sure I've been to bed with women, Carl, but I
was always *the man*." That cracked me up.' Lady and Tallulah
Bankhead had got acquainted in 1948 when Lady was at the
Strand with Basie and Tallu was appearing on Broadway in *Private
Lives*; one of Tallu's virtues had been that John Levy was frightened
of her. She was famous, white, fearless and had plenty of contacts
in the press; if she saw any bruises on Lady there would be hell to
pay, so she could raise any kind of hell she wanted in Lady's
dressing room and Levy was afraid to say boo. We can be sure that
Lady enjoyed all this. 'When we were playing the Riviera in St
Louis,' Drinkard said,

Tallulah came in there with another girl, and I never got it straight who she was because Tallulah kept calling the girl her daughter, but she was really her secretary or companion. Well, Lady goes to their table ringside during intermission, and John's saying, 'Look at the bitch, Carl, look at that. That bitch is going out of her fucking mind, she's all over her,' she's hugging and kissing Lady, and the man that owned the place, I forget his name, he put Tallulah out.

Drinkard knew that Lady's reputation for outrageousness was exaggerated. For one thing, he met too many people who bragged to him about experiences they'd had with her who he knew were lying, sometimes people who didn't know who he was; in one case it was something that was supposed to have happened on the East Coast when he knew that she was on the West Coast.

You know, it's really funny, there's all these stories about what a fabulous lay Lady was, and about these parties where she got involved with her dog Mister, all these stories about Lady having abnormal sex, like *soixante-neuf* was a byword with her, but actually Lady was a straight up and down sex lover. Like she said to me once, 'Carl, you know all these fancy guys with all that fancy head doing all that fancy stuff,' she said, 'I don't really go for head all that much. I like good old-fashioned sex. I'm one of those women that likes to fuck. But I'll be goddamned if that Stump wasn't a bitch' — Big Stump had the greatest head in the world until she met Willie Cook, the trumpet player out of Duke Ellington's band. She had a short run with Willie. He wasn't really her man — he never went into a club and collected her money for her — and John Levy told Willie Cook to jump out a window when he came back to get her in San Francisco, just before they got arrested. But Willie was little and cute, and he played a lot of horn and he was a dope fiend, so they had a lot in common, and she used to like to dress him up just like a mother would, in $300 suits like he'd never had before. She used to say, 'I'll be goddamned if that Willie's head wasn't something else. He has the fastest tongue in the world.' He put those hot lips on her and I guess trumpet players are supposed to have a bad thing from playing triplets all the time. Willie was a bitch, and Paul Quinichette she said was a dog.

Apparently women called Quinichette a dog because 'the first thing Paul wanted was to eat dinner off them'. Another opportunity for Carl to double his wages was when he and Lady toured with Quinichette. In the sort of places Lady was now playing they could always find a good bassist and a drummer, and Paul was a semi-name, and Carl would play piano with him in a quartet as well as backing Lady in a trio. Quinichette played tunes in strange keys and had an odd way of keeping his fingers straight when he played his tenor sax, all so that other musicians wouldn't be able to copy what he was doing, he said, complaining that Stan Getz had tried to steal his stuff. Drinkard thought this was silly, because any experienced rival would only have to listen to know what Quinichette was playing, and anyway, while a lot of people enjoyed his playing, and Drinkard enjoyed playing with him, he wasn't that original. 'I used to wish he'd vary his repertoire a little,' said Drinkard. 'He had a tendency to play the same tunes every night.' And there was the inevitable occasion when Drinkard went to Lady's room about something and knocked on the door: after a muffled commotion from the room, Lady said, 'Who is it?' 'It's me.' 'Come on out, you punk motherfucker, it's only Carl.' She opened the door and there was a sheepish Quinichette, *en déshabillé*. But Drinkard said:

If Lady ever loved a man, she loved Louie. She said, 'That Louie McKay is a goddam bitch. I've never known a man who could fuck like Louie.' And there must have been something to that, because Louie had a girl on the West Coast called Gloria, who was so tough that she had Dinah Washington give her a brand new car. Now the story goes — Louie told it this way and Gloria told it this way — that Gloria turned a trick with Louie and Louie was so good in bed with his straight up and down old-fashioned sex that Gloria gave him his money back and told him she wanted him to be her man. But Louie was a bastard and got me mixed up in it because he wanted to keep it from Lady; so he told me, 'You know, Carl, Gloria really goes for you.' And Gloria was a beautiful girl and I dug her myself, and she was working in the Watkins Hotel where we were staying, so I told her, 'Well, you look pretty good to me too, honey.'
And we left L.A. and went to Frisco and one night I couldn't sleep, so I went down to Jumbo's Bop City on Post

Street, and who should be sitting there at a table with goddam Louie McKay but Gloria, who I thought was my girl. But except for that Louie and I were all right.

They were both hip to Lady's games. On one occasion McKay came bursting into Drinkard's room saying, 'Carl, lock the door, don't let me out. Don't let me get to that bitch.'

I said, 'What's the matter?' There was a girl I was going around with, and she was supposed to have met me in the club one night, and it so happened that I had fallen asleep in my room, so I was late. And this girl came over to their table to ask Louie where I was. Lady *knew* this was a girl I was seeing, she *knew* the girl hadn't come over because she and Louie had anything going; Lady just wanted to start something and create an incident. In the middle of the club, Lady questions the girl about what in the world was she asking Louie about anything for. She got ready to start a fight, and the girl had to flee for her life. Louie tried to grab Lady to calm her down, and he said, 'Carl, that bitch called me a black motherfucker in front of all them white people!' He was so mad he wanted to half kill her.

But Carl and Louis both knew that Lady wasn't as tough as she talked. She couldn't stand any sort of pain (except the sexual pain of being beaten before sex with her main man), and she was terrified of going to jail again. McKay and Drinkard both bought dope for Lady, and 'eventually we got so tight that we talked about it'. They knew that if it were ever necessary to save her own skin, Lady would blow the whistle on both of them. 'But we loved her for what she was, not for what she said she was,' said Drinkard, adding that he also knew that the pair of them would throw him, Carl, to the wolves if it came to it. For that's what it was like, being junkies.

We were a family in a sense. We had to be, because we were privy to each other's secrets. Among the three of us, we had no secrets, but as far as the world was concerned, we *all* had secrets. We couldn't allow anyone else to know anything about any of us, because a weakness known about any of us could be used against all of us.

McKay was the first of Lady's men to understand, said Drinkard, that if he had to keep her supplied with dope as his part of the bargain, it made sense to buy it wholesale, so to speak. At a time when most junkies had never seen a kilo, McKay bought it in that sort of quantity, because it was cheaper that way. McKay did not use a needle, but he was snorting. He took Epsom salts as a laxative every couple of weeks to clean himself out; he told Carl it was to counteract the effects of the dope Lady was putting in his food: 'She wants to get me hooked just like she is.' McKay pretended that he didn't use any dope and Drinkard pretended to believe him – 'She wasn't putting it in his food; he was putting it up his goddam nose.'

All three of them played God where the dope was concerned. At one point during the Levy era when Lady was off the needle, Drinkard hid his works in a corridor between their rooms, so that Lady could shoot up when the coast was clear. 'She would return the works to the hiding place, and leave me a little stuff. But then I got soft-hearted and gave her a set of her own, and she stopped giving me stuff. She was like that.' Later, when McKay wasn't around and Lady was holding the dope, she would hold out on Drinkard all night and all the next day until he started getting sick, keeping him in line until just before show time, when she would give him enough to get straight so they could go on.

And McKay did the same thing to the other two: understandably, the stress of supplying Lady's various needs meant that McKay would need to get away for a while; and anyway he had his own interests to pursue. Lady knew that her men would have girls on the side, said Drinkard, and didn't seem to mind, understanding the appeal of the 'young bitches', but she would goad McKay about going off and getting 'buked'. 'That was an expression that meant, uh, a man getting it from behind,' said Drinkard, 'but you don't have to try to imagine a man getting it from behind from a woman. Lady's point was that Louie was being used by his chippies.'

The trouble was that McKay would often disappear with all the dope. They knew he'd be back in time to see that they were straight for the next show, 'otherwise there wouldn't *be* a show, and he knew that,' explained Drinkard. But junkies always worry when they don't have any dope, and sometimes they had a few days off and didn't know when McKay would turn up. 'He's probably somewhere layin' up with one of those fuckin' chippies sleeping his jaws off; he's probably got his nose full of stuff and that stuff has got him knocked off his ass which means he wouldn't mind sleeping *allll* day long,' said Drinkard. On these occasions Lady relied on Drinkard to cop for them. 'Contrary to the legend that dope fiends can't stand a drop of water on their bodies when they're sick,' Drinkard said, 'Lady would get into a hot tub and say, "I'm not getting out of this tub until somebody brings me some shit." And I knew who that somebody was going to be.'

She usually had enough cash to tide them over; she kept her mad money, $500 a week, in the top of her stocking. If she needed cash she could get it from Joe Glaser, but she always had to listen to his questions: 'You're making plenty of money; why haven't you got any money?' She had several valuable pieces of jewellery left over from her relationship with Levy; Drinkard described a diamond-studded watch that Levy had once pawned, he said, for $10,000. 'He would buy her things like that that were supposed to be presents, but that he could use for collateral for his various business interests.' Drinkard would pawn such an item for a couple of hundred dollars – junkies don't think in terms of getting cash, but in terms of getting dope – and when that money was gone he'd be sent out with another item, and they'd redeem the things later.

Sometimes there was lots of dope around, sometimes not. In Florida there was a Dr Green who would tide them over with morphine, but Lady spoiled that. 'Doctors had to be careful, especially black doctors,' said Drinkard, and Dr Green would drop the morphine on the floor; they had to pick it up, so that he could say that he hadn't actually given it to them. On this occasion Drinkard was in the next room when a commotion broke out, and the astonished doctor entered saying, 'My God, she called me a motherfucker. I've never been called that before.' Lady had decided that if he could take her money in his hand he could give her the dope with his hand, and that was the end of their reliance on Dr Green. Lady sure was unpredictable.

Like, I never in my wildest dreams thought she would fuck up with Dr Green, which now put us in a dilemma. But now, true to form, Lady says, 'Now I'm gonna wait until *some*body comes up with some suggestion,' meaning, naturally, Carl. And I'm thinking, number one, Carl, you need some stuff too; number two, the stuff's not gonna walk in 'cause there *is* no stuff in Miami that we know about. Lady's fucked up your last hope and you can't wait no longer. So Lady says, 'Okay, Carl baby, I don't want to ask this, but would you – could you' – and I know what's comin' next – 'would you fly to New York and cop some shit?'

So Lady gives me my salary for my stuff, and gives me some money for her stuff, and says, 'You pay for the fare, Carl, and I'll give it back when you get back.' But I'm so anxious to get out of there that I'll agree to almost anything. I grab the first plane, which happens to be stopping in Washington DC, and I figure, my wife's in DC, I know people there, so why don't I just hop off the plane and catch a cab to Edna Higgins, where I can cop?

Edna was the wife of Tony Higgins, who was doing a bid in [the slammer]. Tony was an infamous dope dealer, and Edna was carrying on his trade for the duration. She had a whole house set up, she had rooms, sold cocaine, horse, specialized in show people and gangsters. She had two girls, Mildred and Marie, and when I got there at 4 a.m. Mildred came to the door. I said, 'Mildred, I've gotta get some stuff for Lady Day and rush back down to Miami.' She says, 'You got here just in time, Carl. They're lockin' the whole town up; they just busted Sugarfoot Green.' Sugarfoot had been a business administration student at Howard and subsequently became an infamous dope dealer at the Dunbar Hotel where he was an accountant.

Mildred sold me $500 worth of caps which I figured on splitting equally with Lady. But suddenly I had no eyes for flying back to Miami; I wanted to stop and see my wife . . . So I figured, 'Why not put the caps on a plane and have Leon pick them up at the airport?' Leon acted as Lady's chauffeur whenever she was in Miami. So I filled a fuel pump with half the caps, put it on a non-scheduled flight with my own hands, and called Georgia's Tea Room, a sporting establishment where Lady stayed when she was in Miami, and asked Georgia to have Leon meet the plane.

Drinkard didn't hear any more about it, so he assumed everything had gone according to plan. A few weeks later, after an engagement in Philadelphia, he was getting ready to fly back to his wife; on closing night he waited in the lobby to check out; Billy Sharpe came down and paid Lady's hotel bill, but Lady was taking her own sweet time. She finally appeared with Mister and Grady.

I noticed that Lady had an attitude, although she'd been nice to me the whole week. When she hands me an envelope, I'm expecting my salary minus the money I'd been drawing, which should have been $275. But in the envelope is $25. She was subtracting the $250 for the capsules which she now claimed she had never received in Miami.

Leon had delivered the goods to Lady and volunteered to confront her about it, but, Drinkard said, 'the incident was now good and over, so it wouldn't make much difference anyhow.' She was punishing Drinkard for going home to his wife instead of rushing back to her.

This was a perfect example of her vindictiveness and her possessiveness. I was supposed to go back and beg her; then she would have given me a tongue-lashing and finally some help, but I was determined I wasn't going to chase her. Lady was headed for the train station to go back to New York; I left my bags at the hotel because I didn't want people to know what had happened between us. [Apparently she had also stuck him with his hotel bill.] I caught a train to Washington and went directly to Slappy White; he was staying at a guest house on U Street which was also an after-hours joint . . .

Slappy White was an entertainer and Pearl Bailey's ex-husband; he had been part of her act. Drinkard says Slappy used to come to see Lady and stare at the floor, as though remembering how much Bailey had meant to him, 'perhaps *still* meant to him'. The story was that Joe Glaser had convinced Bailey that she would be better off without White; we can wonder what Glaser's reaction was when Bailey subsequently married a white man, drummer Louis Bellson. They had a long and happy marriage, but Drinkard was convinced that Slappy spent the rest of his life trying to prove that he could be a success without her. He worked as a straight man for comedian Redd Foxx, and later turned comedian himself again, working as an audience-warmer for Dinah Washington. He also dealt a little dope.

I told Slappy I had come to pick up the $500 he owed Lady. Every time he'd send her a supply, she'd give him $500 for another supply; this is how I knew Slappy had $500 from Lady. So Slappy reaches in his pocket and gives me five $100 bills. Then I said, 'Well, look here, Slappy – I'm gonna tell you the truth.' And I ran down the whole story. Everybody knew we were always arguing . . . I told him to call Lady in New York and tell her he had given me the money that she had sent me to get. This way, it would clean Slappy up.

We went to a public phone and called Lady and he says, 'I gave Carl those five bills that you told him to get.' She said, 'What? What?' He had to repeat it three times. Lady says, 'Slappy, goddammit, I want you to get some punks, some fuzz, some thugs, give 'em $50, no, give 'em $100, no, give 'em $200, I'll send you the money, Slappy! I want them to beat the shit out of Carl!' She was yelling so hard she was hoarse; we both broke up. Slappy says, 'All right.' Lady says, 'Don't forget now, I'll send you the money. Get him. Carl's gotta pay for this, that dirty little sonofabitch . . .'

I left her nine times and we always got back together.

They even took one of Lady's oldest friends for a ride. 'John Hammond was such a sweetheart,' said Drinkard; 'he knew what was going on.' Lady and Drinkard played the Lighthouse Concert for the Blind at Carnegie Hall several times, and Lady would say to Hammond, 'Look, I can do a benefit, but the musicians' union won't let Carl do any benefits.' Hammond would say, 'Billie, this is a *benefit*. There's no money in the budget to pay anybody.' But Lady would say, 'I can't work without Carl.' So Hammond would pay Drinkard out of his own pocket, and they would spend the money on drugs. 'John knew he was being had,' said Drinkard, 'but he went along with it.' And he got a world-class act cheaply for the charity of which he was chairman; she did that willingly.

Drinkard said that Lady couldn't stand Sarah Vaughan, and told him about how 'greasy' Sarah had been when she was young; she also repeated the canard about Sarah snubbing her in 1948, which Bobby Tucker refuted. Lady was permanently jealous of Sarah, but she adored Lena Horne: 'Lady always spoke well of Lena,' said Drinkard, 'though I never saw them together. But I did see Lady and Dinah together.' Dinah Washington was as tough as anybody, and also had a reputation for liking ladies. But at the Strand Theater Drinkard saw Dinah knocking and knocking on Lady's dressing-room door.

I couldn't figure out why she didn't answer; I knew she was in there. Finally she yelled, 'Who is it?' and Dinah said, 'It's me, Queenie.' Lady opened the door, looked at her and slammed the door in her face. To my surprise, Dinah ran down the stairs all hung up with tears. I don't think anybody else in the world could have done that to her.

Maybe that's why Lady did it. But the last time Drinkard saw them together, at the Blackhawk in San Francisco, they were perfectly friendly, partly, perhaps, because Dinah had lost a lot of weight and looked wonderful. Drinkard pointed out the irony· the pills Dinah took to control her weight led to her early death, in 1962, at the age of thirty-nine.

Lady had a magnetic quality about her that could make anybody love her if she wanted them to . . . she'd bend over backwards if you let her know that you didn't give a fuck for her. But if you let her know you cared, Lady would do anything in the world to cut your heart out, and believe me Lady was a genius at cutting people's hearts.

When Drinkard got married he thought Lady was going to let him lead a life of his own, but before long he knew better.

One time we were in Philadelphia and Lady called Bobbie up to tell her I had a dressing room full of girls, and Bobbie comes over all steamed up and I was sitting there alone. Lady just wanted to start a bunch of bullshit. And Bobbie was doing Lady's hair – Lady had very soft hair, the most you had to do was run a comb through it – and as soon as Lady hears me coming through the door, Lady has it planned, she's yelling and screaming . . and I looked at Bobbie and Bobbie looked so confused, like, 'What is this crazy bitch doing?' And I knew my wife; she was really hurt by this, and Lady's carrying on, 'She deliberately burned me,' and I knew what I had to do. The next day I sent Bobbie home, I put her on a plane to Washington. I explained to her how Lady was.

Lady kept her hair cut short, but she had a hairpiece, a chignon, and every time she got in a fight with McKay in public the first thing that happened was that the chignon fell off. She was inconsistent about wearing it, and McKay would say to her, 'You know, Lady, people aren't fools. If you come out for one set with your hair long, and the next set with your hair short, and then again with it long, they're going to catch on.' She'd just laugh and say, 'It's my hair; I paid for it.'

But it was drugs that exercised their minds and their energy. Ex-junkies have a bottomless fund of stories about their own foolishness, and Drinkard was no exception. One of their suppliers, Slim, was taking so much of Lady's money that out of gratitude he gave them a weighted measure for a while; Drinkard carefully cut the dope so that Lady got only what she was paying for and he had a secret stash. 'I didn't dilute the stuff at all because that would have been sacrilegious to a drug addict. It was difficult to get stuff strong enough to relate to as it was, and Slim's stuff was of superior quality.' That was the only time he ever knew a supplier to display any generosity, and his windfall gave him an extra kick because 'Louie wasn't supposed to be using any stuff, and I knew that he was going to have some hell of a time detouring some of this for his own personal use.'

Another time he was staying in a hotel which had been owned by a doctor who had died; his widow was running the place, and Drinkard found the late doctor's hoard of various kinds of dope. He had hundreds of morphine capsules and would sell them to Lady; he couldn't tell her that he had a stash or she would have used it up in no time. Then the stash was stolen, together with Carl's set of works. Back out in the streets looking for dope, he went to a supplier and saw his own works − 'Every dope fiend recognizes his own works,' he said − and also his stash. 'Where'd you get this from?' demanded Drinkard. The frightened dealer named a musician friend of Carl's. 'You tell him to come to me when he wants his money,' said Carl, knowing that that would be the end of it.

And of course Drinkard not only found dope for Lady, he took the attendant risks. In early 1954 Lady's European fans were finally to get a chance to see her in person; Drinkard was looking forward to going to Europe, when on 15 December 1953 he was arrested in San Francisco. They were playing Joe Tenner's Down Beat in Market Street.

On the bill with us was Jerome Richardson and his band, with George Morrow on bass. Kenny Drew would come in and do a singer to cover up a lull spot. He had been left there by Buddy DeFranco, who took Sonny Clark with him when he left. [Clark and Drew were both fine pianists and both junkies. Clark died in 1963; Drew died in Europe in 1993.] This night started out like any other. We were in the lounge, where people could relax and drink while waiting to get into the club. We'd hang out there while Richardson played ... there was a guy there with whom Louie had earlier had a fracas at a club called the Say When, provoked when Lady walked over to where [owner] Dutch Lehmann and Louie and I were talking, and said, 'Mr Lehmann, I don't know what kind of a place you're running here. I didn't know it was the kind of place where a man could walk up to a woman and call her a motherfucker.' She was saying this to Dutch and looking straight at Louie. We all got the message: love to her meant a man who would go to war for her, and she was constantly trying Louie.

Every time it happened the same way. Lady would set it up with the biggest guy in the place, and Louie, would go in there without question ... he said something — blah blah blah, I didn't hear it — and the next thing I see, Louie puts his hands behind him and twisted his ring around. That was the sign that he was getting ready to Sunday punch the guy. (That was the word that Lady used; whenever Louie knocked her ass out, Lady used to say that Louie 'Sundayed' her.) I know that Louie's about to hit the guy, and I think, Oh my God, here comes the shit again.

The other man went down hanging onto McKay's suit so that McKay went down, too. Drinkard didn't want to get involved, because if he accidentally gave the other man an advantage, McKay's wrath would be unpleasant. 'So instead of trying to restrain him, I started whispering, "Don't kill him, Louie, don't kill him."'

To be honest, what I was really worried about was that Louie was carrying all our dope in his pocket; I didn't want the police drawn in there, because then we'd all be in trouble on

358

account of some bullshit. The fight ended; the guy was kicked out, and Louie had knocked out a mirrored juke box that was built into the wall. Dutch came over, saying the guy was a trouble maker and he was glad Louie had beaten the shit out of him. In all fairness, I think Dutch knew that was the kind of shit Lady wanted to hear; it justified her provocation of Louie.

So to get back to the Down Beat, because Louie had had trouble with this guy before, he comes in the Down Beat looking for Louie. They had words; Louie pulled his gun and ran the guy out of the Down Beat. He's expecting the guy to come back; he's gone to get *his* gun; everybody is expecting the police, because they've seen Louie waving his gun around; he says, 'What the hell am I gonna do with it?' I said, 'Give it to me; nobody saw *me* waving it around.' Louie says, 'Good idea,' and he hands the gun to me. I put it in my trouser pocket, and because of the weight I have to grip the top of my tux trousers to keep them up. We made the next set and came off; the guy hadn't come back, the police hadn't shown up, and I went to my dressing room and stashed the gun there, so I could walk around like a normal man.

There were other, similar incidents. Lady once complained about a man pestering her about drugs, and McKay beat him up; on that occasion, however, McKay later complained to Lady, Drinkard said,

because all she had to say to some guy asking her about drugs was 'I'm not interested,' and that would be the end of that. So he's telling Lady something like, 'Goddam it, any sixteen-year-old girl would have been more goddam help than you were. You're a bitch, you always talk about how goddam tough you are, you coulda took your shoe off and hit that bastard in the goddam head.' That killed me.

But Drinkard also thought that McKay was getting weary of all the aggravation. By now he was about forty-five years old; he was a tough man, but sooner or later he could expect to meet his match.

At the Down Beat, the action seemed to be over for one night. Back in the lounge, 'Lady was rapping her cuff off, as usual,' and a man at the bar stopped Drinkard as he went past, and told him to ask Lady if she'd have a drink with him.

He says, 'I'd be so grateful.' Just as I said, 'Why certainly,' although I didn't think she'd be inclined to leave her crowd to have a drink with a stranger, he says, 'You're Carl; I've heard about you. I used to be Lady's chauffeur; I just got out of jail.' Suddenly I knew who he was. During one of the times I was away from her, this guy had not only been driving for her, he'd been picking up her shit for her, and the cops were laying for Billie Holiday's car, only she wasn't in it, so they booked the chauffeur for possession and impounded her new car. This is why I think the law can be so goddam unfair; they knew whose car it was and whose stuff it was; they didn't have to book this guy. If he'd opened up, he wouldn't have had to do the time, and she couldn't have been paying him enough to be handling that stuff for her – this man had gone to jail unnecessarily because he kept his mouth shut about whose stuff it was.

I was certain Lady hadn't seen this guy. I went over to her and said, 'Lady, look who's here, over at the bar –' She looks over at the bar and stares, as though she sees nothing. 'Lady, your chauffeur; he's just come home.' She says, 'So what? What are you telling *me* about it for?'

After that, Drinkard said, he would have believed anything. He went back to the chauffeur and began explaining; 'As you can see, Lady's hung up with some people . . .' But the man said, 'That's all right Carl, I understand. I know Lady.' Carl concluded that the chauffeur had taken the rap because he loved Lady the way the rest of them did, in spite of everything, and that he didn't even mind getting the brush-off, for the same reason.

Meanwhile, Louis was going round the room telling everyone that the man he had run off with his pistol was a killer, a member of the black West Coast mafia and so forth; the worse that other fellow was, the tougher McKay looked, and that was what Lady liked. But after the next set, Lady and McKay got in a fight. He wanted to go off to Oakland to look after some business, and she told him he was just going off to be 'buked' by his chippies. He stomped out of the club, saying to Drinkard, 'Carl, stay with Lady and take care of her.' They never let her out of their sight because they never knew what she would get up to, and anyway she had been dependent so long that she couldn't get to a gig by herself. Drinkard said, 'Look, Louie, I have nothing to do with your arguments and all this shit. I don't have to suffer every time you and Lady get into an argument. I know what you're going to do; you're going to stay away and make Lady suffer, but don't make *me* suffer. You give me my stuff, and then you do what you want.' McKay knew what time the last set was over, and Lady wouldn't even know he was in the building, so he said he would come to Drinkard's room at the hotel when they got back there. Fat chance.

> After the show, Lady and I go back to the hotel, and I take her to her door. She goes in, steps out of her dress, and I give her her key; I'm not in my room five minutes and the phone rings. I said, 'Lady, you and Louie have had your argument. Neither one of us has any shit, so I'm going to sleep until Louie *does* come in. That way I might be able to make it.' What a fool I was that night.

McKay didn't turn up, and soon the phone rang again. 'Carl, baby, can you come up here, just for a minute?' She kept everybody jumping except when she was asleep, and she knew what Drinkard knew, what junkies know when they haven't got any dope: that they didn't have any dope. McKay never got sick because he carried the stuff, and they didn't even know how much he was buying. 'He issued it out to us every day to keep us from running through it like the average dope fiend, but he could use as much as he wanted,' said Drinkard. It was a nice hotel and Drinkard didn't want to wander around in his dressing gown and slippers in the middle of the night, so he washed and dressed and went up to Lady's room. 'She says, "Carl, godammit . . . that Louis McKay . . . that motherfucker . . . he's going to make us sick all day tomorrow, and blah blah blah . . ."' And Carl knew it was true, and he knew he was going to have to go out and find Lady (and himself) some stuff. So he called Kenny Drew, who claimed to be able to get stuff any time he wanted. He took a cab, picked up Drew and they ran around half the night trying to cop, and all they could find was five $20 papers.

These papers were like iced tea spoons. Stuff on the West

Coast is stronger than stuff on the East Coast, so five $20 papers is enough to take the sickness off you. But with Lady and I, five 20s is just enough. When *we* get back *to* Lady's room, she says, 'Is that all you could get, Kenny?' He hands the money and the papers to Lady. She goes into the bathroom, gets her works out and empties the papers into a cooker. Kenny's mouth is watering in anticipation. His nose had been running when I went to get him, and I know he's waiting to get into that cooker. Now, this is Lady in her truest form; she could be very free-hearted about anything except dope. Kenny's not a dope-runner, he's a musician, and he's been out half the night finding this stuff for Lady; to Kenny, five papers is a lot of dope, but to Lady, five papers ain't *nothing*. In fact, five $20 papers wasn't too much to *me*.

She cooks it up and draws it into her dropper. She's got two sets of works; she enjoyed cooking up for her and me too, rather than giving me mine. This night I would have saved mine, but she had her way of doing things. The droppers are sitting under the mirror on the glass shelf, and Lady's sitting on the toilet seat and she's got her legs crossed – tying up with her silk stocking making a tourniquet for her arm – trying to get her veins to come up so she can hit. Kenny is looking at this cooker so hard, and Lady says, 'I don't know what you're hanging around for, Kenny. You could only get five bags, and five bags is hardly enough for me and Carl. I got some money .. ' Kenny says, 'I don't want no money; I'm sick. I've been running around all night trying to get this stuff, and this was the last that the people had. I bought it for *you* and even if I *had* some money I couldn't get any more .. *Money* don't cook up. I don't want no money ...' He's actually *pleading*.

Well, Lady could have left Kenny a taste. She's taken most of the stuff for herself. She had more than a dropper; she had the stuff all up in the top where the rubber goes. She had left me half a dropper; what she left for me hardly constituted a fix. Lady says, 'Kenny, I got plenty more money. Now if you think you know somebody else ... 'cause I'd like you to get me some more ...' Lady is hurrying to hit herself because she knows Kenny is going to cry and complain until she gets rid of it. She had a hard time finding a vein anyway, and Kenny is making her nervous. I'm sitting there trying to get rid of mine, before Kenny suggests that I give him half of mine; so Lady and me we were both larceny hearted. I managed to get mine put away, Lady got hers put away, and Kenny's still standing there, crying. He saw the last of it slap and he knew it was in our arms and he stopped talking.

Now, Lady isn't gonna trust Kenny with any large amount of money, because she knows she's treated him so foully that if he does find any stuff he's going to go straight home and not come back. Kenny is steaming. She ends up giving him *five dollars* and tells him 'Later!' He expected part of that dope and that's why he brought it back, but nevertheless he brought it back, and the car-fare looking for it would have been five dollars or more. Kenny split, and he had rocks in his jaws, and I was glad I wasn't responsible. This was Lady's transaction.

I told her, 'Lady, I'm going to lie down until Louie knocks on the door. We've got stuff in us and we can make it now.' I was still half sickish, but I went to my room and lay down to go to sleep. Next thing I knew, the telephone rings. 'Oh yes Lady what's the matter? What time is it?' She's let me sleep for two or three hours. We've got all day to go yet, and if Louie hasn't gotten in by this time, he's gonna be gone all day.

Wearily, we must presume, Carl got dressed again and went to Lady's room. 'By rights I should have been allowed to stay in bed all day long, but no, it's all her fault in the first place, and Lady's fuckin' with me. I *know* her. Somebody's gonna have to find her some stuff, and I know who it's gonna be, too.' Sure enough, she gave Drinkard another $200, and this time he called George Morrow, who, like Drew, claimed to be able to find dope any time. 'Eeeevvvverybody knows people they can get it from in a minute. Until you come up with some money and say Okay, get me some, and then there's always some shit.'

They went to see someone who wanted to sell forty $5 bags to Drinkard, but he can't do that, because 'Lady can't relate to those little bags. She's used to loose dope, that she can *dip*.' Back out in the street, Morrow said, 'Goddam, Carl, look, there's my connection!'

The connection is scuttling along very quickly, and looks like a junky; 'I think the reason junkies walk that way is because they're afraid of missing something,' said Drinkard. The connection says, 'Sure, fella, I can fix you up. Let me have the money.' Drinkard looks at Morrow, who says that his connection is trustworthy; he'll be responsible. Drinkard knows Morrow isn't making that much money, and he's got a family; how is he going to be responsible for Lady's $200? But he knows Morrow is sincere; he hands over the cash and waits at the corner of Post and Fillmore for half an hour, an hour and a half, two hours, three hours. He's been beaten.

I know goddam well he could have gone to L.A. and back in three hours. What I should have done was gone back to my room and gone back to bed and said fuck it, but as I was walking into the hotel past the cashier's office a cartoon lightbulb went on over my head, and it was the worst idea I ever had in my life. I drew $200 on my bill, signed the form and went right back out of the hotel. I went to Post Street, and I was right near to where George was rehearsing, so I went over there to tell him what had happened, and he said, 'What?!? Man, aw man, I never knew Joe to do anything like that . Hey, man, I thought you said he'd split. There he is, right there!' I said, Gee whiz, George, and I split because I didn't want to lose sight of Joe.

And I'm wearing my corded gabardine suit and my soft Japanese slippers and my raglan cape-fashion coat and sunglasses, I look so *professional*, and I'm following Joe down the street. Dealers are usually fastidious; they can afford to buy nice clothes, so they wear nice clothes; and Joe is as greasy as a pork chop, looks like he's been living in those clothes for three *years*. Joe isn't really so old, but because of what he goes through to get his daily grits he looked twice his age, he really looked fucked up. It's not cool to look like a drug addict in California, where they have that internal possession law; in New York you can be hanging on a street corner nodding off with your face three inches from the ground, but not here.

I catch up with him: 'Hey, man, where've you *been*? I waited three fuckin' hours!' He says, 'Well, my man, I ran into a little difficulty. I was looking for you, but you had gone. Now look, I gotta go back over to Golden Gate and get your thing now.' If he's already been there, why hasn't he got my stuff? It doesn't make any sense. He's got two other guys with him, and a cop happened to be coming down the street, so they whispered among each other and they said, 'Here's a cab, let's grab this cab.' So I went along too, thinking we're going to Golden Gate. And we stopped at one of those legalized gambling places they used to have in California, like a confectionery store in front where they sell cigars and shit, and we go in the store and Joe says, 'Now look man, I'm going out and two minutes after I go out I want you to follow me to 743 Golden Gate and I'll have your stuff.' Ha. Before anybody can get out of the place, in comes walking Sergeant O'Hara and Sergeant Sergeant, two narcotics dicks, two whities.

Always among police partners, one is a black hat and one is a white hat, and Sergeant O'Hara is the black hat and on this day Sergeant Sergeant is the nice guy. They grab the other two guys first and Joe and I are studying the records on the juke box and trying not to look at them. Sergeant O'Hara walks over to me and says, 'Aha! We're forgetting about this one!' I said, 'I don't understand what you mean.' 'What are you doing hanging out with these guys?' and he flashes a badge, bam. I said, 'Well, officer, I'm new here in town, I've never been in this neighbourhood before, I just came up here to catch a rehearsal around the corner. I work at the Down Beat on Market Street.' 'Aha, a musician. Let me see what you've got in your pockets.' He grabs my wallet, and there's a registration card from Atlantic City, from having used drugs once. 'Goddam, you're one of those goddam junkies!' Well, right then I knew I was going to jail on some kind of bullshit, and all of a sudden I notice that Joe is gone. He's given them the rundown on us, it's a set-up. They call a patrol wagon – the greatest indignity of all. They say, 'Who've you got?' He says, looking straight in my face – 'I've got three fucking niggers, that's who I've got.' I was thinking if I had a pistol I would die myself if I could blow this cracker's brains out, but that's what he wants me to do, make any kind of false move. If I'd only been sure I could kill him first. They put us in the wagon and people are hangin' out the windows watchin' and it's a fuckin' drag.

They shoot us down to a precinct house and into a lineup and I hope it's a nightmare but I'm wide awake, and some guy says to me, subject to hangin' out on Post Street violating the health and safety code of something 434365 of the state of California, and I can't believe my ears. They must be talking about somebody else. *They charged me with practising medicine without a licence!* And the San Francisco jail was like that picture with Paul Muni about Devil's Island; guys they pick up on drug charges plead guilty just to get out of there. It's so crowded we have to sleep on the floor, and I couldn't sleep at all, at all.

The next day they said, 'Carl, we don't want you. All you have to do is give us Lady. We can just walk in on her, but this way you can save yourself. She doesn't have to know about it. What the hell do you want to take the rap for her for?' Drinkard replied, 'I'd like to go back to my cell.' O'Hara's face got red, Drinkard said, he was so angry. Drinkard had called the hotel, asking for the room number, not using any name, to let McKay know what had happened: 'Oh, hello Mrs McKay. This is Carl. Look, I had a little trouble, and I'm in jail.' ' . What?' she said. 'You'd call *me* . . .?' and hung up on him. But McKay sent a lawyer round, who said that Louis wanted to know if he wanted to get out on bail. The hearing was already set for 23 December. 'Louis knows I'm a junkie and I'm sick; what the hell kind of question was that? I told the lawyer, I said, "If I get any time, it's not going to make any difference; I won't be able to go to Europe. There's no need for me to get out on bail now."'

They didn't have much on Carl, except perhaps marks on his arms. Furthermore, he was sick, he was out $200, his trip to Europe was going out the window, and still they couldn't get anything out of him. The gig at the Down Beat had several days to run, and McKay must have been worried that Drinkard would start talking to the law; one way or another, the lawyer got the charges dropped. The European trip went off as planned, but it was a close call. Just a few days in the life of some junkies.

Lady needed a passport to go overseas, but she didn't have a birth certificate; at some point she had visited the Good Shepherd home in Baltimore to find out what she could, and the inmates there were thrilled (and the staff perturbed) when she sang a song for them. They knew at Good Shepherd that Lady had been born in Philadelphia, but nobody knew that the name on the certificate was Harris. Her baptismal certificate, together with a letter from the Mother Superior at the Sacred Heart Chapel in Baltimore, finally got Lady a passport. (Letters survive from Frances Church, who worked for Glaser's office, asking for the help, and from the Mother Superior. The correspondence began on 7 December 1953. Clearly the passport business was a close call.)

The tour was a Jazz Club USA package, organized and promoted by Leonard Feather. Billie was the headliner, with the Red Norvo trio (Red Mitchell on bass, Jimmy Raney on guitar), the Buddy DeFranco quartet (with Clark on piano) and an English trio with vocalist/pianist Beryl Booker, Bonnie Wetzel on bass and Elaine Leighton on drums. There were two bass players and two drummers on the tour, but Feather wrote later that there was reluctance to play with Lady because of her difficult reputation; finally Mitchell and Leighton were recruited, but too late for any rehearsals, partly because a blizzard closed Stockholm airport. The troupe left the USA on 9 January, and the Stockholm concert was on the 11th, but they had to land in Copenhagen and take an overnight train, arriving just a few hours before their first concert.

There were dates in Sweden, Denmark, Norway, France, ten shows in Germany and three in Switzerland. Feather had done his best ahead of time, claiming that Lady was singing better than ever, but was let down by local promoters; some of the halls were too big and some thought the ticket prices too high: the papers in Malmö called the show a 'rip-off'. But the fans were glad to see her. 'No matter what the size of the house was, she was very well received. It expressed itself most openly in Paris.' And everywhere she went she was greeted with fans, flowers and photographers: 'Billie felt a warm glow that had been missing from her dreary domestic rounds of sleazy nightclubs . . .'

Given her usual nervous problem with opening nights, a long tour in different cities every night must have been a trial, but she knew how important this was, and no doubt remembered how surprised and gratified she had been when she first received fan mail from Europe before the war. Everyone is agreed that she had forsworn the needle for this occasion; Feather spent a lot of time with her and saw no sign of it. A needle was found in a dressing room after a concert in Stockholm but was thought to belong local musician who was a known junkie. Marie Bryant, who living in England at the time, said, 'In London, my dear, she only drank gin — till it was coming out of her ears. Because she wanted to do good.' Feather said that the only problem was that she was a little drunk for a couple of shows.

A concert recorded on stage, said to have been at Cologne, is now said by discographer Jack Millar to be Basel on 4 February. On the first tune, 'Blue Moon', she is too far from the mike, but thereafter the sound improved; seven tunes were recorded with the trio, and then two more jam-session style, with all of those named above taking part except Wetzel. She was playing it safe with familiar tunes, as she did increasingly at home, but the recording is a good souvenir.

The group missed a bus in Brussels and had to grab a plane to get to Frankfurt; there was only room for Lady and Feather in the tiny aircraft, and McKay had to be left behind to catch up on his own, but he didn't object. In France, the English singer Beryl Bryden came to see her, and Lady and her entourage then went to see Beryl where she was working; one of the tunes that Beryl was singing was Bessie Smith's 'Young Woman Blues'. Lady said that she loved that song and used to ask Bessie to sing it, and asked Beryl if she would write down the chord changes for her.

When Lady went to England, the musicians' union would allow only Drinkard to go with her. She arrived at Heathrow from Paris on 8 February, on the same plane as dancer Taps Miller, who had been searched for drugs by customs, no doubt increasing Lady's discomfort. Max Jones, Britain's leading jazz journalist and writing for *Melody Maker* at the time, was there to meet them. He had been one of Lady's first European fans, and meeting her was for him one of the greatest joys of his career; his instinctive diplomacy did much to save the day at the airport. He had brought her a half-bottle of whisky and was rewarded with a smile as 'the bottle vanished into the mink' At a press conference, she spotted Max and said to McKay, 'There's the man who saved my life out at the airfield.'

The man from the *Daily Express* wanted to ask her repeatedly about dope; Jones leapt in, asking her how she and Lester Young had got their nicknames, though he knew the answer. Telling the story, no doubt for the nth time, she said that when she had named

I was also the Vice President − of the Vipers
She did say about her cabaret card problem
it had anything to do with race. Max Jones
ecame Lady's fast friends until the end of her
..., and he knew her well enough to write, in his evocative book,
Talking Jazz (1987), which contains an essential chapter on Lady:

> She was, I think, a 'race woman' in the sense that she refused
> to imitate 'white' manners, modes of speech and standards of
> conduct, and ridiculed those that did. But she was in no way
> a 'professional Negro' or, for that matter, a professional
> personality of any kind. What she believed, she said: and
> what she believed was most likely to be the result of her
> personal experience. In Billie's experience, the police were
> part of a system which was subject to bribery, political pres-
> sure, gangster pressure, moral prejudice and all the weaknesses
> of mankind. She thought the withholding of a police card was
> unfair, but she wasn't prepared to attribute it to Jim Crowism
> on the part of the cops . . . As Josh White once said of her,
> 'She's had to fight all her life, and most people hate fighters, I
> can tell you.'

She was often gracious, as when the microphone failed at her
first British concert, at the Manchester Free Trade Hall: she felt
sorry for the fellow who brought her another mike, which also
didn't work. '. . . He apologized so much I felt sort of as if I'd
ruined his show. When you go back be sure to tell him I love him,'
she said. She then rode back to London in Max's car; he had
adjusted the car's cooling system to try to keep it warm inside, and
the radiator hose blew off in the middle of the night, miles from
anywhere. But she forgave everything, saying for example at
London's Royal Albert Hall, 'Any time things aren't just right
when I'm back in America − I'll remember this time and be happy
again.'

Marie Bryant said, 'She called me up − "Marie, I'm so tired of
eating this English shit. It's beautiful, but I want some soul food,
some pig feet and black-eyed peas." I said, "Fine. How many
people?" "Oh, just me and my pianist and my manager and maybe
one other person. We'll do the concert and come over."'

She must have called five times a day before that concert.

With each call there were a few more people invited – 'Could you just manage a few more, Marie? I know it's a drag, but I started telling these people about it and they never had soul food . . .' Me and my husband bought three galvanized tubs. I hyped the butcher into saving the pig tails, three tubs full.

At the concert I never saw the Albert Hall so filled . . . Her voice was rotten, but it still was Billie with that presence, that Lady Day thing. I came on and gave her a special plaque from the *Melody Maker* that just said 'We Love Lady Day'. We were saying, 'We don't care. It's been a drag in America and whatnot, but we think you're great.' She rose to the occasion; they were sitting way up there in the gallery, and that gallery made her go on and on. She sang many songs way after the show was over. She sang 'Strange Fruit', because I know that was a favourite of theirs, and 'God Bless the Child', and 'Porgy'.

After the concert we told her to get these people together and come on over. Billie went out somewhere, got completely stoned and went to Paris with some friends. She called me from Paris – 'I'm sorry, Marie. I blew it, I just blew it.'

In Nottingham, where the women workers in the local lace industry outnumbered the men, Lady got a kick out of watching women dancing with each other. In London she also appeared at the Flamingo Club in Soho, a joint that became popular with black US servicemen, where rhythm & blues soon began having its influence on British music. On one evening of pub-crawling, Beryl Bryden tracked them down at the Stork Club and gave Lady a lead sheet for 'Young Woman Blues'.

Max Jones says that McKay was sociable and picked up his share of the tabs during their evenings out, and he had an eye for the ladies. 'He was a good-looking man,' said Max; the ladies had eyes for him, too. But Max thought that McKay didn't seem to be aware of Lady's talent. 'He never attended any rehearsals, and if he came to a performance he was never out in front listening to her; he'd be backstage.' McKay also took snapshots everywhere, like a tourist, including from the aeroplane window; Lady said, 'He was taking pictures of the *air*.'

Drinkard had warned Max: 'When she's feeling evil, don't cross her.' Maybe Drinkard was feeling the heat. When they left on their return trip there was a minor holdup when Drinkard had mislaid his passport or something; Lady volunteered to Max that Drinkard didn't know it, but his days were numbered. She was about to fire him again.

Lady's first trip to Europe was a personal success; but in 1954 her hard living and her psychological juggling act began to take their toll.

16

Intimations of Mortalit

For most of 1954, for whatever reason, Carl Drinkard was not working with Lady. Perhaps getting arrested at the end of 1953 had shaken him up so that he decided to get off the road for a while; maybe this is when he went to Lexington for a cure. Or maybe it was Lady and McKay who were shaken by the arrest.

Drinkard seems to have been the sort of man who didn't like to say anything bad about anybody, and he may have been seeing Louis McKay through rose-coloured glasses. He soon began to receive indignant letters from the lawyer in San Francisco, accusing him of ingratitude; McKay had deducted the money for the lawyer from Drinkard's salary, but hadn't paid the bill. He also told about occasions when he was trying to get off heroin, and McKay would press a packet of stuff into his hand, for example at the Tiffany Club in Los Angeles just before Christmas, saying 'Here's a little something to make opening night easier.' One of the pimp's time-honoured ways of keeping people in line was to keep them supplied with dope. Fifteen years later, instead of being angry about these things, Drinkard's feelings were hurt, as though he had never understood McKay's ruthlessness.

In 1954 we get another view of McKay, and in that year also, Lady's problems began to close in on her.

Back from Europe, there was a recording session for Granz in New York in April, with Oscar Peterson, Ray Brown, and Herb Ellis on guitar (Peterson's legendary trio), plus Shavers and Ed Shaughnessy on drums. Booze was flowing and the date was aborted; only three tunes were made, one new one and two remakes.

son hinted at a possible problem when he said, 'She had a ... of showing up with an entourage, which Norman detested. ... always called for closed sessions because he felt that outsiders could get in the way of the players.' Lady was sore at everybody, she said later, because she needed the money. She blamed it on an unnamed person who was in charge of the music, saying that everybody got drunk because the arrangements were unusable. 'And when I'd seen Charlie Shavers drunk ... he was my hole card – when he fell, that was it.'

But we know there was never much in the way of arrangements anyway; and making records that way was risky. She didn't want Granz to release the three tracks that were recorded, but he did, and there's nothing very much wrong with them; in fact, they're fine. At the very start of 'How Deep Is the Ocean' she sounds as though she should have cleared her throat first, but she is swinging easily; Shavers' muted trumpet, Peterson's fleet solo on 'What a Little Moonlight Can Do' (uptempo, as on the 1935 version, with Lady behind the beat), and the jiving uptempo second half of 'I Cried for You' lend the date a jam-session quality.

But then there was a real disaster, live on stage. At around this time Granz thought it would be a good idea to have Lady as a guest star at a JATP concert that already had Ella Fitzgerald on the bill, and everybody agreed, including Ella. The first half of the concert was fine – 'She laid waste to the audience – killed them,' Peterson said. But then Lady overdid something in her dressing room. After the interval, 'I took one look at her, and she was like the sphinx, like a graven image.' She kept missing the introduction, and when she finally started singing, she couldn't find the beat. Lady Day of all people couldn't find the beat, and in Carnegie Hall, scene of some of her greatest successes.

Granz had to lead her off stage, and when the concert was over she blamed Peterson for screwing up her music. Granz never asked Peterson to record with her again; not only was Peterson on the road forty weeks a year and making plenty of records of his own, but you didn't mess with him, a complete professional who was becoming Granz's hottest property. Peterson himself said diplomatically, 'He knew I didn't dig being put in that position.' At any rate, Peterson added, 'I saw her several times after that night, and everything was fine, just like before.'

She appeared at the first-ever Newport Jazz Festival in July

1954, backed by Buck Clayton, Teddy Wilson, Jo Jones and Milt Hinton. It was the first time for many years she had performed with Wilson, and the last. Lester Young was there, but had refused to play with her, George Wein said. 'That night Gerry Mulligan made me very mad – he grabbed his horn and he went out on stage, but he didn't belong there. I never told him how mad I was, 'cause I love Gerry, he's a beautiful guy, and I loved his emotion for wanting to be there.' Then the audience got a special treat. 'Prez was sitting off stage, and then he said, "I might as well go on and join the Lady."' *Down beat* magazine hinted that Mulligan's baritone sax had stung Lester into taking his rightful place: 'He shuffled on stage and once again was part of a Billie presentation. They later embraced in the dressing room and the feud was over.'

In September she recorded for Granz in Capitol's West Coast studio. She was singing at the Oasis in Los Angeles, Bobby Tucker was in town, and Granz asked him to do the date. Granz must have been fed up for some reason, because he said something like, 'I don't care what you do; I gotta pay her anyway.' 'I could use the bread,' Tucker said, so he got together Edison, Kessel, Willie Smith on alto sax, Red Callender and Chico Hamilton on bass and drums; he went to the Oasis to find out what she wanted to do. Lady must have been glad to see him.

> It was show time. I said, 'What do you want me to do? The date is tomorrow.' She said, 'Oh, just pick some tunes.' Her ankles were swollen and she could hardly talk. Louis says, 'She'll be all right,' and I'm thinking, Oh boy. She said, 'Do the show with me.' I sat at the stool and she said, 'Move over,' and she sang for a couple of hours sitting at the piano with me. I could hardly play!

The recording session the next day turned out to be completely successful. The music is certainly more organized than on the April date; there is a fair amount of ensemble playing.

Unlike her 1941 recording with Teddy Wilson, her new version of 'Love Me or Leave Me' doesn't include the introduction, but a piquant intro from the band does the job. As we have seen, in the song as written, the first half of the first line has a drop of nearly an octave between 'or' and 'leave', echoed by a similar drop in the second half; in 1941 Billie recomposed the first half so that the interval in the second half came as a greater shock. She did that again thirteen years later, except that she now ignored that first interval with even greater aplomb, simply singing across it, and when she hit that second interval she reached down with searing grace: when she landed on that bottom note, the gravel in her voice, now fully revealed, scattered and made room, just as it did for her beloved Louis Armstrong: nothing will stop her from hitting the note the way she wants to. In the line about love, 'To have it today/And give back tomorrow', she adds a syllable – 'give it back tomorrow' – and of course it sounds as though it belongs there.

'P.S. I Love You', a song by Gordon Jenkins and Johnny Mercer from 1936, was chosen perhaps because it had been revived in 1953 for a hit by a vocal group (with the usual shuffle-beat of white pop groups in that era). In the line 'Write to the Browns just as soon as you're able/They came around to call', she sings 'came around' so that we have no doubt at all who the Browns are: 'I know they're boring, but they're old friends, baby, so drop 'em a line. But when you comin' *home?*' The pop hit is maudlin by comparison.

'Willow Weep for Me' is very slow and very graceful; then 'I Thought about You', a duo for Tucker and Lady, recapturing their old partnership, is the high spot of the date. (What a shame they never did a whole album alone together.) It is very slow, but never drags, and as it follows 'Willow', another (inevitable) identity emerges: Lady was only thirty-nine, but here she is definitely middle-aged, having a few drinks and missing someone terribly.

'Too Marvelous for Words' is a fine romp, and Lady's delivery saves the lyric of 'Softly' from banality. There was one more tune, with Lady credited as composer: it has Hamilton playing a back beat with his brushes and it was issued on a 78, but it is perhaps a bit too slow for its R&B-ish treatment, and she sounds uninvolved. Too bad this one track doesn't quite measure up, because 'Stormy Blues' could have summed up the rest of 1954.

Lady had arrived at the Down Beat in San Francisco in the spring of 1954 without an accompanist and without any music, which made things difficult for Vernon Alley, who was leading the house band there at the time. Alley had started playing bass by playing along with John Kirby on some of her earliest records; he'd known her since about 1945, and adored her.

You got that groovy feeling, just walking down the street with her, you know – 'Are the Stars out Tonight' – I loved her. Her phrasing was the thing that knocked me out the most. She was really a wonderful person; her only vice was herself. She was warm, she was funny . . . I don't think any other singer ever had that presence on stage. Man, she was just like a light.

Alley said in 1971 that McKay had once paid him to keep the dope pushers away from Lady; maybe this was in that spring of 1954.

When there's a junkie around, all the leeches come out of the woodwork. At the Down Beat she was still in fine fettle; she had some mean chihuahuas – they wanted to bite everybody, I couldn't stand those dogs – but all the junkies used to come around to sell her dope, and Louis was trying to keep them away from her, but he couldn't be around all the time.

I knew them all; you could look at them and see. They're usually pretty sharp; they'll scratch, they'll nod, they'll be talking, almost looking like they're going to sleep, real cool, and they hear you but they don't acknowledge they hear you. So when they come around, I said, 'Leave her alone, don't bother her.' And she'd get mad at me, she'd say, 'You damn square, you let my friends in here, man.' I said, 'They're not your friends or they wouldn't be here.' She'd get mad at me, but not really; on the stand she'd say, 'Leave it up to Vernon, he knows what he's doing.'

Memry Midgett, playing intermission piano at the Down Beat, played for Lady during that engagement and subsequently toured with her for several months; they went to the Crescendo in Los Angeles, and soon to Alaska. At the Oasis a few months later when Lady wanted Tucker to play a show with her, he protested – always the gentleman – 'Lady, you've got the *girl*.' Lady always got her way, but Memry didn't mind; she admired Tucker. Memry talked about the role of the accompanist:

It's almost too nebulous to describe, but it's the authority that the singer gives you to help them sing, to make them sing, to give them a platform to stand on. Some think they have to

376

surrender authority, but that's the one thing that makes for a poor accompanist – to be too timid under that person, that is not what makes a singer sing well. To overpower them with florid weavings is bad, but you do have to have sufficient authority to make them feel safe with you.

She was singing her chestnuts at this point in her career, things she'd made famous and liked to sing. When a singer's building a career, there's always new material, but Billie was at the point where she wasn't buying new material; they weren't writing it for her. She was singing what she was comfortable with: 'Moonglow', 'Blue Moon', 'What a Little Moonlight Can Do' – a safe uptempo – and 'Strange Fruit' – people wouldn't let her off the stage until she did it, but she usually only did it once a night – 'Solitude', 'Easy Living', 'Waterfront'. She didn't do 'My Man' too much; too hard to sing and interpret – not so much to sing but to get it across. She didn't do challenging songs. 'Willow Weep for Me' she sang a lot. A lot of times she would turn to me and ask me to choose a song. She didn't stand on the stage too long, so it wasn't like the old days when she'd go on singing.

The audience was very receptive in Anchorage. She was one of the first name acts in Alaska. That was one of the first boom periods there, and at that time they were all transplanted statesiders, very hard working, almost a pioneer type of people.

Memry did not know John Levy, and gives us a very different impression of Louis McKay from Carl Drinkard's. Lady told Memry 'that when she was with Levy he didn't permit her even to wash dishes, because he always wanted her to look like a lady, the illusion that had been built up over the years – the beautiful Lady Day – and every single night he would always send her the orchid, and she had floor-length mink coats.' So Memry thought,

there's the kind of pimp that takes your money and whacks you across the ass now and then but still takes very good care of you because you are his commodity. Louie was not that kind of pimp. He was one of the most ruthless men I have ever met; he exploited her completely. When I was with her she did not have a coat. She went on stage with naked legs and short dresses and runover shoes. When she would get in the bathtub at night she would take her drawers in there with her and wash them out and hang them up so she'd have them dry the next morning. All her jewellery was gone. She was dying of malnutrition, because of Louie. He took all her money. When I was with her she was not on drugs all the time; she kicked the habit. She was functioning. I was with her constantly.

Memry did not know that John Levy had done much worse than whack Lady across the rear from time to time, and that he didn't pay for the flowers if he could help it. Drinkard was an easygoing fellow and tolerated McKay, but plenty had happened by now to harden McKay's attitude. The myth that the law persecuted Lady was already growing: McKay had told Drinkard that it was nonsense, the law could have taken her almost any time. But McKay was apparently never addicted (not using the needle), and perhaps Drinkard's arrest had convinced him that enough was enough for the time being. Lady's mink coat was of such quality, Drinkard said, that there were only a few like it in the country – a pawnbroker had boggled at it – and if the coat and the jewellery had gone for drugs, perhaps pawned when they went to Europe and never redeemed, this would have disgusted McKay, who was at his most ruthless when it came to money. Or maybe he was increasingly fed up and had sold the jewellery and the mink before they could disappear, tired of putting up the money to get them out of hock. Anyway, according to Memry, he was not looking after Lady very well in 1954.

When we went to Alaska for a couple of weeks she had a very small fur, a shoulder wrap, and although we got there in the summertime I have never been so cold in my life. We would just stand in front of the heater all the time; her teeth chattered in the dressing room; she was coughing and her throat was in the worst shape it could possibly be in. I think she was walking around with a low-grade viral pneumonia. Finally we went out and bought a velvet evening wrap, but it still wasn't warm enough.
    Louie saw me as an opportunity to get not only her accompanist but a nursemaid, not only for her but for him too.

So he would put me on a plane with her and send us to the next place, and we might not see him until we were ready to open. She told me that he would lock her in a room – he would lock her up at night and in daytime, and she said he would pull all the shades and keep her in the dark, and all he left her was a can of chitlins, he carried it and the Sterno [alcohol-based fuel in a can, for impromptu cooking in a motel room], and this would be all she ate. He dominated her completely, told her that she couldn't trust anybody but him and that she shouldn't talk to anybody but him. And she'd call me up from her room in Alaska at about 3.30 in the morning; she'd say, 'Oh, I'm so scared; I'm here all by myself.' Louie wouldn't stay with her at night.

She was almost hallucinating sometimes about her relationship with her mother; she seemed to worry a great deal about her treatment of her mother and she became depressed – although her mother had died some years before. But you can get to a low ebb where these guilt feelings come to the surface and drive you mad. She felt that she had not done as much for her mother as she should have; it seemed that her mother needed money at a time when she had a great deal of money; her mother was sick and in the hospital and needed care and she could have provided it and she didn't. She said all this herself. I never got the impression that she loved her mother; only that she felt guilty.

Lady had been bisexual, Memry said, but that was all over now. (Lady and McKay joked about which one of them would be first to screw her, but Memry made it clear she didn't find that amusing.)

Fifteen years later, Memry said that she thought a bisexual person will eventually lean one way or the other, and that Lady was basically hetero, but her relationships with men were such that there was no way out. 'She talked about the kind of men she met, who would have treated her the way we think a woman should be treated – nice guys who would have been kind, protective, providing, and she said herself she didn't know why she didn't like those kind of men, but she didn't.' Lady had had affairs with women, and always wanted to be the man, but could not play the protective role towards a woman. 'That rubbed her the wrong way. Neither did she play the straight role as a woman. That was the twist. She couldn't accept a real man. She didn't choose men who would protect her; she couldn't protect and she couldn't be protected.' Asked if she thought that Lady had been turned against men by her mother, Memry replied, 'It's not far-fetched. You don't ever have to discuss a situation with a child. A child interprets what he sees in our behaviour; children are seldom wrong. Whatever she was, it was programmed.'

Lady continued to drink heavily, but went off heroin while she was with Memry. On the plane to Alaska she was in withdrawal and briefed Memry on what to tell the stewardess: that she had a cold. 'Her use of narcotics was another way of self-punishment, and another way of a pimp exploiting her, of allowing herself to be punished. But I knew she could stop it any time she wanted to, because I saw her do it.' Perhaps going off the needle for several weeks in Europe had reminded her that she could do it; at any rate, she began to depend on Memry, and Memry tried to help. Lady had been eating so badly for so long, Memry thought, that her stomach had shrunk until she'd lost her appetite completely, and malnutrition made her addle-brained.

About her money, there were rumours in Alaska that Louie was buying a lot of land and making investments, but she never saw any of it. Nothing was coming her way. So she leaned very heavily on me. And I said to her, 'There are women with good business sense in New York who can take you at this point in your life. The only trouble with you is that you're malnourished until you're nothing.' I told her she couldn't go on and that she'd die of malnutrition. I tried to get her self-motivated, and that's what turned Louie against me.

We were in Alaska, and I suggested she go downtown and buy herself a coat, and it still wasn't heavy enough; she bought a dress, a short dress to sing in, and of course Louie didn't like it. He said, 'You're trying to dress like Memry. Everything you do is like Memry.' I didn't pick anything out for her; I was just along. That week and several weeks after that, she drew her own salary and kept her own money. This just threw Louie into a rage. She told me, 'This is the first time in years that I've known what it's like to be up and around in the daytime – to even care what I was wearing, or what I put on.' It wasn't as if she couldn't have done it; as long as a pimp was around, she couldn't do it. She kept asking me for strength, like 'What do you think? Do you think I can make it?'

I tried to be objective and honest and encouraging. I tried to get her to get herself a good manager, go back on the circuit for five years, make enough money to retire on; she couldn't do it with him. 'Just get rid of Louie.' I encouraged her to go to Joe Glaser when we got back to New York and ask him for another manager. Clubs hated Louie anyway; he was barred from any number of places where we played. He was barred from the club in Alaska; after a while they asked him not to come there. He was so cantankerous; he started arguments and created disturbances. At the Down Beat, they asked him not to come there; when she was on her intermission, he'd be at the bar with her and he'd start a disturbance.

Memry said that it wasn't Lady starting the trouble. 'We played a club in Philadelphia, and he couldn't come in at all!' (This particular club was one with a piano so bad it was infamous, 'an old upright, and all the ivory had come off the keys'.) 'Anyway, in New York she said, "Memry, I'm going to get up in the morning, I'm going down to Joe Glaser's and I'm going to get another manager."'

That morning she got up and got dressed and we caught the subway together and rode to town. When we got to our stop to go to Joe Glaser's, she couldn't go down the escalator stairs. She just stood up there and said, 'I can't go. I'm too weak.' This is the nature I'm telling you about . . . she loved that punishment. She got *that* close to managing her own life and then she turned around. I said, 'Billie, don't!' She said, 'I can't, I can't.' We stood right on the platform and caught the train back to Flushing.

Memry had tried to do something about Lady's low self-esteem, her lack of any ability to run her own life, and she failed. Yet Lady could still display strength. When they had first got back to New York,

She didn't know where Louie was. So we got to New York, and she tried to procure [buy some dope]. We had driven around all day till about five o'clock in the afternoon, and hadn't been able to procure . . .

That night, or the next day, Carl Drinkard came over and they were supposed to 'tie up' together. Well, I'd seen her withdraw, but I'd never seen her fix . . . I saw her trying to find a vein, and she couldn't do it, and I went into screaming hysterics. It was pathos, not fright. It was like she had done so beautifully in Alaska, and now she was going to throw herself off a building. I kept screaming, 'No, no – don't!' I cried so hard on the floor, and she picked me up and held me in her arms; she said, 'If it's going to affect you like that – to hell with it!' She ripped the thing off her arm and she said to Carl, 'Get the hell out of here,' and Carl left. She picked me up and said, 'Oh, my little baby.' And she didn't fix, and she didn't fix any more as long as I was with her. I must have cried all night, it was so upsetting . . .

And there was another area in which she had reserves of strength until the end: her music. Memry thought Lady was conscious of being a great artist:

One time she said that so many people had tried to bring her down on account of the way her life had been publicized, and she said she never let this touch her on stage. As an artist, she felt that once she had graced that stage, nothing contaminated her talent, and that *no one* was worthy of touching that talent. She said that, more or less. She said, 'That's why I wait until the audience is completely quiet, and that's why I won't do this or that on stage, because *they* don't have the right . . .'

A long story from Memry illustrates this strength. It seems to have been on the Birdland All-Stars tour, which began at Carnegie Hall; there were the Basie and Ellington bands, the Modern Jazz Quartet, Sarah Vaughan, Lester Young (both with Basie and as a solo) and several more, with Lady as the closing act.

We had a rehearsal downtown, and this was one of the times when someone had written [arrangements] for her. I think it was a fellow in Basie's band. Then the piano and the rhythm section took it from there, and everybody can close it out together, without any music; they've been together 100 years . . .

Louie had a little boy and this kid was between four and six years old. He and Louie had been gone for days, leaving Billie and I alone in the apartment; I don't think she even knew where they'd gone. He did most of his disappearing when I was with her; he didn't have to stick close because I was there, and since I wasn't a gadabout he knew she was safe and sound. He came back the night before the concert and brought the child, and the day of the concert was also the child's birthday. So that morning, we went to the rehearsal hall and waited our turn, but it wasn't fast enough for Louie. He told Billie they had to leave. 'Just let Memry tell you what's going to go on; you come on and go downtown and buy this kid a bicycle.' So he pulled her out of the rehearsal . . . She left with him and I stayed at the studio to get the introductions and so forth.

We were to have been at the concert hall no later than nine o'clock. When I got back to Flushing it was close to seven. This poor woman had a house full of Louie's guests, had tramped around all day to buy the kid a bicycle and had been made to cook dinner. They did not realize what they were doing to her. She had cooked all different kinds of stuff, and she had served the meal, and here she was washing dishes, and people were yelling and screaming and drinking and pressing her with all kinds of foolishness; it was crowded, the room was full of smoke, and they were completely insensitive to the fact that this woman was going on stage and she was in no condition . . . She didn't even have her hair done. She wasn't even dressed. Then of course Louie puts all the blame on her for not being ready. She was literally exhausted.

She puts on a dress and manages her hair some way. While we're driving in a limousine from Flushing to New York, she's asking me what she's supposed to sing and asking me what the intros are like, and I'm trying to explain what song has eight bars and what the clip is, and then how we drop from that clip off into another tempo; and of course none of this makes any sense because the people in the car are talking above us, so she can't grasp half of it . . . We finally get to the concert hall and the dressing room is filled with people and Louie keeps asking them to come in. More and more people fill the room.

During the concert, not a single person had got an encore – nobody! They'd gotten good, solid applause, but the impression you had was that [the audience wanted] to see one person, and that person was Billie Holiday.

When she came out on stage, the first thing she did was trip. She didn't trip over the wire because she was loaded; she tripped over the wire because she was so damned weak she could hardly stand up. She got to the centre of the stage and she just phased out. The first number up was 'Blue Moon', and it was an eight-bar introduction at double time, so eight bars sounded like four, and she didn't know what we were playing. Well, you know that Carnegie Hall stage is very big, and the piano is way over on one end, and if we played that introduction once we played it at least six times.

Memry was playing with the Basie rhythm section, and Basie was conducting; he finally decided that maybe the music was overpowering Lady and said, 'Just let Memry take the intro.' 'Then *I* played the intro with the rhythm section, and it *still* didn't make any sense. By this time, the audience knew what the tune was; it was obvious.' There were stage whispers from the band and from the audience: 'Blue Moon'! She turned to Memry and said, 'Memry, can you tell me what it is? What am I supposed to be singing?' And everybody could hear her asking, but Memry didn't have a mike, and Lady couldn't hear Memry from the other end of the stage. By this time people in the front rows were sitting on the edges of their seats; Memry played the intro a couple more times, and finally Lady said 'OH! A – "Blue Moon"!'

And I tell you, that place got turned out! The build-up and that surprised 'Oh!' And she stood there – after she'd done her set – and sang encore after encore after encore. I played tunes for her that I'd never played before, like 'I'll Be Seeing You', 'All the Things You Are' . . . It was an inspirational moment. After she'd gotten past all this other shit – then she could sing. And the people laid their hearts out and showed their love; I'll never forget it, because it started so pitifully and pathetically . . .

And after the concert was the fight, literally, between her and Louie and me, in Birdland. It was my first time there. I said something like, 'I think you did marvellously well, under the circumstances of the day . . .' And she hadn't made a rehearsal. And Louie made some sort of remark like 'Why the hell *wouldn't* she do well? After all, she's Billie Holiday!' And he began to loudmouth and verbally bludgeon. She then began to take up for me, which made it worse, and he had such a knack for starting an argument. He did something which so put me on the defensive, I picked up a bottle to hit him, and that started a big rumble in Birdland. We ended up in the street and he literally knocked her across the street . . .

He was violently angry with me, till I didn't dare go back to the apartment that night. I started out for my ex-mother-in-law's apartment, but not knowing the subway system, I rode the train all night. My clothes were there; I finally got back to Flushing to Billie's at about four in the morning.

Lady let Memry in, surprised to see her; Memry was even more surprised to see everything lovey-dovey. The story is a good one: Lady's health was beginning to fail and she was exhausted, yet in the end she pulled it off for her audience; evidently she had also been questioning her own motives to the extent of allowing Memry to mobilize a rescue attempt. But Memry was only twenty-three years old in 1954; she had got close to Lady because she was a black woman, but from a completely different sort of background, and didn't use drugs or drink very much; these very differences meant that she did not understand what she was involved with. She discovered what she was up against only as she went along.

To begin with, the reason Lady was shivering and coughing in Alaska was partly that she was in heroin withdrawal, and she didn't eat properly because she was both a junkie and an alcoholic. (Memry says she drank at least a full bottle of hard liquor every day.) Then at home in Flushing, McKay was doing what a man in his position was supposed to do: play the big shot. He was entertaining his friends (and Lady's too, as Memry admits: 'Some of them seemed to have known her for a long time'). He was a man who not only had a star under his wing, but a star who cooks a meal and does the dishes while the big shot plays the host. On top of this, Lady was widely known to be a good cook and to enjoy cooking; and having cooked a lot of food perhaps she ate some of it, which would have been all to the good.

As far as the concert was concerned, Lady was not well known for her punctuality, was not often known to do a great deal of rehearsing, and had not sung with any big-band arrangements for years: Basie was probably right; the band was overpowering her. There is no excuse for McKay's violence afterwards, but we are more used to that than Memry was, and by this time she might have known better than to threaten to hit McKay with a bottle. She didn't know what to expect when she got back to Flushing, Memry went on, 'but I certainly didn't expect them to be in a love tryst together. Now I understand it perfectly. This is typical of this kind of person, that needs punishment. After they've gotten the punishment, they've been so completely gratified that they can enter into a sexual or a love tryst.' Quite. Lady's taste for punishment was not yet exhausted.

Not surprisingly, Memry's time with Lady was almost up. From Carnegie Hall the concert went to Boston, and then to Philadelphia. 'She didn't have any engagements after Philadelphia; we were to have gone to Detroit, but that had been cancelled.' And in Philadelphia Memry felt that she was in danger:

> Louie began to accuse me of theft. When we left Los Angeles we had a valet, and this valet had disappeared into thin air behind some narcotics charge, and I got the feeling that Louie had planted it on this guy. It was something he could have done to me very easily. I began to see him get to the place where he was uncontrollable in his hostility to me. As her respect for me grew, he saw me as a formidable enemy . .
> At that point, I had my mother send me a telegram saying that my father was ill, and I showed it to them and told them I had to go home right away. I said, 'When I get home, I'll let you know whether or not I can return,' and of course when I got home I sent them a wire that I couldn't come back.

Young Memry was well out of it. A lot of what she says is confirmed by Dorothy Winston, who lived in Oakland, California, and had known Lady since 1951 Lady visited Dorothy once or twice a year, whenever she came to the San Francisco area. She never talked to Dorothy much about drugs. 'She saw me as a naïve little housewife, and she wanted me to stay that way.' Lady was interviewed on local television in 1953 or 1954 and said she had kicked the habit, but when Lady left, Dorothy would find her best silver spoons in the garbage, bent so they would be level for cooking up. She thought it was Louis who threw them away. 'He was the thoughtless one.'

> Louis was bullshitting us that he was cutting off the stuff so she would get less and less of a dose until she was getting only a minimal amount, tapering her off, so we thought, Oh good, at last she's got somebody in her corner. After Memry started travelling with her we found out what Louis was like. Louis told Memry that he was going back to his family in Jersey; what made him think she wouldn't go back and tell her? That was the rottenest thing.

McKay apparently had two families; he told everyone that the children in California were 'a trick's babies', but he was supporting them with Lady's money.

> He'd go visit his family out here, and sometimes his little boy would stay with us, and Billie would go out and buy him clothes. Louis was buying property, he said in Canada. Billie couldn't have it in her name because of her record; that was his excuse for putting it in his name. It took a long time to see through Louis, that he was a big bag of wind. He'd buy her a coat and tell her it cost $350 and it only cost $150 . . .
>
> I remember one night she was very late for a show at the Say When, and she said to me, 'Don't leave me! No matter what anybody says, don't you go away!' She grabbed me by the hand because she was scared to death that they were going to say something because she was late, and she stuck her head in the air and marched into the club as though, 'Don't you dare say a word to me,' and we went back to the dressing room and nobody said boo. She'd give this image to other people that she was hard as nails and would bite their head off, but she really wasn't like that.

The longer Dorothy Winston knew Lady, the more sentimental and lonely Lady became and the more she opened up. She spoiled

Dorothy's two daughters and added them to her list of godchildren.

Carl Drinkard soon came back, got fired again and came back again. On Valentine's Day 1955 there was a recording session for Granz, this time in New York; seven tunes resulted. Drinkard has always been credited with playing on this date, but in fact he quarrelled with Lady and with bassist Leonard Gaskin and was fired; Jo Jones was in the studio and called Billy Taylor. Gaskin still thought years later that it was Drinkard who had played; he remembered being disappointed with Drinkard's approach to 'I Wished on the Moon', because he loved her original version from 1935, with Kirby. It is just possible that Drinkard played on some tracks, but reissue producer Phil Schaap is sure it was Taylor, and Taylor agrees.

The date is not one of Lady's best. Shavers was there, ex-Woody Herman guitarist Billy Bauer, Cozy Cole on drums, Budd Johnson on tenor sax and Tony Scott on clarinet. Musicians' union rules required someone to be listed as leader; this was pianist and arranger Leroy Lovett, though what he did isn't clear. There isn't much in the way of arrangements, but there is too much obbligato from Scott. Scott was an old friend of hers, but a clarinet obbligato behind a singer requires *chalumeau*, or low-register playing, of which Benny Goodman was the master. What might be called 'early hi-fi' sound doesn't help either, shedding harsh light on the proceedings.

But perhaps the main problem is simply that the rhythm section doesn't cohere; Lady consistently outswings them. She works her usual magic with lyrics: she comes in well behind the beat on 'Say It Isn't So'; she gives us the introduction to the verse on 'Everything Happens to Me', which becomes an autobiography, and this time she also sings the introduction to 'I Wished on The Moon':

> Every night was long and gloomy,
> Shadows gathered in the air,
> No one ever listened to me,
> No one wondered, did I care.
>
> None in all the world to love me;
> None to count the stars that hung.

388

Then the moon came out above me,
And I saw that it was young.

I wished on the moon . . .

It had been a very long twenty years, and Lady was almost
through wishing.

Drinkard soon came back again. He related an example of her
very high status in the music world, from the Charlie Parker
memorial concert in May 1955, only a few weeks after Parker died.
Carnegie Hall was full of big names; the concert was four hours
long, but not everyone got on stage. (Babs Gonzales was one of
those who didn't perform, but he said to Drinkard, 'What jivers
these people are. When Bird was alive they wouldn't give him
enough money to buy a bag, but now they all want to play at his
concert.') Hazel Scott was organizing the show, Drinkard said,
and had the problem of who would close it. She didn't want to
offend anyone, so she gave the big spot to Lady, 'and nobody
wanted to argue with that'.

In Los Angeles in August came the recorded rehearsal session with
Jimmy Rowles. Recording dates had been scheduled, and the day
before the first, Rowles wanted to rehearse. The only decent piano he
could find was at bassist Art Shapiro's home, where Shapiro turned
the tape recorder on. As well as the anecdotes already quoted, such as
Lady's first meeting Rowles almost fifteen years earlier, there is a lot
of badinage; the old friends had a good time while they got some
work done. At one point you can hear Lady's dog barking.

Rowles always wanted some rehearsal, because when you've got
two chording instruments (piano and guitar) it is useful to decide
ahead of time about keys and other things. Granz didn't care
about rehearsals, and Rowles was also irritated with Granz because
Granz would record Ella with sixteen instruments, but never
allowed Lady anything more than a combo. This was the way
Granz wanted it, and was probably an accurate appraisal of
Lady's proper setting by this time in her career, but Rowles was a
partisan. There was also the matter of economics: big bands cost
more, and by now Ella's albums were outselling Lady's.

Rowles also said that in accommodating Lady's voice they got
into some pretty strange keys. Going over 'Nice Work If You Can
Get It', some of the discussion went like this:

SHAPIRO: You've got Jimmy working in
LADY: Yeaaah!
ROWLES: You goddam bitch, you've col
    awfullest key in life.
SHAPIRO: That's all right, it's a good key . .
LADY: And write the lyrics out too una   .11 of that,
    because I won't remember it tomorrow See, I'll
    be in a different mood ... That's why I can
    never sing the same way. I can't do it 'cause
    I've never, I don't always feel the same. I just
    can't do it. I can't even copy *me*!

Recording the next day were Rowles, Kessel, Edison, Larry
Bunker on drums, John Simmons on bass, and on alto sax, as well
as leader and arranger, was Benny Carter, who is still composing
and playing beautifully, eighty-five years old and apparently age-
less. Here is Rowles on Carter:

Then we had Benny Carter, and the respect they paid Benny
Carter ... He shows up and everybody had best cool it. I
don't know why. He's got a charisma, a strong personality.
He could almost whip Joe Louis if that's how mad he got.
He's the only man in the world who could tell Ben Webster to
go sit in the corner. I've even thought of going to court to
change my name to Carter. I'll go under the name I've got,
but I want him to be my pop. I'm not kiddin'. When I was
learning to play, I played his records and studied his solos,
'cause he's a *teacher*. When he picks up his horn, you better
watch out.
    Lady loved him. Respect. She'd tell one guy, 'Oh you
motherfucker,' but then to Benny, 'Uh, Benny, would you
mind ...' Deference. Of course. Idolized him. Everybody did.
Benny Carter is something else.

On 23 and 25 August, sixteen tunes were recorded, with one of
the best lineups Lady ever had. At the informal rehearsal session
her voice sounded rough; on the records she was in very good
voice, yet she was relying more and more on the lyrics: here and
there on the 23rd she had some trouble holding the pitch on a long
note, but two days later she was even better. All the results are
magic: what a difference the band makes. No wonder Sinatra

...d Sweets to play behind him; and Carter knows what to do ...hind Lady, just as Prez had.

Five smoochy tunes are followed by the uptempo 'Please Don't Talk About Me When I'm Gone'; Simmons's bass is especially fine as his old sweetheart tosses off the lyric: she's casual, but she's not kidding. Next comes 'It Had to Be You', with more Carter, and 'Nice Work' picks it up again. Sweets takes the mute off for 'I Got a Right to Sing the Blues' ('A certain man in this old town keeps draggin' my poor heart around . . .') On the beautiful 'What's New?' Rowles switches to celeste and Carter solos. Rowles is so lean on 'A Fine Romance' he might be the Miles Davis of the piano, and then come obbligatos from Carter and Edison; never too many obbligatos from *these* people, but the horns sit out on 'I Hadn't Anyone Till You', and the intimacy is stunning. 'I Get a Kick out of You' gets a Latin treatment for the vocal choruses, but the soloists turn it into a straight swinger. Lady recomposes 'Everything I Have Is Yours', and finishes with 'Isn't This a Lovely Day?' It sure was. For all her problems with love, she knew more about it than she could tell us any other way.

Her schedule of engagements began to become hectic. She was not a natural big-show person, not very good at changing gears and psyching herself up for this or that, and now her strength was failing; yet in August 1955, at around the time those wonderful recording sessions were taking place, she doubled at a club, the Crescendo, and the Hollywood Bowl on the same night. In one place or the other, maybe both, she could not have been at her best; yet later that year, again at Storyville in Boston, Dom Cerulli wrote in *down beat* that she held the audience spellbound.

Also in July and August 1955, she had been talking to Jeff Kruger about an eight-week tour of Europe in August and September; he was offering her $500 a week minimum, which doesn't sound like much, but if he had got her firm commitment he could have got more gigs; she could not get him to state clearly whether the money was after travel expenses. Glaser was getting good bookings for her in the USA and he was opposed to a European trip; Kruger was quoted in the British press as saying that he was negotiating directly with her rather than with Glaser, and Glaser took out an advert saying that he was still representing her, which may have made clubs unwilling to accept a booking from Kruger. Anyway, it didn't happen; she no doubt wanted to return to Europe, but as scatter-brained as she could appear to be, she was no fool when it came to contracts. This was hardly fair to Kruger, though; she kept him hanging until the last minute, and he must have lost money advertising gigs that never happened.

Early on 23 February 1956, while she was at the Showboat Club in Philadelphia, McKay and Lady were both arrested when their hotel room was raided and drugs were found. It was soon after that that McKay paid Jimmy Monroe $2,000 for his cooperation, and McKay and Lady went to Mexico and got her divorced and themselves married. She was married to Monroe for nearly fifteen years; she had told a reporter in 1952 that she wanted to retire soon and just stay home and be Mrs McKay, but the reason he finally married her was so that she couldn't testify against him. He had treated her badly and stolen her money long enough without being her husband; now it was clearly time to 'cover his ass', as the saying goes.

Jimmy Rowles, Bobby Tucker and John Levy the bassist all had the kind of intimacy with Lady that you can only have on the road together, and they all talked about how beautiful she was. Carl Drinkard loved her too, but he did not achieve that kind of intimacy until later; by the time he was helping her in and out of the bathtub, she was in much worse condition. She had gained and lost so much weight over the years that her skin was sagging and stretch-marked; she had already suffered for years from swelling in her legs and her feet; as strong as she was, she had stacked the deck against herself. She carried a kerchief on stage, chiffon in a colour to match her gown, to cover the needle-marks in her hands; then she wore long gloves to cover her hands and her arms. She had indeed had beautiful, smooth, translucent skin, Drinkard said; the trouble with such skin was that it didn't take well to being punctured: her body was covered with scars from small ulcers that had erupted. Knowing what she really looked like, he marvelled at the fact that she remained so photogenic.

We don't know what Sadie died of, but she suffered from problems with her legs; and Lady's great-grandmother had suffered from dropsy (oedema); the genetic tendency towards circulatory and other problems was there, and this being the case, Lady's lifestyle was appallingly bad for her health. After the arrest, she went into a clinic for a battery of tests and an attempt to wean her from narcotics by means of substitute drugs. She was clean for a while, but she drank more than ever, and it wasn't the drugs that killed her in the end, but the booze. She had already collapsed for the first time. It was probably in early 1956; Drinkard was there:

She was the sort of person who had never been sick a day in her life, and she took pride in telling people about it. But when it really came down on her, Lady showed it, and I knew it was possible for her to die like anyone else.
We played a date in L.A. at Jazz City, on Hollywood Boulevard. Closing night – we were being followed into the club by Miles Davis – Lady fell out. In her room she felt dizzy and lay down on the bed, she just collapsed, and nobody knew what was wrong with her. She had been treated in some small way for her liver, but nobody suspected it was as bad as cirrhosis. Louie had the hotel to call a physician. The next morning when I walked into her hotel room – it was the Adams Hotel – she was in a tent, one of those things with the fumes coming out, not oxygen, but a little machine to enable her to breathe, similar to an inhalator. When I looked at her, her cheeks were sunken and she looked like an altogether different person. That's when I knew that Lady could go, just like anybody else.
The second day she was beginning to snap around. That was the result of her crutch – the drugs she was taking. Heroin works in a funny way; in the long run, it can possibly kill you, but it has the tendency to arrest whatever's wrong with you. It doesn't cure it, but it will put it to sleep; it enables you to function while under the effects of a particular illness, in this case cirrhosis of the liver, the result of all that drinking.
We were on tour for Granz; from L.A. we went to Frisco, Seattle, Victoria in Canada, back to Portland. In Seattle she fainted again, but it was never as bad as the first time. She'd just go see a doctor wherever we happened to be, but from that point on, it was only a matter of time; she had illnesses increasingly often.

In the summer of 1956 she went to the Dunes in Las Vegas, appearing on a bill with Jerry Gray and his band. Gray was a Swing Era veteran who'd arranged 'Begin the Beguine' for Artie Shaw, composed 'String of Pearls' for Glenn Miller and many more; once again Lady turned up without an accompanist, and Gray's pianist was Corky Hale, who was twenty years old:

She wasn't on any kind of dope at all, but she was drinking I don't know how much gin. There I was at a rehearsal, and she said, 'Who's the piano player here?' And I began to shake, and Jerry said, 'This is our piano player,' and she looks at me like, dumb little white girl playing the piano – what is this? And we did one number together, [she] threw some charts down, and I read them off – and we hit it off immediately. We did three weeks in Vegas together, July and August.

I was like her maid. I sat around the dressing room with her and mixed her drinks and helped her get dressed and get herself together, because she was, first of all, may she rest in peace, such a darling woman, but I would say Billie's intelligence was about twelve years, or [maybe] by that time the hard shit and liquor had just taken a toll of her brain. She was like a little child. You couldn't carry on any kind of conversation with her, her brain was dazed, maybe it was from people beating her up. She was like wandering around. It was like an effort getting her up on stage . . .

She had a diaper on her dog and gave it water from a little doll's bottle. She talked about wanting children   she was a battered human being. She wrote the inscription [in her book] 'To my little girl, Corky'. That should tell you something. I was *mothering* her; I had to help her under the arm. I don't know what the hell Louis was doing; he was out running around with girls. He came on with me. He put her down all the time . . .

She asked me to continue on with her after Vegas, and I went on into Jazz City in L.A., by this time I was very unhappy – they were paying me a lot of money, like $400 a week – I think Louis was paying me – I did two weeks with her there, but it was getting hard for me, depressing. She was even worse by the time we got to L.A.; she made every show, but I had to help her onto the bandstand and help her off. In the Dunes it was a big band, but in L.A. it was a trio and I was in charge of everything. I was very uncomfortable. She wouldn't come in [in the right place], we had to go back a couple of bars, panic every night as to whether she was going to get through the numbers.

I remember opening night José Ferrer was there, evidently friendly with her, a big fan ... He brought her several big gardenias and pinned them on her shoulder. I remember her arriving with them; I remember him sticking his hand down the front of my dress – 'You look pretty, better than male accompanists.'

She went on to Hawaii, and Louis said, 'I'm going to give you $500 a week if you come with us,' but I wouldn't go. Because it would have been a scene with him – I was scared of him; it hurt to see her every night, and I was making money in the studios in Hollywood and I couldn't leave.

She was darling to me ... Louis was terrible, horrible, made fun of her, but I don't think she was even aware, she was so out of it. I helped her get dressed and Doe Mitchell, Red's wife, was always getting her together, doing her hair.

She was a walking zombie .   punch-drunk ...

And so Corky gave up what must have been one of the saddest gigs she ever had. In Las Vegas, John Chilton reports, Lady's hairdressing had been a problem, because her head had been bruised by coming into contact with a telephone; but the gig at Jazz City was said to have set a record for the club because of the publicity over the book Corky mentions: Lady's ghost-written autobiography was a last burst of fame before her final decline.

17

The Triumphant Decli *Lady Day*

396

In 1954 the news had got out that Lady and Bill Dufty were working on a book. She told Memry Midgett that the idea was to make some money and possibly sell it to the movies.

Dufty, a journalist at the *New York Post*, was Maely's new husband; he met Lady in 1953, and she was godmother to the Duftys' son, Bevan. Dufty said that the book was McKay's idea. Books about alcoholic stars had done well: Lillian Roth's *I'll Cry Tomorrow* and Diana Barrymore's *Too Much Too Soon* were both being filmed. First they hired a black journalist from Johnson Publications, who published *Ebony* and *Jet*. This attempt at collaboration was soon aborted, and Lady turned up at the Duftys' apartment in high dudgeon. As Dufty wrote later,

> Unless you were an avid reader of *Ebony* and *Jet* in the forties and fifties, you couldn't know what she was salty about. The ads were full of pale-faced, beige-skinned lovelies selling hair straightener and pomade. The prose was even lighter than that. Staff writers had ghosted several first-person stories over Billie's by-line. She came out sounding like a freshman at Sarah Lawrence.
>
> After Billie loosed her fury on everyone involved in her biographical project, she had me on the floor with laughter, as usual. To me she was quite simply the funniest lady who ever lived. Her stinging Afro-Irish wit raised profanity and gutter grammar to the level of poetry.

Dufty started work on the book. When he first began interviewing Lady, she told him about an article which had appeared in the

PM magazine by a black journalist called Frank
(Greer Johnson said that it was about 1939, that he had
d to arrange it, and that the article was called 'The Hard
e of Billie Holiday'.) This had been the first substantial biographi-
al piece on Lady, full of the sort of factual errors that resulted
from her embroidery whenever she opened her mouth, and it was
the starting point of the book, which every journalist since has
relied upon to some extent, even though we all knew better. For in
the end it has become a sort of American classic; if all the stories in
it were not literally true, they may as well have been, and Dufty
seemed to have done a good job of allowing Lady's voice to come
through. But some of her friends hated the book; a photograph was
taken of Lady at a typewriter wearing glasses, but she said she
never even read it, let alone wrote it.

They had wanted to call it *Bitter Crop*, a phrase from 'Strange
Fruit', but the publisher changed the title to *Lady Sings the Blues*,
which they both disliked. Lee Barker of Doubleday bought the
book:

> I don't remember how the thing came to me, honest to God.
> They sent me a chapter and I was electrified with it ... I
> bought the book on the basis of that [first chapter] plus a
> short outline. I thought Dufty's work was terrific. He took her
> down very simply in her own language and that's what made
> it such a damn good book.
>
> I didn't know much about her before I bought it, except as
> a big name in the field. I'd been interested in Negro celebrity
> books for a long time; I handled Ethel Waters' book back in
> the early fifties which was a great hit – *His Eye Is on the
> Sparrow*. I had a wonderful time with Ethel; she was great ...

The irony is that Ethel Waters has been described as 'a rotten
bitch, she hated and resented everybody', which is why although
'Lady, Lena, Dinah, Sarah, all of them got something from Ethel,
they never gave her any credit.'

The book had to be read for libel, and Barker seemed to
understand that Cousin Ida and others had been 'fictionalized' so
that they were unrecognizable, and anyway most of them were
dead. One line that had to be taken out was about Peggy Lee:
'She stole every goddamn thing I sing.' Tallulah and Charles
Laughton had to be excised. 'I was trying not to name-drop,' said

Dufty, 'but these people had given her recognition; artists like Paul
Muni and Franchot Tone had come down and become friends . . .'
'The crazy part,' said Barker, 'was that the material in the book
we took out was not libellous material. It seemed very innocuous
to me . . . It wasn't a vituperative book at all.' An item about
Tallulah coming to Lady's house to eat spaghetti had to be cut.

Charles Laughton was gay, which is no secret now but was still
a delicate matter then, and Laughton of course was still working.
'He used to keep a negro valet on his payroll all year long so when
he came to Harlem [the valet] could take him up there,' said
Dufty. 'He came up balling, looking for kicks . . . To Billie he was
Henry the Eighth; she'd seen him in that movie.' There are stories
about the dignified, portly British actor with the posh voice asking
people in Harlem, 'I say, do you have any pot?' 'When Sadie saw
him, she knew he wasn't interested in Billie . . .' In fact, Laughton,
to give him credit, is said to have been in favour of being included
in the book: he said, 'Tell 'em anything you want,' according to
Dufty, but then conditions began to be set. In other words, agents
and lawyers got in the way.

Some of what Dufty says is clearly hearsay, but he tells an
interesting story about the time Lady was arrested in San Francisco
with opium in her hand. Lady told Dufty that Bankhead had clout
in Washington because her father had been a prominent politician,
and that she arranged a three-way telephone conversation between
Lady, herself and J. Edgar Hoover: again, a story which ought to
be true, if it isn't.

> She was clubbing Hoover over what he had done to this
> woman, who was a friend of hers. Hoover was saying that he
> doesn't have any responsibility over narcotics arrests
> [Hoover's and Anslinger's bureaus were always rivals], and
> Bankhead was saying, 'Don't tell me that; you're the most
> powerful man in Washington. You know that every artist has
> to have a little something, sir, help give her the lift every once
> in a while,' and Billie was saying, 'Bankie, shut up, you're
> gonna get us all in jail.'

But at the time the book was being published, Dufty goes on,
Bankhead was involved in a lawsuit with a secretary who had been
'caught with the goods', and one of the things the secretary would
have come up with was the relationship with Lady. Bankhead won

her case, but in the meantime Barker had sent a section of Lady's book to her for her approval.

> Shortly after I sent it to her, I went back to have Thanksgiving dinner with my mother . . . While I was there, the phone rang and my sister came in looking very shocked and said, 'There's somebody named Tallulah on the phone for you.' I rushed to the phone and got the usual routine: 'Dahling, how are you?' I said, 'Fine.' She said, 'If you publish that stuff about me in the Billie Holiday book, I'll sue you for every goddam cent that Doubleday can make.'

In a happy and optimistic letter to the Rev. Norman O'Connor in November 1955, Lady wrote, among other things,

> My new album for Granz is out and it's called 'Music for Torching' . . . Who knows it may get a good review from *Deadbeat*. If it does I hope you'll like it anyway.
>
> My book is about to go to the printers. We are still haggling over a couple of places where I want to libel a couple of people and the Publishers and Lawyers think I'd better not. We may have to go to arbitration.

For the rest of her life Lady was hurt by her old friends' refusal to be associated with her, and would periodically threaten to tell everything she knew. The letter to the Rev. O'Connor was neatly typewritten; her handwritten notes are legible, but look as though she wrote them in a hurry. In 1956 she sent an undated one to the Duftys:

> Hi Bill and Maely
> Well I don't know if you people have been digging But my Book is just a bitch did you see that shit that man from my birthplace Baltimore Wrote He even said my Mom and dad were stinkers for having me I haven't said anything to louie as yet but you can believe me I am sick of the whole goddam thing you tell people the truth and you stink I didn't hurt anyone in that book but myself oh the guy's name is [J. Saunders Redding] from Afro American Baltimore papers. Please have Bill to look into this for me or I will take other means to take care of him he needs a lesson hope you can understand my beat up writing . . . How is my GodSon Kiss

him for me God knows I hope when he gets to be a man he won't have to go through this kind of shit When I get to New York I will read this letter for you I am at the St Clair Hotel please write or call me Miss you love you

Billie Holiday

PS . . . Now you know why I don't write i can't

The book sold 12,000 copies the first year, Barker said, which was not spectacular but satisfying, and meant good business for Lady in the clubs. The book is still selling today, and still doesn't have an index.

'We really had a lot of fun with the book,' said Lee Barker:

It was great. We went up during the publication – my wife, daughter and I – to the Apollo, where Billie was singing; I went backstage. I didn't know what her talent was until I heard her sing that time . . . She sang all the way around the tune; you carried the tune around in your head, listening to her do the variations. She was attractive, damn attractive. She had beautiful bones . . . I thought she was lovely . . . and she was extremely gracious to my wife and daughter, who was eighteen then . . . she was a nice dame.

I met Louis, her husband, and her arranger; we all went down to a joint on 43rd Street for drinks and so on. She was on heroin and her chihuahua was on gin. The dog drank out of a shot glass and got plastered. We had a great evening.

At the time, Barker said, Doubleday had received a few threatening letters associated with the book, but 'the funny thing about this was the way everybody vanished thereafter'. Not quite everybody. Nowadays a publisher will try to buy all the rights, but in 1956 Lady and Dufty had retained the film rights, yet Barker said 'there were various people representing themselves as being associated with the book in some way . . . Several lawyers came in that said they were acting on her behalf. Well, it was not so much funny as peculiar. The movie business bugged us for a long time . . . We never had the movie rights.'

There was constant talk about a film, and Dufty was writing a script. Lady still had a fascination for Hollywood and all things glamorous; in London in 1954 she had told Max Jones that she didn't like going to people's homes, 'because the drinks don't come

up fast enough, honey, and you can't leave when you want to'. But
she agreed to go with Max and others, including Dick Kravitz, of
Esquire magazine, to the home of painter Vasco Lazslo in the
middle of the night, because Kravitz wanted to put her on the
cover of the magazine. Sure enough, she complained, 'Who's
pouring the damn drinks here? They ain't comin' up very fast,'
according to Max; and the cover story in *Esquire* didn't come up at
all. But as much as Lady wanted glamorous recognition, she had
been stung when she made a second-rate film supposedly about
jazz in 1946, and she was not about to accept second-hand treatment from Hollywood a second time.

She knew that in the later fifties she was too old to play herself,
but she intended to record songs for a soundtrack; at one point it
was mooted that Dorothy Dandridge would play Lady, and she
apparently approved But later Ava Gardner's name came up, and
Lady was not happy When the third film version of Jerome
Kern's *Show Boat* (released in 1954) had been made, Gardner
played the part of the mulatto Julie; Eileen Wilson dubbed the
singing, but Big Stump said that Gardner had wanted Lady to do
it 'Lady thought that was a waste of time, certainly. Lady was
Lady; she didn't want. "If you want the song sung, get me; why
this?" This let-down thing. "I'll be standing in the shadows and
there's Ava Gardner out front using my voice – why?"'

A few years later, Lady went to a club where Annie Ross was
working, Annie said, and Lady was livid. She said, 'I heard that
you told Dorothy Kilgallen that I wanted Ava Gardner to play
me.' Annie was innocent, and Lady was apologetic after she
calmed down. In July 1957 Lady was quoted as saying, 'Even if
they get a white actress, the character she plays will still be
coloured. If they change that, there's no story.'

In May 1956 there was another recorded rehearsal session, this
time at Dufty's home in New York. Tony Scott was there, as well
as Maely Dufty and young Bevan. This was a more chaotic
rehearsal than the Shapiro recording, but Lady enjoyed herself,
imitating Sophie Tucker singing 'Some of These Days' and 'My
Yiddische Mama', and even turning to 'Roll Out the Barrel'. Scott
teased her because she had never recorded a song he'd written for
her called 'Misery', and the only time she recorded it was at this
rehearsal: it is an attractive artish effort, in the same bag as 'My
Man' and 'Gloomy Sunday'. There was also another Scott tune,

called 'Israel', which he'd written with Herz\
that she expressed any interest in it at all.

Another new tune was 'Lady Sings the Blu\
and Herbie Nichols. Nichols, one of the finest p\
ers of his generation, made a living playing in \ ⸺ ⸺ ıt
was Dufty who arranged the collaboration with\ ⸺ ⸺etting her
together with Nichols at his apartment; the lovely composition
chosen had been called 'Serenade'. Dufty said that Lady wrote the
words; two of the greatest black artists of the decade collaborated
in their living room, and the only audience was Bill, Maely and
their baby. Years later, Nichols's close friend, trombonist Roswell
Rudd, wrote that out of all Nichols's brilliant tunes, it was 'his
most popular song. Why? Because a famous singer adopted it.
Thank you, Lady Day, for believing your ears.'

Then there were recording sessions for Granz. In June in New
York eight tunes were recorded in two days, mostly remakes;
again, unfortunately, New York sessions were flawed in much the
same way as in the previous year. Wynton Kelly played piano,
Quinichette was there, and Scott's arrangements are clunky; the
only studio recording of 'Lady Sings the Blues' has an introduction
and a finish with a drum-roll and open trumpet, sounding like
bullfight music. 'Strange Fruit' also gets open horn, and for once
Shavers indeed sounds overbearing, partly because of the recording
quality. In addition, Lady was having trouble with her intonation,
resorting to the trick of hitting a note high and dropping to the
pitch she wanted.

On two days in August on the West Coast, again as in the
previous year, better results were obtained, eight more tunes being
mostly new ones, with Rowles, Edison, Kessel, Ben Webster and
Stoller, with Joe Mondragon on bass on four tracks and Red
Mitchell on the last four. Her voice is so naked that it sometimes
comes out as a chant; as Joel E. Siegel has pointed out, however,
Webster could sing the song for her so that she could concentrate
on the lyrics. Her vibrato is becoming wobbly, yet here and there
her debt to Louis Armstrong is more obvious than ever. On 'We'll
Be Together Again', in the line 'We'll have a lifetime before us',
her pitch leaping on the syllable 'life' is as though she was
frightened and whistling in the dark; Webster makes everything all
right on the bridge, and continues with an obbligato to her last
chorus. She had not recorded with him since 1938.

recorded rehearsal in May was said to have been for an
asual Carnegie Hall concert to promote her book. It took place
in November. There were two concerts, at eight and midnight; the
first was recorded. Gilbert Millstein read four long excerpts from
the book to an audience which was said to have been patient while
it waited for Lady to sing; he said later that he'd picked the parts
to read without knowing what she would sing. At a rehearsal,
Lady seemed to have trouble concentrating, but

> that night, it was utterly superb. She was thoroughly profes-
> sional, alert, took her cues perfectly, made not a single mistake.
> It was the most haphazard [thing] with which I've ever been
> associated in my life and yet it came off as though it had been
> machine-tooled.

She did thirteen songs, two of them accompanied by Scott at the
piano; on the others Drinkard was there, as well as Roy Eldridge,
Coleman Hawkins and a rhythm section. She was in good voice
and the audience loved her; one of the tunes turned out to be her
revival of 1944s 'I'll Be Seeing You' Nat Hentoff wrote in *down beat*
that it was a night when she was on top, 'the best jazz singer alive'.
Most of the tunes were her own; the concert version of 'Lady Sings the
Blues' is her best recording of it.

In an undated letter from the Duftys to Lady and McKay,
Dufty says that the Cowans had sat next to them at the Carnegie
Hall concert; this was producer Lester Cowan, who said afterwards,
'What is this girl doing at Carnegie Hall? She should be doing
two-a-day at the Palace, like Judy Garland.' And there is a burst
of enthusiasm from Dufty about a movie of *Lady Sings the Blues*:
Cowan claimed that you could make 'honest movies about people
who stay brown all year round' if you wrote off the South, made
up the gross from Europe, and raised capital to make the film from
exhibitors in the North, who would then show the film no matter
how controversial it turned out to be. *The New York Times* had
already reported in September that Cowan had a deal with United
Artists, the director was to be Anthony Mann, four new songs were
being written by Ann Ronell (Mrs Cowan), and Dufty's script had
the approval of Geoffrey Shurlock, administrator of Hollywood's
production code. On the question of a white actress, Cowan said,
'My principal concern as a producer is to find for the role an
actress who can do justice to it.' He said that all Lady had said

was, 'I'm not prejudiced.' A few months later Dorothy Kilgallen reported: 'Casting rumours . . . get sillier and sillier . . . now the producer reportedly is trying to get Lana Turner . . .'

Meanwhile, it was back to the West Coast for Lady, where she went to Jazz City over Christmas, and a marathon five sessions across seven days in January 1957 followed: she recorded eighteen tunes with the same crew as in August (Mitchell on bass, Stoller on drums and probably Bunker on the last four tracks). The band also recorded an instrumental on 'Just Friends' at one session while waiting for her. These were her last studio recordings for Granz and the last in the small-group context she was famous for.

The first track was another version of 'I Wished on the Moon', without the introduction to the verse, and slightly uptempo, casually tossed off, as though now she is now no longer wishing, but remembering having wished. On 'Moonlight in Vermont', her naked voice sounds at first, eerily, as though she were younger than she ever was, little-girlish and with something of the clarity of Ella Fitzgerald; but within a few bars the wobbly vibrato and the yearning past-tense in the lyrics reveal her as older than she ever was. Webster is beautiful; the band, as in August, selflessly reinforce her, but they are able to do so because they are backing not so much a singer as another musician: she is among equals.

On the first two dates she recorded only three songs each; resting between, she improved, and ended up doing some of the best of all her work for Granz. 'Let's Call the Whole Thing Off' has no less silly a premise than it did as a brand-new lighthearted film song twenty years earlier, but it no longer matters; the important thing was the swing, and the abrupt ending on the word 'off' is a delight. On the very last of the eighteen tunes, Don Redman's 'Gee Baby Ain't I Good to You', it's the old sassy Lady back again.

Again she resumed touring, and she began working with Mal Waldron, who became her last accompanist. He was at home in New York when he got a call from Dufty, who asked him to go to Pep's in Philadelphia to play for Lady; Quinichette was in charge of the group. Waldron said he rushed out and bought all the Billie records he could find, and he must have listened to them all night because the next morning he left for Philadelphia. Like every other musician, he was in awe of her. Chilton quotes him:

I soon found out why most musicians who knew her called her Lady, because even though I didn't please her completely she spoke to me as a big sister and gave me many helpful hints. She also told me that I wasn't playing funky enough, and from that day on, I worked at playing more and more bluesy and earthy for her.

Waldron was thirty years old and a house pianist at Prestige Records, making albums under his own name and with the young John Coltrane and others, including Quinichette: one wonders if it was not Little Prez who recommended Waldron, who was already a composer of distinction; he later became better known than anyone who had played for Lady since Teddy Wilson. Earl Zaidins, Lady's lawyer, said that Waldron took his share of abuse, but when Lady went on a tirade, he would just agree with her and stay neutral. He was as faithful as Bobby Tucker had been: Zaidins said, 'Waldron carried her plenty, believe me.' Apparently he meant in the financial sense; towards the end Lady didn't have much money, but Waldron was always there.

Waldron said that she was still deeply attached to McKay, and that on one occasion in Detroit, when McKay was late to the club and she didn't know where he was, she decided to sing 'Lover Man'. 'It sounds corny, but by the time she'd finished there were tears in everyone's eyes.' Yet McKay had only a few months left as the centre of Lady's life.

In July Lady played the Newport Jazz Festival, with Waldron, Joe Benjamin on bass and Jo Jones on drums. The six tracks recorded at Newport have been described as 'her most pitiable recording', but that is a questionable judgement; Lady is the sort of artist who deserves to have her work listened to as a whole, and her decline is still part of a continuum. True, she sounds desperately tired, putting special poignance on lines like 'Tired? You bet.' But she had always lived through her music; that's what made her a great interpreter. She repeats a lyric on 'Lover, Come Back to Me', but the singer who has never screwed up a line probably doesn't exist; she had done it at her (highly praised) Carnegie Hall concert a few months earlier. At the end of 'Willow Weep for Me', and to a lesser extent 'My Man', she stretches the time unmercifully, as though she was trying to escape time altogether. She negotiates Nichols's sinuous melody on 'Lady Sings the Blues', and

*** PORTRAITS OF BILLIE ***

Right: Circa 1941. Photograph by
Murray Korman. *(Rialto Archives)*

Above: Circa 1940.
(Rialto Archives)

Right: At the
Off-Beat Club,
Chicago, 1939.
(Rialto Archives)

Previous page:
August 1935.
Photograph by
Timme
Rosenkrantz.
(Rialto Archives)

Right: Recording at Decca
Studios, circa 1949. *(Rialto Archives)*

Left: March 1945. Photographs by
Skippy Adelman. *(Rialto Archives)*

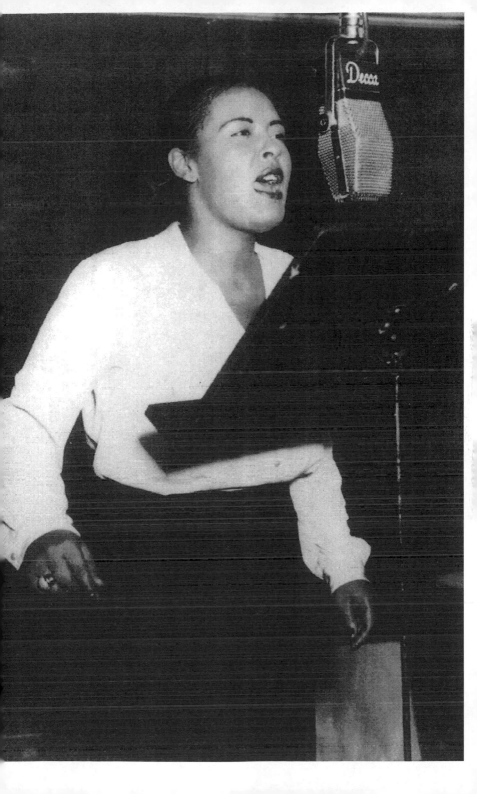

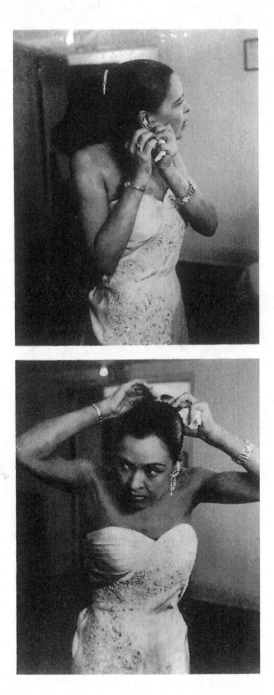

Left and right: Backstage at Newport Jazz Festival, July 6, 1957 Photographs by Bert Block. *(Courtesy of Barbara Carroll)*

Following page: Billie Holiday at her last recording session for MGM Records, March 1959. *(Rialto Archives)*

the roughness and tiredness in her voice adds to a memorable experience.

In August she went to the Shakespeare Festival in Stratford, Ontario, and on to a club date in Toronto; *Melody Maker* gave her high marks from both places. Bill Dufty had written to Lady that his sister had a summer place across the river from Detroit, so maybe she got a chance to relax there. She then went to the Avant Garde in Hollywood, but illness caused her to cut short that engagement, and when she went back to New York she left McKay in California. The following year she started divorce proceedings.

In early 1957, after many adjournments, the Philadelphia arrest of the previous year had been resolved in probation. There is a transcription of a telephone call from Louis McKay to Maely Dufty dated 'Winter 1958 time of record session LADY IN SATIN'. It is incomplete; McKay had received a wire from Lady, something about some money, and was angry; he complained to Maely about

> all the money I made and all the things I bought her . . . this girl ain't never had a dime to buy nothin' . . . Ain't going let nobody make a fool out of me   . good as I been to this woman. You talking about I been bad, Maely, I ain't been bad to this woman. I treat this woman right. She know I was getting some money out of this girl. She took the money and used it up so why talk about me . . . If I got a whore I get some money from her or I don't have nothing to do with the bitch . . . She never gave me a goddam quarter. I took care of her. I kept the woman alive.

He was in his gangster bag, threatening appalling violence: '. . . Holiday's ass in the gutter in the East River somewhere . . . I'm going to do her up so goddam bad she going remember as long as she lives . . .' But part of the conversation is tantalizing:

MAELY: Louis, both of you are involved in a case in Philadelphia; you better not start fucking around.

LOUIS: I don't give a goddam about that case in Philadelphia. Shit, that case been beat a long time ago. People worried about that case, I ain't worried about it. I ain't worried about that case at all, because the right people are behind that case.

MAELY:	What do you mean?
LOUIS:	Every motherfucker that I know tried to get me to turn that bitch loose and let her go ahead and get some time, don't worry about it.
MAELY:	You mean she's supposed to do time?
LOUIS:	She ain't going to do no time. I mean that's what happened two years ago. They told me to split her out from the case and then cut me loose. No, I said, she can't make it. If I make it she make it. And here this dirty ass bitch done pulled her shit on me . . .

This is likely to be just McKay bragging. But he probably had underworld connections, and he may have thought that Lady would not survive a jail term; is it just possible that he had managed to protect her in some way, by bribing the law to get her on probation? That he had even married her not to protect himself but to protect her? Drinkard says that after the arrest McKay also hired a black policewoman to travel with them, and to keep an eye on Lady so that she didn't get into any more trouble (and that the starry-eyed, attractive young policewoman regarded her duty as an exciting holiday).

Lady was superstitious, though she would never have admitted it. A hat on a bed, shoes on a shelf or a broom against her feet while a room was being swept, said Drinkard, would make her angry. She never signed a will either: her lawyer, Earl Zaidins, says he drew one up for her, but then she wouldn't talk about it, because she was superstitious. She was not divorcing McKay because she was ill. Yet although it had taken her fifteen years to divorce Jimmy Monroe, she now wanted to get rid of McKay after little more than two years of marriage. She later claimed to have 'put the whammy' on John Levy the pimp, whereupon he died, implying that McKay had better watch out.

John Levy still owned the house in St Albans, and during the mid-1950s had tried a scam so daring and ingenious that it made all the newspapers. Tonda said he was always a whiz at anything electronic; he installed a fancy radio aerial on the house and was trying to receive instant results from a confederate at a nearby racetrack, whereupon he would place bets with numbers runners before the betting closed. This once again involved the whole family; Ron Levy said that he was the only ... arrested, and the authorities even pestered Ton ... married his current girlfriend for the same r ... married Lady: so she couldn't testify against ___ began investigating Levy's tax affairs, an area where he must have been vulnerable; but he told Ron that he could never go to prison because of his claustrophobia. High blood pressure ran in the family — Ron is the first male Levy to live well into middle age — and on Thanksgiving Day 1957 John had a cerebral haemorrhage, dying in December. Ron said that the Justice Department came to the funeral to make sure he was really dead and arrested another member of the family they'd been looking for; Levy's obituaries described this cruel but complicated man as something he never was: Billie Holiday's ex-husband.

Years later, Zaidins said he had helped to get some of McKay's chippies out of trouble, and also told about Lady coming round to his apartment to hide from McKay. Zaidins locked her in his bathroom while McKay came banging on the door, saying 'I got a pistol.' Zaidins threw him out, he said, and wanted to call the police, but Lady talked him out of it, and also would not press charges against McKay, which was only fair, given the number of times she must have provoked him. Her friends disliked McKay, but they allowed that she was no doubt hard to live with; both Lady and McKay have been described as 'pathological liars', but that kind of lying is a desperate struggle on the part of people who have started at the bottom to bend the world into some sort of reasonable shape. We do not know what finally caused the split, but perhaps she realized that she could not take any more of the punishment he was used to dishing out, or perhaps he understood that there was no longer much point in treating her like dirt. Zaidins said that she resented McKay's having married her, but we have only his opinion on that. You could only take advantage of Lady in ways of which she approved; marriage to her was a serious business, and she complained to others about the heartache: her man, such as he was, had left her.

At the end of 1957 came the last truly great experience we have of Lady Day on record. It was the 'Sound of Jazz' CBS TV show, sponsored by Timex, in the series *Seven Lively Arts*, produced by John Houseman.

This had been a series fraught with difficulties, an attempt at a

of twentieth-century news magazine in the days when most
TV was still done live. The first programme had been about 'The
Changing Ways of Love', as exploited through the century in the
various media; and the presenter of the series, John Crosby, was
himself controversial. A fearless critic for the *Herald Tribune*
syndicate, 'his charisma was essentially literary,' as Houseman drily
put it in his memoirs. Crosby was having trouble with his contact
lenses, refused to wear glasses on screen and tried to memorize his
business instead of reading a monitor; he froze at the beginning of
the broadcast, and the resulting eighteen seconds of dead air made
television history· the series was judged by that, and only eleven
programmes were broadcast instead of the scheduled twenty-six.
After it was cancelled it won awards, too late; but the penultimate
programme in that innovatory series will never be forgotten.

Bassist (and photographer) Milt Hinton talked about it, introducing it with a little history. About recording with Teddy and Lady
in the thirties, and Charlie Parker a little later, he said:

We never thought of these [records] as being something that
would be a matter of history. When a session was over, it was
another good session and another good time. Most of us never
even bought the records, because the joy was in the playing.
That whole era was like that. It's gone and there's nothing
like it. The Street's gone and the players are leaving and
there's no school like the Street, for new jazz players to break
in and learn and receive that sort of environment and be
engrossed in and sort of fulfil themselves . . .

1957. All right. I'd already won the first *Esquire* award in
'44, so I'm entrenched; in *Metronome* I'm fifth in this poll and
I'm second in the international poll, so now I've traced myself
as a member of this jazz society. You're recognized as a
player; there's no more worries about getting a gig. It's just
which one I want to do. So in 1957 we're aware of who we
are and what's been happening and we're doing our own
particular things and making our own little individual monies
wherever we can scrounge in and make them.

But now you want to know, where is everybody? Billie's
going off and she's singing in Pittsburgh and they're giving
her a fairly high price, but in order to do that they can't
support her with the kind of musicians she should be with,

like the ones who made her records that they've hired her because of. So in some little joint they pay her whatever her price is and they get some local musicians, which is just ridiculous because they haven't had the experience, and they just don't *know*. They'll probably be great later but now they're just terrible and they're getting $50 a week, and she has to scuffle through a performance with this kind of background. In the meantime, I'm over here with somebody else because they can pay me the kind of money I want, and I'm playing with some other guy . . .

But my name is out in front and his isn't, so he's not getting any bread and I'm not happy because I'm not playing with Osie Johnson here, and this is going on all over with us. Ben Webster's going crazy because he's getting his $500 a week in Rochester but they got three high-school kids playing with him, and he's got to sit down in the afternoon and teach them *the* chords to the tunes which they'll forget by the time they get on the bandstand, and with his greatness, coming out of Duke's band with all that beautiful background music, he's got to insert his cottontail into this sort of a background . . .

We're all making our individual bread but we're all unhappy, because nobody's ever going to say to Ben, 'Why don't you hire Milt?' Because if Ben hires his rhythm section, now he's got to pay me. I won *Esquire* awards, I need $100, I need $200. If he's gonna get $500, I gotta get $250, and they can't afford that. Roy Eldridge is having this problem, Billie Holiday is having this problem, and we're all very, very unhappy, and along comes the producer of this TV show and says, 'Let's get them together.'

So here we are, and now we're really happy; this producer, whoever he was, he was most gracious, and he knew who he had and he just let us mingle and didn't disturb us. There's Basie — I live right next door to Basie, by the way, he's my neighbour — and there's Monk, and we're talking and the cameras are running and they're saying, 'When we gonna get on the set?' And the director's saying, 'Well, let them talk for a minute.' And there's Billie Holiday, and I'm taking a shot through the piano, with her long pigtail standing next to Basie, and Basie's playing this thing and there's Jo Jones, his majestic self standing there, and Roy Eldridge is there and

Danny Barker and Red Allen, and there's Gerry Mulligan, king of the baritone sax, sitting there in the saxophone section with Coleman Hawkins, Ben Webster and Prez. And here we are together and we can't possibly stop.

Whitney Balliett and Nat Hentoff helped to put the programme together, and when Hentoff told Lady that the idea was informality, that everyone should be wearing street clothes, she complained, 'I just spent 500 goddam dollars on a gown!' But the producers knew what they were doing. A rehearsal was recorded on 5 December, with the Mal Waldron All-Stars, which included Hawk, Ben and Prez, the three greatest tenor players in the first fifty years of jazz; Doc Cheatham on trumpet, a veteran of Cab Calloway's band; Vic Dickenson on trombone, Barker on guitar, Jones on drums and Jim Atlas on bass; three days later the live broadcast added Mulligan and Roy Eldridge, with Hinton and Osie Johnson on bass and drums. In September it had been announced in the *New York Post* that Lady was to sing 'Strange Fruit', but that would have been all wrong in this context; it was 'Fine and Mellow', and it was just right.

She didn't have to try very hard to sing this song: 'Just treat me right baby, I'll stay home every day; but you're so mean to me baby, I know you're gonna drive me away.' Once again a particular song at a particular time seemed to mirror her life: in December of that year her love life was virtually over, and her easy yet meaningful delivery of the verses is classic Holiday magic.

The rehearsal session was better recorded, and Prez blew a little obbligato during her first chorus, followed by the leanest, sparest solo he ever did – only the love was left, but it was enough. Webster followed, another chorus from Lady, then Cheatham, then Hawk, Lady again, Dickenson, and Lady took it out. It was less than six and a half minutes long.

The live broadcast was preceded by a recording of Lady's voice, as the camera followed her walking in among the musicians, everybody smiling at each other, the room full of love: '. . . There's two kinds of blues – there's happy blues and sad blues . . . I don't know, the blues is sort of a mixed-up thing, you just have to feel it. Anything I – I *do* sing, it's part of my life.' Cheatham blew a muted obbligato during her first chorus, then Webster soloed, followed by Prez. Both Lady and Prez sounded more tired than at the rehearsal, but on the television recording you can see them watching each other, listening, smiling, and we are reminded that jazz is a *live* art. The performance ran for over eight minutes; there's room for a solo from Mulligan, and Eldridge's solo is almost angry: 'Hey, where've you guys *been*? Why can't we do this more *often*?'

There were a few other, similar jazz programmes on American television in that era, and that was it. All were memorable, but one short segment of one of them is special, because of Lady, and because of the way she smiled to herself during Prez's solo.

'Prez was out of it that day,' said Hinton:

> It was just that beautiful thing that he did. It wasn't that he wasn't so well, it was just that he was so much out of it. We didn't feel too bad. We just let him sit on the side on a bench. I even got pictures ... There wasn't too much sadness. I don't remember anyone saying, 'I think he's going.' We had no thoughts like that.

In 1957 Lady had also sat in at the Five Spot until 4 a.m. one morning with Waldron; after-hours sessions were overlooked by the police, probably because performers didn't get paid anyway. She also sang in concerts, which didn't require police permission and were becoming more common because the artists themselves were tired of being restricted to booze parlours. In June at a midnight concert at Loew's Sheridan Theater in Greenwich Village were the Charles Mingus Quintet, the Modern Jazz Quartet, the Randy Weston Trio and vocalist Barbara Lea. In July in Central Park, Jazz Under the Stars in the Wollman Memorial Theater included Gerry Mulligan, George Shearing, Dave Brubeck, Erroll Garner and Lionel Hampton. Dufty described how she would walk home afterwards to Columbus Circle, and 'It was like the Queen walking through the Casbah, people saying, "Hi, Billie!" "Hi, baby!" in a neighbourhood atmosphere of love. She would make jabbing remarks about the cabaret card.' Singing in the Park, she felt as though she had put one over on the city.

She had met Earl Zaidins in New York in 1956, while they were walking their dogs. He was fresh out of the University of Wisconsin, and she asked him to negotiate contracts for her; he soon realized that she knew all there was to know about contracts, but wanted him principally to obtain advances, because she needed the money but hated to ask for it. In late 1957 she signed a contract with Columbia Records.

> She had broken off from Verve because she was unhappy; I went into the accounting out in L.A. but I couldn't make a full accounting because the books weren't available. I always felt she never had a decent accounting from anybody but E. B. Marks [publishers of her songs]; they were square on their accounts, the others were not.
>
> I never went through Glaser. She was upset that I set up the Columbia deal instead of him; yet from the day I met her she griped that he wasn't booking her for enough money, and she could never get a count out of the guy; she wanted me to go up and get an accounting. We set it up but it never came off. Glaser would set it up so that as contract time drew near she would be in debt to him, and then he'd let bookings slide a bit so that she was short of money and she would sign with him again.
>
> I was general counsel for Milt Shaw, and he promised that he could do better for her than Joe was doing. I brought Milt over to Lady's apartment and she immediately liked him; he was a down cat, he'd get down on the floor with you, and she liked him, but felt guilty about signing with Shaw because it was as if she were cutting off a part of her life.

But Zaidins knew how helpless Lady was; and how do you look after someone like that? 'In retrospect I think Glaser did a good job for her. To many people he was a father image; when you were broke you went to him and got some money, whether you needed a coat, a car or just to get home. He was there when she got in a jam; he got her out of a lot of trouble.' Zaidins and Glaser were on opposite sides for a while; they eventually made it up, but by the time of the Columbia contract Zaidins was well and truly part of the family.

In February 1958 she made an album for Columbia Records called *Lady in Satin*, her most controversial recording. A lot of people hated it, and other people (like Jimmy Rowles) still become angry if you say anything bad about it. She had become a fan of Ray Ellis, arranger and conductor, from hearing one of his mood music albums, *Ellis in Wonderland*, and it is possible that Granz or somebody else wanted to make a Lady album with strings, because

Ellis had received an earlier inquiry: whatever it was, he couldn't do it because he was under contract to Columbia. Maybe Lady gave up her contract with Granz because she wanted to make an album with Ellis; years later Ellis said that the next thing that happened was that Irving Townsend, then an executive producer at Columbia, asked him to keep several days open in October 1957 for an album with Lady. Townsend said Ellis called him and that he was surprised at first: 'It would be like Ella Fitzgerald saying she wanted to record with Ray Conniff.' But if Lady wanted to do it, Townsend was dying to do it.

Townsend was experienced at dealing with singers. Many years earlier, he said, he had witnessed Sadie cooking for Mildred Bailey, and Lady helping, and Mildred being bitchy; then he was still working with Mildred at the end of her career:

I'd been doing this all my life . . . I went through fifteen years with Mahalia Jackson, I had a long long thing with Mildred; their insecurity, their terror of going downhill and not being a star any more, their fear of losing their physical and vocal prowess, and you keep reassuring them that they look pretty and sound great and the people love them, and they want to believe you so all you have to do is feed it. Except that Billie was closer to the end than most stars . . . People didn't give a damn what her voice was like, because she was Billie Holiday, with a style and a voice like no other woman ever had, and what she once was would carry her through with any audience.

Singing with strings is very different from singing with jazz backing; the string section has to play what's on the music paper, and the singer feels that she has to follow them, not the other way round. 'Johnny Mathis or Nat Cole aren't scared by strings, but when I recorded Mahalia with Percy Faith I had to keep her from walking out of the hall: "What do you mean, doing this to me? I can't sing opera!" It's her favourite album now. *Power and the Glory.*' Lady had sung with strings before and knew she wanted to do it again, but nearly ten years had gone by, and 'She was losing confidence in herself,' Townsend knew, 'and as a musician she knew that her voice wasn't what it should be, and she was drinking to bolster her nerve and the more she drank the worse it got.'

Ellis met Lady when she signed the contract; they picked some songs and Ellis started writing arrangements, and 'she blew about twenty-five appointments,' Ellis said, which was why the album wasn't made until February. Zaidins said that the conditions of her attendance at recording sessions were written into the contract.

Ellis was busy making albums with Johnny Mathis, Sarah Vaughan and others, but he wanted to record with *her*, Ellis said, and she gave him a very hard time because 'she was so out of it'. Choosing songs, they riffled through sheet music, and she had never heard of some of the songs or couldn't remember them; she chose them on the basis of the lyrics. He set the recording sessions for 11 o'clock at night and told her 10, figuring she'd be late; she'd turn up at 12. He ended up yelling at her and she swore at him, and this is what she probably needed. Lady had always been quick to learn a song, but those days were over.

> You know what I did to her? First, she was cutting the whole thing out. 'I hate that . . .' I cut two songs out, and I finally realized that this bitch doesn't know the song, and she's putting *me* down because *she* doesn't know it. So I said, 'Look, baby, I'm gonna give the band a fifteen minute break, and you learn that goddam bridge.' I had to treat her like a school kid. She stood there and pouted. She went over to the corner with Hank and she learned that bridge . . . The reason this woman was stoned all the time was she had absolutely no confidence in herself. She always came completely unprepared, so she figured if she came stoned, she could cop out. She would get a little help and do it . . .
>
> What she ended up doing was a recitation to the music. I didn't realize what she was doing.

Finally they had most of the album done:

> We still had one track that wasn't picked, so I said 'Hey baby, we're still doing another session tomorrow, I still have one song that I haven't [arranged] and I can't write it because . . .' She said, 'All right; let's go to the Colony.'
>
> It was about 3 o'clock in the morning and she'd been drinking straight gin all through the session. I took her to the Colony Record Shop. She really looked bad, dilapidated, dissipated. So I get her into the cab, you know what the black

and white scene is, even now, we get double takes ... I'm trying to get her out of the cab and I'm trying to pay the cab driver and I'm holding her up and I think she's going to fall, so I lean her up against the telephone pole, the lamp post, and I say, 'Hold it, baby' ... I live in Larchmont, which is a very nice wasp community, and I don't know what two of my neighbours are doing on 52nd Street at that hour, but they see me, and they cross the street, because they don't want to embarrass me. Can you imagine this? They don't know who this is and all they could figure is I'm out with a black hooker, and what bad taste, because she looks like a disaster.

She was looking through the sheet music and she was out of her head; she's cursing everybody in the [music shop] ... She picked 'You've Changed'.

Anyway, we finished the album and I was completely bugged, frustrated, disgusted, finished with it. So Irv Townsend says, 'We're going to try to mix it next week; you're coming to the mixing?' I said, 'Irv, you know something? I don't even want to hear this thing again. Forget it. *You* mix it! ...'

Later, he called me. It was summertime, my family was away. 'I've made a test of this thing, and I think you should hear it.' So he sent it over, and I put this on and listened to one side of it. And I got into the car and drove to New York. I couldn't stay in the house by myself, that's how despondent it made me. It hit me finally. It didn't matter whether she sang the right note or the wrong one, because she sang 25,000 wrong notes on that one. She poured her heart out ...

What they had made was an album about the story of her life. Some of it is very painful listening, but it's still Lady; part of the pain is caused by the fact that some of the songs don't lend themselves very well to the sort of *Sprechstimme* she was now doing, and some of it by the contradiction between the lush production and her condition. Hinton took a famous photograph of her listening to a playback during the *Lady in Satin* sessions; it is a heartbreaking image, as though she thought that this time her message might not get through.

The sessions were full of good musicians, such as Waldron or Hank Jones on piano, Billy Butterfield on trumpet, Gene Quill on alto sax, and on most tracks Hinton on bass, Osie Johnson on drums and Barry Galbraith on guitar, the premier New York rhythm section of the period. (Zaidins says that she rehearsed tunes with both Drinkard and Waldron.) By this time Lady's voice was weak, even her time was shaky, she needed to be well lubricated with gin before she could start and she no longer found it easy to learn new songs. So what did Columbia do, the world's greatest record label, as it then was? The orchestra was too big, a chorus was added on some tracks, the arrangements called too much attention to themselves, and Columbia gave her the kind of big, close studio sound that was the result of years of 'hi-fi' hype. It was as though they were trying to highlight her imperfections rather than the truth that was still there.

As Hinton put it, 'It was just that she was at that time of her life when [the album's production] was too much commercialism.' Yet there is no greater evidence in Lady's recorded career than *Lady in Satin* of the fact that interpretation of lyrics was her greatest strength. *Lady in Satin* is painful listening because it is the audio equivalent of shoving a video camera in the face of someone who is grieving; yet it grows on you, because it's Lady. 'You've Changed' is the best thing on it, because the song works well; she said she was crying when she recorded it. The critics (and Lady herself) also like 'For All We Know'. Her voice on these tracks is the voice of every loyal woman who's ever begun to suspect that she's being wronged.

She made a broadcast recording with strings perhaps as early as 1949, with Percy Faith, whose later albums too suffered from vulgar sound, to say nothing of the commercial necessity of recording rock songs in string arrangements. But Faith was the most talented of the arrangers of this kind of music, and her recording of 'You Better Go Now' with him is a textbook example of how this needed to be done: again, she is a woman no longer young, but still yearning for love – she doesn't *really* want him to go – and Faith's greatest skill as an arranger was in writing counter-melodies. The orchestra caresses her and provides a setting for her, rather than thrusting her at the listener. The string orchestra in popular music is a path that led nowhere, because the arrangers were confined to the studio, where commercial values were paramount; perhaps it is significant that Faith began as a concert pianist and was trained by teachers in the classical tradition.

(Lady and Faith also did 'Them There Eyes', a jaunty performance from her with a 'swing band' arrangement and no strings.)

During the summer of 1958 Lady appeared twice on a TV show, Art Ford's Jazz Party; and Dan Morgenstern wrote, 'Some say that what Billie does now is no longer singing; whatever it is, it sure as hell communicates.' There was a 'Jazz at the Plaza' party at the Plaza Hotel in New York; two tunes by Lady were recorded.

During the 1950s, the foolish controversy over 'traditional' and 'modern' jazz was still going on, and people like Leonard Feather were trying to break it down; he produced 'The Seven Ages of Jazz', which was a sort of history of jazz in concert form. There were two September concerts, in Warwick, Rhode Island, and Wallingford, Connecticut; the latter was recorded. 'She was added as a favour to me, really,' said Feather. 'She was not working that steadily at the time, and she sang very well on both occasions. Backstage at one of the concerts, talking with my wife, she opened up a bit, about how lonely she was, what an awful thing it was for a man to leave you . . .'

For the Wallingford concert she stayed at Irving Townsend's house in Westport, and he took her back and forth. 'Between the station and my house, it's only five miles, the floor of the car was grey with ashes, like ash trays had been dumped on the floor. She was very nice and gentle, warm inside no matter what bitterness had cost her.'

She was at the Blackhawk in San Francisco in early October. Vernon Alley was advised by friends not to go and see her, indicating how word was getting around about her condition; but Vinnie Puleo, who had worked in clubs all his life, from 52nd Street to the Blackhawk, and hadn't seen her for fifteen years, she not only remembered but greeted warmly. He said it was as though she knew she didn't have much time left and she was trying to make amends. She made all the shows, but 'She'd start apologizing for her performance,' Puleo said:

She'd say, 'Oh, pretty soon I'll get it all together. Tomorrow night I'll be much better.' Sure enough there would be moments when she was fantastic, then erratic again. All right, she wasn't the singer she used to be, but whatever tune she got off sounded great to me.

On 5 October she appeared at the first Monterey Jazz Festival and she was clearly in poor physical condition. Jimmy Lyons was the producer:

> Backstage it was very dark; when she came out into the lights she was disoriented. Gerry Mulligan grabbed her hand and escorted her over and laid back on his horn and just propped her up. She was like a husk or a shell or something that was there.
>
> The next morning I went to the hotel in town where all our artists were housed; this was our first year in Monterey, and John Lewis, Monte Kay and Ralph Gleason and I all had breakfast together and did a post-mortem on the whole deal. Then we walked out through the lobby, and Billie was sitting there.

Gleason wrote that she asked, 'Where you boys goin'?' and added, 'They got *me* openin' in Vegas tonight.' She seemed profoundly lonely, and Lyons added, 'There was nothing you could do.'

The Monterey tapes disappeared for over twenty years; when they were rediscovered and the album came out in the early 1980s, some said it should not have been issued. This live recording has more than its share of shortcomings, with jet planes overhead and backing that is more or less clunky, but the crowd was in no doubt: Lady had to do two encores. Her strength was waning, but what she had left was for her audience, and one hears what Puleo heard at the Blackhawk. She is in decline, but her phrasing, even on what were now set pieces, and the sound of her voice on certain words, serve to remind us that it is always necessary to *listen* to Lady Day.

She had gone to Hawaii at some point in 1958; Maya Angelou met her coming back through Los Angeles. Angelou had a bright and talkative twelve-year-old son who astonished Lady with his torrent of childlike energy and questions, but her love of children reasserted itself: she checked her salty language in front of Guy and sang songs to him. When she sang 'Strange Fruit', however, Guy asked, 'What's a pastoral scene, Miss Holiday?'

> Billie looked up slowly and studied Guy for a second. Her face became cruel, and when she spoke her voice was scornful. 'It means when the crackers are killing the niggers. It means when they take a little nigger like you and snatch off his nuts

and shove them down his goddam throat. That's what it means.'

Angelou and her son were stunned, and Guy was upset for days. There are several pages of Lady's boiling cynicism in Angelou's book *The Heart of a Woman*; Angelou's autobiographical books are valuable because they are about the resilience of a black woman thirteen years younger than Lady who knew only too well what kind of a childhood Lady had and who was bringing up her own son in a different but equally complicated world.

During this period she ran into an old friend, guitarist John Collins, an underrated musician kept in lucrative obscurity recording with Nat Cole during the 1950s. He had been introduced to Lady by Art Tatum in Chicago around 1937; later he knew Lady on the Street, and they'd been more than friends.

I would see her, like in Chicago, and she might not be letting anyone in her room, but if I called, she'd say, 'John, come right up.' We'd get high, and have a taste, and I'd know when to stay, when to leave . . In 1938 I went to New York to live, because I was with Roy Eldridge . . . And she might say, 'Hey, let's hang out tonight.' Okay. So we'd go over to my place and get high and enjoy everything, and tomorrow night, like no hangups. This was the type of person she was. Roy was the kind of guy you couldn't say anything around, because he'd repeat it; but with Lady, nobody owned her. You just loved her. She was a free soul.

The only thing I regret, and any musician who knew her regretted, was that she got hung up on shit. We lost her because whoever was her man at the time could control her with the drugs.

In 1958, when Collins was playing with Cole in California, just before the last show a waiter came to him with a message from an insistent woman, asking him to meet her at a certain table:

We did the show, and I went over to the table, and there was Lady. And she sat at the table and she cried and reminisced. She was working some of the clubs and there was a sympathetic audience wherever she was, but it wasn't the same, that's all. It really surprised me that she came on like this, but I was glad she could let it out, and she could let it out with me. 'John, I'm so sick of this shit, I've tried everything, I've

tried to kick this habit, and I can't kick it. I don't enjoy
fucking, this, that, I don't enjoy anything any more.' It was
really sad.

But she was a fighter, definitely a fighter. This was the only
time I ever saw her down. This surprised me, because she was
definitely a fighter.

Earlier in 1958 Lady had been offered a tour of Europe; Harold
Davison had announced a concert at the Royal Festival Hall in
London backed by Kenny Baker's Dozen (Baker is still one of the
best British trumpeters). There were also plans to record songs in
France for the soundtrack of *Lady Sings the Blues*, but it all fell
through when the Algerian crisis forced the French government to
close all the concert halls. In October, however, she left for her
second and longest tour overseas. A gig in Milan was a disaster;
she was apparently booked into a theatre on a bill, as Dufty put it,
with all the jugglers and dog acts that hadn't yet been exported to
the Ed Sullivan Show. (She sent the Duftys a wry postcard about
the impresario on this trip, saying that he could speak as much
French as she could, but there were still people everywhere who
didn't know who she was: an American club-owner once billed her
as 'the sensational comedienne'.) Also in Milan, however, a fan
booked her into one of the small halls within the local opera house
for virtually private gigs: it happened to be the most famous opera
house in the world, and Lady Day sang at La Scala.

In France the audiences at the Olympia were good, reviews not
so good. She accepted a gig in a jazz club, and reviews were better,
but she wasn't making much money. Hazel Scott saw her there
and began to cry. 'She backed me into a corner and in a cold, dry
voice said, "No matter what the motherfuckers do to you, never let
'em see you cry."'

Lady did not visit England on this trip; she sent Max Jones a
telegram from Paris telling him what hotel she was in, but jazz
journalists don't make much money, certainly not in England;
Betsy urged him to go to Paris, but he didn't, and regretted it the
rest of his life. He was also trying to get her a gig or a record date
while she was so close to London, but nobody would book her;
recording sessions cost money, and the record labels were being
offered Holiday material, such as airchecks from Storyville, if they
had wanted it.

She had no sooner returned from Europe in January 1959 than she had an ominous call from the Customs Department. An obscure piece of anti-narcotics legislation passed in 1956 now required anybody who was using or carrying narcotics to register with customs upon leaving or re-entering the country; and it applied retroactively to anyone who had ever had a narcotics conviction and a sentence of more than a year. 'What a difference a day makes,' Dufty cracked; Lady had been sentenced to a year and a day in 1947, and had now been overseas without checking with the puritans. She was frightened, but she told Dufty she wasn't going anywhere without a lawyer: she'd done that in 1947 and she'd been paying for it ever since.

'I didn't want to go to Glaser,' Dufty said, 'because he was her agent and she didn't want anybody to know about this.' Dufty didn't know if Zaidins had ever been inside a courtroom; he brought in Wilkes & Kennedy. 'Casting to me is terribly important – Wilkes was a white Southerner, he had been in the Federal District Attorney's office, so he knew the routine, and Flo Kennedy did a Pearl Bailey number then – so I thought they were good, and they got her out of this thing.' None of them had ever heard of the 1956 legislation, but in February Lady had to go to a federal building in Brooklyn for a grilling by three US District Attorneys. She was on her best behaviour, according to Dufty; accused of being arrested in 1947, she replied, 'They were real nice people, just like you; they just talked to me.' After they had justified their salaries, they decided not to prosecute.

The same month, February 1959, Lady made a three-day visit to England for a television appearance; she sang with a band for two numbers, and the faithful Waldron played for her on a third 'No one who saw the programme,' wrote Chilton, 'could have doubted that Billie was seriously ill.' But she saw her friends Max, Betsy and Beryl one last time.

Ellis had switched labels to MGM, and Lady wanted to make another album with him; she called on him unannounced, and an ignorant receptionist was about to have her thrown out when Ellis's secretary happened to come along and saved the day. In March 1959 the album *Billie Holiday* was made, her least-known work. One suspects that some sort of helpful electronic gimmickry was used; on the Cole Porter tune 'All of You', for example, her voice sounds too high, as though she had been recorded singing along with a slowed-down tape of pre-recorded backing. (This was perfectly possible in 1959: Zaidins says that a couple of backing tracks on *Lady in Satin* had been pre-recorded for her because she hadn't learned the tunes in time.) She sounds like a sprightly seventy-year-old making a comeback instead of a forty-three-year-old wreck. On 'There'll Be Some Changes Made', there's a new twist to the lyric: 'even Sinatra has been changin' his jokes'. The torch songs on *Lady in Satin* were perhaps difficult for her now; the songs on *Billie Holiday* are less demanding fare, from 'When It's Sleepy Time Down South' to 'It's Not for Me to Say', then a recent Johnny Mathis hit.

The soloists from *Lady in Satin* returned, plus Jimmy Cleveland on valve trombone, and best of all, Sweets is there. Ellis has improved: the fiddles don't get in the way too much; there are twelve strings on four tracks, only four on another four, and on four more none at all. She sings 'Don't Worry 'Bout Me', and we don't. A few tunes are faded out at the end, the only time they ever did that to Lady; but it was her last album, and not a bad way to go out.

Meanwhile, Lester Young had returned prematurely to New York from a gig in Paris, gritting his teeth against the pain, and on 15 March he died. Lady had only four months to live.

18

The Loneliest Girl in the World

Lady took Lester's death badly. After the funeral, she remarked, 'These things come in threes.' She mentioned somebody else's name – Bill Dufty couldn't remember who – and Lester, and said, 'I'll be number three.' Leonard Feather also heard the remark. A few nights later Dufty received a frantic telephone call; could he come right over? And he'd better bring his typewriter

Earlier, Lady had been irritated because Prez had been living with a white woman who, Lady said, laid down the law, saying things like, when they were walking down the street, 'You have to walk on the right side of me, and do what's right, because you're with a white woman now.' Where Lady heard this, or whether she made it up, is not known, but now this woman had come to see her, and the true horror had come home to Lady in several ways.

Lester Young had a house in St Albans but lived in a hotel room in the centre of town, listening to Frank Sinatra records and watching the action in the street from his windows, which overlooked Birdland. He smoked a lot of marijuana, drank too much and rarely ate anything. This girl had done her best to look after Lester (who like Lady was short of money), even to the point of shoplifting. Maybe she wasn't white; according to Dufty:

> There was a very light-skinned, bourgeois [girl], college trained, from New Jersey, and she was living with Prez ... He had been separated from his wife, but she claimed his body and so on, and here was this woman who had given up a lot for him, out. And Billie was shaken by this, because she thought Lester had somehow been luckier than she, and was

doing well economically and the other way, and the smell of the reality she got from this woman shook her up. She had thought Lester was all right, and what astonished her was her own naivety This scared Billie, that there was this legal right of the spouse to come in and take full charge of the funeral rights while this woman who had boosted and stolen to take care of him was barred.

This woman was there. Billie wanted me to help her write a book about Lester; let's tell it like it is. And Billie proceeds to tell me the story of how this woman came from a high-class family, and she was crazy for Lester, and she got hooked, she started out boosting books and selling them and taking chances to get money, and Billie began to cry; she said, 'It's a beautiful fuckin' love story.'

You could just collapse because she told such a horror story, but what she was really saying was, 'How could I have been so naïve to have believed, because I was not a part of it, that he was insulated, and I didn't know he was going through the same shit as me.' But here was a man who had found a woman to take care of him, be a buffer for him, which was incredible, something she had never found, and she was in awe of this. She said this bitterly crying.

Nothing came of the book idea, but the woman told Dufty that 'when she became marked as Lester's chick, all the guys that were imitating him felt they had to fuck her – *sine qua non.*'

Lady's last months were the loneliest she ever had in her life. In happier times, Dufty said, 'I'd been out with Billie when it was like being in a ladies' restroom and they forgot I was there. Like Thelma Carpenter. Annie Ross, Blossom Dearie; and you could always tell when they were really in session when Thelma would call her "William" or "Bill".' Some of these friends still came round, but as Annie put it, 'There were so many people flocking around her when she was at her height, but when she became ill they didn't flock around no more.'

Sylvia Syms ran into Lady in the street at about this time. She hadn't seen her for years, and they saw her getting out of a cab.

She was the worst I had ever seen her look, but like I always said, her worst was like somebody else's best. She called to me, 'Hey, baby.' I called back, 'Hey, Lady.' She said, 'Baby, everyone I love is dead – and you dead and I'm dead.' I said, 'No, Lady, Mama's dead, but you're alive and I'm alive.' She said, 'You mean it?' I said, 'Yes, Lady ' She said, 'Call me, baby.'

Dufty tried to help her with money. She told him that Charles Laughton was once financially embarrassed (from spending all his cash on marijuana), and gave Lady and Sadie a cheque; they thought it was a scam, that as soon as he got back to England he'd stop payment. Lady was so furious that she wanted to tear it up; she thought if she went into a bank to cash it she'd be thrown in jail. But Sadie wanted to save it as an autograph, so they pasted it in an autograph book; and years later, Lady presented it at a bank and was astonished when they cashed it. This story may be apocryphal, but Dufty said that her pimps had convinced her that it was against the law for an illegitimate child to have a bank account; this was one of the ways they stole her money

> Her idea of luxury was to call the local liquor store and have them deliver a bottle of booze. But I told her that this was a way of establishing credit, if you gave a cheque for $20 and got some change for it, so I said, 'Why don't you let me prove it to you?' This was a time when she had some money. I said, 'Give me $100 and I'll open an account for you and be back in a minute.' She didn't want Louis to know about it, so it was care of me; I went to the nearest bank where I had an account.

But she was totally helpless about money, and the account was soon a mess. Zaidins tells a similar story

> I opened an account for her in the Chemical Bank – she and I – and she screwed it up in no time. Overdrawn. Any bread that came in was spent before she carried it; she was constantly drawing advances .. She would authorize people to draw money for her and then she would forget it. Or she would draw a cheque and pay it over and as far as she was concerned she didn't get it.

Presumably she hadn't seen the cash. Zaidins said that he occasionally paid her rent, and that Glaser paid it when she was threatened with eviction because she wasn't paying it. She had rented the flat in the name of Eleanora Fagan because of her bad reputation; the landlady found out who she was just before she moved in, Zaidins said, but she got the flat anyway. 'It was very important to her to have her own place to live.'

Like everyone else who knew her, Zaidins was haunted by her for ever afterwards. She sometimes paid him for his legal services, he said, but not much. That wasn't the point.

> Everybody wanted something out of her. She made herself vulnerable, attracted this kind of thing. I used her, too. It was good for my ego, and public relations. 'Who do you rep?' 'I rep Billie Holiday.' In fact, I went back to Milwaukee and got married in '58 and they ran a piece in the newspaper with my wife, and the thing read according to the clients I repped .. She invited people into her life; I got into her life very easily But I couldn't get out so easily.
>
> I had the feeling she was dependent upon me. She was honest with me; she was a good friend ... She could be abusive. She'd apologize for it – 'You know baby, I wasn't feelin' right' ... At the Leow's Sheraton concert in '58 I brought Neal Hefti around, thinking about doing an album with her; brought him backstage and she was very nervous and bitchy before the concert, and he walked out. Her bitchiness was like barking; I don't even know if she knew what she was saying or doing. I think it was a basic lack of confidence; she confided in me that she didn't understand why people loved her ...

The function of her friends was partly to reassure her. As John Levy, the bassist-turned-manager, said, 'I found this out, the ego of all performers, they have to have their ego constantly fed.' (He thought that was Maely's function.) A lot of these people, apart from the musicians, describe each other as opportunists; Zaidins is the only one who admits, 'I used her.' In the end, they all served their purpose at the court of Lady Day.

Thelma Carpenter, Babs Gonzales and a few other friends came round; Annie Ross washed Lady's hair, giving her a vinegar rinse, which Lady got a kick out of because she'd never heard of it before.

Alice Vrbsky looked after Lady more than anyone else from the summer of 1957 until the end. She was a diabetic, and so at least had access to clean needles. Alice was not into drugs or drinking. 'One guy once offered me marijuana, and I said, "No, thanks; I get drunk on the music." I didn't drink in those days either. And the guy looked at Lady and she said, "She gets drunk on the music." She liked that.'

After Alice heard Lady in Central Park she spoke to her, saying that she had an album that she hadn't brought with her because she never dreamed that she'd get to speak to her, and would she sign it?

I was trying to tell her how much I admired her, and she said, 'Fine, bring it down.' So the next day I showed up with the record, and she said, 'A woman of her word.' We hit it off; I can't explain it. Then she wrote, on the album, 'Thank you for loving me'. And this killed me, because I had the feeling she needed something, somebody, but didn't know what.

I was sort of between jobs; then her husband asked me, would I be her secretary, and I'd get to see the nightclub business, and I thought that was great, because I'd see some of the country. I was really surprised that they asked me. I zipped her up, and sometimes I'd zipper up her skin too; I was a novice. But I got to hear her sing. He paid me cash, I think $65 for the first week, and he sort of disappeared, faded in and out. She paid me after that.

One of my main jobs was making out her parole reports for Philadelphia. She thought they wouldn't bother her as long as she sent them in. Once a month she had to report where she would be working.

Alice went to California with Lady in the late summer and the autumn of 1957, and the next year, among other places, to Baltimore twice, and to Las Vegas just before Lady went to Europe. 'In Baltimore she had to stay in a Negro hotel,' Alice said, and was surprised that Las Vegas was no better: Lady stayed at the hotel where she was working because she was the star, and an arrangement was made, but the musicians had to stay somewhere else and black people couldn't come to see Lady's show. A newspaper reported that she complained about the 'Faubus-like attitude to accommodation,' a reference to the segregationist governor of Arkansas.

Guido Cacianti, manager at the Blackhawk, said that she did only three days of a two-week gig there, the only time she ever appeared at the Blackhawk, and her last appearance in San Francisco. Glaser's office asked him to let her go to Las Vegas to replace Prima, where she could make twice as much money. She sent a postcard back to Cacianti, 'saying that she was sorry she went down there because they're treating her like a dog down there.' No wonder she looked lonely when Jimmy Lyons and Ralph Gleason saw her on her way to Vegas: twenty years after having to use the freight elevator at the Lincoln Hotel in New York, and now in failing health, she still had to deal with Jim Crow.

Lady told Alice that when people saw them together, a black woman and a white woman, it would be assumed that Alice was trying to pass for black, or that it must be a lesbian relationship; it couldn't be any other way. Alice said that she knew there had been 'some of that' (lesbianism) in Lady's past, but that it was all over when she knew her. Lady couldn't afford to take Alice with her to Europe; then in 1959 the engagements were becoming fewer, and Alice remembered a lot of talk and reminiscence.

> She wasn't one to pick on people who'd done her wrong; she'd say about somebody like Dinah Washington, 'Oh she's black-hearted,' or something like that, but she wouldn't go into specifics. But the people who did good things to her she really always remembered, extra special. This was a positive thing, in a way surprising, for someone who'd been kicked down.

All her life she had had friends who were funny. Bobby Henderson talked about her unrestrained laughter; later there were Slappy White and Redd Foxx, and Bobby Tucker talked about a comic called Willie Lewis who could make her so helpless with laughter that she didn't dare let him in her dressing room just before a set When he stuck his face in the door, she'd yell, 'No, no, Willie, not now, go away, go away!' Now she complained to Alice that people thought she didn't enjoy life, thought that she didn't want to laugh any more. The image of Billie Holiday as a tragic figure was already growing, and she was aware of it.

Lady talked a lot about her mother and all the squabbling

they'd done, and now wanted to take the blame, telling Alice that she'd won the battles by yelling back at Sadie until Sadie began to feel that she must be in the wrong. 'She said, "I haven't spoke to anybody the way I speak to you since my mother died."'

The only white girl who could really sing the blues, Lady said, was Kay Starr (Prez admired Kay Starr, too). She spoke warmly about Ella, Louis Armstrong and Mahalia Jackson; she admired Ella's instrument, and the fact that Mahalia lived the way she sang: she didn't sing gospel music and then go round cursing and drinking. And when Lena Horne was starring in *Jamaica* on Broadway in 1957–8, Lady got in touch, and Lena was as sincere and caring as always.

Once when Alice was playing opera records and Lady was enjoying them, Maely was there, and said, 'Ohhh, I didn't know *you* liked opera,' and Lady was indignant. Alice said that Maely was a 'gruff and aggressive type person', and that Lady told her that Maely didn't like Alice travelling with her, as though Alice must be after something. 'At one point something happened; I had done something that Maely must have thought was all right, and she said to Billie, "She's not stupid." Something like that. It just struck me as strange, this whole attitude.' Reading interviews with Alice and seeing television interviews with her, it is clear that Alice was one of the least opportunistic of all the people who were involved with Lady; Alice was in no doubt that 'Maely thought she had a corner on Billie, and didn't want anybody getting in.' Bill Dufty said that when he first met Lady in 1953 as Maely's new husband he'd felt as though he had to pass muster; in the end, Alice said, Lady got on better with Bill than with Maely.

Lady didn't really need a lot of looking after, and Alice was not a full-time servant; she would come and do the shopping, but Lady did her own house-cleaning. They went to the movies together; Lady would want to go out late to an all-night double feature. Finally there came a time when Alice had to get a job – Lady didn't have much money, and as Alice put it, 'I couldn't live off my parents for ever.' For the last few months, Alice said, she visited Lady whenever she wanted some company.

Frankie Freedom, a young man originally from Chicago who had theatrical ambitions, ran errands for Lady. 'Billie always liked someone,' Dufty said, 'usually a young man, which isn't unusual, someone who wouldn't bug her, who would take care of her clothes . . .'

Frankie was flamboyant – she had several guys around like that, and he would run errands for her and do all the unmentionables, and one didn't know who these people were, but one always hoped that they were out for her own good. But her problem was that she couldn't cop. This was the source of the power of these guys, because she was in this vulnerable position, and no one would come near her, only one time I was aware of, I was in her apartment and she got nervous and I sensed something, some connection, and I said, 'Want me to leave?' and she said, 'Yes.'

She was scrupulous not to want you to know something, because it was a way of getting involved. She knew the whole legal thing backwards and forwards. You're vulnerable to the degree that the most naïve person [can be arrested] even if there's only one [marijuana] cigarette in the room, and in order to be let go they have to tell everything they know, and they don't know what is important and what isn't. So she had to protect herself by not letting people know anything, and this is something she lived with constantly. And unless you knew that, the whole choreography that went on around her was completely mysterious.

Drinkard knew Frankie, too. 'Frankie was a hip little dude, a little black bastard, just as hip as anybody I've ever seen in my life and a shrewd son of a bitch. If you didn't watch out, he'd take your fuckin' socks off your feet without removin' your shoes.'

In April there was a birthday party for Lady in her basement apartment on 87th Street; it went on all night, all her friends coming and going. Annie Ross was there, and remembered that Lady had made potato salad, chicken and ribs. Alice used to try to get Lady to eat breakfast, but by this time she was eating next to nothing; yet she still liked to cook for others. 'One time I cooked something for her,' said Annie, 'and she took a whiff of it and said, "Shiiiit."'

Also in April, Lady made her last appearance at Storyville in Boston, with Waldron, Roy Haynes on drums and Champ Jones on bass. She pulled it off one more time: local critic John McClellan wrote that there were eight tunes in each set, and he could remember when if he was ten minutes late he missed her whole performance: 'The voice now cuts through like a painful knife. But there is a ripe, mature beauty . . . and as Nat Hentoff once wrote, "Other singers sing about emotion, Billie actually projects the emotion itself." ' George Wein said there were five shows a day and Saturday matinees and he stayed for all of them:

> She had a lightness in her voice that I hadn't heard for years. I went up to her and said, 'Lady, what's happening? You're singing out of sight!' Before her final show, she was very nervous. She asked me for a glass of water. I put my hand on her heart and it was pounding. But she sang fantastic. She said, 'George, I'm straight now. You gotta help me.' Those were her last words to me. I said, 'Let's do it.'
>
> A few weeks later she was singing in a little place in Lowell, Massachusetts, the Blue Moon Café. I said to someone, 'Let's go up to see her.' He said, 'Don't go. Don't go and see her. Remember her from how she sang the last week at Storyville.'

Back home again, Lady had a visit at home from old acquaintances, Dr Terkild Vinding and his wife. They had heard she was feeling poorly, and she was glad to see them. She asked after their daughter, who was an aspiring jazz singer, and told them to tell her to learn 'Violets for My Furs', one of the songs on *Lady in Satin*. She played the album and they loved it; she gave them an autographed copy of it. 'But she was in bad physical shape,' Vinding wrote later:

> Her legs and stomach were swollen from oedema due to her liver cirrhosis to a degree I had never seen before . . . I told her she must go at once to a hospital and get the fluid drained out. She refused to go. I told her that since I did not have a New York licence to treat her, we would drive her to a hospital of her choice. But again she refused.

On 25 May, there was a benefit for the Phoenix Theater, raising money to keep it open. Lady got there early; so did Steve Allen:

> Leonard Feather had asked me to do a benefit, and comics are always doing some benefit or other. You don't even ask; you know it's for a good cause and you just go. I like to get there early, to check out whether the microphone is as tall as I am, and whatever I can check out . . . There was somebody backstage, like a stage manager or a stagehand, and I asked,

where do I go, I'm Steve Allen, I'm on the show tonight, and he said, go anywhere, so I just walked into a room, and there was this little old Negro lady sitting on a cot or something, and just to be polite I said, 'Hello, how are you?' She said, 'Fine, how's it going?' something like that. It was a very old theatre, there was a single light bulb in the room, very poor lighting . . . And since I didn't know her I just looked at my fingernails for a moment, and suddenly I had a creepy feeling and I did a slow doubletake, and the little old lady was Billie, looking forty years older than I expected to see her . . .

When the time came for her to perform, I introduced her, and somebody had to help her on stage, and it was Leonard Feather and me. We finally got her to the mike and we left her there, and she sang terribly of course, her voice was all scratchy, no vitality, no volume, nothing.

In his book, *Mark It and Strike It* (1961), Allen said that he had suggested to Lady that she lie down for a while before she performed; she said, 'No, I don't want to do that. When you do that, you *die*.' Elaine Lorillard, who had been associated with the Newport Jazz Festival for several years, had been at Lady's birthday party and thought she was not in good enough condition to sing at the Phoenix, but Joe Glaser had said she would be okay.

Feather had been shocked to see her in her dressing room; she was drooling, and there was spittle on her chin. Lady said, 'What's the matter, Leonard? You seen a ghost or something?' Annie was there and said that Lady heard Feather wondering out loud whether she was well enough to go on, and got sore at him. 'Like, what d'you mean? I'm fine; don't worry about me. I'll do my thing.' Mal Waldron helped her into Tony Scott's car afterwards, and Scott drove her home; they were all concerned, but none of them knew she had made her last public appearance.

Feather was more worried than the others. The English-born jazz writer had been one of Lady's closest friends for many years. He had known her since 1936, when John Hammond invited him to the first recording session under her own name, when 'Summertime' was recorded. By the time of Lady's birthday party, Feather had already been writing to Max Jones in England, urging him to find gigs and recording sessions for Lady in Europe (not that Max needed any urging). Feather thinks to this day that

Lady would have lived longer if she had got out of New York, but that is to be doubted; she was dying not of dope but of liquor, and she was still drinking heavily every day. Feather had noticed that she had been losing weight, but at the birthday party she had crossed the line from weight-loss to emaciation.

On 26 May, the day after the benefit at the Phoenix, Feather called Joe Glaser and Allan Morrison of *Ebony* magazine, and they all went to Lady's apartment to try to convince her to go to the hospital; Glaser would have taken care of the expenses. She refused to go, saying that she was opening in Toronto on Monday and she would be all right by then. Feather wrote the same day to Jones, because he knew how much Max cared for Lady, to break the news that Lady would probably never get back to England. He wrote that it had been all he could do to keep from bursting into tears in her dressing room at the Phoenix; as bad as she looked at her birthday party, she'd been the picture of health compared to the way she was now. Feather wrote that Glaser, who hadn't seen her for some weeks, was broken-hearted at her appearance and would continue pressuring her to go to the hospital; but if she didn't go, Feather predicted, it would be weeks rather than months before it was all over.

It was Frankie who was there on 31 May, feeding Lady mild breakfast foods that Dr Eric Caminer had prescribed, when she collapsed in her apartment. Frankie called Caminer, who called an ambulance, and she was taken to Knickerbocker Hospital, where she was logged in at 3.44 p.m.; she received a thorough examination, was put into another ambulance at 4.47 and taken to Metropolitan Hospital in Harlem, a city hospital, arriving at 5.30. She was conscious the whole time. Caminer arrived at the Metropolitan shortly before 6 and found her still lying on a stretcher; he soon had her in an oxygen tent. It is still not clear why she was turned away from the Knickerbocker; maybe they didn't know that Glaser would be paying the bills. But in the newspaper stories and exchanges of letters that followed, the hospitals acquitted themselves fairly well; Caminer pointed out to Dufty that it wasn't a question of racism: the staff at the Metropolitan were mostly black and overworked, and she was registered as Eleanora McKay; they didn't know who she was. America's health-care problems are not a new story.

It was Memorial Day weekend, and Dufty had been away; he found out she was in the hospital when someone on the night side [of the *New York Post*] called and said there was an item in Earl Wilson's column. And you know how Earl loves everybody; it was as if she'd just gone in to have a hangnail removed. I think Maely went to the hospital on Wednesday and found out she was on the critical list and only next of kin could get to her. She was in an oxygen tent. When we finally got in to see her it was the day before the first *New York Post* article appeared. I figured somebody was going to do a story about Billie Holiday, so my impulse was to get it straight and get it out; and after the big drama with the first article everybody knew me; before that I had to sign in, but then I came up with my dirty raincoat and walked right in and nobody said boo. I was a reporter and they were afraid of me, and of course the joke was that as soon as they found out she was a celebrity, everybody in the hospital wanted signed copies of records and books.

Lady was weak from malnourishment and had skeletal hollows in her temples when Dufty first saw her, which frightened him. She began to rally slowly, which was exaggerated in the newspaper articles. 'My notion was not to present a picture of a dying woman. The business I wrote about the flowers was a lie; she was receiving calls but there wasn't a thing arriving. I put in the names to shame people into sending things.' As soon as she was out of the oxygen she resumed smoking; Dufty changed brands so that he could leave her cigarettes as though he'd forgotten them. She was being fed intravenously and began to gain weight.

She said that Frankie had panicked because he thought she was dying, but she wasn't bitter. Dufty said,

> She would rather have died in her own place and been left alone. Going to the hospital was the beginning of trouble because your body belongs to the state once you get in there, and she understood this instinctively. *I* wouldn't want to get into a hospital because they can do anything to you; I would want three guys in the hall outside my room at all times.

In those days the hospital had neither an intensive-care unit nor the more sophisticated antibiotics they had later; in any case, Lady was not expected to live, and she told Zaidins that she didn't think she would.

Her central problem was liver cirrhosis, but her heart, kidneys and other organs were affected by general infections caused by the cirrhosis and by her poor physical condition. The problem of drugs, her friends knew, would be if she didn't get any 'There were no withdrawal symptoms because she had drugs on her,' said Dufty. She could not suffer withdrawal symptoms at the same time as she was being treated for all her other problems.

A struggle immediately began: on Lady's side were the doctors who had the nerve to stick their necks out, the Mayor's office (Robert Wagner was inclined to be sympathetic) and Lady's friends, who knew a whole lot more about drugs than the law did. On the other side was the law, which effectively wanted to kill drug addicts by denying them proper treatment. 'I was talking to a Chinese doctor about this,' said Dufty, 'an intern who was standing by on call, and we agreed about the irony, that the danger in going to the hospital is that they give you too many drugs, but she would have got none.' The reason why Lady had tolerated Caminer was that he was Viennese and probably took a more enlightened attitude; many doctors were frightened of the whole subject.

'Glaser, oh Glaser, he was tremendous,' said Dufty. They talked about moving her to a private hospital, but they would have had the same problem with the drugs. Besides,

> The oxygen tent was there, even though she wasn't covered, and she was being fed intravenously, and Joe did not want to take the risk of moving her. I said to Joe, 'The thing to do is get her out of the hospital as soon as you can, and put her on a plane to Bermuda or any British possession which is better than Canada.' That was the game plan. Joe was willing to pay for everything.

As she gathered strength after the crisis she said, 'They'll call this a comeback.' Alice said she called Zaidins to tell him that Lady was in the hospital; when he turned up, they asked her, 'Do you know this man?' She said, 'What the fuck you mean? That's Earl, my lawyer.' Zaidins brought a record player and a copy of her new MGM album, and he talked about the MGM option on another record. 'Look, Lady, they're good business people, check into things, they already talked to the doctors; would they pick up your option if they thought you were going to die?' They joked about making another album right there in the hospital room and calling it 'Lady at the Met'. She phoned Zaidins in the middle of the night to complain about a dripping tap that was keeping her awake. 'Drip-drip-drip,' she said; 'I wouldn't mind, but it don't *swing.*' He told her to put a towel under it.

She also had visits from a psychiatrist. She had earlier talked about this with several people, but always concluded, 'Why should I see a psychiatrist, when I'll just end up telling him he's nuts?' Now the joke was, Dufty said,

> Out of all the psychiatrists in New York, it was a young pansy she knew. He was a very good-looking guy, very handsome, very swish; he came in one day when I was there, and she said, 'That's my psychiatrist.' He was carrying on, doing his whole number and laughing. After he left she told me she knew him in the Village and he was a white freak.

Ron Levy came to see her. 'She was never a tragic woman to me; she was a fun-loving woman,' Ron said, and even in hospital people were coming and going. Glaser, his assistant Francis Church, Frankie Freedom and Alice were on the list of visitors Lady was allowed. Jimmy Fletcher, the now-retired narcotics agent, came to see her and couldn't get in, but she was pleased to hear that he'd called. 'Bless his bones,' she said. She was cheered up by bags of cards and letters from ordinary people, some of which Alice answered for her.

Kay Kelly, who was the daughter of Phil Gough, once married to Sadie, and who passed herself off as Lady's sister, now turned up from Philadelphia. 'By now Earl Wilson's column had been printed everywhere,' said Dufty. 'Maely hadn't been able to get in at all, and she ran into Kay Kelly saying she was Lady's sister, and she's black; what the hell do they know? People were calling us: does Billie Holiday have a sister?' Lady said, 'She ain't my fuckin' sister.' But Dufty said that Kelly had put up $500 bail when Lady had been arrested in Philadelphia in 1956. This seems unlikely; surely McKay, also arrested on that occasion, would have been able to put his hands on that much money, or Glaser would have taken care of it, but Dufty believed that Kelly really had been useful to Lady in the past. Anyway, 'She was running around to department stores buying nightgowns for her sister.'

Then Lady said to Maely, 'You watch, baby, they're going to

arrest me in this damn bed.' At least that's what Maely said she
said. A few years later Maely was the one who wrote:

> 'Loverman, where can you be?' was a cry for a glassine
> envelope full of heroin more often than a man. But for rare
> exceptions, such as her last marriage, the two were usually
> mutually inclusive . . . The night nurse claimed she had found
> heroin in Billie's handbag, which was hanging on a nail on
> the wall – six feet away from the bottom of her bed. It was
> virtually impossible for Billie – with hundreds of pounds of
> equipment strapped to her legs and arms for transfusions – to
> have moved one inch towards that wall.

The only thing certain about Maely is that she was a rotten
journalist. It was widely reported at the time that a nurse had
caught Lady with junk in her hand and powder flecks on her nose.
'What's that?' the nurse demanded. 'Mind your own damn business,' Lady snapped. Dufty said that the dope was found in a box
of paper tissues at her bedside. On 12 June she was arrested and
charged with possession of narcotics; her radio, record player,
flowers and telephone were taken away, and two guards were
posted on her door to protect the public from her. Lady claimed
she had brought the junk with her in her handbag, but the cops
didn't believe that; they grilled her on her bed, first two detectives
and then three, and threatened to take her away to jail regardless
of her condition. Maely said that she yelled at them that they
couldn't arrest anyone who was on the critical list, and that they'd
taken care of that: she'd been taken off the critical list. But it is
hard to trust anything Maely said. Frankie Freedom was arrested,
charged with illegal possession of sleeping pills, and soon disappeared. The only person allowed to visit her was McKay, and he
had to get permission for each visit from a nearby police station
and could approach her bed no nearer than three feet.

Carl Drinkard heard the news:

> The first thing I heard was that she had gone into the
> hospital. The second thing I heard was that she was beginning
> to recuperate and was doing so well. Then I was playing a gig
> in New Jersey, walking across the yard, and it came over a
> loudspeaker: 'Jazz singer Billie Holiday was arrested in her
> hospital room for possession of narcotics, in New York ' I

looked at Be-Bop Sam, a little trumpet player, and I said, 'Lady's gonna die.' I knew it just like I knew my name. I knew that Lady could not fight liver cirrhosis and kicking the habit at the same time.

Now the struggle broke into the newspapers, and Lady's friends struggled behind the scenes. 'This was a horrifying outrage, arresting somebody in their hospital bed,' said Dufty, 'but how to impress it on people's consciousnesses?' He began trying to get up a petition to be sent to the Mayor's office.

> There was the problem then between Mayor [Robert] Wagner and the police as to whether people should be thrown in jail or treated in hospitals. Dorothy Ross [a press agent] and I were calling people like Frank Sinatra, Steve Allen, Basie, Ellington, Ella, Sidney Poitier. And nobody responded. Sinatra said, 'Wagner hates my ass.' Earl Brown of *Life* magazine was one of the first black staffers on a national publication, and had a committee proposing a rational alternative to abandoning the motherfuckers to the police, but as far as the police were concerned, Lady's arrest had proved their point, that if you let addicts into hospitals, you would ruin the hospitals.

The puritans were oblivious to the point that allowing doctors to treat addicts in a rational way might reduce the dope in hospitals, as well as being more humane. In fact Dufty acknowledged elsewhere that James Baldwin, Dan Wakefield, Nat Hentoff, Ruth Brown, Dakota Staton, Mal Waldron, Denzil Best 'and a thousand or so people uptown' had responded to the petition.

The *Post* had printed an article about the arrest on page six, but the *New York Daily News* played it big. The police attitude, said Dufty, was just like towing away a car. 'Nobody's responsible; somebody else did it.' They had clearly overplayed their hand, ignoring due process in grilling Lady in her bed without even informing a lawyer; it all amounted to imprisonment without bail or a hearing.

Wilkes applied for a writ of *habeas corpus* against Stephen Kennedy, Police Commissioner of the City of New York, granted by Judge H. Epstein of the New York State Supreme Court on 16 June. To judge from the transcript, Assistant District Attorney

Irving Lang felt pretty helpless; he said that 'All this is doing, your honour, is keeping three policemen at a hospital door –' In his defence, he said he was under the impression that 'this drug' was slowly killing her. 'If the detectives had prevented her from jumping off a bridge they would be considered great heroes. In effect they're doing the same thing by taking this heroin away from her.' No doubt he believed that. Wilkes said that the hospital had classified her as 'terminal', and at another point that she would never leave her hospital bed, and Lang agreed. So what had been the point of arresting her?

Lady was paroled in Wilkes's custody, but it took at least eight hours for the guards to be removed from her room. Dufty wrote in the newspaper that some cops were asking for autographs while other cops wouldn't let her sign anything. Wilkes had to threaten another writ before the news got to the 23rd Precinct.

Coincidentally or not, Lady had been arrested seven days after the Wagner Program for the treatment of addiction as a medical not a penal problem had been announced. 'Anna Kross had been fighting for this for five years,' Dufty wrote. On 18 June Earl Brown's Special Narcotics Committee of the City Council held its first public hearing; Kross followed Inspector Edward Carey, who had announced Lady's arrest, with a sermon. Why, she asked, had a nurse turned Lady in to the police instead of to the medical authorities? If she needed medication, why wasn't she getting it from them in the first place? To the argument that Lady's arrest proved that hospital treatment of addicts would ruin the hospitals, she replied, 'Do you gentlemen know what a monumental task it is to keep drugs out of our city prisons?'

The churches were involved, setting up clinics to give medical help to addicts; Dufty mentioned the Rev. Gene Callender and his Mid-Harlem Community Parish. The police department wanted to be 'more repressive than anything Anslinger proposes'; they wanted to be able to arrest any two addicts found together. 'This is presented as a bill to break up "shooting galleries", but would close up every clinic in town . . . they could not even hold meetings open to all, addicts, former addicts and their families to help out in this problem; even Narcotics Anonymous would have to disband.'

Dufty was so deeply involved with the lawyers that he saw a conflict of interest arising, and was summarizing events for Adam Clayton Powell Jr, as well as briefing John Bott, another journalist.

He wrote to Powell that he was suspicious because the nurse had disappeared for four days, only to turn up suddenly in Lady's room:

> It is a miracle that Billie didn't just hit her with a pop bottle or something. Instead she had the self-control to order her out of the room, and never to touch her. The slightest incident would have been or could have been magnified into a story 'Hopped-up Singer Assaults Nurse' etc. Then the nurse shortage in city hospitals could be blamed on the narcotics programme of Wagner's and it could be stopped before it began.

He wrote to Bott, 'There is some hanky-panky about the charge. Originally, announced by the police, it was 3305 Public Health Law, possession of less than one-eighth of an ounce, a misdemeanour; now, apparently, since they're proceeding with a Grand Jury, it must I guess be an indictable offence, a felony at least.' No sooner had the writ been granted than the District Attorney decided that Lady's condition was no longer grave and scheduled an arraignment at her bedside on 22 June. On that day they told McKay that the arraignment had to be cancelled, because the chief prosecution witness, the nurse, was ill; McKay replied, 'The nurse? What about the patient?' They may have succeeded in fingerprinting Lady on her deathbed.

The cancellation of the bedside arraignment may have had something to do with the fact that the hospital was being picketed that day by the Rev. Callender's Committee, some of the signs saying 'Let Lady Live'. One of the Committee's press releases stated that over 150 addicts had been helped by their one clinic already, and told the story of a former addict who had been arrested and charged with possession of a tranquillizer, only to have his case dismissed for lack of evidence after three and a half weeks in jail. The Committee complained that the police department had its own agenda, and wanted to know who was running the city.

> The police have a function in this area. Let them halt the flow of narcotics into this country. Let them arrest the top echelon of importers and distributors of narcotics here. But unable or unwilling to do so they harass the ill and defenceless,

sabotage the Mayor's constructive and enlightened programme and interfere with efforts by concerned community leaders . . .

On 24 June, Wilkes wrote to Melvin Glass, Assistant District Attorney of the County of New York; he began, 'I thank you for your letter of June 23 informing me that if I should have my client . . . at the Grand Jury Room on Leonard Street on June 26 at 10.30 a.m., "she will be given an opportunity to testify in her own behalf."' In three pages of impressively controlled sarcasm, he reviewed some of the events already described, and ended:

My friend, I say that this adds up to a very, very shabby performance on the part of the State of New York — and the horror of it all is that it is a typical performance.
   But I trust you gather from the tenor of this letter that this time, your usual method of doing business will be contested every step of the way.

Louis McKay had arrived in town broke, according to Dufty; he would go to Joe Glaser for money and do whatever Glaser wanted, so that all the information was filtered through Glaser. Zaidins had been fired. 'I came up to the hospital and they put it to Lady and she said she wanted me to represent her, and Joe Glaser said he was paying for it and he would pay anybody but me. I was a pain in the neck to him; I was threatening accounting and I was repping Shaw.' Maely brought in Donald Wilkes and Florence Kennedy. There was eventually an *entente cordiale* among all concerned, but Dufty had as little to do with McKay as possible, because he knew that McKay would try to take advantage of Lady.
   In fact, he wrote later, Zaidins and McKay were trying to get Dufty and Lady to sign away their film rights to the book. Lady and Dufty played Alphonse and Gaston, said Dufty, each refusing to sign and trying not to antagonize McKay. Finally, 'McKay gave up. He couldn't wait for her to die. He came in and read the 23rd Psalm to her. She told me afterward, "I've always been a religious bitch, but if that evil motherfucker believes in God, I'm thinking it over."'
   Knowing that Glaser was paying for private nurses, Lady said, 'Wait till he finds out he's paying for the nurse that busted me.'

Glaser had brought in a doctor from Rockefeller, Dufty said, who had enough clout to recommend that Lady be given methadone, a synthetic narcotic that blocks the withdrawal symptoms. But no doctor could legally maintain a narcotics addict beyond a certain number of days. She continued to improve slowly as long as she was on methadone; she was gaining weight and looking better. But the methadone stopped after ten days.

When she first went to the hospital, Dufty knew that she needed dope; he thought that she may have been shooting up in the hospital for a while. 'I was in no position to get the drugs for her, but I could get the bread. And it was $20 here and $50 there, but I didn't have that kind of money, and I also thought it would be great for her morale – I thought of it as a green transfusion.' He went to a literary agent, but *Playboy* wasn't interested and *Esquire* already had somebody Then he realized that *Confidential* was the only magazine Lady ever read.

> I went down there and I told this high priest that I was doing an article on Billie Holiday, and he said, Oh, yeah, but it's all been done – you've got to have a new angle. And I said to myself, new angle, new angle, new angle, and I was desperate, so I said, how about 'Heroin Saved My Life', and he said terrific. They were concerned with one thing, that they get it in the magazine while she was still alive, and I couldn't guarantee that she would live. They completely did it over, the headline was 'I Needed Heroin to Live'; I don't know why they rewrote it, but they wanted it in their style. And Jerry Tuck went up with me to the hospital and he brought along the cheque and she signed it, and I said you've got the money, give her the cash. And of course the important thing was that Louis McKay didn't know about this.

After she had been admitted to the hospital, Maely had been denied access to Lady at first; Dufty had written a series of articles for the *New York Post* and thereafter had no trouble seeing her. But in a note to his City Desk in early July, he said that for some reason his access had been restricted, and even Maely had to go through red tape because she was a reporter's wife. Lady was being guarded round the clock by private nurses and the hospital police; 'photographers have been chinning themselves outside her window.' Seeing Dufty outside the door of her room, Lady shouted,

'Baby, you need a haircut.' Soon the restrictions were eased; Dufty could be cleared by doctors and hospital staff and visit her as a friend, but 'That Danton Walker item about me doing recorded interviews at the bedside is a press agent's dream.' (This was apparently something printed in another paper.) Yet it was during this period, after Wilkes's writ had got rid of the New York Police Department, that Detroit Red walked right in and paid a visit; she said there was nobody on the door at all.

Dufty also wrote that he and McKay were persuading a top liver specialist from Rockefeller Institute who had done research into the effects of narcotics on the liver to come in as a consultant; they were still planning to move her to a private hospital. Lady continued listening to her new album, especially enjoying 'Just One More Chance'.

> At this moment, specialists I have talked to insist that no one has been known to survive more than four weeks after a liver coma, but Holiday breaks all the rules. Meanwhile, she is gaining strength and weight. She is alert, raising hell with doctors and nurses. Yesterday she got them to order her a beer.

Lying in a hospital bed on a sweltering day listening to radio commercials for cold beer, she persuaded the staff to allow McKay to run out and get her one. She watched as a nurse poured the beer into a glass of foam, and teased, 'What kind of trained nurse are you, baby, if you can't pour a beer?' The next day she tried and failed to get another one.

'She has her hair fixed and nails done,' Dufty wrote, 'with two coats of polish. She directs her secretary to send thank you notes for the flowers, wires and gifts . . [one card said] "Get Well Soon, Lady, so you can sing for my children." Gary Cooper sent a yard long telegram full of the Holy Ghost and his newly discovered Catholicism . .'

On 6 July Dufty sent a special delivery note to Glaser; Lady had begged him to tell Glaser that she wanted to leave the Metropolitan as soon as possible. On 10 July a food pass was signed allowing her gifts of 'candy, ice cream, & fruit – not salty goods'. She talked with Dufty about writing a song called 'Bless Your Bones', apparently inspired by Jimmy Fletcher's attempt to visit her. She signed a contract for a film and made plans for a wardrobe conference.

At one point she sneaked a cigarette and a nurse complained that she'd set herself on fire; Alice, Dorothy Winston and others said she was a careless smoker, burning holes in everything. Lady shrugged: 'They already arrested me a month ago. What are they going to do for an encore?'

Then suddenly she was back on the critical list.

'The room was very small,' Dufty said, 'and it had glass from the waist up so they could see in, and there was this outer chamber, so that I would be in this room while she was sleeping.' The nurses would bathe her, and they found the money from the *Confidential* article.

That was 1959, and there are certain things you can write, and *Jet* magazine came out with the business and I know that at this time there's no other reporting being done but mine and everyone's rewriting me including Nat Hentoff, so in *Jet* magazine I read that she had a roll of $50 bills taped to her leg.

What she did, she wanted a piece of Scotch tape, because she rolled the bills tight, tight, tight, and she put a piece of Scotch tape around them to keep them from springing open, and it was up her vagina. Talk about a place to hide things. They didn't find it until about an hour before she died.

A nurse came out and said, 'Are you Bill?' and he thought at first that somehow they'd found some more drugs, but the nurse was completely astonished by the money; Lady had given it to her and sent it out to Dufty. Up to that point, Dufty knew better than the nurses: 'When they told me she was terminal or she was in a coma, I would squeeze her hand and she would squeeze back. But when she sent the money out with the nurse, that was her signal to me that she was checking out.'

He told the nurse to take the money to the office as part of her property. 'She was in extremis for something like twenty-four hours,' slipping in and out of consciousness, and there was 'a kind of animal thing that was above and beyond consciousness, where the body goes on and the will to live is there, and the will to live was there until the end'.

At about three in the morning on 17 July, 'her face relaxed, in an incredible repose'. The nurse felt her pulse and said, 'She's gone.'

19

Coda: The Lady Is an

Lady did a radio interview with Mike Wallace on 3 November 1956. Art Tatum had died three days earlier; she talked about how much she and Sadie had loved Tatum, and asked if he was a kind man, she replied, 'You can tell from his music. Yeah. He was a doll.' Then Wallace asked her, 'Why do so many jazz greats seem to die so early – Bix Beiderbecke, Fats Waller, Charlie Christian, Charlie Parker?' Lady replied,

> The only way I can answer that question, Mike, is that we try to live a hundred days in *one* day, and we try to please so many people. Like myself, I want to bend this note, bend that note, sing this way, sing that way, and get all the feeling, eat all the good foods, and travel all over all in one day, and you can't do it.

During and after Lady's last illness, newspapers had a good time perpetrating their usual inaccuracies. Her age ranged from forty-two to forty-six; she was of course 'the blues singer', and one writer indulged his very own fantasy, making her 'the dreamy-eyed blues singer'. Two more writers, one of them probably cribbing from the other, recycled the story of her discovery at Pod's and Jerry's, adding a piano player called Lester Young who asked, 'Can you sing, girlie?' Simple truths about Lady have always been in short supply, let alone more complicated ones.

Wilkes & Kennedy, Attorneys at Law, issued a statement dated the day of her death from 'Vinod Pethek and George Morris, producer and writer respectively, of the movie *The Flaming Nude*, the filming of which is to begin in September . . .' They had to play the part of Nellie, and they had written a song lled 'Tired and Disgusted', which was all about 'the pain athos and heartbreak that go with living.' They wanted to he world know that filming would go ahead and that they ere 'proud to have her name associated with the production', even though she was gone. So much for the funniest woman Dufty had ever known; the loneliness and illness of the last couple of years of her life were to stand for all forty-four of them.

When she died, Joe Glaser patched up his quarrel with Earl Zaidins, who said that Glaser knew Louis McKay was going to be trouble, and if Glaser was paying for the funeral he needed all the allies he could get. The funeral was at St Paul the Apostle Roman Catholic Church, on 60th Street near Columbus Circle, and 2,500 people were there, said the newspapers.

McKay asked Alice to be a receptionist at the funeral, but she refused. He offered her one of Lady's coats, Alice said; 'I told him that wouldn't take her place, but he didn't understand.' She couldn't listen to any of Lady's records for a year. Zaidins said, 'I actually cried for a couple of weeks after this woman died ... I was very emotional about it. I didn't know I would be. She meant a lot to me.'

Dufty wrote that a wealthy Catholic layman, Michael Grace, who was also a jazz fan, arranged for the funeral at St Paul's. Bill Dufty didn't want to go to the funeral – 'I had seen enough jazz funerals' – but he went and he was glad he did.

Nobody said anything, no Reverend Licorice with an idiotic sermon, but a Requiem High Mass, with a choir and everything, so that the only obscenity was on the steps, seeing all these people I'd talked to on the phone and suddenly they're all there and they're all pallbearers and everything. That's the way it goes . .

I had a picture of her and I didn't want an embalmer to ruin it. It wasn't gruesome, it's just that I hate those things. I remember somebody at the *Post* took a picture of people on their knees beside her in the coffin and tried to show it to me, and I just said, 'Don't.'

Michael Grace had also, in 'a new expensive Catholic cemetery in upstate New York,' said Dufty, 'paid $5,000 for a burial plot – between George Jean Nathan and Babe Ruth'. But McKay sent a

telegram to the Duftys dated 19 July: TAKE NOTICE REFRAIN
FROM MAKING ANY ARRANGEMENTS REGARDING MY WIFES
(ELEANORE MCKAY A/K/A BILLIE HOLIDAY) FUNERAL WHAT-
SOEVER OR USE OF MY NAME. He couldn't stop the funeral at St
Paul's, but he saw to it that Lady was buried with her mother in
St Raymond's Cemetery in the Bronx, which is what she may have
wanted. McKay was said to have paid $30 to have the grave opened,
and Lady buried on top, but the cemetery says Sadie was moved to
Lady's grave in 1961. 'Louis was somethin' else,' said Annie Ross. 'I
mean after she died, he called me and said, "I got Lady's mink. She
always wanted you to have it." I suspected him right there. "I'll let you
have it for $500." That was Louis.'

On 25 July, a black newspaper called the *New York Age* printed
a story headlined '*NY Post* Lied About Billie Holiday: Husband'.
'Sitting quietly in the office of his attorney and friend, Earl
Zaidins, McKay . . . bit his lip, and continued.' He claimed to have
been in the hospital when Lady died. He complained that a letter from
Dufty printed in the *Post* quoting Lady used profanity, and said, 'She
never used that type of language.' He said that the original
manuscript of her book (written by Dufty) had been full of hate, and
that he, McKay, had insisted on changes. The article quoted McKay:

> The main reason Billie got into trouble was that she was
> depressed by not working regularly In the eight years I was
> with her, we did not work ten weeks straight. Then when she
> did work, she had to have a maid and a good pianist. This is
> why we were never able to accumulate any money.

He blamed this on the cabaret card problem, but did not explain
how he had supported two families on her money He complained
that Dufty had said in his obituary that he and Lady were
'estranged' at the time of her death.

> 'Estranged' means you don't have anything to do with one
> another, this is not true in our case. We called each other at
> least once a week. I left June of 1958 because of a bleeding
> ulcer. I never told Billie how sick I really was . . . I promised
> her two days before she died, I would never again leave her
> side, and I meant it.

It is not impossible that life with Lady gave McKay an ulcer, but
he left nearly a year before that. Dufty wrote an undated list of

events in chronological order: Lady and McKay had not even been married when the book was written, and during her last brush with the law McKay was in California. They had been estranged, Lady had started divorce proceedings and made out a will (but never signed it), and Dufty had documentary proof of all this.

> The night she died, McKay went off with this white woman he was going around with . . . She was alone. McKay was not there. Wilkes and Kennedy . . . represented me and filed an action against the *New York Age*, Clyde Reed, the author of the article, and McKay. The *Age* shortly thereafter went out of business. Donald Wilkes, partner of Miss Kennedy, left the country for ever under mysterious circumstances – and the action just fell between chairs. Sometime later, a Negro weekly called the *Citizen Call*, the successor to the *Age*, appeared. I had become separated with my wife [who] took a job with this paper as a columnist to embarrass me. She aligned herself with McKay for a while but that didn't last long . . . I have never spoken to McKay since Holiday's death, despite many overtures from him, through Miss Kennedy. I refuse to have anything to do with the sonofabitch . . . I will remain grateful to Miss Kennedy for all she did for Miss Holiday in her last days – at a time when it counted. I want to make that clear. She was never paid for any of the extensive legal work she did. Neither was Mr Wilkes. Both of them performed brilliantly and devotedly on her behalf. As for Miss Kennedy's actions since that time, her legal action on behalf of Mr McKay, I don't understand it. That is all I can say with charity.

Glaser received a bill from Wilkes & Kennedy and expressed astonishment at it; they wrote back expressing astonishment at his astonishment. We do not know if Glaser ever paid up, but Lady's death had helped to sell quite a few records; *down beat* reported at the end of the year that her royalties had amounted to $100,000 since her death. We do not know what 'Miss Kennedy's . . . legal action on behalf of Mr McKay' was, but clearly there was still money to be made from her estate. Dufty seems to have been one of the best friends Lady had, and it cost him his wife and his lawyer friends.

A year after the funeral, somebody noticed that Sadie's and Lady's grave was the only one in their row that didn't have a tombstone. *Down beat* started taking up a collection from readers; McKay objected, announcing that he intended to have Lady's and Sadie's remains removed to the St Paul's section of the cemetery, and that he would erect a monument at a cost of $3,500. A funeral director needed to be involved; McKay gave the cemetery the name of Erskine, but the cemetery could find no funeral director of that name.

Some time in the 1960s, one of the USA TV networks ran a programme about Lady, and Carmen de Lavallade portrayed her in a dance sequence. Kennedy complained to the network on McKay's behalf that they hadn't had the estate's permission, and that the dancer didn't look anything like Lady; Carl Drinkard remarked that Lady would have liked being portrayed by a dancer with such good legs.

In the mid-1950s, a Columbia LP called *Lady Day* had appeared, reissuing some of her most famous recordings from 1935–7. In 1962 a three-LP set, *The Golden Years* was released, soon followed by *The Golden Years, Volume II*, making a total of 108 tracks from the period 1933–42 available, with no duplication. Many of the Commodore, Decca and Verve recordings were more or less continuously available on various albums; royalties must have been paid on these to McKay and his heirs. Some people have thought that this was unfortunate, but she married McKay, and she did not divorce him; she loved children, and she was kind to his children; by now perhaps some of McKay's grandchildren have gone to college, helped by Lady's recordings.

Dufty wrote a series of articles in the Boston *East West Journal* in the 1960s, from which I have already quoted. His script was never filmed; 'the book was optioned again for a film,' he wrote. 'This time they didn't want me to write the screenplay. They didn't even want me to see it. A double agent in the film organization sent me a copy of the script anyway. I made myself read it. It had Lady having a baby in the fifth reel. That one never got made either.'

But finally, in 1972 came a film of *Lady Sings the Blues*, starring Diana Ross, who had come from a Detroit housing project to be the star of the Supremes and a solo diva after 1970. This was a Motown movie.

Berry Gordy was one of the most successful black men in

America, making pop records in what in retrospect looks like a golden era, because most pop since has been so dismal; the Supremes alone had four big hits in 1964, the year there was no *Billboard* black chart because white and black kids seemed to be buying the same records. Gordy was more successful than any black record man could have been during Lady's lifetime, but he was a hands-on record man, and when he left the studio he did less well. Leonard Feather, in his review of the movie, wrote that the producer, Jay Weston, told him that the original script, 'so authentic that it was tantamount to a documentary, proved unsaleable'. Only when it was rewritten did Gordy decide 'that he had found a strong vehicle for Miss Ross' screen debut'. The writers are listed as Terence McCloy, Chris Clark and Suzanne de Passe; the director was Sidney J. Furie.

Gordy had made records which were new and unique, but his movie was just another Hollywood biopic. The result, wrote Feather, was 'a production with Academy Award potential in the star performance, with brilliant work by Billy Dee Williams and Richard Pryor – and a story line in which the anachronisms, distortions, errors of omission and commission are almost continuous.' The film is set 1930 to *circa* 1945; John Hammond, Benny Goodman and Artie Shaw refused to allow their names to be used; maybe they'd seen the script. Lester Young, Jimmy Monroe and Count Basie aren't mentioned. Louis McKay is in it, though. He had nothing to do with Lady's life during that period, but he was a 'technical consultant' on the film.

The line 'Baby, I'm going to get you into Carnegie' must have made Ernie Anderson feel ill; then the Carnegie Hall sequence had Lady accompanied by a large interracial orchestra with strings. The picture has Lady touring with a white band whose pianist introduces her to heroin: Jack Batten, reviewing the film in England, wrote that Les Burness, Shaw's pianist in 1938, should have consulted his solicitor. This farrago was no better than *The Glenn Miller Story* in 1954, which didn't mention Tex Beneke, the star of the Miller band, because the Miller estate was sore at him, and put 'Little Brown Jug' in late 1944 in order to jerk tears from June Allyson, although the record was a hit in 1939. Hollywood had learned nothing in twenty years, but at least the music in the Miller picture was better. The talented black composer Oliver Nelson was hired to do the music for *Lady Sings the Blues*, but didn't like the script because it wasn't really about Billie Holiday; Michel Legrand did it instead. The French-born conductor and composer of mood and movie music had won an Oscar in 1968 for 'The Windmills of Your Mind'; his was a score 'colourless and lacking in the jazz vitality it needed', wrote Feather.

Everyone praised Diana Ross, whose talent did not bring her anything more than tokenism in the Hollywood of the 1970s. Thelma Carpenter and Sylvia Syms agreed that the film of *Lady Sings the Blues* had at least introduced a new generation to Lady and her tunes, and must have helped sales of her records; somebody who saw it on Hollywood Boulevard said that the whole audience booed, but the film is still making money today on television.

By this time Lady was becoming a cultural icon. Photographs became postcards, there have been innumerable caricatures, and her face even appears on a T-shirt. When I first began writing this book I thought I wanted to play down the icon as much as I could, but I've changed my mind. True, pop icons are a dime a dozen these days, because the media are so willing to be manipulated, but today's icons disappear as soon as the hype stops. Lady became and remained an icon without any hype; the reason the film was made was that she was already an icon. Of course, she was black, and her life certainly had its tragic aspects, appealing to the bleeding-heart liberal in many of us; and she was a great artist. But there are other greatly loved artists whose records are still selling many years after their deaths; and a surprising number of them, both black and white, led tragic lives and died young. I think there is even more to it than all that.

Some observers say that Sadie attended Mass regularly; Lady was not much of a churchgoer, but she never lost touch with her Catholic religion. She had written her chatty letter to the Rev. Norman O'Connor because she'd borrowed some books from him; she wrote that she had consulted an Irish friend of hers, who agreed with O'Connor that it was perfectly possible to be a good Catholic and still enjoy the finer things in life, adding 'He's for you for Pope for sure!' Bobby Tucker said that when his little girl was ill, she prayed for the child until she got better.

Father Peter O'Brien, like O'Connor, was a 'jazz priest'; he had been pianist/composer Mary Lou Williams's manager for years. Mary Lou became a Catholic in 1956 and told O'Brien that she and Lady had been sitting together, possibly at a funeral or a wake. 'And Billie says to Mary Lou, "Mary, talk to me, I'm Catholic too." And she holds up her fist and she has her rosary wrapped around her hand.'

It is interesting that Lady decided to adopt Theresa as the name she had been given as a child in the Good Shepherd home in 1925. There are two St Theresas; one was an activist in the religious politics of her day, but Lady is said to have chosen the other, who was quiet and contemplative, and is associated with roses. Thelma Carpenter is also a Catholic:

> One night we had to go to Jersey for her to sing and she asked me would I take her. And on the way to Newark, that big bridge, you know that ramp that sort of goes round and round, whatever it is . . it was a funny thing that whenever I took her someplace my brakes would go on me and she would always know it. So she said, 'Brakes gone,' and I said 'Yep,' so I figured I'd hug the highway and we sort of prayed real good and finally we made it. And she turned and said about Saint Theresa, she said, 'She let some of those rosebuds fall down on us.'

In conversation, Father O'Brien, Thelma and Michelle Wallace, a black feminist and a Catholic, agreed that some of Lady's songs were effectively prayers; that some of the stories in her autobiography, if they were not literally true, nevertheless betrayed strong feelings about sex, death and guilt; that Lady was in some way ashamed of her background, but that she remained a searcher.

Being a Catholic can load you with guilt, or it can allow you to get away with anything as long as you go to confession, or both. Bill Dufty was also a Catholic. He speculated that if Lady's Catholicism had come all the way from an Irish slave-owning ancestor, the knowledge of mortal sin may have begun that far back; and that being a Catholic for a black person was different from being a Baptist or a Methodist, because there weren't many black priests and you got your religion from the same place as other (white) Catholics got it from: Rome. 'Nothing was left to chance.'

When Dufty was interviewing Lady for the book, he asked her how old she was before she started telling fibs at confession, and she was startled by the question. 'I been questioned by all kinds of fuzz. Some of those feds are pretty sharp . . . I was before a Grand

Jury once in New Jersey . . . They asked me all kinds of things. But nobody ever asked me a question like *that*.' She asked him what he had fibbed about, and he told her that masturbation had been a more serious sin in Michigan than in Illinois, 'where you could do it all night long, wash your hands under the pump in the morning and go to confession'. He had had a fantasy as a teenager about taking a bus to Chicago, going to confession and taking in a baseball game while he was at it.

They were sitting in a Chinese restaurant, and just then the waiter arrived with paper tubs of sauce. 'Ask him to take away that damn mustard,' she said.

> I hate the smell of mustard. I sat in a tub of mustard for eighteen damn hours one time, killed my baby so I wouldn't be a bad girl. Having a baby without being married. My mother worried about that. It happened to her. And all she prayed for was it wouldn't happen to me. I didn't want to hurt her so I sat in a damn tub full of hot water and mustard. God will punish her, the nuns used to say. He damned well did, too. The only thing I ever wanted was that baby.

'That's what you couldn't confess?' asked Dufty. 'Hell, no,' Lady said, 'I wouldn't mind confessing that. Everybody was doing that. I stopped going to confession long before that.'

Lady told Alice that when she was first married, after sex she would lie with her feet in the air, hoping that would help her to conceive a child. Much later, she told several people that her dream was to retire to a big place in the country and adopt a lot of kids, all different colours. (She may have heard about Josephine Baker, who had done exactly that in France. Baker called her children her rainbow tribe.)

Leonard Feather, Mike Gould, Dorothy Winston, Rosemary Clooney, the Duftys, her Italian fan who had her sing at La Scala, and many others allowed Lady to be godmother to a child: Feather named his daughter after Lady. Lady asked Sid and Mae Weiss if she could be godmother to the child they were expecting and was disappointed when they told her they'd already promised somebody else. It would be wrong to assume that Lady was a neglectful godmother; Dorothy Winston said that she spoiled her two daughters: 'She'd take them to the variety store and buy them little things.' And she sent Bevan Dufty a postcard when he was no more than a toddler, saying 'I hope you're not still sharpening your teeth on your daddy . . .'

Rosemary Clooney said:

Billie is my oldest daughter's godmother . . . I was pregnant with my second child. And she looked at me and said, 'I think you've got a girl child in your belly this time. And I think I should be her godmother, because it takes a very bad woman to be a good godmother.'

The important thing is not what kind of godmother Lady was. The important thing is that she knew what it meant to *have* a godmother.

It is really quite remarkable that throughout her life many people, seeing Lady, somehow saw themselves, as in a mirror. For example, there are conflicting reports of Lady's last birthday party. Elaine Lorillard was there for a while and said that Lady was incoherent and bitter; her laughter was hostile. Her nose was running and her ankles and feet were swollen, 'but she was still beautiful, in an evening gown, with a flower in her hair'. Lady sat on the floor, with records strewn around her and somebody was taking pictures. But Lorillard was there around 5 or 6 in the morning, and by that time Lady had been up all night; others had a different memory of the party. Leonard Feather said that it was a happy occasion, although he was alarmed at the weight Lady had lost. Maybe she wasn't in the mood for a photo shoot at 5 in the morning; evidently she'd changed clothes for it, because Feather said that she'd been prancing around in toreador pants. He saw no sign of drugs; Lorillard said people kept nipping in and out of the bathroom, and complained that Lady didn't speak to her, didn't seem to know who she was.

It was as though people saw what they expected to see, as though Lady herself didn't exist. Some said she was all soft and warm inside, and others saw her bad girl act, which she put on because that's what people wanted to see. Squirrel Jackson was a junkie in Baltimore who shot Lady with heroin:

I had to hit her in order to get some drugs for myself. And my friend is telling me it's Billie Holiday, which is like telling me it's Tom Jones or Lucy or somebody I'm not concerned; I'm sick and she's sick; we're two dope fiends . . .

If she hadn't been a singer, she'd have been a prostitute. That's the type of attitude she had.

To Billy Eckstine she was a little girl; bassist Al McKibbon, who met her in a club in Detroit around 1940, was frightened of her:

> We were a bunch of youngsters to her, not that much younger, but in experience. She had a rough scene with her man, from the Cats and a Fiddle group. They had fights. She would fight anybody. She whipped a couple of girls while she was there . . .
>
> I was afraid of her, sure. One time I was in the men's room and she came in, she went in the urinal standing. We talked. What could I do? I thought it was a hell of a thing for a woman to do; I was shocked but she wasn't. She was another guy.

One of the most graphic accounts of the reactions Lady could arouse in people just by being herself comes from a white club-owner in Philadelphia. The man apologized to Dufty because he didn't book her five or six times a year; she was his all-time favourite performer. But there was always trouble. 'He talked as though I should know what he was talking about,' wrote Dufty. It wasn't race – the club was happily integrated – and it wasn't drugs. It was sex.

> A guy brings his wife or his girl friend. A chick brings in her man. They have a few drinks. That's what we're selling, right? Lady comes on. Sure, she's beautiful. But I've had better looking chicks singing in here and they don't cause no trouble. Lady does her number. Sure she's sexy. But she don't work at it like some of them. I've seen girls throw themselves at two guys at a table, and their wives think it's cute as hell. Billie don't do nothing. She just sings 'Love for Sale' Or anything. Follow me and climb the stairs. Some man at a table of four starts looking at her. His wife has had one drink too many and she starts looking at the way her husband is looking at Lady. Ice starts rattling and purses start bang-ing and chairs start scraping and people start coming apart. Why, I've seen as many as twenty-seven fights start in one week while Lady's here. She really stirs things up.

It doesn't happen with Ella or Dinah or Sarah or Della . .

'He seemed to have had an actuarial somewhere on the catharsis quotient of various attractions,' wrote Dufty. 'He regarded it as the highest kind of tribute that Lady could turn a table of customers into an encounter group in nothing flat.'

Lady's love life may have been dysfunctional from our point of view, but all her lovers, whether they knew it or not, were being tested in some way. If people wanted her to play a role, they had to reciprocate. She was willing to be used – we all have to allow ourselves to be used – the question for her intimates was, how well can you do it? The test was especially tough, because especially complicated, for black men, as Jimmy Monroe found out; and she must have known at some level that it would be. Perhaps this is one reason she also went with women: to rest from the violence of racism. But she also knew that the bottom line is that we are each responsible for our own behaviour, no matter what colour we are.

Many of the people reading this book will already be Billie Holiday fans; perhaps others will grant that she was a great and influential stylist. But so what? It will be pointed out that nearly all the songs she sang were about romantic love, which (some say) is itself an illusion, invented in France in the eleventh century: in the ideal of courtly love, the lover is supposed to be able to sleep next to his lady without touching her. In the real world, an ideal is nothing to build a relationship on, nor is sexual attraction, hence today's divorce rate, now that social pressures have lessened and divorce is easier. But most of the songs are very good songs, and the way Lady sings them, they become something more than romance. They become songs about human relationships; they are about whether or not we are able to have any respect for each other at all. And did not Lady retain her friendships with Bernie Hanighen, Jimmy Monroe, Freddie Green, Ben Webster, John Simmons, John Collins and many others who had been her lovers?

Some time in the late 1950s, Lady met William Faulkner. The reviews of *Lady Sings the Blues* concentrated on her drug problem and her early career as a prostitute; Faulkner must have come to New York now and then to see his publisher and evidently wanted to meet her. Thelma Carpenter says that Bill Dufty probably set it up and that there was a newspaper article and a picture.

Lady called Thelma; she was worried because Faulkner was a

Southerner. 'She wanted to know who was Faulkner,' and Thelma tried to explain. 'And they got along beautifully .. he understood her perfectly.'

Flannery O'Connor was another Southern writer, from Georgia, and an invalid; she died younger than Lady, in 1964, of systemic lupus erythematosus. Some of her stories, too, are about people you might not want to live next door to, but who are touched with grace. She called one of her stories, and titled a collection, 'Everything That Rises Must Converge'.

Grace is a theological concept. It is an unmerited favour of God, a divine inspiring influence. The point of it is that none of us merit it; and similarly, if Lady had had no talent, we would never have heard of her, or if she had been a middle-class girl, she might have sung her songs to her ironing board and we wouldn't have heard of her then, either. Lady is an icon – not a triumph of marketing but a real icon, an image of something sacred, itself regarded as sacred – because she was granted grace. Her art went to that place where things converge; she was sent to test us, and we mostly failed.

When it came to the cabaret card law, Lady did not blame anybody in particular, and she did not blame it on racism. The public was not being protected from a dope fiend: she could sing in places where children could hear her, while the clubs in which she could not sing were full of drug pushers, gangsters, pimps and prostitutes, as well as tourists and ordinary jazz fans. She simply pointed out that the law was foolish and unfair, and nobody listened. The cabaret card was finally abolished by Mayor John Lindsay in 1967; meanwhile, Zaidins said that Morris Levy, a music industry gangster who was part owner of Birdland, had offered Lady a card if she would give him six months a year in his club. She had no doubt that he could buy her a cabaret card, but she didn't want it badly enough to sell herself to a hoodlum. Morris Levy, who was also active in the record industry, was finally indicted for commercial fraud in the late 1980s, but died before he could be sent to prison; he didn't even know he'd been tested.

But if we know that we have been tested, and even more if we know that we have failed, then perhaps we have glimpsed grace, even if we cannot possess it.

'What do I remember?' said Jimmy Rowles. 'Oh, I remember her turning around and looking and laughing, or maybe you'd

458

play some tune and she'd turn around and hug you and say
something like "I love you." If she said "I love you," boy, you
heard it. She used to say, *I love you*, she used to growl it out, and it
would mean like the next two weeks of your life.' Let Rowles have
the last word:

One time my old lady fixed her hair a certain way and Lady
liked it, so she fixed her hair that way too. They were tight.
When Dorothy first met Lady was in '42, and all the bands
would come in on Sunday afternoons, like Count Basie,
Jimmie Lunceford, Duke, and I remember one Sunday, the
first time I brought my old lady out, and Lady sat with us.

This was before the days of complexes, when somebody
says 'Hello' and somebody else says, 'What did he mean by
that?' It was very uncomplex, in those days, living. It had its
own complexity, but there was nothing on the outside to fuck
it up. It was just up to you to get to it, not like going through
twelve doors first.

Anyway, Nat Cole was playing, and Buck Clayton was
playing, and Lady starts screaming at him, 'Go on, play it,
you blue-eyed sonofabitch, you motherfucker, let 'em have it!'
And Dorothy's hanging on to me and saying, 'What's happening?' I had cautioned her out front, but she'd never heard it
like that before. But she got used to it and started enjoying it.
And Prez would be sitting over in the corner saying, 'Isn't
that nice. Isn't that nice.' And he'd see a chick and he'd say,
'Damn, I like that.' And he'd empty his whisky glass and he'd
get up there and start blowing and wipe 'em all out. It was
really wild. Those that were there will remember . . .

One time in New York I came out of the Roxy Theater
and going into this Chinese joint across the street I see Lady
coming along, and she has Pepe with her, and Pepe wants to
get down and chew all the garbage, and she's cursing at Pepe,
and everyone's stopping and saying, 'Look at that terrible
coloured girl,' and the language is all coming out. And I'm
standing behind her and she says, 'What are you doing here?'
I said, 'I'm with Evelyn Knight at the Roxy,' And she says,
'That fuckin' bitch. She's doin' the Roxy for $10,000 a week
and I'm still doin' the Apollo for $1,500. *Fuck her. And fuck
you.*' And I hadn't seen her for two years! I said, "Wait a

minute. You're puttin' it all on *me*.' And she says, 'You motherfuckin' white ofay,' and she goes through all of it, and Pepe goes into the garbage can and she's screamin' and the people are standing there and they're gettin' ready to call the police. Oh I loved her. Oh how I loved her.

Lady Day liked to have you tell her you loved her. Of course, I told her. Everybody used to tell her; you couldn't help it. She'd do something, and you'd have to say, 'Jesus, how I love you!'

Another time she says to me, 'Louis is out of town, so you've got to take me home.' So I wait till she's ready. 'You gotta feed me. I wanna go to a Chinese place.' So all right; if she wants to go to Tokyo, we go.

So we go to a Chinese place a block away, and we sit down, and we order, to go – because I want to take her home, she's going to have her food and I'm gonna go home. So we're sitting there and all of a sudden this coloured cat walked into the kitchen with a tray, and she flipped. She started throwing things, swearing, yelling, 'Did you see that? There's not a Chinaman on earth who would let a black motherfucker in his kitchen or a white motherfucker either. This ain't no Chinese restaurant, this is a bunch of shit!' Then the owner comes over, and she chews his ass off, and finally the guy comes with the food, and we take the food, and I'm trying to drag her out, Come on Lady, I'm laughing and she's still screaming, 'You fuckin' slant-eyed motherfucker, you Chinese can't, I bet this shit's gonna taste –'

I get her in the car, take her home, get her into her room, put her into bed, tuck her in with her food – 'There's your shrimp, your foo young, you've got it all here. Now you're straight, now good night, you lovely bitch. (Kiss.) Talk to you tomorrow; now eat your goddam food, drink the rest of your gin.' Then she'd get coy. She's in bed, and her titties are sticking out and all that shit. 'Louis is out of town, you know.' I know it. I wouldn't ball her, because I wouldn't spoil it for anything. I'll fuck her after I die. If I'm playing for them, I don't want to be fucking them. Oh, I did it a couple of times, but that was different. That wasn't permanent.

With Lady Day, you thought permanent.

Index

Made in the USA
Lexington, KY
30 August 2015